Practical Event-Driven Microservices Architecture

Building Sustainable and Highly Scalable Event-Driven Microservices

Hugo Filipe Oliveira Rocha

Apress®

Practical Event-Driven Microservices Architecture: Building Sustainable and Highly Scalable Event-Driven Microservices

Hugo Filipe Oliveira Rocha
Ermesinde, Portugal

ISBN-13 (pbk): 978-1-4842-7467-5   ISBN-13 (electronic): 978-1-4842-7468-2
https://doi.org/10.1007/978-1-4842-7468-2

Managing Director, Apress Media LLC: Welmoed Spahr
Acquisitions Editor: Smriti Srivastava
Development Editor: Laura Berendson
Coordinating Editor: Shrikant Vishwakarma

Cover designed by eStudioCalamar

Cover image designed by Pexels

Distributed to the book trade worldwide by Springer Science+Business Media LLC, 1 New York Plaza, Suite 4600, New York, NY 10004. Phone 1-800-SPRINGER, fax (201) 348-4505, e-mail orders-ny@springer-sbm. com, or visit www.springeronline.com. Apress Media, LLC is a California LLC and the sole member (owner) is Springer Science + Business Media Finance Inc (SSBM Finance Inc). SSBM Finance Inc is a **Delaware** corporation.

For information on translations, please e-mail booktranslations@springernature.com; for reprint, paperback, or audio rights, please e-mail bookpermissions@springernature.com.

Apress titles may be purchased in bulk for academic, corporate, or promotional use. eBook versions and licenses are also available for most titles. For more information, reference our Print and eBook Bulk Sales web page at http://www.apress.com/bulk-sales.

Any source code or other supplementary material referenced by the author in this book is available to readers on GitHub via the book's product page, located at www.apress.com/978-1-4842-7467-5. For more detailed information, please visit http://www.apress.com/source-code.

Printed on acid-free paper

As with all the best things in my life, this book included,
started with a suggestion from my wife.

To the love of my life, Eduarda, and my dear daughter, Olívia.

Table of Contents

About the Author

 **Hugo Rocha** has nearly a decade of experience working with highly distributed event-driven microservice architectures. He currently is an engineering lead for the leading global eCommerce platform for luxury products (Farfetch), providing services to millions of active users, backed by an event-driven architecture with hundreds of microservices processing hundreds of changes per second. Before that, he worked for several reference telecommunications companies that transitioned from monolithic applications to microservice-oriented architectures. Hugo has managed several teams that directly face the caveats of event-driven architectures every day. He designed solutions for critical pieces of the platform's highly distributed backoffice platform, handling hundreds of changes per second, concurrently, scalably, and with high performance.

About the Technical Reviewer

Daniel Gomes has been working in software development for 16 years now. He has a degree in Software Engineering and a post-graduate degree in Software Engineering for enterprise software applications.

He started his career working mostly on software development for an ERP (enterprise resource planning) in the areas of accounting, human resources, laboratory management, energy projects, quality assurance, and innovation certification.

Over the last six years, his focus has mostly been on the design and implementation of microservice and event-driven systems to support an eCommerce platform (Farfetch). Currently, he is the engineering lead for two tech teams that deliver software based on microservice and event sourcing architectures.

Acknowledgments

The monumental journey of transforming knowledge into a truly useful book requires an inconspicuous amount of people besides the sheer will of its author.

I want to thank everyone at Apress for making this book possible, especially Smriti Srivastava, Shrikant Vishwakarma, and Laura Berendson who were deeply involved in the book's development. I also want to thank my technical reviewer, Daniel Gomes, for his thorough technical review and detailed suggestions.

I want to thank everyone at Farfetch for providing the real-world experience of many technical subjects, for enabling a trustful and open environment, for giving everyone the opportunity to tackle the difficult challenges of a highly distributed platform, being committed to their personal development and doing what's never been done. A special thanks to the members of my teams, for embracing every challenge that I throw at them easily and enthusiastically. And a very special thanks to Daniel Gomes and Ricardo Felgueiras for being committed to my personal development since the beginning, for inspiring me and challenging me to tackle new challenges, and for their honest and heartwarming camaraderie.

I want to thank my parents for their support and love throughout the years. I want to thank my two-year-old daughter who sat on my lap or next to me watching cartoons while her father wrote this book and furiously rambled about event-driven microservices for innumerable hours.

All the greatest achievements in my life, personal and professional, can be traced back to a conversation with my wife, this book included. More than anyone, I want to thank my wife, Eduarda, for challenging me to write this book, for her unwavering support and everlasting patience in the countless hours I spent writing it in the last year, for her unfaltering faith in me, resolute and undying love and care throughout the years, and for being everything I ever wished for and much more than I ever deserved.

Introduction

Applications and systems came a long way since the traditional use cases of the turning of the century. You might recall measuring large data in a few gigabytes, waiting for a web page to load for a few dozens of seconds, or the scheduled maintenance that included a few hours of downtime. These were common practices perhaps 20 years ago; today, however, they are completely unacceptable. In fact, serving functionality in dozens of milliseconds and 100% uptime are properties users started getting used to and expect from any application. Achieving them at scale, however, requires a substantially different approach to how we build software and different paradigms to software architecture design. When dealing with data in several orders of magnitude larger than traditional applications, serving information in fractions of seconds globally and consistently with varying throughputs, and achieving higher availability by being resilient to most failure modes, is a fundamentally different challenge that traditional architectures weren't made to solve.

Besides non-functional requirements like performance and scalability, time to market is paramount to the success of competitive businesses. The evolutionary nature of event-driven architectures paves the way for the technical infrastructure to react to changeable business needs. The success of recent tech companies proved that the close relation of the business and their tech solutions and the solution's inherent flexibility and adaptability are pivotal for the company's success. The technical decisions are as essential as the business strategy, and an inadequate strategy can become as disastrous as a bad business decision, being able to constrict business growth without the proper concerns and strategies in place.

In recent years, event-driven architectures arose as a powerful approach to software architecture design and as an answer to the difficult challenges applications face with increased usage, distributed data, and sharing data at scale. A notable characteristic of event-driven architectures is the focus on the event streams: it goes beyond applications simply reacting to events; event streams become the heart of data sharing throughout the company. Data no longer sits solely on a database and is accessible only through synchronous interfaces; instead, it is shared in event streams readily available for every current and future consumer. The event stream becomes a medium to share all relevant data occurring in real time and provides a way to understand how it changed in the past. It is also a powerful way to stream data to other services. Each consumer can plug into the stream and create a personalized view of the state. The highly decoupled nature provides more resilient properties than traditional architectures and flexibility to changing requirements. Data is readily available to new consumers in a scalable and decoupled way.

However, event-driven architectures aren't without their downsides. Although single-process applications and monoliths have their limitations, walking into a distributed architecture is a whole different hell which companies are often not used to or ready for. An adoption without deliberate strategies to tackle its challenges and unawareness of its caveats can be a disastrous decision as other companies experienced in the past. Kelsey Hightower once said "You haven't mastered a tool until you understand when it should not be used." It's hard to achieve that level of realization without the experience of using something for long enough in production. This book proposes to shed light on when and where to use an event-driven architecture and how to fully reap its benefits. It proposes patterns and approaches to deal with its most difficult characteristics and how to incrementally and sustainably adopt an event-driven architecture.

CHAPTER 1

Embracing Event-Driven Architectures

This chapter covers:

- How monoliths can hinder business growth and their main limitations

- Understanding microservices, their advantages, and how they relate to event-driven architectures

- Recognizing the potential in adopting event-driven microservices and how an event-driven architecture works

- How to identify the need for your business to move to an event-driven architecture

- Knowing the challenges in adopting a microservice event-driven architecture

© Hugo Filipe Oliveira Rocha 2022
H. F. Oliveira Rocha, *Practical Event-Driven Microservices Architecture,*
https://doi.org/10.1007/978-1-4842-7468-2_1

You might have struggled, the same way as I did, with the limitations of monoliths. It starts with a small team delivering value in a fast iterating working mode in a single application. The business succeeds, and the use cases grow and get more diversified. More developers join to keep up with demand. High-priority features and urgent fixes blur the lines of single responsibility and slowly turn the practices of clean code into remnants of the past. The team outgrows the application, and we soon struggle with merge requests with hundreds of conflicts and complex lockstep releases. The first time I migrated a monolith to a distributed microservice architecture, it felt like a glimmer of hope in the inhospitable big ball of mud[1] we so often and easily fall into.

It often starts smoothly: the first microservices stand as living proof of how time to market and team's autonomy can be software engineering pillars even in large teams working with complex architectures. The inconspicuous detail is the fundamentally different hell we are walking into that most people are oblivious to. While working in a global eCommerce platform, I recall a situation where one of the teams had to migrate the product's stock information to a new service. The operation was simple: the new service would fetch the stock information from the service holding the inventory data, perform some straightforward operations, and save the data internally. One of the operations the service had to do was fetching the location of the warehouse storing the stock, which involved requesting data from the location service. The inventory service, a crucial component in the platform, had plenty of resources, and the added throughput of the operation was accounted for. However, no one considered the impact in the location service, a component with apparently limited importance and relevance in the platform. The added throughput of the operation in the location service caused the service to crash due to high load. What we soon noticed was that the apparently minor and peripheral location service was being used in the order fulfillment flow and other vital parts of the platform. The apparent harmless data migration of a new service ended up stopping the main order fulfillment flow. To me, it felt like the gilding on the microservice architecture cracked to reveal the imperfections underneath.

When an apparently innocuous change ends up affecting a completely unrelated functionality, a distributed microservice architecture doesn't seem all that different from a monolith. In fact, we might get the worst of both worlds and end up with a distributed monolith instead. This consequence is one of the many challenges we need to address

---

[1] A common anti-pattern in software architecture, https://en.wikipedia.org/wiki/Big_ball_of_mud

when building a distributed microservice architecture. One of the most sustainable ways to address those challenges is through an event-driven architecture.

In a microservice event-driven architecture, several decoupled services react to each other and gracefully choreograph to accomplish a business goal. They provide an immutable sequence of events that enable you to understand the purpose and the evolution of the data and interpret their business processes. The hauntingly beautiful potential of event-driven architectures is the ability to provide streaming of data with history and meaning, enabling each consumer to take the vision that is more fitted to the consumer's context and build value on top of it.

Although event-driven architectures aren't new and were very popular with ESB (enterprise service bus, detailed in Section 1.3), the ability to provide high volumes of messages to distributed components sustainably and in real time certainly is new. Without a doubt, for most use cases, the most valuable data is the most recent one, but being able to offer an accessible stream with the history of the data unlocks robust solutions to difficult problems. Take migrating data for example. Instead of complex syncing solutions that have to deal with data being changed while the migration is running, doing it with event streams becomes trivial and organic.

Microservices pushed the limits of traditional applications, but sometimes to unravel more difficult ones. Synchronous communications traditionally used with microservices (like REST) become problematic due to the inherent coupling. Although much safer than in a monolith, changes in services might still affect the underlying ecosystem inadvertently. The complex web of synchronous calls between services is hard to track and create a breeding ground for cascading failures. We also choose microservices due to the scalability capabilities, which can become hindered by the synchronous dependencies between services (further detailed in Section 1.4). Although we still need deliberate approaches to these problems, event-driven architectures provide a higher level of decoupling and enable a genuinely evolutionary architecture from the ground up. New consumers can join without affecting existing services. Old services can be decommissioned without affecting their dependencies.

However, the asynchronous, distributed nature of event-driven architecture poses difficult challenges that we often take for granted in a monolith. Event-driven isn't also a silver bullet and shouldn't be used in every use case. In the end, complex businesses ultimately reflect their complexity in the technical solutions we develop. Our duty and our mission is to model that complexity in a way that enables the business to grow, either in scale, velocity, or new functionalities. An event-driven architecture proposes a way to do just that.

1.1 The Truth About Monoliths

This section will discuss the advantages and limits of monoliths and how they can constrain business growth. Often monoliths are treated as an anti-pattern, strongly associated with legacy applications. However, there's a lot of misconception about the meaning and usage of monoliths. Monoliths can be an adequate architectural decision depending on the situation, failing to acknowledge this, limits our options. Microservices and event-driven architectures aren't a one-size-fits-all solution; neither monoliths are a one-fits-none solution. We will further detail this in Subsections 1.1.1 and 1.1.2.

We can adopt many strategies to circumvent the monolith's limits, but some limitations reach the point where we need a more sustainable approach. The business growing pains start aching typically in monolithic applications and manifest themselves through a myriad of symptoms. When not tackled with a deliberate approach, this might limit the business's success and be a ball and chain hindering its advance. The common drawbacks of monoliths are detailed in Subsection 1.1.3.

However, deciding to move to a microservice event-driven architecture requires a deliberate decision and a strong reason. Event-driven microservices might be the solution to many of the monolith's limits, but they are also the source of more complex challenges. Moving to a distributed architecture requires thoughtful preparation and the right fertile conditions to strive. We detail the movement to event-driven microservices in Subsection 1.1.4.

This section approaches these topics to give you an overall context. The detailed migration from a monolith to an event-driven architecture, with a use case and strategies to do this, is discussed in Chapter 2.

1.1.1 Anatomy of a Typical Monolith

Businesses start somewhere, sometimes with a piece of software. New functionality is added to that software; sometimes it is a success, sometimes it's not, and the business chooses a different route. If we are lucky enough, that business prospers and that piece of software grows. New functionality spawls inside the application, and old functionality, even when removed, leaves a footprint due to design choices or technical debt. Without deliberate effort to decouple domains and a disciplined organization, it quickly grows into an application that's hard to maintain.

Patchwork Monoliths

Also known as big ball of mud, the most frequent type of monoliths are the ones that have been built during several years with no clear boundaries and logic entangled together. I like to call them patchwork because you usually see cores of domain logic concentrated in one place and then all over the place, like a patchwork quilt.

They are also the ones most troublesome to deal with and to maintain. The application is a single artifact and is deployed all at once. All of it is a single process running in a machine. Through the years, the domain logic becomes entwined and hard to read.

Figure 1-1 illustrates the example of an eCommerce platform with several domains. Without a deliberate effort to maintain each domain divided and decoupled, all the logic from the different domains becomes mushed together.

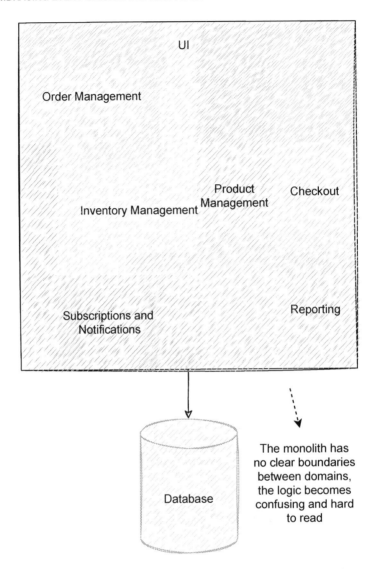

Figure 1-1. *Example of an eCommerce patchwork monolith with no clear boundaries between each domain*

This kind of monolith is the one that is more susceptible to the drawbacks explored in Subsection 1.1.3.

Modular Monoliths

Modular monoliths are divided into modules with clear boundaries; the code is decoupled and able to evolve independently. Modular monoliths benefit from all the advantages monoliths have (and yes, they do have some, detailed in Subsection 1.1.2) and don't suffer from the complex challenges distributed architectures have.

Monoliths usually have a negative connection because most of them are patchwork. Still, a well-structured modular monolith can be an architectural option as valid as a microservice, SOA (service-oriented architecture), or event-driven architecture. Figure 1-2 shows the same example as before, but all the intertwined domains are organized in clear boundaries.

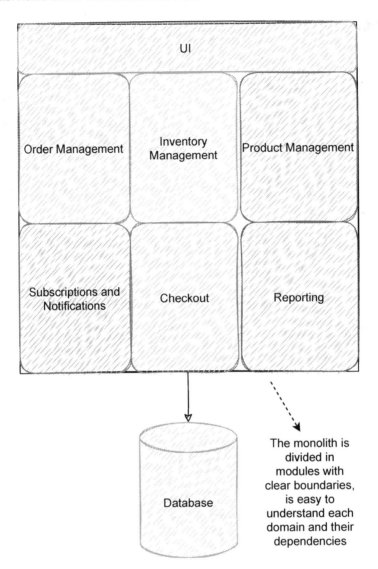

Figure 1-2. *The same eCommerce platform with a modular approach; each domain has clear boundaries*

The dependencies between each module are contained, organized, and visible. The modules should be able to evolve without affecting the other modules; even when we need to remove one of the modules, it is possible because the dependencies are explicit and the domain is contained.

The common pitfall is how easy it is to violate that principle; the dependencies need a deliberate strategy to remain decoupled. That can be done with APIs for each boundary or automate tests for explicit dependency validation (this article[2] details how Root did this). It is still a single application that is deployed together; even if you change just one module, it often requires the deployment of all modules.

1.1.2 What They Don't Tell You About Monoliths; It's Not All Bad

Although monoliths have a terrible reputation, there are advantages to maintaining a single application with one codebase. We often miss those advantages due to being overwhelmed with their limits. There are fundamental, well-known developing principles that we often use on traditional single-process applications that become deficient when using a distributed system and require a different approach. A distributed system is more complex and doesn't have some of the characteristics we always took for granted in monoliths. This section will detail the main advantages of monoliths and how they can ease the delivery of features.

Business Flow Is Visible

With a single codebase, we can inspect the end-to-end flow quickly. We can effortlessly find any feature we want since all functionality is in one repository. It is also easier to see the impacts of new developments since we can see the dependencies of that flow. The business flow can become hard to read with event-driven architectures due to the asynchronous interaction between several services. To understand the business process, we need to understand the flow of events between each service. It is harder to understand the bigger picture, and the bigger picture is always important when adding new features, either to account for possible impacts or to understand if the development is the correct one for the feature. In a monolith, it is possible (although sometimes laborious) to understand how they fit in the overall flow.

---

[2] See Dan Manges, "The Modular Monolith: Rails Architecture," Medium, January 23, 2018, `https://medium.com/@dan_manges/the-modular-monolith-rails-architecture-fb1023826fc4`

No Network Overhead and Limited External Dependencies

All the different modules call each other directly inside the application. There are no remote calls through the network through external APIs or event brokers. This characteristic can enjoy a performance boost (although constrained to the scaling limits) since there is no network overhead. It also doesn't need to deal with API or event versioning and backward compatibility; if there is the need to do a breaking change, we can do it in a single release; all dependencies are inside the application. This characteristic simplifies the development and the release of features that need more profound changes.

We should always avoid a breaking change (as we will detail in Chapter 8), but sometimes they are unavoidable. In an event-driven architecture, we would need to support two versions of an event temporarily, or two versions of an API, to allow the consumers of that event to adapt to the new one. These changes are complex since they possibly affect several services. There is a need for coordination between different teams to align the shift to the new event. There is a considerable development overhead due to the development of the two events' publication and consumption and then removing the old one. In a monolith, this is straightforward; we just change that one application and release it.

Local Validation

In a monolith, it is possible to locally run the whole environment (although I saw applications that took several minutes just to build and additional several minutes just to start up locally). Often we can add and validate a feature by running a single application. However, on an event-driven architecture, we will be adding the feature to one of the several services in the workflow. It's often hard to run the whole workflow locally due to the complexity of the flow and the high number of services it requires, each with their specific configurations and unique dependencies (sometimes even in different languages and environments). Most of the services we might not even know that well since they belong to other teams.

Code Reuse

Since all the code is right there inside the application, it is easy to reuse and build on top of existing functionality. In an event-driven architecture, every service is isolated with their codebase, many of the services will need similar functionality, and obviously, it's not possible to share code. Creating custom frameworks to use across services can be useful, but it isn't as straightforward as using the code inside an application like a monolith and introduces coupling which might be hard to manage later on. Frameworks can also be difficult to debug and can be a nuisance if we need to update all services with a new version. Usually microservices prefer to duplicate code rather than reuse to avoid coupling. Reusing code also makes the code less useful, since it needs to deal with every possible use case. Frameworks are still a valuable asset on common infrastructural functionality like logging.

Monitoring and Troubleshooting

Monitoring a monolith is straightforward since it is only one application. There is a reduced number of machines to monitor, and the logs are trivial to fetch. Troubleshooting an issue is also easier since the scope is reduced to one application. In an event-driven architecture, there are several instances of dozens or hundreds of microservices. This requires a whole different strategy for monitoring and pinpointing incidents. There is a need for a pre-existing infrastructure to manage all those microservices' signals and metrics. Understanding an incident can also be a detective's journey worthy of a short novel without the deliberate approach. On the other hand, a monolith is much more straightforward since the information is far more localized.

End-to-End Testing

End-to-end testing in a monolith is considerably simpler than an event-driven architecture, and I will dare to say, more than simpler, it is actually possible. Since it is a single application, we can have automated tests that validate the whole application's flow. Often end-to-end validations are contained in that application since they don't depend on external services (other than databases, caches, etc.) and can be managed as a single piece. On an event-driven architecture, the approach has to shift from a single piece approach to not having end-to-end tests (or a significantly reduced amount) and having other processes to guarantee quality (we will further detail these processes in Chapter 10).

Simpler Deployment Strategy

Since there is only one application, the deployment pipeline needs to account only for that application's needs. A microservice architecture has to support the deployment of several different services, possibly written in several other languages and with several different dependencies. The overhead of building that kind of pipeline can be lesser or greater depending on the environment's diversity. The deployment topology is often much simpler (and cheaper) with a monolith than with a microservice architecture.

Data Is Centralized

For better or for worse, the data is typically centralized in one or many accessible databases. If a new feature needs some kind of data, it can just go and fetch it from the database. It is simpler to develop, but it has dire consequences when the application reaches a large scale. Although an advantage on the implementation side, it is also one of the most common reasons to leave a monolithic architecture. One of the challenges in event-driven architectures is fetching and managing data dependencies from other services (further detailed in Chapter 8).

Possible to Scale

We can scale monoliths by installing several instances of that application behind a load balancer (also known as cookie cutter[3] scaling). The application does need to be ready to deal with concurrent requests. However, it is limited to the scaling of the application, not the database; when the issue is the database, vertical scaling is often the only option. On the other hand, event-driven architectures are built for horizontal scaling from the ground up and are much easier to scale.

Consistency

Monoliths often use relational OLTP (online transaction processing) databases, which have strong consistency guarantees. These types of databases on monolithic applications typically enjoy ACID (atomicity, consistency, isolation, and durability) guarantees, which provide the traditional consistency guarantees we are used to; for example, a change happens

---

[3] See "Cookie Cutter Scaling," November 29, 2011, https://paulhammant.com/2011/11/29/cookie-cutter-scaling/

everywhere at the same time. On event-driven architectures, due to the asynchronous nature of events, the consistency is often eventual consistency, which can be challenging to deal with (we further detail approaches to deal with eventual consistency in Chapter 5).

Concurrency

In monolithic applications, we can deal with concurrency with the traditional strategies to handle race conditions, like locks or using the database. However, there might be multiple instances of a service on separate machines in an event-driven system, not being possible to do an in-memory lock. Also, depending on the database technology the service uses, it might not support transactions. Dealing with concurrent events requires different approaches that we further detail in Chapter 6.

1.1.3 When Monoliths Become the Business Constrictor Knot

This subsection will discuss the usual problems we associate with monoliths and how they can limit business growth. Monoliths can be an adequate solution in several contexts; however, as companies outgrow them, their handicaps become an increasing concern, especially with patchwork type monoliths. Companies typically struggle the most when reaching a large scale, both in data, usage, and developers. When the business pulls one of these factors because it needs or was successful, the monolith's limits pull the other way around. Like a constrictor knot, the more you pull, the tighter it pulls back. Given enough time, it can bring the business to a halt. It is essential to have a clear reason or a specific problem to tackle when migrating to an event-driven microservice architecture; often it is one or a combination of the ones discussed in this subsection.

Coupling and Lack of Boundaries

The main issue with monoliths is, given enough time, they become unbearably complex and coupled. Since all functionality is inside a single application, it is relatively easy to compromise each domain's boundaries. With time, they fade and become entwined and hard to read. A single change might affect several parts of the system and has unpredictable impacts, for example, changing the subscription logic affects the login. It becomes a nightmare to maintain and change reliably. Since a microservice event-driven architecture relies on events, it is decoupled by design, being easier to maintain the boundaries between domains through time.

Team's Autonomy

As the development team grows, it gets increasingly harder to work on a single application. Even with clearly defined modules, the development still requires communication and alignment, the deployment of the application needs coordination between the different teams. Depending on the development workflow, feature merges also become problematic. Feature branches will often lead to large merges with a high number of conflicts. The overhead of communication, quality assurance, and coordination increases with the number of developers working in the application. We often talk about scaling the application resources, but monolithic applications often limit the scaling of the team.

Release Cycle

The release cycle of a single monolithic application is usually larger than a microservice. Even if a company adopts continuous delivery, the cycles will be inherently larger due to every release; no matter how small the change, the whole application must be validated and deployed. Validating the entire application at once requires a gigantic test suite that can take a considerable amount of time to run (assuming there's no manual validation that often there is). Small changes make the deployment more controllable and enable fast feedback, making it harder to achieve with larger release cycles.

Typically, businesses that rely on monoliths don't deploy that often (e.g., every day) due to the risk since we always deploy the whole application. Not deploying that often accumulates features, and it is harder to have a continuous delivery mindset. That alone is a common argument to move away from a monolith.

Scaling

Although scaling is possible, as we mentioned in the previous section, it is limited to the application. It also implies the monolith has the mechanisms to deal with concurrency with several different instances. When they don't, they require extensive changes to be able to deal with concurrent requests.

Most of the time, monoliths also nurture a monolithic database, which is very hard to scale. When the data starts to have a very high volume, it becomes problematic, especially with queries that require a lot of joins. Vertically scaling (increasing the number of resources, e.g., memory, CPU, etc.) is always an option for both the database and the application, but it gets costly very fast. If a business grows to a stage that needs geo-distribution to provide low latency to every location, a monolithic database might limit its ability to achieve it. A microservice approach shines in this particular aspect since each microservice owns its own database (or at least should), paving the way for a more scalable distribution of the data. Event-driven microservices by design are very easy to scale since they handle events from a queue and largely benefit from the associated decoupling.

When we scale a monolithic application, we scale the whole application. Most of the time, only a single or a part of the modules need scaling. But since every module is bound together, the only option is to scale the whole application. By using a microservice approach, it is possible to scale only the part of the architecture that needs scaling and leave the remaining parts with minimal resources, optimizing costs and resources.

Outdated Technology Stack

Most of the time, monoliths are applications that have several years. Meanwhile, some of the technologies might have been discontinued. It goes beyond the usual technology hype of adopting something just because it's the new best thing. If the application uses technology that is no longer supported by the company that made it, it is a concern. Suppose we face a compatibility issue with new versions of the operating systems or choose to adopt a different way to deploy the application (if we choose to deploy a .net framework application in a Linux environment, for example). In that case, it will limit our options if the monolithic technology doesn't support it. It can be a deal-breaker for new functionalities and can seriously hamper our ability to evolve. Most of the time, changing the whole technology stack on a monolith requires a monumental effort with unimaginable impacts.

Technical debt and no longer needed functionalities can be challenging to remove due to the coupling between boundaries. Although we can achieve this with a modular monolith (Shopify did this with their tax engine[4]), most of the time, removing or replacing a functionality involves touching the whole application and can have unforeseen consequences. Although any service can have an outdated technology stack, event-driven services are highly decoupled; implementing an existing service in a new technology is greatly simplified.

---

[4] See Kirsten Westeinde, "Deconstructing the Monolith: Designing Software that Maximizes Developer Productivity," February 21, 2019, https://shopify.engineering/ deconstructing-monolith-designing-software-maximizes-developer-productivity

Reliability

The risk of deploying a monolith is that any change can bring the whole application down. Even a change in a less critical part of the application can produce an issue (like a memory leak or unforeseen CPU usage) that can affect the whole application, and the whole application is every functionality.

Event-driven architectures might not improve reliability directly since by using several instances on several different machines, we are increasing the number and types of failures that might occur. A deliberate approach to solve these issues is crucial. However, we can deploy smaller parts of the system independently, which (hopefully) won't bring the whole application down.

1.1.4 Using Event-Driven Architectures to Move Away from a Monolith

In the last few subsections, we discussed the advantages and limits of monoliths. In this subsection, we will discuss the transition phase between a monolith and an event-driven architecture. We will slightly approach the considerations we need to make to move to this architecture and how we can start. These topics will be further detailed in Chapter 2 with a real use case.

It is important to notice that an event-driven architecture isn't the ideal solution for every use case. As we discussed in Subsection 1.1.2, monoliths have a set of properties that make development easier, and the limits discussed in Subsection 1.1.3 can also be managed at least until a point. Moving to an event-driven architecture considerably increases the complexity and has costs associated with it. For example, it is debatable if a startup should adopt an event-driven architecture from the beginning. A startup typically is still trying to understand which products work and which don't, needs a fast time to market, needs to be innovative, and might need to restructure a large part of the solution. All that with limited funding, an event-driven microservice architecture has associated costs due to the infrastructure (deployment, monitoring, etc.) that might be overkill in such an early phase. Also, we can apply it best with a considerable understanding of the domain and its boundaries. Changing the boundaries after they are in place can be costly and laborious.

It is also essential to understand why we want to move to an event-driven architecture. Often the potential of this architecture (detailed in Section 1.6) and the hype generated around it can be enticing. Still, one or combined factors mentioned in Subsection 1.1.2 are much stronger than the hype. Perhaps we are already struggling with one of the monolith's limits, maybe we are already struggling in scaling the application or the database, maybe our team is getting too large, perhaps we want a tool that enables us to adopt an Agile and continuous delivery mindset with ease. We should always have a strong reason to do the shift, and it should be a top priority while migrating. After electing that reason, we should measure how we are doing against it and understand if we are making progress or not (this is further detailed in Chapter 2).

To make a move is vital to know where to start, what domains exist, and how they interact with each other. Figure 1-3 illustrates the possible steps to start the migration from a patchwork monolith to a modular monolith. If the monolith is a patchwork monolith and most of the logic is coupled together, an important first move could be to refactor that monolith into a modular monolith. It wouldn't be unprecedented if most of our issues with a monolith disappeared when refactored to a well-structured modular monolith. Sometimes it's a complete nightmare to do that shift in a monolith. Either way, the exercise of trying to do that is pivotal to understanding the domain and associated boundaries, even if we don't change to a modular monolith. By knowing the boundaries, we can reason which would be the most adequate domain to start migrating. By knowing their dependencies, we can plan how to address them both on the monolith and the new architecture. If the monolith is modular, then part of this work is already done, the boundaries are defined, and it's easier to understand its dependencies.

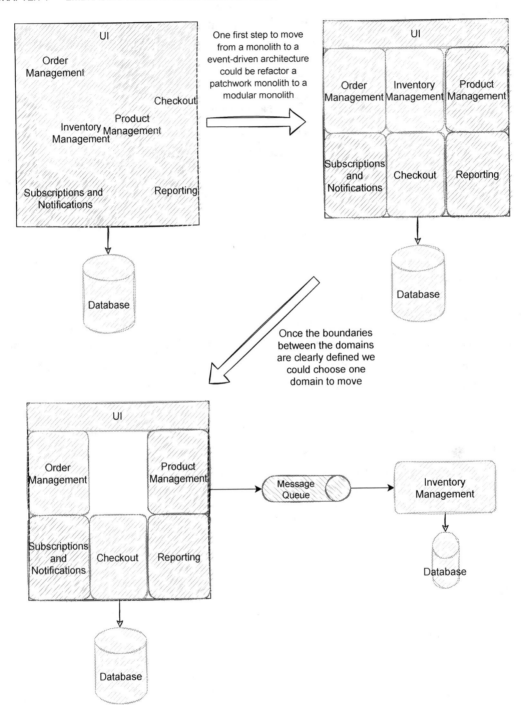

Figure 1-3. *An example of the steps to start the shift from a monolith to an event-driven architecture*

Choosing which domain to move to the new architecture isn't always easy; the decision has to weigh the risk, value, and viability. Risk is the business domain's criticality, value is the benefit we might obtain from migrating that domain, and viability is how practical and viable it is to migrate it.

Once we choose an appropriate domain, we can use an event-driven approach to decouple that domain from the monolithic application. In the example of Figure 1-3, we moved the inventory management module to an independent service that reacts to changes occurring in the original monolith. However, this change introduces all the challenges distributed event-driven architecture has, which this book approaches.

The process of migrating a monolithic application to a microservice event-driven one is hardly a full one-shot migration, where we descope the monolith and create the whole new architecture from scratch. I have rarely seen this happen; most likely, you already have a monolith and might be starting to migrate it to a distributed architecture. Doing a greenfield event-driven microservice architecture also isn't the right option in most cases. It is essential to have a strong understanding of the domain and its boundaries before moving to this kind of architecture. It is hard to have an in-depth mastery of the system's domain without an existing application. In the beginning, those domains can change considerably; adopting an event-driven architecture early on can have substantial costs by reorganizing and redefining the domains.

Adopting a small increment migration enables us to understand what is working and what is not. It allows us to face the challenges of distributed event-driven architectures one step at a time while maintaining the business running. It gives us the space to fail, understand why we fail, and adapt accordingly at a low scale. It gives us room to adapt, learn, and act without having the world crashing down on us. Event-driven architectures also introduce a level of decoupling and reliability different from synchronous microservices. Event streams enable sustainable ways to access the data even from monolithic applications. We further discuss these strategies and the migration from a monolith to a microservice event-driven architecture in Chapter 2.

1.2 What Are Microservices and How Do They Relate to Event-Driven

In the last section, we discussed the monolith's characteristics and limits and how they can constrain business growth. We also approached the various considerations when starting a migration to a microservice event-driven architecture. In this section, we will discuss what microservices are and how they fit into an event-driven architecture.

An event-driven microservice is a simple, specific purpose service that reacts to events to do its work. In an event-driven architecture, several of these services interact with each other to accomplish a higher-level process. Usually, the interaction is composed of a sequence of events between the different services.

An event-driven architecture accomplishes its business processes using the flow of messages through these loosely coupled services. Each service belongs to a given domain or bounded context and has a specific role and limited responsibilities inside that domain. Each domain has the responsibility to process the relevant data in that domain and communicate that change to other domains.

Using the example in Figure 1-4 of an eCommerce platform, when buying a product, the process of accomplishing that order would be the interaction of several boundaries, in this case, the order, inventory, and pricing boundary. The order management boundary processes the order, the inventory boundary manages the stock, and the pricing boundary manages the taxes and final prices for that country. Instead of being the synchronous flow in a single application is the choreography or orchestration of several individual services, each one with its role. Having single-purpose services enables organic bounds for each service and consequently for each boundary.

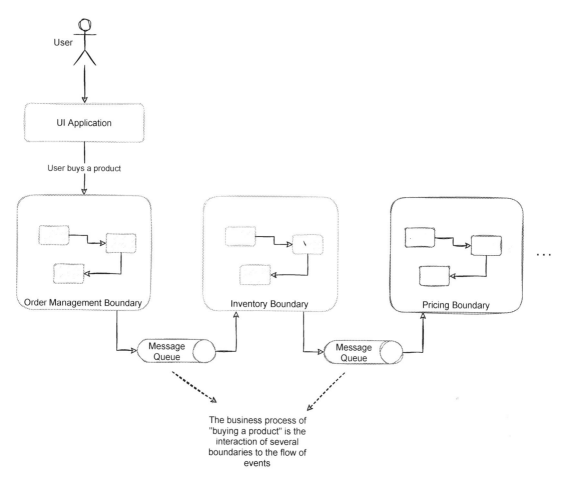

Figure 1-4. *The user purchasing a product triggers a business process composed of the interaction between several boundaries*

In event-driven microservices, each fully decoupled service reacts to each other through technology-agnostic messaging to complete a higher business process.

1.2.1 Deployment

We should also make event-driven microservices independently deployable; a common anti-pattern is the need to deploy several services together. When we need to do so, it rapidly becomes a nightmare to manage and guarantee reliable releases. Also, the deployment should be automated; the teams should be focused on delivering business value rather than laboriously pushing their release live through an intricate release process. The right tools need to be in place for an automated deployment with the required validations. Developers should rely on those deployment tools rather than release or DevOps teams.

1.2.2 Decoupled and Autonomously Developed

We should develop each service autonomously without dependencies from other services. They should also be fully decoupled, easily achieved due to the message brokers between the services. Event-driven enables the architecture to be highly evolvable (as mentioned in the book *Building Evolutionary Architectures*[5]); changes in a given service will hardly affect the whole architecture, and we can deploy the service independently. This characteristic also makes the architecture highly pluggable since new services can simply listen to the events already flowing through the architecture.

1.2.3 Data Ownership

Each service should own the data needed for its domain and expose it through a straightforward interface, typically messaging in an event-driven architecture (although an API is also an alternative). Owing the data is pivotal to achieve independent and autonomous developments. Otherwise, often a change in one service requires other services to change at the same time. Changes in the schema, manageable when in a single service, become a nightmare to release.

1.3 SOA, Microservice, and Event-Driven Architectures

SOA (service-oriented architecture) and microservice architecture often come up when talking about event-driven architecture. There's even some confusion about the differences between SOA and event-driven. This section will detail the characteristics of these three architectures and mention the differences between them.

Sometimes you might hear, "Yeah, event-driven microservices have already been doing that since 2000 with SOA, nothing new." SOA is composed of services that choreograph to accomplish a complex workflow instead of the synchronous flow of

---

[5] See Neal Ford, Rebecca Parsons, and Patrick Kua, "Building Evolutionary Architectures," www.thoughtworks.com/books/building-evolutionary-architectures

a single application like a monolith. It also uses messaging to communicate between services. At first glance, it indeed sounds similar to event-driven architectures, but they are fundamentally different.

1.3.1 SOA

SOA typically tries to build business functionality using reusable components that communicate through a decoupled medium like a network or service bus. We will focus on SOA with ESB (enterprise service bus), which is similar to event-driven architectures. The typical organization of an SOA architecture is illustrated in Figure 1-5.

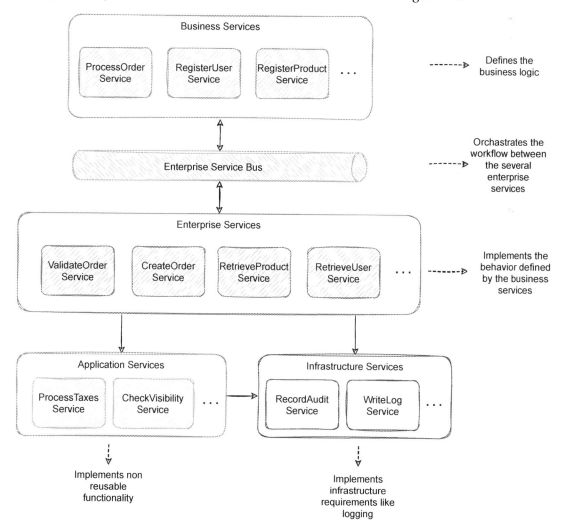

Figure 1-5. *Typical service organization of SOA architectures*

Illustrating with the same example of a user buying a product on an eCommerce platform, we could define a business service named "ProcessOrder" to handle the business logic associated with processing the order. This service determines in an abstract way what is needed for that business to process the order. The enterprise service bus orchestrates the calls needed to the enterprise services. The enterprise services implement specific behavior defined by the business services. In this case, the service bus would call each enterprise service in the correct order to process the user's order, and the enterprise services would do the actual work and manage the state. Enterprise services are designed to be reusable for any workflow; the application services, on the other hand, implement functionality that does not need to be reusable, like processing the order specific taxes that would be relevant just for the order workflow, for example. Infrastructure services implement cross-cutting functionality like logging or monitoring.

The mindset behind the application services is to make functionality reusable, and this is a core design concern in this kind of architecture, opposed to microservices and event-driven where sharing functionality is limited (even avoided). While SOA focuses on abstract, reusable functionality, microservice and event-driven architectures focus on organizing their components around domains.

Also, in SOA the service bus tends to become increasingly larger. Business logic tends to be added to the bus instead of the services. The bus also accounts for several responsibilities besides orchestration. The bus is usually the component that routes and knows to communicate with each service and often has logic to adapt and transform requests. The enterprise service bus tends to grow and become a monolith in its own right although the whole architecture is distributed, often having the worst of both worlds.

1.3.2 Microservice Architecture

A microservice architecture comprises several specific purpose services that interact together to accomplish a given process or workflow. The services are grouped according to a bounded context and in the scope of a given domain. They are decoupled and interact with each other using a message broker or HTTP requests. Figure 1-6 illustrates the same example of an eCommerce platform in a microservice architecture.

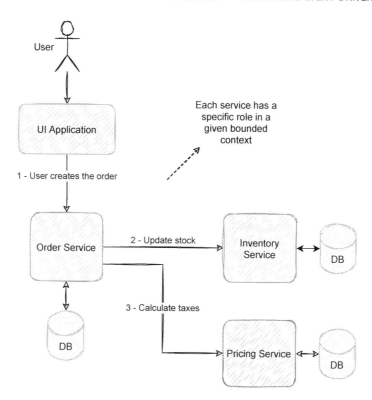

Figure 1-6. *An example of the same eCommerce platform with specific microservices for each bounded context*

The order service is responsible for handling the request for the new order. The service then communicates with the inventory service to manage the product's stock and the pricing service to manage the taxes. Each service is responsible for a single action and is modeled around a domain concept (order, inventory, and pricing); the workflow of processing the order is managed through the interaction between the several services. It is also important to note that each service has a database instead of a shared store; they also expose interfaces for other services to interact with them and expose only the relevant data. Opposed to SOA where reusability is a significant priority, microservices avoid sharing. Instead, they are focused on that domain and bounded context.

This kind of architecture is highly decoupled since there is a physical boundary between components. They have to communicate through the network; this poses natural bounds on each service. The organization of specific bounded contexts in the scope of a given domain allows the domain to change without affecting other unrelated components.

1.3.3 Event-Driven Microservice Architecture

As defined in the previous section, a microservice event-driven architecture shares many of the same microservice architectures' principles. But the interaction between services is focused on the usage of events. Figure 1-7 illustrates the same example of Figure 1-6 with an event-driven architecture.

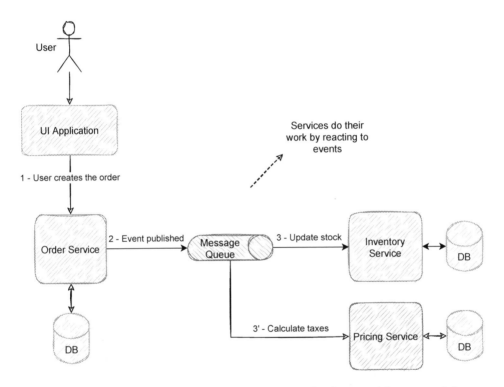

Figure 1-7. *An example of the same eCommerce platform with event-driven microservices*

Instead of a synchronous call between the order service and the other services, the inventory and pricing service react to the order created event from the order service. When consuming the event, they do their work asynchronously, the inventory service updates the stock, and the pricing service calculates the taxes.

By handling the communication between the services with an event broker, we further decouple the services. The order service doesn't know any of its subscribers, and the inventory and pricing service only know the event contract. It is also easy to add new consumers; we just plug them into the event queue. Imagine we had to add a subscription service that notified the users on the order's reception, we could just plug that new service into the message queue, and we don't need to change the order service. This further increases the ability to change each component and evolve their domain without affecting unrelated components or boundaries.

Architectures exclusively composed of event-driven services you will probably find in books or in proofs of concept. Most real-world architectures are a mix of asynchronous and synchronous services. Some use cases require synchronous functionality or won't simply benefit from the complexity of an asynchronous queue, and an API will suffice. The interaction between the two types of services raises challenges and needs deliberate strategies to deal with. The challenges of event-driven architectures are further detailed in Section 1.6.

Event-driven architectures go beyond just reacting to events; they introduce a novel way to share their data. Typically, this was done with synchronous requests through an API, for example. APIs are useful for a real-time fetch of a small set of the latest data. Moving a large data set is difficult and can have impacts on the service and its database. We don't share databases due to the schema coupling or the impact an application can have on another. Synchronous HTTP requests can have the same effect we try to avoid when deconstructing a monolithic database.

In an event-driven architecture, it's also possible to understand the evolution of the data. Often the most critical data is the most recent data. Typical messaging produces an event and disappears once the service consumes it. However, the ability to keep the event and maintain it to be consumed again freely by the same application or future applications unlocks powerful possibilities. The event stream becomes a medium to share all relevant data occurring in real time and provides a way to understand how it changed in the past. It is also a powerful way to stream data to other services. Each consumer can plug into the stream and create a personalized view of the state. This property enables the service to combine data from different sources and model it in the best way to its domain and querying needs.

1.4 The Promise of Event-Driven Microservices

Until now, we discussed monoliths' characteristics, the differences between the types of architectures, and what defines an event-driven architecture. This section will discuss the advantages of microservice event-driven architectures and how they can be an effective solution to many of the limits we usually find in monoliths. We will also discuss how event-driven can benefit a regular microservice architecture.

When Toyota developed lean manufacturing, the focus was on identifying and preserving value for each product; a key concept was eliminating waste and everything that didn't add value to the customer. For example, if you are buying a car, you don't care how long the car's doors travel inside the factory, although the longer the parts' path, the higher the impact on productivity and consequently on the car's cost. The factory should be composed so it minimizes the door's transport; you just care if the car has functional doors. Sometimes we find event-driven architectures compelling due to the technical challenge. Still, when a customer submits an order, it doesn't care if it is processed by a monolith or a cutting-edge architecture. The focus should be on delivering value quickly, safely at scale. How do event-driven architectures enable this?

1.4.1 Evolving Architecture

The services that compose the architecture are contained and decoupled and have a specific role in a given domain. These characteristics limit the impact of changes in the architecture; changing one service will hardly affect others. The natural segregation by bounded contexts enables the domains to change along with the business without affecting other domains. It is easy to add new services to the architecture; often the only change needed is to add the new consumer service, which doesn't require changes in the upstream services.

Having small components decoupled by message queues also enables an experimentation mindset; it is easy to try something with a new service, and if it doesn't work, decommission it. Technical debt is also naturally contained in a component or boundary due to the high decoupling between each component since each service is a different solution and an independent process. It creates the opportunity when the refactoring is too complicated and involves changing the whole service, to create a new one and descope the old one, as long as the bootstrap of a new service is straightforward.

1.4.2 Deployment

As we discussed, monoliths' deployment is risky and usually is associated with test regressions and large release cycles. Instead, event-driven microservices, due to each service's granular and decoupled nature, enable independent deployments without the need to coordinate services. It paves the way to continuous delivery; it is possible to change small increments of functionality throughout the system with little impact, quickly and sustainably. In the example depicted in Figure 1-7, if there were a new way to calculate the taxes in the pricing service, we would change the pricing service to calculate the new taxes and deploy only that service.

It also provides the foundation for a cultural change. When the organization has one application, where developers typically would be focused on the building stage, now it has dozens or hundreds. The focus needs to change to the whole application's life cycle; the teams need to manage developments and services from the developing phase until the deployment in production. There is a fascinating article[6] from Microsoft which associates code ownership with more quality. This cultural change enables that ownership and autonomy.

1.4.3 Team's Autonomy

Instead of coordinating changes in a single application, teams will own and autonomously develop a set of services. Due to the services' decoupled nature, it is easy to autonomously develop those services without dependencies and coordination from other teams. These properties mean decisions can be made quicker and by the people who get most impacted by them – the ones in the trenches working with the services every day and who are called to solve their incidents. It also empowers the teams to make those decisions.

Having teams owning sets of services enables functionality to be added to different domains simultaneously. Usually, the only coordination needed between teams is the contract definition; once agreed upon, both teams can develop their own services in parallel. In the example of Figure 1-7, if the pricing service needed to add a feature to calculate the shipping costs from the order's address, the order service might need to publish the order's address in the event and the pricing service would need to do the calculation. But once they agreed on how to reflect the address in the event, they could do their development in parallel, autonomously without dependencies from each other.

This characteristic is the building block to increase the number of teams. We often refer to technical scalability, but this allows the engineering team to be scalable. By enabling a decoupled architecture, with defined boundaries and ownership between services, we structure the way to add more teams sustainably and grow organically.

---

[6] See "Don't Touch My Code! Examining the Effects of Ownership on Software Quality," September 5, 2011, www.microsoft.com/en-us/research/wp-content/uploads/2016/02/bird2011dtm.pdf

1.4.4 Flexible Technology Stack

We often hear the phrase "use the right tool for the right job." I find it to be very overrated, there are several tools for the job, there isn't a right one, it's often about weighting the tradeoffs and preference for a set of properties above others. Despite this, some technologies are clearly more suitable for some roles than others. For example, if we need geo-distribution between several data centers without significant query capabilities, using Cassandra for that use case could be a good choice, but it would hardly be a good choice to use in all the platform services due to the query limitations. It would be hard to manage different database technologies in a single application like a monolith (although possible with a modular monolith but we don't often see that). On the other hand, on an event-driven architecture since all components are independent and decoupled, it would be easy to adopt different technologies for each service.

Another argument we might see a few years ago would be to use a full-stack JavaScript application to facilitate development with a single programming language. Meanwhile, we learned that it's not a good approach[7] and polyglot programming might be preferable.[8] Having decoupled services enables a polyglot environment, which in a monolith would be very hard to do.

1.4.5 Resilience and Availability

An event-driven architecture enables higher resilience in the sense a single fault can't, or hardly will, crash the whole system. Monolithic applications are more susceptible to this since a critical fault in an infrastructure part of the application (like a memory leak) can crash the whole application, even the modules that weren't changed. In an event-driven microservice architecture, these kinds of faults are naturally bound to that component, so if one fails, the others will keep operating.

Event-driven achieves a higher resilience than synchronous microservice applications due to the decoupling provided by the message queues. In a distributed microservice application with a network of HTTP requests, we often see that they are

---

[7] See ThoughtWorks Technology Radar, "Node overload," May 19, 2020, www.thoughtworks.com/radar/platforms/node-overload

[8] See ThoughtWorks Technology Radar, "Polyglot programming," April 29, 2020, www.thoughtworks.com/radar/techniques/polyglot-programming

susceptible to cascading failures. If one service fails, it will impact all the upstream services and the failure will propagate along the chain. We illustrate this situation in Figure 1-8. This topic is further detailed in Chapter 3.

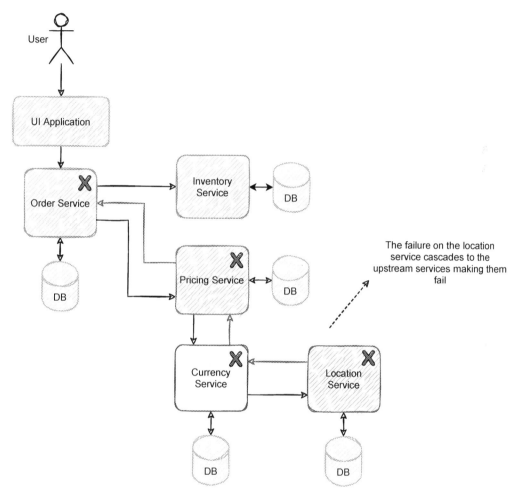

Figure 1-8. *Cascading failure on microservice architectures with synchronous requests*

In this case, the location service fails or is offline and propagates that failure to the upstream services producing a cascading failure. This kind of network of synchronous requests leads to complex dependencies and to instability. Event-driven microservices are naturally resilient to this since even if a service has an issue, it will remain localized to that service due to the event queues.

The decoupling provided by event brokers also means higher availability; even if a component or part of the system is unresponding, the remaining components will continue to process and answer requests. It is further enhanced by the ability to add new instances of event-driven services organically. We can achieve fault tolerance this way; one instance might be unavailable, but the remaining instances will keep processing.

1.4.6 Tunable Scaling

As we saw in Subsection 1.1.2, we can scale a monolith, but it is all or nothing; we scale the whole application, not just the modules we need. If the platform received a peak in orders, we would hardly need to scale the reporting module, for example. Microservices enable to scale only the services that need scaling. This enables the system's resources to diminish or expand with the business needs. It is also cost-effective since we are mobilizing our resources to the components that need them.

Event-driven microservices are often consumers on an event broker; adding new consumers is usually straightforward. The ability to effortlessly add new consumer instances provides natural horizontal scaling without the need for load balancers. Scaling in monoliths is also usually limited by the database; by having services with independent databases, we distribute the data between the services, removing that limitation from the system.

1.4.7 The Past on Demand

As we discussed in the last section, event-driven architectures can share data through events. The sharing isn't limited to the information that is happening at the present time; instead, it provides the full history of events until now. In typical systems, to migrate data from one service to another, we require long processes that query the originating service API, usually with throughput limitations to restrict the impact on the system. It also has complex logic to deal with changes happening during the migration. For example, if we are running a process to migrate stock, a product might have two units of stock at the start of the migration. While the migration is running, a user might have bought those units. So the migration process must account for changes while the migration is occurring, which is prone to tricky corner cases.

With event-driven architectures, we handle this naturally since we start reading from the beginning of history; when we reach the end, it is guaranteed that every change that happened in between is reflected. Streaming data is more sustainable than querying;

it depends solely on the service that needs the data. There is also value in the past; the business can use it to learn and infer. If a new projection of the data is needed, we can use that stream to create a unique projection; the data didn't disappear and is readily available for anyone to use.

1.5 When Should You Use Event-Driven Microservices?

This section will briefly discuss what signs might be relevant when considering a move to an event-driven architecture. We will also question if it is the right decision to make. Microservice, in general, has been a fashionable technological choice and has been adopted by many companies, many times thoughtlessly, what ThoughtWorks names Microservice Envy.[9] As we saw in the previous section, combined with event-driven, it has powerful properties. But should we blindly rush to adopt it?

When I started using C# Linq (a language component that adds native querying to .net) many years ago, I started using it for everything. Need to select the first element of an array? Linq it is. Until someone, much wiser than me, asked me if I wasn't overdoing it. Me at the time, a know-it-all youngster, baffled by the comment pretentiously recited all the benefits of Linq in every possible use case. I did mend my ways regarding Linq, but isn't that what we often do with popular technologies? Currently, microservices suffer the same thoughtless adoption. There's an interesting quote by Kelsey Hightower that says, "You haven't mastered a tool until you understand when it should not be used," which symbolizes this very well.

The first thing to ask when moving to an event-driven is why are we adopting that architecture? As we saw in Subsection 1.1.3, there are limits to monoliths that can draw the business growth to a halt. We look to solve many of those limits with microservices. We need to have a clear reason, which should be a top priority to solve while migrating. As engineers, we try to base our decisions on data and metrics; it would be great to say "Ok, after 30 days without releases we definitely need to move to microservices." Obviously, it doesn't work that way. However, there might be strong signs indicating we might benefit from a microservice event-driven architecture:

---

[9] See ThoughtWorks Technology Radar, "Microservice envy," November 14, 2018, www.thoughtworks.com/radar/techniques/microservice-envy

- The team outgrows the application: The communication and coordination overhead dramatically exceeds the development effort. Feature merges are gigantic and error-prone, with common conflicting touchpoints. These can still be managed with a modular monolith, assigning modules to different teams promoting independence and autonomy, but only goes so far. The natural bounds of microservices are often a good fit.

- Scaling: We can't scale anymore. This is a tricky one; when you think you can't scale, most likely you still can; probably it is just too expensive. As we mentioned, we can scale monoliths with duplicate instances of the same application; this is a valid alternative. The database, however, is typically the pain point. Usually, it can only scale vertically or with a different technology. Event-driven microservices are designed to be horizontally scalable, which helps solving this issue.

- Deprecated technology stack: The application technology is no longer supported or is outdated. It would be possible to upgrade the existing application incrementally, especially in a modular monolith. However, most of the time, it is challenging and expensive.

- Embrace a continuous delivery mindset: Although more challenging, nothing prevents a monolith from adopting a continuous delivery mindset. If the release cycles are massive, imply lengthy regressions, and if the solution is unbearably large, a possible solution could be a modular monolith. However, often transitioning to a modular monolith is hard; microservices need a foundation of automated releases and DevOps culture, which can promote the transition.

Most of these signs require a significant scale; we wouldn't say every startup needs to start with a monolith,[10] but they often are good examples of how they don't benefit[11] from a complex microservice architecture from the ground up. A recent company is still trying to figure out what works and what doesn't; we as developers are still trying

---

[10] Further detailed by Stefan Tilkov, "Don't start with a monolith," June 9, 2015, `https://martinfowler.com/articles/dont-start-monolith.html`

[11] Further detailed by Martin Fowler, "MonolithFirst," June 3, 2015, `https://martinfowler.com/bliki/MonolithFirst.html`

to understand what domains exist and their boundaries. Without stable boundaries between domains, we might have to redraw them later, which can be costly in existing microservice architectures.

We discussed how the decoupled nature of event-driven architectures and the localized scope of microservices can facilitate swapping components. This characteristic can seem antagonistic to the associated cost of redefining boundaries. Large restructures of domain boundaries usually impact several services from different boundaries. They often require the domain to change, and that usually impacts changing the domain logic and models, database schemas, and event contracts of several services, which often impact several teams and have complex dependencies. We should avoid this kind of profound changes to the architecture due to the sheer effort they imply. Often it is more beneficial to have a single broad application where we can understand what boundaries exist without hampering time to market. When we have a sound understanding of the domains, we can start migrating to a distributed architecture.

While a single application is easy to monitor and observe logs, event-driven microservices require a solid foundation of release maturity through pipeline automation, centralized logging and monitoring, automated testing, and message brokers. All of these have an associated cost to bootstrap and maintain that the company needs to account for. It definitely pays up in complex large businesses but is debatable if a small business would benefit largely from it.

A large number of components in microservice architectures also benefit autonomy and ownership, but centralized decision becomes hard. Often, SOA architectures with ESB had a centralized team that decided the message contracts, for example. With event-driven microservices, that management becomes problematic and a bottleneck; although standard guidelines are useful, we should delegate the autonomy of the decision to the teams, which might not be the best situation for a company that wants to retain central control.

1.6 Overview of the Challenges in Event-Driven Architectures

As we discussed in the last sections, a microservice event-driven architecture can solve complex problems and be the foundation of a truly scalable, resilient, and evolutionary architecture. Adopting one also means we are opening a Pandora's box of new kinds of challenges. Many of the characteristics we always took for granted in a monolith suddenly disappear. Distributed systems also carry a new tier of challenges of their own and require deliberate strategies to deal with. This section will briefly discuss those challenges.

A fundamental step to designing an event-driven architecture is getting the size and scope of the services right. There is no formula for this and it can become subjective. The most useful strategy is to follow DDD (domain-driven design) and get the bounded contexts between the services right. This, however, requires a strong knowledge of the system and its domains. As we saw in the previous sections, changing these boundaries later on might be costly and time-consuming. We detail the service design and DDD in Chapter 3. Chapter 4 discusses patterns to organize microservices.

In a monolith, we are used to enjoying strong consistency; any change is seen anywhere in the application instantaneously. The presence of event brokers between the services turns each service asynchronous. The asynchronous nature of the services produces what is known as eventual consistency; given enough time, all changes will eventually propagate throughout the system. However, while the changes are still propagating, different system parts might return old data to customers and other services inside the architecture. This raises the challenge of how to deal with stale data. Chapter 5 further details and proposes solutions to handle eventual consistency.

Eventual consistency and the asynchronous nature of the services require a different approach to UI design. Typical UIs induce the user into false strong consistency, as updates might take some time to occur. Messages like "updates might take some time to be reflected" on the UI are common and also a dubious user experience. Chapter 9 further details this topic.

Dealing with concurrency in a single application is also straightforward; we can use traditional ways to deal with concurrent threads like locking or mutexes. In an event-driven architecture, however, we scale by having multiple instances of the same service. In-memory concurrency mechanisms no longer work since concurrent requests or events can target different instances. Message ordering can also be an issue if the order of events is switched, if the service ends up processing an old event after the most recent one can become inconsistent. Although there are brokers that guarantee the order, most don't, and retrying can disorder messages. Chapter 7 details how to achieve better consistency with idempotent messages. Chapter 6 details strategies to deal with concurrency and unordered messages.

Event-driven architectures enjoy a high level of decoupling. The domain flow itself couples them as business processes progress through the boundaries. Often, the only sharing point between the services is the message's contracts. Contracts become pivotal to the system design as the event schema and its size often is a topic of lively discussion. Events can be small or large; depending on how we design them, both approaches have tradeoffs. However, they heavily impact the systems that need them and the overall architecture, as we detail in Chapter 8.

Support teams often need to do quick data fixes on applications. Monolithic applications support this since a monolithic database typically backs them up. When we move to a distributed architecture with dozens or hundreds of services, these quick fixes aren't so straightforward. In an event-driven architecture, correcting something often means sending a command with the opposite operation (if we add stock using an AddStock command incorrectly due to a bug, we need to do the reverse operation and send a RemoveStock command, for example). Usually, to do so requires custom tooling from the ground up to allow these kinds of operations.

As we discussed before, in an event-driven architecture, the message brokers allow the components to be highly decoupled. The decoupling enables the architecture to be highly evolutionary and the components to come and go as they wish. It is a great property to allow the system to evolve along with the business. However, when we have many decoupled components, it gets hard to understand the flow between the services. Testing the end-to-end flow, it's impractical due to the interaction of several components. Each component is also independently deployable, raising the challenge of guaranteeing the quality of the end-to-end flow every time we deploy a single component. Chapter 10 further details the challenges and strategies of quality assurance.

Different teams are responsible for different sets of services. Adding a business feature might impact several teams, as features often involve several domains. Although the decoupling between the services promotes parallel working, sometimes complex dependencies between several teams arise. Chapter 10 further details the organizational impact of event-driven architectures.

When technologies become popular, people tend to see them as a magic solution to most of our problems. We sometimes rush to turn a blind eye to their issues and focus on the benefits they can bring. However, it's always about weighing the tradeoffs. There are types of challenges that we can only feel their true extent in production. Certainly, proofs of concept are great to test a specific objective, but most of the time, we need to run a technology at scale in production to really learn them and understand the reach of their limitations. The added complexity, the distributed characteristics, and the asynchronous nature of event-driven architectures pave the way to complex challenges. To manage them, we require deliberate strategies. This book approaches those challenges and proposes strategies to deal with them.

1.7 Summary

- There are different types of monoliths; the hardest to deal with is patchwork monoliths due to entwined logic and lack of boundaries.

- Modular monoliths can be an adequate architecture choice and offer several advantages and reduced complexity over distributed architectures.

- Businesses can outgrow monoliths, and given enough time, monoliths' limits can constrict business growth.

- Event-driven architectures can facilitate the migration from a monolith to a microservice architecture by promoting high decoupling between components.

- Event-driven architectures accomplish higher-level processes through the flow of events of several small, specific purpose services.

- An event-driven architecture facilitates a medium to share past and present data in real time to any service. By easing the decoupled sharing of every data that occurred and is occurring in the system unlocks powerful possibilities.

- An event-driven architecture's components enjoy a set of properties that are the foundation for a scalable, evolutionary, and decoupled architecture.

- There are situations where event-driven architectures aren't the best option. We also need an exact reason when deciding to move to a microservice event-driven architecture; that reason should be a top concern while migrating.

- The distributed, complex, and asynchronous nature of event-driven architectures has difficult challenges we must address from the ground up.

CHAPTER 2

Moving from a Monolith to an Event-Driven Architecture

This chapter covers:

- How to incrementally adopt an event-driven architecture

- How to decide what functionality to move first

- How to move data from a monolith to a microservice architecture in an event-driven mindset

- Using CDC (change data capture) to move data

- Using events as the source of truth for both the old and new architecture

- How to deal with event-driven microservices that need monolith's data and vice versa

- How to gradually move traffic from the monolith to the new services

- Implementing two-way synchronization and understanding the impacts associated with it

© Hugo Filipe Oliveira Rocha 2022
H. F. Oliveira Rocha, *Practical Event-Driven Microservices Architecture*,
https://doi.org/10.1007/978-1-4842-7468-2_2

Splitting a monolith is often like an onion. There are legitimate recipes to eat it whole, depending on the dish we are serving. But to release their flavor compounds and achieve their true potential, we have to cut it. Onions, like monoliths, are manageable as a single piece. When we start to cut them down, they become hard to handle. As we cut them, we are never sure how small is small enough, the layers inside the onion start to fall apart and run away from our hand, and depending on the way we cut them, it can rapidly bring tears to our eyes.

In the last chapter, we discussed the advantages and limitations of both monoliths and event-driven architectures. This chapter will tackle how we can start migrating functionality to an event-driven architecture and discuss several patterns to migrate data using an event-driven approach. We will illustrate how we can achieve this by using an example of an eCommerce platform.

Starting a migration from a monolith can be daunting. Monoliths are often very intricate with complex and tangled logic, often the result of years of unchecked growth, with unsure business requirements and pressing urgency. Modular monoliths are the exception but also rare to find. Even to know where to start the migration and what to migrate first can be hard to decide. On the other hand, event-driven architectures aren't always the best option. Sections 2.1 and 2.2 will help you decide if an event-driven architecture is the best option and how we can start migrating functionality.

Moving data is one of the parts people most struggle with while migrating to a new architecture. Stateless functionality, like a service that applies a fixed tax to every order without relying on state, is relatively straightforward to migrate. It is greatly simplified by not needing data migrations and keeping data in sync with the old and new architecture. Event-driven approaches provide an alternative to traditional methods by exposing data sustainably and seamlessly. They offer an organic way to keep data up to date in (potentially) real time.

Moving functionality from the monolith to a new architecture usually isn't done (and it shouldn't be done) with a big bang release (transitioning to the new architecture and descoping the old one instantaneously). Most of the time, we need to deal with the new services requiring data from the monolithic application and the monolithic application still using the new service data. Event-driven architectures also aren't composed of only event-driven services. Often they are composed of both synchronous and asynchronous services. Section 2.6 will discuss how we can deal with dependencies between the monolith and new services in both situations.

Even after moving functionality to the new architecture, users and clients don't change all at the same time to the new architecture. We need approaches to gradually move traffic from the monolith to the new services. Furthermore, there is functionality that depends on several different boundaries. We might migrate one of them, but we need to maintain the interaction between the others. Requesting data from the new services is an option, as discussed in Section 2.6, but depending on the use case, it can be hard to do (e.g., if there is considerable logic in stored procedures). Section 2.8 illustrates how we can migrate functionality incrementally and maintain two sources of truth.

2.1 Is Migrating to an Event-Driven Architecture Your Best Option?

Chapter 1 discussed how a modular monolith might be a good architectural choice and how it can enjoy several properties we often look for in microservice architectures without the challenges of distributed components. This section will teach you to challenge whether an event-driven microservice architecture is the best option and to question if it is possible to solve the issues we face without the added complexity of a distributed architecture.

A survey[1] by Kong indicates that most technology leaders believe the failure to adopt a microservice architecture will hurt their company's ability to compete. Microservice architectures have been adopted by many companies as a means to solve scalability and productivity limitations and most of the issues Chapter 1 mentioned. Without a doubt, they bear advantages other architectures struggle to provide.

However, we often rush to blindly adopt technologies that work for other companies. By focusing on all the limits the current architecture imposes on us, we often fail to see the simplicity and safety they always provided. Adopting one without careful deliberation often leads to dreadful results. As discussed in Chapter 1, the added complexity, the distributed challenges, and asynchronous nature are often mischievous challenges and difficult to tackle with the strategies we often use in a monolithic application.

---

[1] See this article by Kong, December 11, 2019, `https://konghq.com/press-release/2020-digital-innovation-benchmark/`

Take Istio, for example; the community decided to change from a microservice architecture to a monolithic approach gradually. Istio, a service mesh for microservice communication, would apparently benefit from the same architecture that helps others build. However, they soon found[2] out the deployment overhead and configuration complexity of several moving parts, the difficulty in debugging, and the overhead of network requests and caches never fully paid off. So they moved back to a monolithic deployment for the Istio control plane, which makes sense for that project.

Segment is also another interesting example; they moved from a monolith to a microservice architecture just to move back to a monolith a couple of years later. They shared an article[3] explaining how a small team struggled to cope with the considerable increase in complexity. A single update to a shared library with the old architecture would take a single deployment now would take dozens, one for each service. The developer productivity greatly plumbed due to the large number of services that kept growing. Operational overhead increased steadily with each new service. Eventually, they needed to do something and moved back to a monolith and benefited largely from it.

"Ok, well, obviously you shouldn't have done things like that" is often a common (and naive) argument when an architecture fails. Instead, we should be asking: "Is a microservice architecture right for that use case?" Sometimes it isn't; a monolithic approach might be much more adequate. As we mentioned in Chapter 1, it is about delivering value to the customer and the best way to achieve it.

The questions we should ask are: "What am I trying to solve? What will I get from it?" And a cutting-edge, cool, brand new, shiny architecture isn't the answer. Business goals should support the answer and be in line with the actual value delivered to the customer. Using the same architecture or refactoring it in a structured way might yield even better results than a premature microservice adoption.

Let's illustrate with some examples of answers to that question that might not be a solid reason to advance with an event-driven microservice architecture:

- "We will be able to scale horizontally more efficiently.": Although that is true, event-driven microservices allow for selectable scalability; as we saw in Chapter 1, we can scale a monolith; isn't that an option?

---

[2] See this article by Christian Posta, "Istio as an Example of When Not to Do Microservices," January 8, 2020, `https://blog.christianposta.com/microservices/istio-as-an-example-of-when-not-to-do-microservices/`

[3] See Alexandra Noonan, "Goodbye Microservices: From 100s of problem children to 1 superstar," July 10, 2018, `https://segment.com/blog/goodbye-microservices/`

- "We will be able to develop autonomously.": Teams working in a modular monolith can also enjoy a high degree of autonomy. The way the company organizes the teams and how autonomously they can work is often a shift in the mindset rather than a technological shift.

- "We will deliver features faster.": Depending on the size of the team, it can actually hurt productivity moving to a distributed architecture as segment experienced. It is often valuable to understand the root cause of why features are slow. A huge team would indeed benefit from a microservice architecture, while a smaller one might not be able to gain as much and often suffer from other kinds of limitations unrelated to the application's architecture.

- "It will be simpler to add features for an isolated domain.": Despite this might be true in most cases, the isolated domain systems are still part of an ecosystem of services, and adding features or new data to entities often lead to the other systems to adapt to the new data or features. Sometimes dependencies between services are hard to manage due to the team roadmap priorities and introducing breaking changes, for instance.

- "We want to adopt a continuous delivery mindset.": Although a good reason, we should always ponder if we can't do that with the existing architecture. It is possible to adopt a continuous delivery mindset with a monolith, although it gets more challenging as the teams and application grow.

Here are some examples that often are strong reasons:

- The database can only be scaled vertically and reached a point that it isn't cost-effective. Monolithic databases tend not to be horizontally scalable. Scaling often reaches a point where a better approach is more effective (especially cost-wise).

- The size of the team. Although the number of teams can be manageable in a modular monolith, it often gets to a point teams outgrow the application.

- Using different languages and technologies or the need to change deprecated ones. Although it is always possible to update an existing monolith, it is often tough and error-prone. Also, it might not be possible to support different technologies in the same application.

We should always question if there aren't other options and if a microservice architecture is the best approach. We should also have strong reasons or concrete limitations to solve. A large scale amplifies most of the advantages we mentioned in Chapter 1, both in usage and developers. If a company didn't reach that stage, it will likely struggle with the complexity more than enjoy the benefits.

As we mentioned in Chapter 1, not having clear domains and boundaries is also a strong reason to postpone that migration. In the early life of a company, domains are prone to change. Changing the domains and boundaries in an event-driven microservice architecture is costly and laborious. Having a monolith (even a bad one) at least guarantees there is a physical place to validate the existing domains and refactor them with less effort.

However, often teams tend to outgrow a single application. Managing changes and releases becomes harder as the teams and application grow. Guaranteeing the isolation properties of modular monoliths becomes increasingly harder. Event-driven microservices provide a good alternative to solve these problems, provided we have a clear objective.

2.2 Moving to an Event-Driven Architecture, How to Decide Where to Start

This section will discuss how we can choose the most appropriate functionality to migrate from a monolith to an event-driven architecture. We will illustrate an example of an eCommerce platform monolith and explain how we can choose one of its modules to create a new service.

Most complex applications have several domains, and they interact with each other to achieve a higher-level process. A bounded context is focused on a piece of the overall functionality and contains a given domain model. For example, an eCommerce platform might have several bounded contexts, being one of them the order management. The order management bounded context could have a core domain model that conceptually illustrates orders (bounded context is a domain-driven design term that we detail in Chapter 3; for now, see it as a domain boundary).

In a perfect world, we would just stop product development for a few months while re-architecting the whole system. This situation is rarely the case since the business must still operate and evolve as the new architecture is being built. An important consideration is to migrate functionality incrementally; bear in mind that often we need to have both old and new systems running simultaneously. It is imperative to build a sustainable way to gradually migrate functionalities to the new architecture to avoid big bang releases. Migrating gradually also provides a way to deal with the event-driven architectures' challenges on a lower scale. It also is easier to guarantee a safe way to roll back the changes if needed. We will get some parts wrong; it is vital to guarantee the business's reliability and give us the space to learn from our mistakes. Event-driven and the patterns we describe in this chapter are built in this mindset to allow incremental delivery of functionality.

The first step to start moving functionality to an event-driven architecture is understanding the existing domains and bounded contexts. Often monoliths feel like the example illustrated in Figure 2-1.

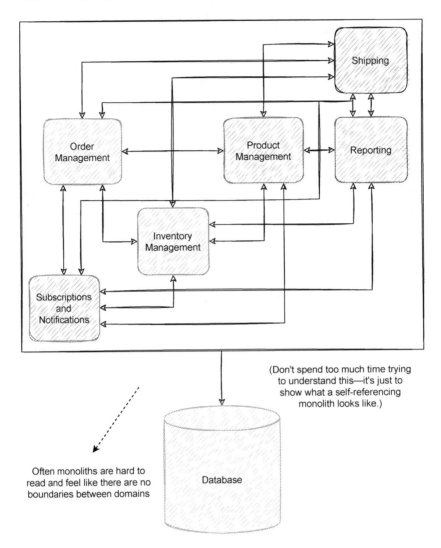

Figure 2-1. *Example of how we often feel about monoliths. Illustrates an example of an eCommerce platform where everything references everything*

It might be overwhelming to analyze all the bounded contexts in massive patchwork monoliths. The first few tries might feel like everything references everything, and there is no clear distinction. DDD (domain-driven design) has techniques that can help with this, further detailed in Chapter 3. However, having an existing application that already describes these relations can help in understanding how a business operates, hence the importance of sometimes starting with a monolith and then moving incrementally to an event-driven microservice architecture.

If you are dealing with a patchwork monolith, it might be useful to refactor it to a modular monolith. By doing so, we might even solve the initial reason that made us consider moving to an event-driven architecture. It will also underline the existing bounded contexts and make their dependencies visible. If we can't build a well-structured monolith, why do we think we can create a well-structured event-driven architecture? With that information, we can make an informed choice on which module to migrate first. Do not underestimate this effort as domain knowledge is essential to build the new architecture.

Even if we don't choose to change the existing monolith, trying to understand how we could change it to a modular monolith and the underlying exercise of comprehending the boundaries and bounded contexts is pivotal to understanding which domain to move first. Eventually, we will reach a design similar to pictured in Figure 2-2.

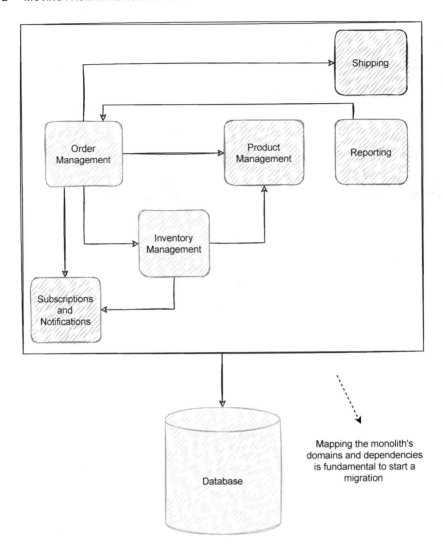

Figure 2-2. *Example of an eCommerce platform with several interactions between bounded contexts*

Once the business features and how they map with each bounded context are clear, we can design the domain model. These steps are fundamental to start the migration. Those bounded contexts will eventually map to different services responsible for managing the operations in each domain's scope.

We have our bounded contexts and dependencies mapped (as detailed in Chapter 3); now what? We need to decide which module to migrate first. Often it is a weight between the difficulty in moving a module, how that module would benefit from the move, and how lenient the consistency guarantees can be. As we discussed in Chapter 1, event-driven architectures feature eventual consistency; a functionality might allow smaller or larger inconsistency windows depending on the impact of that weak consistency model. It is wise to start migrating features that allow lower consistency constraints to give us space to tune the system to guarantee the inconsistency is small enough that won't impact the system's users (how to tackle eventual consistency is discussed in Chapter 5).

In the example in Figure 2-2, the order management module might benefit significantly from an event-driven architecture to ease the process of scaling in the face of load peaks. However, it might not be easy to remove the module because it depends on the other four modules. The shipping or reporting module could be a good alternative since each one only has one dependency. Shipping might need stronger consistency guarantees than reporting, which typically is asynchronous; often reports don't need to be accurate to the last second. Following this line of reasoning, reporting could be a good option to migrate first.

We should try to find functionality that is easy to migrate, that largely benefits from the migration, and it is not critical to have strong consistency guarantees. All modules are liable to be relocated, but doing an easy part first can be an excellent way to get feedback on how the migration is going and pave the way for the system's more challenging pieces. It also guarantees you face the challenges of distributed architectures gradually and can sustainably respond to them.

It is also important to understand how the migration to the new architecture is going. We are doing this because we are trying to deliver value to the customer or solve an issue in the current architecture. Our gut feeling is important, but as engineers, we try to drive our decisions with data. What should we measure? It is often related to the answer we gave to the question in Section 2.1 on the reason we are migrating.

If we are trying to improve the team's autonomy and productivity, it might be interesting to measure the dependencies between teams, feature branch longevity, or merge requests. Long-lived branches are prone to get stale due to other teams conflicting changes in the master branch. It is often the source of complicated merges and a high number of conflicts; it is one of the typical challenges teams have when they outgrow one application.

It can also be useful to measure the deployment process. If we are trying to shift to a continuous delivery mindset, the number of deployments, cycle time, and lead time might be interesting metrics. They also relate to the number of dependencies between teams since with high coupled code typically found on monoliths, features sit on ready-to-merge state longer. The shift should improve the overall time a feature takes to be deployed.

If we are trying to improve our scalability capabilities, the number of incidents due to load peaks or measuring response time might be useful. The tier of the current machines for both the application and database might also give some insight into the capacity the application has to support a growing business. As we discussed, often monoliths struggle with load and when the only way to scale is vertically (by increasing the machine's resources) it can constrain the business growth. As we migrate to an event-driven architecture, gradually the load will be distributed between the new services, so the high-tier machines shouldn't be needed anymore.

We also can unconsciously overwork metrics, and with enough creativity, they can reveal anything. To some extent, we should base our decisions on metrics, but it is as important to know the feeling of the people working with the system. Understanding their problems, concerns, and opinions on the state of the migration can give an overall view of how it is going. Be sure to check with the team regularly to understand their experience; their feedback is the most valuable metric you can find.

2.3 Using an Event-Driven Approach to Move Data from a Monolith

The last sections discussed the decision to move to an event-driven architecture and how we can decide which module to move first. This section will approach how we can expose and transfer data from the monolithic application to the new architecture.

Using the example in Figure 2-3, let's say we decided to migrate the reporting module to a new service. Remember how we discussed why it is essential to do an incremental migration? We could start by building the reporting service outside the monolith.

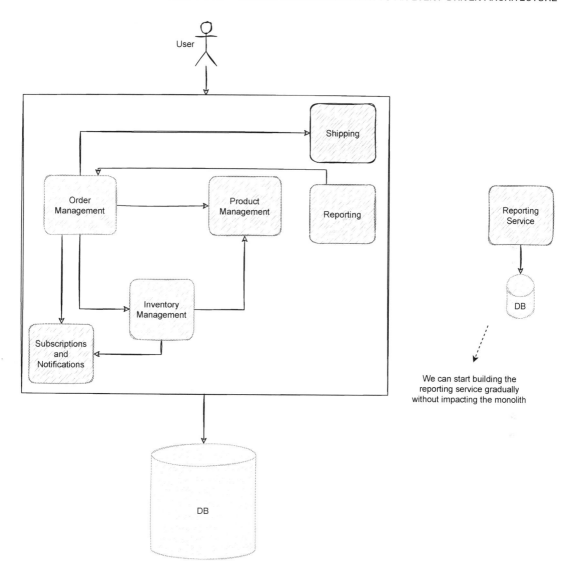

Figure 2-3. *First step in migrating the reporting service to an event-driven architecture. It is important to do the steps incrementally by building the reporting service independently from the monolith*

By building the reporting service without any interaction with the monolith, we can avoid any impact on the other teams working on it. We can also incrementally add functionality to the reporting service. We could first deploy the service in the live environment without any functionality and then gradually add feature by feature until the service has all the monolith's reporting functionality.

A common question is whether to copy the code as is in the monolith or to refactor it. It depends on the monolith; on a well-structured and organized monolith, it might make sense to copy the code as is; it will save us time. However, most often than not, the monolith's model might not be up to date to the incoming requirements. The migration is a good opportunity to refactor it and build it more cleanly if needed. We will soon add an event queue between the reporting service and the monolith so they can have different models and behaviors as long as the monolith obeys the event's contracts.

Just bear in mind that while we are migrating, both services have the functionality. A change in the monolith's reporting module due to bug fixing or new features means we have to change the reporting service accordingly until we descope the functionality in the monolith.

Let's say the reporting service generates and saves a report for each fulfilled order. We already migrated the functionality to create the report. But we need the order information to trigger the report creation and to fill the report's data. As we see in Figure 2-3, the monolith's reporting module has a dependency on the order management module due to fetching information from that module. We need to somehow expose the order information to be consumed by the reporting service. The next step is to step up a queue between the service and the monolith; the reporting service will use that queue to react to events and generate the reports, illustrated in Figure 2-4.

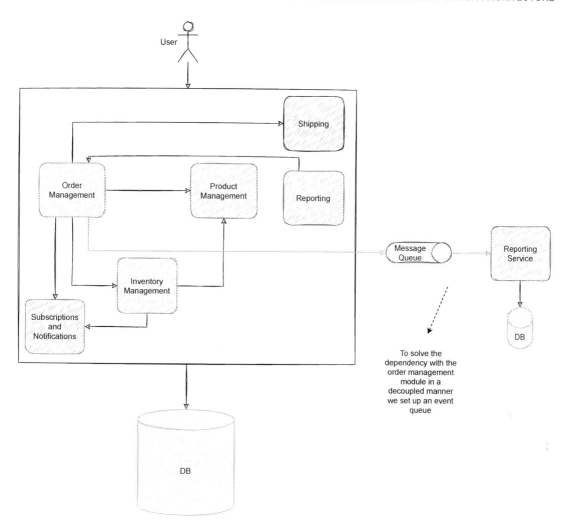

Figure 2-4. *Second step in migrating the reporting service to an event-driven architecture. Set up a queue with the order management information to be consumed initially by the reporting service*

An essential step in building the reporting service is defining the contracts that the service will listen to. Event schema usually triggers a lively debate and is a core design that affects the downstream services. It is crucial to design them right; otherwise, they can trigger difficult challenges to the services that consume the event. How to design the event schema is further discussed in Chapter 8. At this point, let's worry about creating a contract that fulfills the needs of the reporting service.

Once we set up the order management event publishing and the reporting service event handling, we are already able to expose functionality in the reporting service. For recent orders, users can already use the reporting service to obtain the reports. But what about all the reports that were created until now? We just migrated functionality, not data.

There are several strategies to migrate data from existing databases. You probably had to do this one time or another and likely will know how hard it is. Section 2.9 approaches some of these alternatives. Without events, we could run a batch from time to time to synchronize the monolithic database to the new service, introducing higher complexity with higher delay. We could temporarily access both databases with all the issues that can cause.

The beauty of event-driven services is that they provide a way to seamlessly expose that information without these complicated ad hoc processes. Events are the source of truth, and we can use them to transfer data to any service that needs it. We can leverage the fact we already handle events and use the same strategy to migrate all the existing data that we need along with the data that is happening now.

In the example of Figure 2-4, we could trigger a job in the order management service to publish all the order information to the event queue. When the reporting service starts to consume, it will consume all orders and generate all reports that it needs. It would also be a great way to validate the service's correctness; the generated reports would have to be the same as those existing in the monolith.

Using an event broker that keeps the events and doesn't delete them upon consumption also opens the way for exciting possibilities. Imagine we introduce a bug in the reporting service, and we need to generate the reports again. We could simply start reading the queue from the point where the bug was introduced. If there was a feature to change the reports to have different information, we could simply start reading from the queue's beginning and generate the new reports. Operations that otherwise would be cumbersome to do, with error-prone manual interventions, are suddenly built in and can occur organically.

But we are not done; we migrated the functionality and the data, but the user is still using the monolith to obtain the reports. Now we can inform the consuming applications to change to consume the reporting service. We can also have a proxy on the layer above the monolith redirecting the calls to the new service. Section 2.8 further discusses these options.

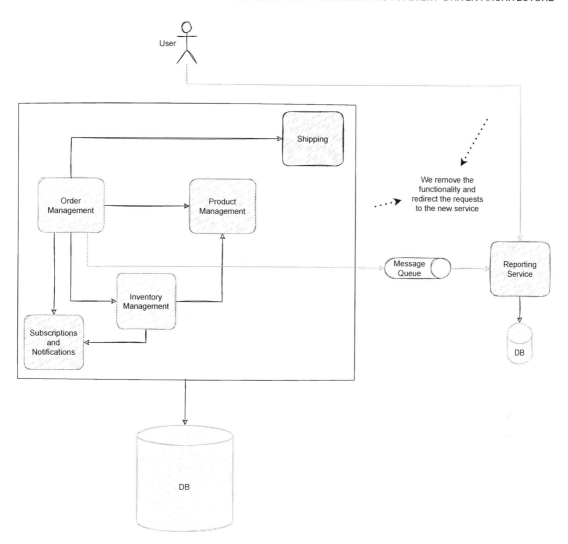

Figure 2-5. *Third step in migrating the reporting service to an event-driven architecture. We finalize the migration of the reporting functionality by removing the old module*

Once there are no calls to the monolith's reporting module, we should remove it from the monolith, as depicted in Figure 2-5. If we incrementally do this to each module, we gradually decompose the monolith into smaller services.

We also built the foundation for other services to build on top. If another module needs the order management information, it's already exposed. We can start building the service and plug it into the existing message queue. Even the order management module itself, when we create the new service, can migrate the data by merely streaming the events in the queue by reading it from the beginning. Once we migrate the order management module, the reporting service would consume events from the new service rather than the monolith. The decoupled nature of event-driven services allows the order management service's migration without changing the reporting service. In a traditional microservice architecture with synchronous requests, this change would need coordination to at least shift endpoints from the monolith to the new service.

This way, an event-driven approach enables data streaming from the monolith to the new services. It avoids other complex alternatives to split or share the database without a custom batching process or other manual options. Streaming the data serves both as a way to share real-time information to the new services and as the history of data, easing the migration process. It is also a very intuitive, scalable, and organic way to distribute data throughout the architecture.

Adopting an event-driven service has its drawbacks; as we mentioned in Chapter 1, the reporting information is now asynchronous and might not enjoy the strong consistency guarantees it enjoyed while inside the monolith. In this particular case, reports are typically asynchronous, so it seems a good fit. However, other functionalities might have stronger consistency guarantees, for example, guaranteeing the consistency with several tables by using transactions. Achieving consistency is still possible through process managers and Sagas, as detailed in Chapter 7. How to deal with eventual consistency is discussed in Chapter 5.

2.4 Using Change Data Capture (CDC) to Move Data from a Monolith

The previous section discussed how we could share the monolith's data by publishing events in internal modules. However, capturing every functionality that might change information can be challenging. Monoliths also tend to have a considerable amount of logic in the database's stored procedures, making it even harder to publish changes to an event broker. This section will discuss how we can use a similar event-driven approach but using CDC (change data capture) to extract the data.

One of the situations where I experienced firsthand the difficulties of extracting monolith's data was when the team was trying to migrate the inventory management module from the backoffice application (a large patchwork monolith) of an eCommerce platform. The first approach we tried was to call the new service every time any functionality changed inventory data. By making two requests, one to the new service and maintaining the monolith calls, we were able to verify if both databases held the same data. After changing a few missing flows, it looked great; the regressions we did on every functionality were working fine; both databases were the same in every quality environment.

When we reached production, however, it was a completely different story. The new service data somehow was slowly diverting from the monolith (the current source of truth). Although the high majority of flows were calling the new service, we found out there were still some stored procedures (with some hundreds of lines each) that changed the data. The support teams, from time to time, also did some data fixing directly on the database. There were also mushroom applications outside the monolith that changed the data. Mushroom applications are ad hoc applications that often pop up throughout the company, created outside the standard architecture to achieve a small objective. It can even be an excel sheet accessing the database. Many companies have several of these created by operational teams to help with ad hoc operations like data analysis or automation of a common task. Due to these reasons and others, we soon found out that completely covering all flows that accessed that data would take a substantial effort. There are times where it is overly complex to change an existing monolith to follow, for example, the approach in Section 2.3. Sometimes it's not even possible when using third-party vendor monoliths.

CDC is a pattern to identify and capture individual changes made to a database or application. Using CDC can be a valid alternative in these situations since we can capture every change directly on the database. There is also built-in functionality on many databases that support CDC and provide easily accessible ways to extract data.

Instead of natively extracting and publishing data, there are also several frameworks to extend this functionality; for example, Kafka Connect uses CDC and connectors to the database to extract data and load it to Kafka. Apache NiFi is also a reliable option that provides the same functionality. These frameworks are easy to bootstrap and offer an easy way to extract data from the database, mostly through configuration. It is also possible to create our custom transformations.

However, these frameworks have a few drawbacks:

- If we are trying to track down a live incident, it's hard[4] to locally debug the connectors. Building unit and integration tests can be challenging due to the references to all the internal Kafka classes.

- The level of customization might not be the most adequate for our requirements and might have limitations. If we need to enrich the data with an external source on the connector, it becomes hard to extend (although we should keep that logic out of the connector, it isn't always easy).

- These frameworks tend to expose the underlying database data models adding additional coupling. We might prefer a custom application in charge of extracting, creating, and managing its events. Often it is preferable to endow the events with domain meaning. An update of a few fields might have more business value than the technical definition of a few columns that were updated. Maybe updating the stock column means making a reservation business-wise. The events themselves should reflect that business intent. That can become hard to translate using these frameworks.

Depending on your requirements, building a custom solution to analyze the database CDC can be a preferable option and give you higher flexibility. On the other hand, using a framework can significantly reduce the implementation overhead and set up a solution with little effort.

In the same example in Figure 2-2, how could we migrate a module using CDC? The first step would be to set up a service or a connector to the database, depicted in Figure 2-6.

---

[4] See "Why We Replaced Our Kafka Connector with a Kafka Consumer," December 16, 2017, https://hackernoon.com/why-we-replaced-our-kafka-connector-with-a-kafka-consumer-972e56bebb23

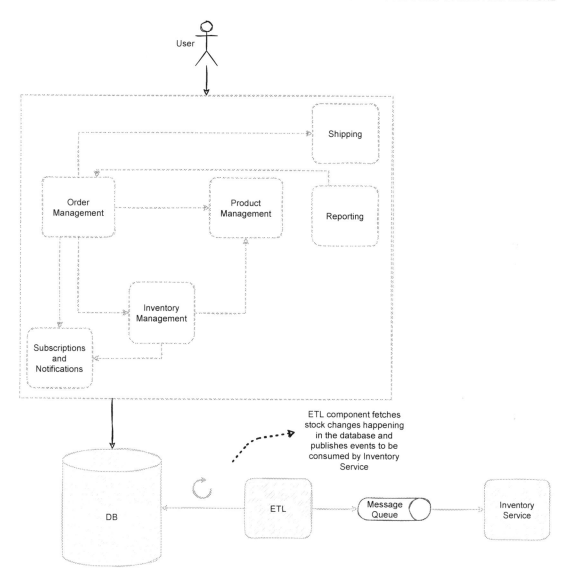

Figure 2-6. *Using CDC to migrate data from a monolith's module. We set up a component to read the databases' changes with CDC and publish them to a message queue*

The ETL (extract, transform, and load, although the load is to a message queue) component processes the changes, converts them to events, and publishes them to a message queue. In the same example with the reporting service, the component would poll for changes in the databases' CDC mechanism in the order tables and publish them to the message queue. It also provides the role of decoupling and hiding the undesired data CDC provides to external events. If we use the frameworks mentioned before, they might expose more information than needed and leak information about the underlying data models. A custom component would abstract these concerns and publish events that made sense to the new services.

The ETL would probably need to bootstrap the current information by fetching the current state and publishing it to the message queue to bootstrap the new service. To descope the reporting module on the monolith, we could then build the reporting service and listen to the events in the queue. After that, we would change the consumers to the new service and descope the current functionality. Our final mission is to descope the ETL component and have the new service be the source of data.

An important consideration is as the new architecture grows, we should continuously add functionality to the same ETL component or add different individual components. Well, it depends on the use case, but here are some guidelines to help you decide. If there is only a small team using the ETL component, then one component is probably preferable; using a framework such as Kafka Connect could also be a good option. When there are several teams with diverse bounded contexts, building an ETL per bounded context might be advisable. The implementation overhead will be larger, but it will give each team independence to create the events for their context without dependencies between other teams and models. It will also encourage them to understand how the data is organized on the monolith, what events make sense, and how they interact with the new services.

2.4.1 Event-Driven and Change Data Capture (CDC), a Real-World Example

Custom querying is one way to implement CDC. We can extract the data by querying the database, with or without filters. We can also bulk load all data to the message queue, sinking all existing information to an event stream. After the bootstrap of all existing data, the process would load changes after a given watermark, which can be a timestamp or an incremental id or version. We would publish all changes that occurred after the watermark to the message queue.

It is also possible to customize the query to filter only a set of records. For example, if the table has a type, it might be relevant only to publish the records of a given type or segregate types into different queues.

Any database supports querying, so it is always an option even if the database technology doesn't have a built-in CDC process. It is also very flexible since we can adjust the query to the way we want the data. On the other hand, the more complex the query is, the higher the impact on the database's resources.

It also relies on a last updated column, which might skip multiple updates to the same record. Most of the time, this isn't an issue, but if we want to capture the user's intent and how the data evolves through time, it won't be as accurate since it might merge several updates. Squashing several updates might be an issue depending on the way the old and new architecture is designed. For example, if we have a table with generic properties that each has a type, we might have decided to separate each property in independent models on the new architecture. If so, an update to the type would mean the deletion of the old resource and creating a different one. Having information on only the latest state might not be enough to apply the same state to the new architecture.

Deletions are also hard to detect for the same reason unless we implement soft deletes (by having a state column). Soft deletes consume more resources since the record isn't removed. Besides that, it surely wouldn't be unprecedented if someone hard deleted a soft delete table (by actually deleting instead of updating the column).

Many database technologies have an internal operation log that records every change operation that occurs in the database. That log is also used to restore the database to a correct state if a catastrophic failure occurs or to replicate information to other instances. It is a fascinating mechanism very similar to event sourcing and event-driven principles. Many of them also provide CDC functionality by using the operation log to expose the changes that occurred in the database.

Using the CDC functionality, we can fetch every change operation that occurred in the relevant tables. Unlike custom querying, even if a record is updated multiple times, it will provide information for each update. It also records deletes, allowing for a more realistic view of the data evolution without soft deletes. Performance and resource-wise log scanners have less impact than querying since it relies on the operation log rather than querying specific tables.

However, they are highly dependent on how the database technology exposes this information. They might not have all the information needed or rely on internal identifiers that are hard to track. Most technologies that expose this functionality have detailed information on each change, which often implies they expose the underlying data model, raising the need for an adaptation and encapsulation of only the relevant information.

CDC Example Using SQL Server and Kafka

Let's illustrate an example of moving data using CDC with SQL Server. Using the same example monolith of Figure 2-6 and assuming we want to move the stock data from the monolithic database to a new service, we could build a topology similar to Figure 2-7.

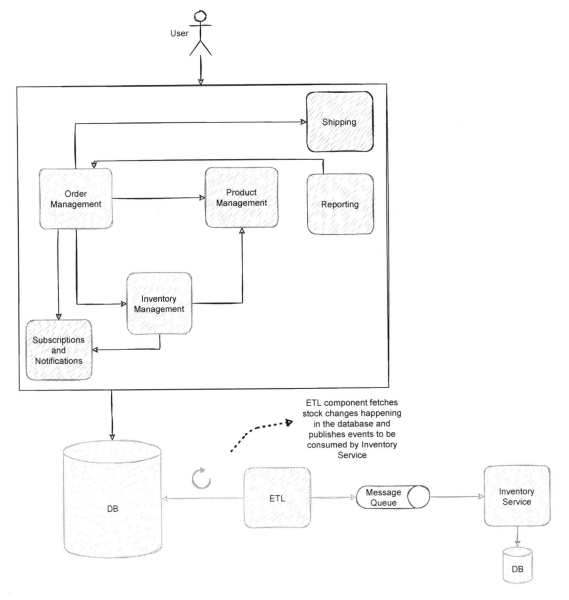

Figure 2-7. *Example of using CDC to move data from a monolithic database to a new service (inventory service)*

We can access SQL Server CDC information through CDC specific tables that the database creates when enabled. SQL Server has a transaction log with every change that occurs on the database. This log is essential to guarantee that the database is in a consistent state. CDC uses this log to understand what operations are happening in the database and populates the CDC tables with this information and some metadata. We can use the data populated in those tables to understand the changes that occurred in the database.

Let's say we have a Stock table that has the stock for each size of each product. Listing 2-1 shows that table and how to enable CDC for the database and that table.

Listing 2-1. Create Stock table and enable CDC

```
1    -- Create table stock
2    CREATE TABLE Stock #A
3    (
4        ProductId int,
5        Size varchar(10),
6        StoreId int,
7        Quantity int,
5        primary key (ProductId, Size, StoreId)
4    )
7
8    -- Enable CDC at the database level
9    EXEC sys.sp_cdc_enable_db #B
10
11   -- Enable CDC at the table level
12   EXEC sys.sp_cdc_enable_table @source_schema = 'dbo', @source_name =
'Stock', @role_name = NULL, @supports_net_changes = 1 #B
```

#A Create stock table definition
#B Enabling CDC at the database and table level

Every time a change occurs on the Stock table, the agent records the change in the SQL Server transaction log (even without CDC enabled). The transaction log reader agent will read the changelogs from the transaction log and insert those changes in the CDC tables. The CDC table was created once we ran the command on line 12 in Listing 2-1, and we can fetch the changes happening in the database by querying that table.

Listing 2-2. Changes to stock records and retrieval of CDC logs

```
1    -- Some changes to stock records
2    insert into Stock values(153854, 'XS', 914, 1) #A
3    update Stock set Quantity = 2 where ProductId = 153854 and Size = 'XS' #A
4    insert into Stock values(153854, 'S', 914, 1) #A
5    delete from Stock where ProductId = 153854 and Size = 'S' #A
6
7    -- Fetch changes
8    SELECT * FROM [cdc].[dbo_Stock_CT] where __$start_lsn >
0x00001058000007110003 #B
```

#A Some changes done in the Stock table
#B Retrieving the CDC logs in the table dbo_Stock_CT (the value will change
from your use case)

Listing 2-2 shows some changes done to the Stock table. We inserted two rows and then updated one and deleted another. Querying the CDC table retrieves the result illustrated in Figure 2-8.

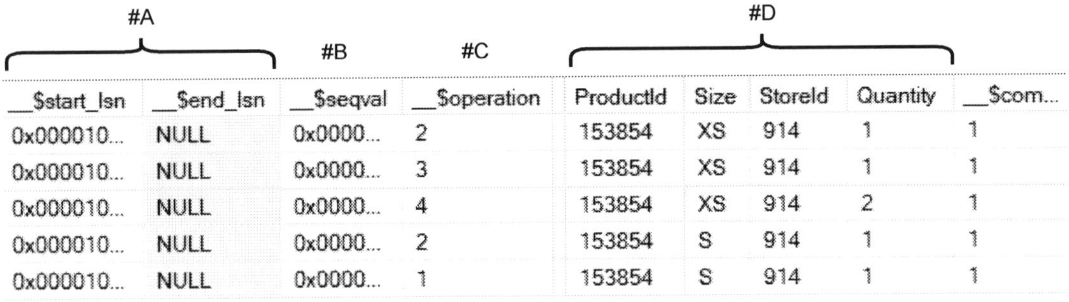

#A		#B	#C	#D				
__$start_lsn	__$end_lsn	__$seqval	__$operation	ProductId	Size	StoreId	Quantity	__$com...
0x000010...	NULL	0x0000...	2	153854	XS	914	1	1
0x000010...	NULL	0x0000...	3	153854	XS	914	1	1
0x000010...	NULL	0x0000...	4	153854	XS	914	2	1
0x000010...	NULL	0x0000...	2	153854	S	914	1	1
0x000010...	NULL	0x0000...	1	153854	S	914	1	1

Figure 2-8. *CDC table results from the changes in Listing 2-2*

The CDC tables have some columns directly related to SQL Server but might be relevant to some use cases:

- __$start_lsn and __$end_lsn (#A) are the log sequence number (LSN) assigned by the SQL Service.

- __$seqval (#B) gives information about the order of the operation related to other operations in the same transaction.

- __$operation (#C) indicates what was the operation performed on that row (1 is delete, 2 is insert, 3 is the row information before the update, 4 is the row information after the update).

- All the stock table columns (#D) with the data when the change occurred.

The query in line 8 of Listing 2-2 would be in the ETL component. This component polls the database to fetch the records that happened after the last LSN that it processed (the SQL Server function fn_cdc_get_all_changes_dbo_stock could also be used to fetch the changes on a specific interval). The query would return the changes to the table between the last polling iteration and the current time. An important consideration is to fetch only a max amount of changes (like 1000 rows each time) due to performance reasons and resource optimization.

Once we load the changes, we would map the data fetched from the database to the stock events. For example, operation 2 (insert operation) could generate a StockCreated event, and operation 4 (update operation) could generate a StockChanged event. Once we map the data from the database to the events, we could publish them to Kafka. The inventory service would handle those events and update its internal state with those events.

The CDC table gives a lot of information about each change and how the data was before the change. Update commands provide details on how the data was before and after the change. Some use cases might need this kind of detail if we don't need only the latest state but also need the state before the change. For example, we could move stock across two products if we updated the product id in the Stock table. Depending on how we design the system, it could be necessary to remove stock from one product and add stock to the other. Reflecting the change on both products might need two different events with information before and after the update.

CDC has the disadvantage of recording a large amount of information about each change. This can lead to excessive resource consumption in high usage tables and databases. We might need to implement an aggressive retention policy in those cases. In the case of SQL Server, there is also another option using Change Track, which is relatively similar to CDC but compares changes between two versions. It doesn't give the detailed data evolution CDC does, but when we need only the latest state is fairly lighter than using CDC.

2.5 Migrating Data from a Monolith: Event-Driven As a Source of Truth for Both Systems

The last sections detailed how we can extract data through events from a monolith. This section will discuss how we can use events to be the single source of truth for both the monolith and the new services.

A pivotal mindset to embody while adopting an event-driven architecture is to embrace events as the source of truth. Until now, we discussed how we could shift the source of truth from the monolith to the new services. However, as long as the information relies on the monolith, it will be the source of truth. Shifting consumers to the new applications might not be an activity we can do autonomously; some of them might be external consumers that might need to adapt to the new services. If so, the shifting action can take a considerable amount of time, during which we are stuck with the monolith being the source of truth or having simultaneously two sources, as we will discuss at the end of this chapter.

An interesting approach is to have the monolith react to a queue. Adding a queue can be harder or easier depending on the monolith. Some monoliths already react to message queues, so plugging a new service into the same queue and routing the messages accordingly to the new and old architecture would be a good approach. If the monolith doesn't have a queue, we could transform the requests into messages. The transformation could be done by the external consumers, an intermediate component, or in the monolith itself.

Although similar, it differs substantially from the approach described in Section 2.3; instead of the event publishing being a new secondary operation from the initial flow, it becomes the trigger to the existing process. This way, the message becomes the source of truth for both the old and new flow.

This alternative is illustrated in Figure 2-9 using the same example as before; a message queue is the input for both the monolith and reporting service. Having a queue to trigger the process promotes the mindset shift to prioritize event design since the message is pivotal for both systems to operate.

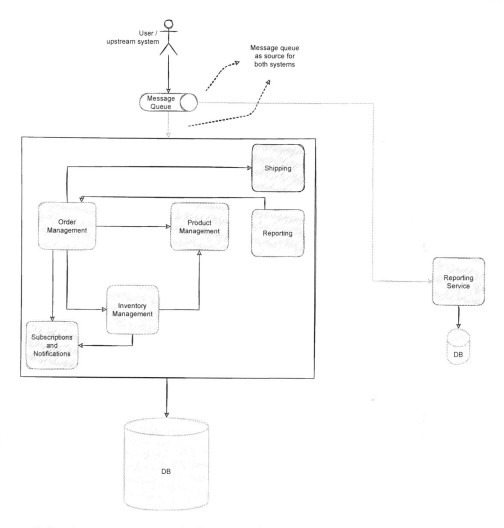

Figure 2-9. *A message queue is the input for both the new architecture and the monolith, being the only source of truth*

Once we get the queue set up, we could gradually change the message consumption from one system to another. We could roll out based on the messages' content; if we are publishing order information, then we could roll out by country, for example, starting with all orders from "CA" instead of all countries at once. Once the reporting service is consuming all countries, we could remove the monolith's reporting module.

If it's not possible to change the upstream systems to publish to a queue or add an intermediate component, we could split the monolith flow. The first step would be to receive the request, send a message, and then continue with the rest of the flow by handling the message. The monolith itself has only limited benefits to having a queue but would set the new system's pace. It would also be a good trial to see if the functionality can deal with the weaker consistency guarantees the queue introduces.

2.6 Incremental Migration from a Monolith to an Event-Driven Architecture: Managing Dependencies

In the last few sections, we detailed how to migrate data to new services using an event-driven approach. This section will discuss approaches when a new service might still need data from the old architecture and when the monolith has the same need for the new services.

We might find some use cases in the monolith relatively decoupled from the rest of the functionalities due to not needing many dependencies to work with. The example of the reporting module, although it needs order management information, is not a central functionality that is referenced everywhere. As mentioned in Section 2.2, we should use these modules to start the migration; it's often better to start with a small, easy part and build our way on top of that than trying to migrate a central functionality that is referenced throughout all modules. However, we will reach the point where we might migrate a functionality but still need data from an unrelated module inside the monolith. More than reacting to its changes, it requires the module's data to process its logic. Since the data is in the monolith, we need strategies to access that data in the service. The inverse can also be applied; other modules in the monolith might still need data that we migrated to a new service.

2.6.1 Managing a Dependency from a New Event-Driven Service to a Legacy Monolith

Using the same example in Figure 2-2, let's now look at the inventory module. The inventory module might need product information to process stock changes; every time someone changes the stock, the inventory module fetches product information and associates that stock change to the product. This use case differs from the reporting module since it is not reacting to the system's changes; the inventory module fetches information in the flow of its domain.

The order management calls the inventory module to remove the stock quantity the user bought. Instead of calling the inventory module directly, the order management module would publish an event signaling the user created an order. The new inventory service would react to that event but would still need the product management module information. The first most direct approach would be to request that information from the monolith, as illustrated in Figure 2-10.

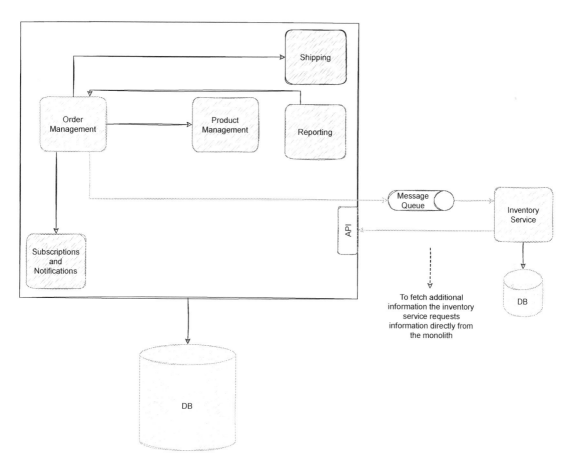

Figure 2-10. *When the inventory service needs additional information that still exists on the monolith, it requests the information directly through an API*

This alternative is very intuitive: we treat the dependency in the inventory service as we would call any other module inside the monolith, but instead of being inside the same application, it now makes a remote request. We often are reluctant to add functionality to the monolith, and we should be; however, adding functionality to the monolith might be a stepping stone to build the new architecture.

However, the inventory service now has a direct dependency on the monolith. If the monolith struggles with performance issues or has a catastrophic failure (like a memory leak), it will cascade to the inventory service. Scaling the inventory service will also impact the monolith; if we add more resources to the service, it will trigger more requests to the monolith. These issues were the very thing we were trying to avoid with the decoupled nature of event-driven architectures. It is a viable choice, and we might use it sparingly to promote the migration of functionalities that need this approach. However, it must be temporary and something we should use only sparingly.

An alternative to this option is to publish the product data and use an internal view of that data inside the inventory service. This way, the inventory service remains decoupled, and we avoid the remote request to the monolith, illustrated in Figure 2-11.

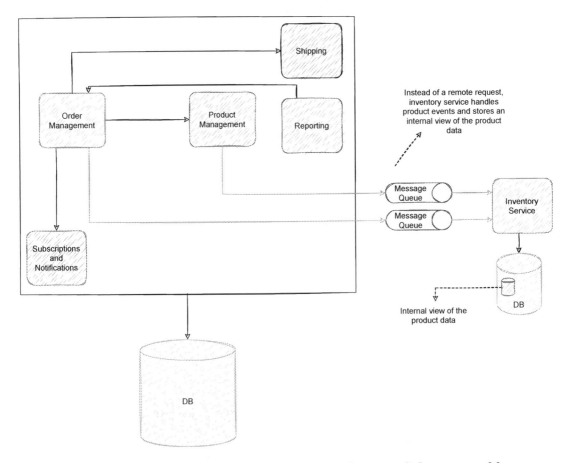

Figure 2-11. *Instead of a direct remote request to the monolith, we are able to avoid a direct dependency through an internal view of the product data inside the inventory service*

The inventory service, by having an internal view of the product data, would be able to process its domain logic by using that internal state instead of requesting data to the monolith. The state doesn't necessarily need to be saved inside the database; Kafka, for example (we will discuss Kafka in more detail in Chapters 3 and 6), if we use Kafka Streams, provides a way to keep that information in KTables. It is also possible to opt for other solutions to save data, discussed in Chapter 8.

We are preferring to denormalize the data in the service over having a centralized place to hold it. Besides the higher decoupling, this solution provides a performance boost since accessing local data is often faster than making a remote external request. But it also has an infrastructure and maintenance overhead of saving and maintaining that data.

2.6.2 Managing a Dependency from a Legacy Application to a New Event-Driven Service

As we discussed, by migrating modules from the monolith, we also move the data associated with those modules. There might be use cases where other modules inside the monolith require that data. A common example is UIs that display diverse information and often aggregate data from several domains.

Using the same example we used before, let's say the order management module needed to validate if the product being ordered had enough stock to fulfill the order when receiving a new order. To do the validation, the module would have to fetch the current stock information. If we move the inventory service to an independent service, the data no longer exists in the monolith.

We could follow the same approaches we discussed before. The most intuitive approach would be to request information from the new service, as illustrated in Figure 2-12. When the order management module needs the stock information, it would request data from the inventory service much like it would do if the module was still inside the monolith, but instead of running the request in memory, it makes a remote request.

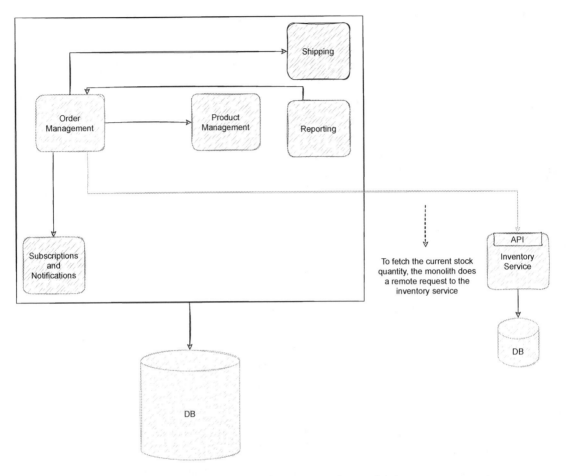

Figure 2-12. *The monolith requests information from the inventory service through a remote request*

Although this approach suffers from the same issues we mentioned before, they aren't as troublesome. We might still have a cascading failure if the inventory service fails, but it is less likely to happen since the service has a minimal scope. On the other hand, any change in any bounded context of the monolith has the potential to bring the whole application down. If we need to add load to the monolith, it will trigger more requests, but the inventory service is easily scalable; scaling a monolith is harder. Since this approach is straightforward and easy to implement, we might use it as a building block, and when we move the order management module, opt for a different strategy.

We could also adopt a strategy to feed the monolith's existing state with the inventory service's events. This way has the advantage of keeping both architectures decoupled, as illustrated in Figure 2-13.

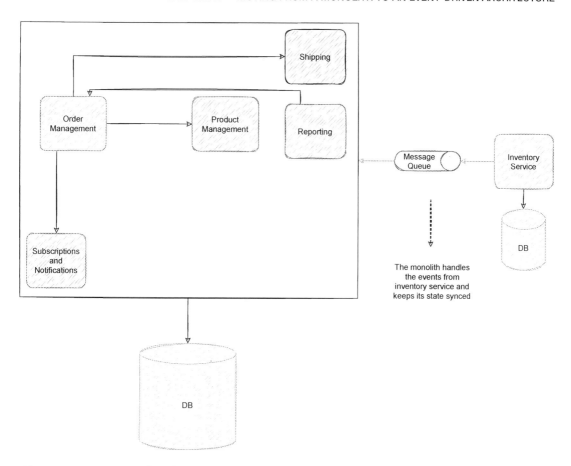

Figure 2-13. *Monolith handles the events and keeps its internal view of the inventory data synced*

Often monoliths have internal views that join a large amount of diverse information together. Joining information is possible since all data is stored in the same database; when deconstructing the database, maintaining this kind of functionality is challenging. A sustainable approach is to sync the information back to the monolith and feed its internal state through the new services' events. The new services are the source of truth, making the monolithic database a denormalized view of the different domains. This approach is often required since joining diverse information through HTTP requests isn't possible without requesting a lot of information and joining it in memory, a cumbersome process both performance and resource-wise.

2.7 Gradually Moving Traffic to New Microservices

In the last sections, we discussed how we could move functionality from a monolith to individual services. However, we didn't detail how to shift traffic from the monolith to the new services. This section will detail how we can gradually move that traffic without a big bang release.

Previously, we discussed that we could shift traffic to the new service once the new service is fully functional and descope the old functionality. However, we should guarantee the transition has the necessary quality guarantees. Whenever possible, we should avoid big bang releases; it is much safer to gradually deliver functionally than releasing it all at once, in a single moment.

The event-driven approaches we discussed in the previous sections allow us to build the new services gradually without impacting the current application. Exposing the data on the event queue also enables the service to asynchronous bootstrap its database. Since the message queue decouples the service and enables it to process the information asynchronously, as that process advances, it provides a way to compare the information in both databases to guarantee the data is coherent. Event-driven queues also retain the messages even after consumption; if we detect an issue that corrupted the data, we can simply read the queue from the beginning and regenerate the state. Once we are confident the data is coherent, we can start to shift requests to the new service, as illustrated in Figure 2-14.

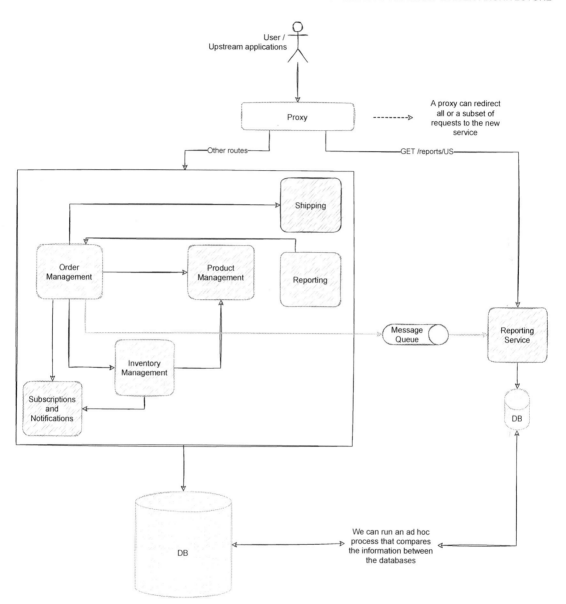

Figure 2-14. *The proxy between the upstream applications and the downstream services can route the monolith or new service requests*

We also don't need to route all requests at once; we can route based on the content; the proxy can filter a subset of requests to the new service and the remaining ones to the existing application, guaranteeing a gradual rollout. For example, as illustrated in Figure 2-14, the proxy can forward part of the requests based on the route. If we consult reports by country, we could forward requests for a country to the new service and keep the remaining in the existing application.

If it is impossible to set up a proxy between the upstream systems, we can use the monolith to serve as a proxy and forward the requests to the new service. We can change it to receive the request and internally call or send a message to the new service. It's not ideal since we will still be using the application we want to discontinue, but might help as a temporary solution. At the same time, the monolith's consumers can adapt to the new services.

We can also apply content routing to messages. If the monolith is already receiving messages, like the approach in Section 2.5, we can forward a subset of messages to the new service and the remaining to the existing application. For example, messages with country code "US" would be consumed by the new service and ignore the others, while the monolith would do the inverse. We could also use different queues, one for the new service and another for the monolith, although we would have to duplicate the messages for both queues. This way is also possible to gradually shift message traffic between the two applications.

It is also important to maintain a rollback strategy in case things go wrong. Event-driven queues retain the messages in the queue. If we build systems that rely on those queues to process their domain logic, it's often straightforward to roll back the system and reprocess the messages after the point the issue was introduced. Chapter 7 further details this rollback strategy.

2.8 Migrating from a Monolith: Two-Way Synchronization and Living with Two Sources of Truth

In Section 2.6, we discussed how to feed the monolith's state after migrating the source of truth to the new services. In the previous sections, we discussed how to migrate the monolith's functionality and data to the new architecture. However, we discussed use cases where the transition is immediate or spans during a short period. There are situations where this transition isn't as immediate, and we might need to maintain both the old and new architecture for a considerable amount of time. We should always avoid two sources of truth; it's complicated and hard to maintain; however, in the real world, often migrating functionality is messier than simply descoping old functionality instantaneously.

In any migration to an event-driven microservice, our key goal is to turn the new service into the source of truth; the entry point of that domain's information is the new service. A single source of truth is a fundamental objective we always must aim for in any situation. However, there are times we must maintain functionalities in the old application that can't or are too hard to migrate to in a short period. Functionalities that span several domains can be hard to discontinue since each domain often belongs to different teams. Some teams may need to advance in the migration at a different time than the others. As mentioned in Section 2.7, we should always do this migration gradually, so even if the timing was right, synchronizing a release between several teams is more often than not a recipe for disaster. Section 2.6 mentions strategies to keep the monolith's state synchronized, but how does that play out when we mix strategies like those mentioned in Sections 2.3 and 2.6? We could descope the monolith's functionality and feed the state back to the monolith in a single moment, but this is risky and such short time migrations are rare.

When we discussed CDC in Section 2.4, we described it as an interesting approach because there might be functionalities entangled throughout the whole application. When the monolith's domain we are trying to split has logic spread across the entire application and in stored procedures, it can be exceptionally hard to decouple it from the rest of the application. Several entry points are often dependent on other domain logic or on consumers that can't change to the new service quickly. In the company where we were trying to migrate the inventory management logic I mentioned in Section 2.4, we used CDC and it was going well; with CDC, we were able to capture every change and synchronize it to the new service. However, that also meant the entry points were still in legacy. Although we were able to change many of the clients to access the service directly or proxy the monolith's call to the new service, some of them were unfeasible due to the associated coupling and complexity. There were stored procedures that changed stock that joined a large amount of information from different domains like order and product. These were also business-critical functionalities; descoping or making them unavailable for a period of time wasn't acceptable. We were able to descope them later on and move them to the new applications but only after most of the other domains left the monolith, which took years to do so; meanwhile, we had to live with two entry points and two sources of truth.

Doing so allowed the stock information to be available in the new architecture, enabling the building of new services and applications on top of that information instead of legacy applications. This while still maintaining some of the monolith's functionalities that we couldn't move.

Using the same example in Figure 2-2, let's say the user could edit the reports generated by the reporting service. The user can edit reports in the new service, but editions can also be done in the monolith due to functionality we couldn't move. Combining the approaches we discussed until now, we could publish changes from both the monolith and the reporting service to a message queue and both would listen from those queues, but only the changes that weren't from that system would be consumed.

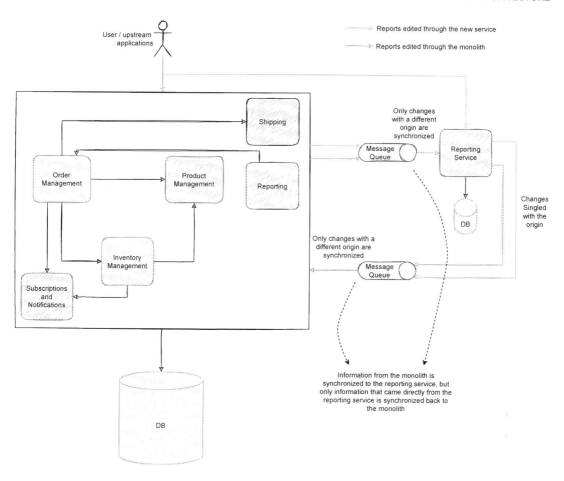

Figure 2-15. *A way to maintain both systems synchronized. Both systems publish changes, and both systems process them but ignore the changes that were originated by themselves*

One of the catches in this solution is breaking the cycle; we can do that, for example, with a header signaling the origin system. In Figure 2-15, if a user edits a report in the monolith, the monolith would publish the corresponding event to the message queue. The event would also need to inform the origin system of that change. The reporting service would consume that change and publish a similar event signaling the same change to its queue. The monolith is consuming that queue but ignores the change because it originated in the monolith. Changes in the reporting service have the same flow and are published to the service's queue, consumed by the monolith, published again by the monolith, and ignored at the service.

We aim to descope the monolith's message queue; all new services should plug into the reporting service's queue. As we descope the monolith's functionalities, fewer messages should flow in the monolith's queue. Once no messages are flowing in the queue means the monolith no longer has any functionality that affects the reporting service, and we finalized the migration. Then we should also descope the monolith's queue.

There are also other details we need to consider; for example, if the user changes the same report at the same time in both systems, how would we manage the collision? We should identify events with a version or timestamp and the latest should prevail. So when consuming the messages, the systems would need to validate the message date and only update more recent changes than the system's internal state. However, these challenges aren't exclusive to two sources of truth; any horizontally scalable event-driven system can encounter parallel changes due to concurrency between instances or loss of the event's ordering. We will discuss approaches to these challenges in Chapters 5, 6, and 7.

Maintaining two-way synchronization, in the long run, is extremely hard and the source of ongoing issues. Not only are incidents harder to trace since they can originate from entirely different systems, but new functionalities are also limited to the monolith's design choices. The domain logic also needs to stay coherent between the two systems. It is possible to evolve the new system without affecting the monolith due to the decoupled nature of the message queues, as long as the message's contract remains the same, but only until a point. Most of the time, we can avoid having two sources of truth, and we should do the utmost possible to prevent it. It is a solution we might keep in our toolbox, but near the bottom, other solutions are often preferable.

2.9 Summary

- An event-driven architecture has a complexity boost associated with it, and we should question whether it is the best option for our use case. We should always ask ourselves what we are trying to solve and have a clear reason to advance with the migration.

- We should always strive to do an incremental migration. Doing so will allow us to face the challenges associated with it in a sustainable manner.

- Often good candidates to be migrated first are modules with fewer dependencies and that largely benefit from the migration.

- Event-driven provides a high decoupled solution to free data from a monolith. It also provides the tools to build the new services asynchronously without impact to the monolith and the teams working with it.

- When functionalities are too coupled, too complex, or simply can't be migrated seamlessly, CDC is a valid option to access the data changes and convert them to events.

- We can use events to trigger both changes in the monolith and new services. Doing so places the source of truth in the events further promoting the mindset shift to adopt events as a single source of truth.

- When other modules are depending on the data of the functionality we are migrating, we can use events to feed that state inside those applications. A view of the state can be maintained both in the monolith and new services and be used to solve those dependencies.

- Some migrations don't need to be done fully in a single moment; we can gradually change traffic to the new applications.

- There might be use cases where a full migration can't be done in a short timespan and might take several months. It is possible to use two-way synchronization to maintain the harder functionalities in the monolith while proceeding with the migration of the remaining ones. However, it is a complex option with several impacts; we should always strive for a single source of truth.

CHAPTER 3

Defining an Event-Driven Microservice and Its Boundaries

This chapter covers:

- Understanding the structure of an event-driven microservice, associated message patterns, and common topologies

- Comprehend DDD (domain-driven design), how to apply it, and its concepts

- Using DDD to extract the domain's bounded contexts and leverage the services' boundaries

- How to avoid common pitfalls when designing the aggregate size and understanding its impact on downstream services

- What different characteristics to weight when organizing service boundaries

- Understanding the difference and the impacts of request-driven and event-driven services

- How to decide between adding functionality to an existing service or creating a new one

© Hugo Filipe Oliveira Rocha 2022
H. F. Oliveira Rocha, *Practical Event-Driven Microservices Architecture*,
https://doi.org/10.1007/978-1-4842-7468-2_3

It's funny how sometimes computer science feels more art than science. Perhaps not more, but it often has a soft brush of artistic inspiration mixed with it. We often fail to see the practical value in learning all the computer science fundamentals in class or learn about new patterns in books or articles. Usually, we use them as building blocks or extract their underlying ideas to combine and adapt them as solutions to unique problems. They often serve as an inspiration to other solutions in different contexts. Sometimes creativity plays a role, and your personal style gets associated with it. How often have we looked at someone's code and underline the invisible traces that define a coworker's style? We can feel the style the same way we would if we read several poems of a unique author – who is probably sitting next to you, trying to exit Vim.

When defining domains and boundaries, it can also get fuzzy and often feels more like art than science. There isn't a magical formula we can apply and obtain a result, but there are approaches that can help us extract business domains and decide what is the best approach. This chapter approaches those strategies and helps us understand the application's domain and translate it into a logical model.

In Chapter 2, we discussed how to extract functionality from a monolith to a new service. The different types of services and topologies we can build in an event-driven architecture are the building blocks we can use to evolve that architecture. Understanding them is paramount to maintaining and building these architectures.

As we evolve the architecture and depend on several different components, the need arises to define the services' boundaries, how they interact with each other, and what domain they manage. Different organizations have different priorities; often deciding the adequate boundaries is a tradeoff between the different approaches. We will discuss the various considerations when defining boundaries in Section 3.2. DDD is an approach we can use to understand and extract the domain concepts. When modeling complex domains, the entity's size (the aggregate in DDD terms) is often hard to measure. In an event-driven architecture, how we design it can have repercussions to the downstream consumers; this impact is detailed in Section 3.4.

Adding new functionality usually falls into one of two choices, creating a new service or adding functionality to existing services. Sometimes the choice isn't clear; the high decoupled nature of event-driven architectures promotes the birth and decommission of components. However, continuously adding services further increases the system's complexity. Section 3.6 further details these tradeoffs.

3.1 Building Event-Driven Microservices

This section will discuss the typical architecture of an event-driven microservice and its standard modules. We will discuss the typical messaging entities and messaging patterns that we will use in the rest of the book as building blocks in the architecture. At the end of this section, we will discuss common pitfalls, their impacts, and how to avoid them.

In Chapter 2, we moved functionality from a monolith to event-driven services. We represented it with a square, but what is inside that square? Each service is a single-process application, and inside it, the code is organized typically according to an architecture. Usually, we divide this architecture into layers. One of our missions is to model business concepts and processes into code. As the business grows, the application also grows in complexity. Organizing the application with logical layering is one way to manage that complexity.

Dividing an application into layers according to its responsibilities aligns with the separation of concerns principle. It's also a way to help developers understand the application and easily find functionality. Maintaining the same architecture through several microservices minimizes the overhead of understanding an application and implementing new functionality. If someone never worked in one service and now has to change it, although the domain might be different, the application's organization is the same, so it is easier to understand.

We can use a layered architecture to encapsulate functionality inside each layer, promoting the code to change without affecting other layers. The functionality can also be reused throughout the application standardizing common functionality in a single implementation. We can also use a layered architecture to limit coupling and restrict how layers communicate with each other. They also become useful to develop unit tests since the separation of concerns promotes simple single-purpose tests.

There are several types of layered architectures. Due to the natural decoupling of event-driven services, we don't need to use the same in every service, as we don't need to use the same technology in every service either. However, it is advisable to choose one and maintain the consistency between services. As we will discuss in Chapter 10, if other teams need to change services in the ownership of other teams, the development is more straightforward if every service has similar architecture. If the structure of applications is familiar, the focus of discussion shifts from technical details to the domain implementation, which is often more valuable.

3.1.1 N-Tier Architectures

The most common architectures feature a separation of the application code into several layers. There are several variations; the number of layers depends on the application's needs (thus the name N-tier). Figure 3-1 illustrates a typical three-tier architecture.

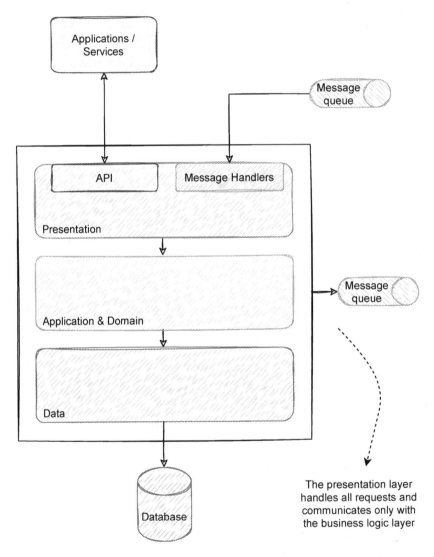

Figure 3-1. *Three-tier application architecture with three layers: presentation, application and domain, and data*

In this architecture, the presentation receives all external requests; if the microservice has a UI, we also place it in this layer. Microservices without UI expose an API that other applications and services use to access the data. Typical event-driven microservices communicate through events. Event handlers receive the events and call the other layers to process their business logic. The presentation layer only interacts with the application and domain layer, which has all the business logic. The application and domain layer manages the state through the data layer, which has all the data access objects and the database technical implementation.

The most important part is the business logic that resides in the application and domain layer. One of the drawbacks of this architecture is the direct dependency of the application and domain layer to the data layer. Often this means the business logic depends on data access, which shouldn't be relevant for the domain logic itself. The database implementation details often influence the implemented business logic. The existence of a database also often becomes a required prerequisite to the business logic. Testing might even become an issue due to database coupling. Often to test the business logic, we require a staging database; we can avoid that with dependency injection, which often leads to a different kind of architecture that we detail in the following.

3.1.2 Clean Architecture

An alternative to N-tier architecture is Bob Martin's clean architecture.[1] As we mention in the following, if we adopt the dependency inversion principle (the I in SOLID[2]) and depend upon abstractions rather than implementations, we often reach this architecture. It is also designed to build the domain logic in the core of the application. Domain logic shouldn't depend on or reference anything else; the order management business logic doesn't need to know we use SQL, for example.

Other architectures are typically designed upon the same practical concept the clean architecture translates. The hexagonal architecture[3] (also named ports and adapters) or the onion architecture[4] provides a similar approach based on the same principles.

---

[1] See Robert C. Martin, "The Clean Architecture," August 13, 2012, `https://blog.cleancoder.com/uncle-bob/2012/08/13/the-clean-architecture.html`

[2] See "SOLID," `https://en.wikipedia.org/wiki/SOLID`

[3] Further details in "Hexagonal architecture (software)," `https://en.wikipedia.org/wiki/Hexagonal_architecture_(software)`

[4] Further details in Jeffrey Palermo, "The Onion Architecture: part 1," July 29, 2008, `https://jeffreypalermo.com/2008/07/the-onion-architecture-part-1/`

They strive to provide a clean separation of concerns through the segregation of the software into layers. They also emphasize the business logic as the focus of the application. The business logic also has no dependencies or references, the outer layer references the domain models, but the domain models don't reference anything. Figure 3-2 illustrates a typical microservice with the clean architecture.

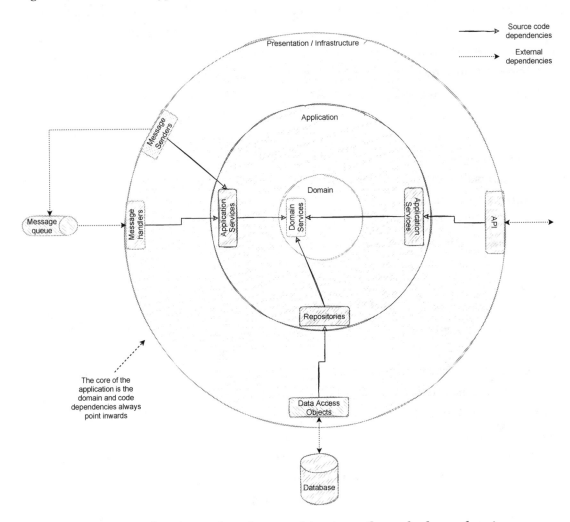

Figure 3-2. *An application using clean architecture; the code dependencies are always inward. The domain layer is the core of the architecture and hasn't any references to other layers*

We only reference external dependencies in the outer layer. Code in each layer can solely depend on references to the inner layers. The core layer holds the domain logic and domain entities and can't reference anything in the outer layers. This way, anything in the outer layer can't impact the inner layers. Outside layers typically have concrete implementations, while the inner layers grow more abstract as we advance to the core. Figure 3-2 only shows three layers, but it is just an example; an application can have as many layers as needed. The application layer, which holds the application business logic, can have an additional layer with interface adapters in charge of adapting data between the presentation layer and application logic.

Having the external dependencies on the outer layer means we reference every tool, driver, or framework in that layer. Having external dependencies referenced only on the outer layer promotes the separation of the application and domain logic from external tools. Often, the limitations of these frameworks or technologies entangle themselves on the application's logic. Moving them to the outer layer promotes the modeling and evolution of the logic without the influence of outside tools. We often hear "If we need to exchange databases, we can do it without affecting the inner logic." Separation of concerns is an essential coding principle, but how often do we exchange databases anyway? Database constraints tend to leak toward application logic (e.g., managing transactions between several models) or framework updates that span all applications. The outer layer helps prevent these common issues.

Also, domain logic shouldn't know anything about what we implemented in the outer layers. The independence from outside references (like the data reference in the N-tier architecture) helps the business rules evolve as needed and reflect what the business intends. Changes in how we authenticate users, how we publish events, or how we log changes shouldn't affect the business rules. Having this kind of separation and isolation, they won't. Figure 3-3 illustrates two services using this architecture, interacting through a message queue.

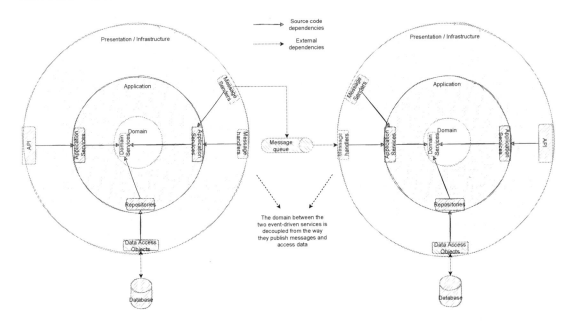

Figure 3-3. *Two event-driven services with clean architectures interacting through a message queue. The domain is isolated from the way the applications send events and access data*

If, for example, the messaging framework we are using in both services becomes deprecated, upgrading it will only affect the outer layer. It eases the replacement of external dependencies, and it also promotes single-purpose unit tests in each layer.

We can apply to each microservice the clean architecture. Still, as we add more functionalities and new services, we might create smaller services that aren't that rich in domain or application logic. First, as we mentioned in Chapter 2, it is advisable to develop services that encapsulate a subset of the system but a more extensive and autonomous domain. Creating larger coarse-grained services, in the beginning, will naturally contain the expansion of the number of services to a sustainable pace. They will also depend less on external services that are easier to manage while building the architecture. It will reduce the number of remote calls each service has to do and lessen the impact of weak consistency since each service will manage its domain locally. As we mentioned in Chapter 2, we should gradually build the system, adding coarse-grained services first and then, when needed, advancing to fine-grained services with lesser responsibilities.

As we evolve the architecture and create more fine-grained services, we might have smaller services that own part of the overall architecture's responsibilities. Figure 3-4 illustrates an example where there is a service to manage the domain logic.

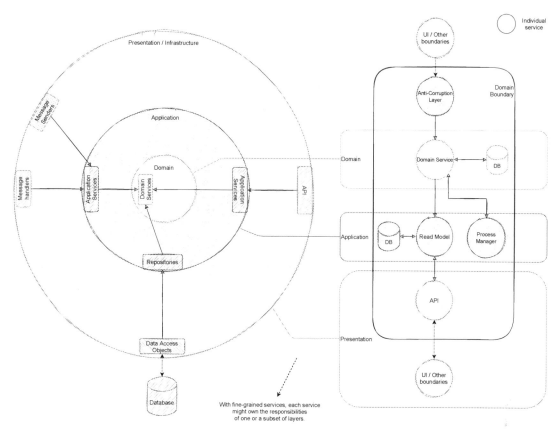

Figure 3-4. *As we create more fine-grained services, a subset of services inside a domain boundary might map with one or a subset of clean architecture layers*

Other services like the read model and process manager operate the application logic, and the anti-corruption layer works as an adapter between external and internal information. The API service exposes the boundary's information.

There are pitfalls associated with having fine-grained services that we need to avoid. Such a small scope often increases the risk of having lockstep releases, where a functionality spans several services and requires coordination to deploy them in the live environment. Microservices should be autonomous, and a release of one service shouldn't affect others. Also, services with a small scope will rapidly increase the number of services, increasing the system's complexity, and exponentiate the challenges of distributed systems discussed in Chapter 1. We can contain those challenges by organizing the services into boundaries, as illustrated in Figure 3-4. However, creating coarse-grained services first and using fine-grained services later is a better approach to decompose the system incrementally.

3.1.3 Event-Driven Microservices: Durable vs. Ephemeral Message Brokers and GDPR

The availability of messages after consumption and the underlying messaging semantics are the foundation for data streaming and provide a novel way to share data. Message brokers can have durable or ephemeral messages depending on the broker we choose. Typical messaging has ephemeral messages; however, having durable messages potentiates the useful use cases we mentioned in Chapter 1 and which we will detail throughout the book. In this section, we will discuss the two approaches of using durable or ephemeral message brokers.

Traditional message brokers are built to have short-lived messaging; published messages typically are removed once consumed. A famous example is RabbitMQ that is designed for destructive consuming semantics; once the consumer acknowledges the message, the broker removes the message from the queue. RabbitMQ also features[5] an append-only log data structure and will provide non-destructive messages besides the current destructive semantics.

With the rise of the Internet and continuous data growth, event streaming became increasingly relevant, along with durable message brokers. Durable messages remain readily available even after processed by the consumers. Streaming is about enabling a distributed and ordered flow of events. Durable messaging allows the stream to be processed as many times as needed. A famous example is Kafka, which is a distributed event streaming platform and provides a persisted event log. Like the event stream in Kafka, durable events are always available even after an application has consumed them. Other consumers can access the event stream, or existing consumers can reprocess the same messages if needed.

As with many of the technologies we use, the decision is about weighing tradeoffs. Using durable or ephemeral message brokers in every use case might not always be the right decision; it depends on what we need them for and its use case. Ephemeral message brokers like RabbitMQ have a high focus on point-to-point communications and routing messages to specific channels. Short-lived messaging is usually best for consumers who can process the messages fast and don't retain the broker's messages for long periods. These brokers often struggle when large numbers of messages pile up

---

[5] See Brian McClain, "Understanding the Differences Between RabbitMQ vs Kafka," November 16, 2020, `https://tanzu.vmware.com/developer/blog/understanding-the-differences-between-rabbitmq-vs-kafka/`

in the queues and are best used for instantaneous low-scale communications. In our experience using RabbitMQ for years in production on a high-throughput platform, we struggled sparingly with message load peaks that affected the whole cluster. When the entire cluster struggles, it will likely affect unrelated services and have daunting impacts, even imperiling the whole platform. Looking back, the use case for RabbitMQ might not be the best in that situation because we didn't need short-lived messaging.

For event-driven architectures, durable message brokers have high synergy with the event-driven mindset. Exposing the application state and maintaining it for any consumer in the form of events potentiate powerful possibilities and provide a sustainable way to share data throughout the company. Brokers like Kafka can also horizontally scale and manage vast amounts of messages, often achieving[6] better throughput and performance than typical short-lived message brokers. However, non-destructive message semantics usually has an associated cost and overhead of adding new brokers due to the need to replicate the data between nodes. Overall, event-driven architectures greatly benefit from durable message brokers, and many use cases become notoriously simple by having one. As we will see, many of the patterns we discuss in this book benefit from durable message brokers.

The Right to Be Forgotten and Other Security Concerns

Durable message brokers imply a challenging concern about securing the data. There is a lot of value in every event being available in the broker for any consumer even after consumption and requires dedicated security strategies. Typically, data that is no longer needed often is a security risk. Durable event brokers also raise several challenges guaranteeing compliance with regulations like GDPR (general data protection regulation). Compliance with the right to erasure or right to be forgotten is particularly challenging in an event-driven mindset. As we discussed, durable event brokers persist the event stream and provide access to it to any consumer. When a user wants to be removed from the system, we also store data associated with the user in the message broker, and we need a way to destroy that data. Ephemeral message brokers naturally comply with these requirements since they remove messages after consumption.

---

[6] See "Benchmarking Apache Kafka, Apache Pulsar, and RabbitMQ: Which is the Fastest?", August 21, 2020, www.confluent.io/blog/kafka-fastest-messaging-system/

Deleting an entity in an event-driven mindset is often accomplished by an event signaling the deletion of an entity (e.g., if the entity is an order, the service deleting the order would publish an order deleted event). This concept is often referred to as a tombstone; Cassandra, a popular NoSQL database, for example, when deleting a record, doesn't immediately purge it from the disk; instead, it writes a value signaling the record was deleted.

Theoretically, event streams reflect what happened, the history of the entity with all its evolution; every event is the reflection of a unique operation and shouldn't be deleted, the same way we can't delete history and what happened in times past. Many durable event brokers don't have straightforward, built-in ways to delete specific events and often require ad hoc solutions.

For example, the right to be forgotten introduces a unique challenge; if we shouldn't delete events, how can we comply with that requirement? Ephemeral message brokers deal with this naturally since the broker effectively deletes messages after consumption. Since the broker deletes them, it organically complies with the requirement, and we do not need a strategy to deal with data deletion.

An approach to solve this challenge is using crypto shredding. Crypto shredding is a strategy to destroy data by losing the encryption keys needed to understand the data. Encrypted data can only be understood by decrypting it with the corresponding key. By deleting or overriding the key, the data is inoperable. Encryption is also a common requirement and needed to achieve compliance with GDPR, having a synergy between encrypting the events and using crypto shredding to destroy data. Figure 3-5 illustrates how we could apply crypto shredding to event-driven services.

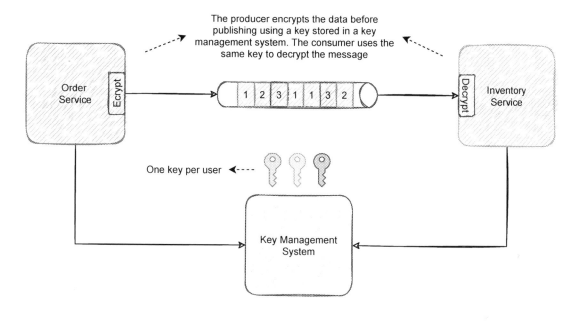

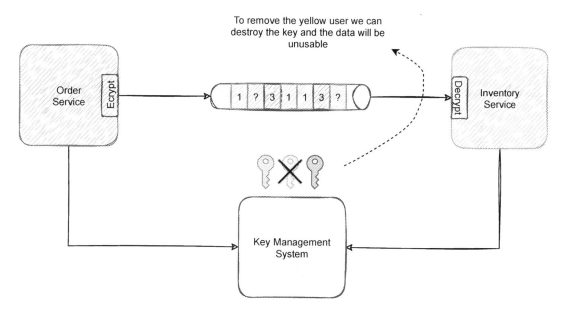

Figure 3-5. *Example of using crypto shredding to destroy messages associated with a user*

The order service encrypts the data using a key in a key management system. Each user has a different key, and we encrypt each user's events with the respective key. The inventory service to use the data has to decrypt the events by using the same key used to encrypt. If a user wants to be removed from the system, we can destroy the key associated with that user and the data will be unusable.

Applying this strategy to a complex architecture with several microservices can become challenging since each one of them would have to implement this strategy. Often, not all services need encryption and deal with sensitive data. Identifying and isolating the sensible data to the services that need them and applying this strategy only to those services can also be a good approach. There is also the option to use this strategy at the infrastructure level avoiding the implementation effort in all services. We can proxy the requests to a common module which has the responsibility to encrypt the data before publishing them to the broker. David Jacot details this approach in an interesting presentation[7] by shipping containers with that additional module (known as a sidecar pattern) using Kafka.

3.1.4 Event-Driven Message Types

Traditional messaging uses messages somewhat indifferently; they are just a means to propagate data. In event-driven architectures however, there are different types of messages that have different purposes and different meanings. In this subsection, we will discuss the different types and in which situations they should be used.

Messages are usually composed of a header and a body. We can use the header to pass additional information common to all messages, much like HTTP headers. A typical example is the correlation id, which we often use to link several messages related to the same entity. For example, if we create a product and then edit its brand and category, each of the changes would publish a different event (e.g., the generated events correspondingly: ProductCreated, ProductBrandChanged, ProductCategoryChanged); all three events could have a header with the id of the product signaling they are all related to the same product. Although there isn't a formal definition of what headers should a message have, we benefit from having a predefined set for the entire system. The correlation id we discussed before is a good example, but having other message

---

[7] See David Jacot, "Handling GDPR with Apache Kafka: How to Comply Without Freaking Out?", May 13/14, 2019, www.confluent.io/kafka-summit-lon19/handling-gdpr-apache-kafka-comply-freaking-out/

headers like a message id that uniquely identifies each message can be useful for debugging purposes. The headers' information must be chosen carefully in order to avoid flowing information that will have logic associated on the consumer side, like specific flags for specific processes. Often this kind of information can be forgotten, leading to errors on the consumption process or even assuming default values for the headers; Chapter 8 will further detail this subject. Having an event version or timestamp is also helpful for managing idempotency, as we will discuss in Chapters 5 and 6.

The message body has the full information we want to publish. Messages can be commands, events, or documents. Queries are also a common concept, and typically, they aren't a message but a common concept in event-driven architectures.

- **Commands** are orders to perform a given action. We should name them with a verb in the imperative form, for example, CreateOrderCommand. A command is a request to a given service to perform an action and thus can be rejected or fail a validation. We can change aggregates by sending a command to perform a given action in that aggregate and often reflect a user's action. Typically, commands affect one service and a specific domain; they usually aren't published to several subscribers, only one. Although often commands are messages, a command can also be an HTTP request if the service receives changes through an API instead of a message broker.

- **Events** notify something that has changed in a given domain or aggregate. They are named in the past participle verb and inform that something has happened, for example, OrderCreatedEvent. They are facts and, unlike commands, aren't liable to be rejected; they are something that already happened. Events are the most common block of event-driven architectures and are used to pass information and signal relevant changes throughout the architecture's components. They are often published to several consumers and can accommodate new consumers in the future, unlike commands that are related to a single system.

- **Documents** are much like events; the service publishes them when a given aggregate or entity changes, but they contain all the entity's information, unlike events which typically only have the information related to the change that originated the event. Although they often are triggered by changes in the aggregate, they often don't give information about what change triggered the document, unless we specifically add it to the document. If someone changed an order address, the generated event could be OrderAddressChanged and contain the information about the new order's address. The same change could trigger a document, for example, OrderDocument, which would have all the order information; each receiver would have to interpret it in the way that made sense to that service.

- **Queries** are requests of information issued to a given system to obtain the service's data. Typically, they aren't messages and are often synchronous requests like an HTTP request. They also don't change state; they simply request information.

Figure 3-6 illustrates an example of an interaction between these entities.

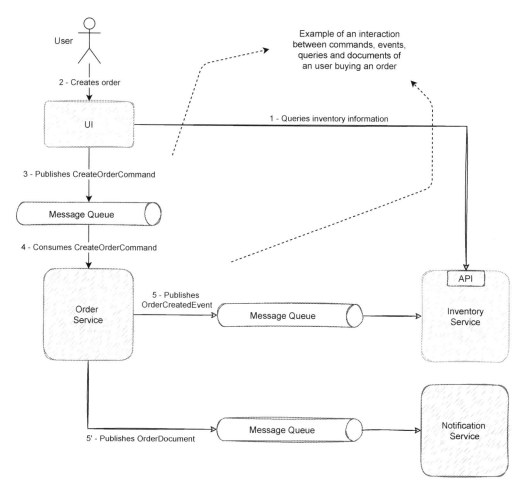

Figure 3-6. *The interaction between commands, events, documents, and queries*

A user placing an order would query the product's stock to the inventory service and then trigger a CreateOrderCommand by submitting an order that would be consumed by the order service. Once the service creates the entity, it publishes a CreateOrderEvent and an OrderDocument which are consumed by the inventory service and the notification service, respectively. Commands, events, documents, and queries are the foundation for the patterns and topologies we discuss further in this chapter.

3.1.5 Event-Driven Microservices: When to Use Documents over Events

In Subsection 3.1.2, we discussed we could use either events or documents to notify changes in entities. Choosing to publish an event or a document can be debatable, and they often accomplish the same goal. However, they are fundamentally different, and we should use them in specific use cases. In this subsection, we will discuss several topics that will help us decide where to use documents or events.

Events represent a specific change and have domain value by themselves since they represent something the user did or a change in the domain. Documents just inform the entity's latest state, so they lose the domain value carried by the event's meaning. For example, in Listing 3-1, there is an example of a partial event and a document representing the change in an order's address.

Listing 3-1. OrderAddressChanged vs. OrderDocument

```
1    OrderAddressChanged
2    {
3        OrderId: 15251212,
4        Address: "9980 Rock Maple Street",
5        UserId: 12162
6    }
7
8    OrderDocument
9    {
10       OrderId: 15251212,
11       Address: "9980 Rock Maple Street",
12       OrderLines: [
13               {
14                   ProductId: 1147421,
15                   Quantity: 1,
16               }
17               ],
18           OrderedAt: "2021-01-23T18:25:43.511Z",
19           UserId: 12168
20   }
```

If the receiving system needs to react only to changes in the address, it is more beneficial to use the event. For example, if a billing service had to update the address in the invoice, whenever the user changes the order's address, it would be easier to handle the OrderAddressChange. Using the OrderDocument would need to save the orders internally after each event or request the order from the order service to understand the address had changed.

However, documents often simplify consumers that need more information from the entity than an event would make available. For example, if we need to notify the user with all the order information every time an order changes, we would benefit from using the document in Listing 3-1 since all the information is available in the message. It would prevent the service to request or store the additional information that wasn't available in the event to send the notification; this would greatly simplify the consumer. With partial events, it also becomes complex to maintain all the entity's data. For example, if the order entity would grow and have more and more properties, it would probably imply that we needed to create more and more partial events. If the consumer needs to maintain all the order data, it is more complex to handle several different events than one with all the information. Another advantage of using documents is that if the user changed the address and quantity simultaneously, that would mean two different partial events. In contrast, if we use the document, we only need to publish one.

An exciting approach with Kafka is to use compacted topics. Compacted topics in Kafka have a periodic mechanism to remove messages with an older version for a given id, maintaining only the latest ones. So if we combine compacted topics with documents, we have a message queue with all the orders' information, much like a database table but in the form of events in a medium oriented to be shared with other consumers. In the case of the example in Listing 3-1, we could use the order id and publish the OrderDocument for each order; this way, the topic would have all the orders' information, much like the lines on a SQL table but in the form of messages ready to be shared. Consumers can plug to the topic and stream the data directly to their application. This way, we provide a way for applications to receive the data without impacting the origin service and its database. Since the broker is durable, we can read the topic from the beginning if we need to replay the data or new consumers need initialization.

Overall, it becomes simpler to use documents when we need a large part of the entity's data. However, we lose the meaning and the inherent change behind the event; if the consumer needs that meaning to process its logic, it will have to infer the meaning internally. In those cases, we are better off using partial events. It is often more useful to use events that reflect the user's intent, and this should be our go-to approach. But we always need to have the event consumer's needs in mind and adapt accordingly. In some use cases like we mentioned before, documents are useful; we will further detail this concept in Chapter 8.

3.1.6 Common Event-Driven Messaging Patterns

In Subsection 3.1.2, we discussed the types of messages and how they differ from each other. This subsection will discuss how they are typically used and the different patterns they are organized into.

As we mentioned in Chapter 1, event-driven architectures are composed of services that publish events to event brokers. Other services react to those events to accomplish their business rules. The services are built to be horizontally scalable, and several instances of the same service can consume from the same queue, having the load distributed between all of them.

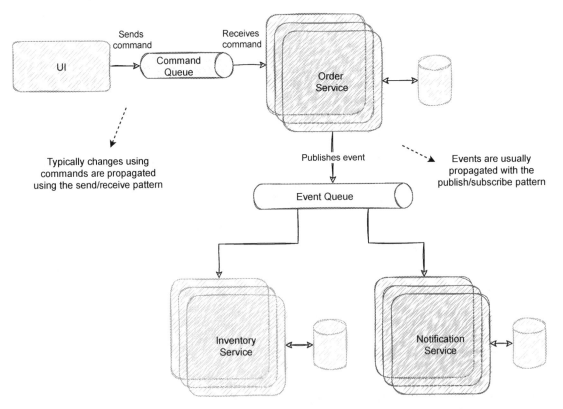

Figure 3-7. *Typical messaging patterns used in an event-driven architecture*

Figure 3-7 illustrates a typical architecture, much like the examples we discussed until now, using an order, an inventory, and a notification service. Changes are triggered by the UI, where the user changes, for example, its order information. To change the order, the UI sends a command to the order service, which publishes an event that is handled by any application that needs order events. Notice, however, several squares are representing the services, meaning each service can have multiple instances.

Send/Receive Pattern

The interaction between the UI and the order service is a send/receive pattern. Typically, commands are requests to change a given entity or aggregate information and have a very specific receiver. The request to change the data is only relevant for the order service; no other service needs or should receive that command. Send/receive is typically a point-to-point communication between two services with a specific purpose, often a request to do a given action on that service.

It is essential to distinguish the publication pattern along with the types of events. Commands are typically send/receive; events are typically publish/subscribe. Commands often have a very specific purpose and have a close relation with the domain they are changing; it is important to guarantee only the desired service reacts to the command.

Publish/Subscribe Pattern

The interaction between the order service and the inventory and notification service is a publish/subscribe pattern. The order service publishes changes that happened in its domain, and interested services subscribe to those changes and process them. As the previous pattern, typically they are fire-and-forget; the originating service only guarantees that the message was published to the broker.

Multiple services can handle the events and will process them at different rates. Each service might have several instances, as depicted in Figure 3-7, and each instance will receive various events and process them at different rates in parallel. This is the basis of horizontal scalability, which also introduces complex challenges on how to handle the concurrency between the several instances, out-of-order events, and eventual consistency associated with it, which we will discuss further in this book.

Request/Response Pattern

The interaction between the UI and the order service is intrinsically asynchronous due to happening through a message queue. The UI also doesn't know when the changes took place. The UI can notify the user the changes took place by handling the corresponding event. Once the service handles the command and applies the changes, it will publish an event signaling those changes. The command and the event can be correlated by an id which can be used by the UI to understand that the requested changes were applied. This way, the UI can be a publisher of commands and a receiver of events, implementing the request/response pattern. The changes can be linked together by a correlation id that would be published in the command and transmitted in the event. Figure 3-8 illustrates how the patterns we discussed before can be applied conceptually.

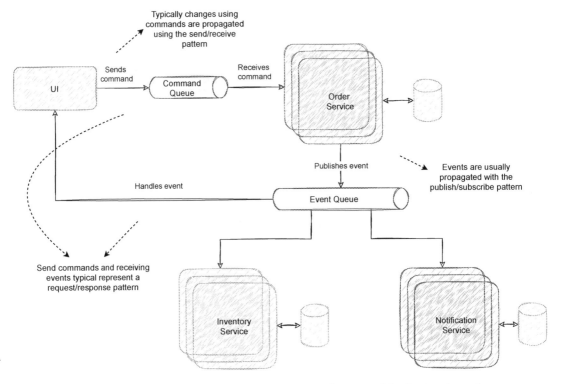

Figure 3-8. *Simple examples of the patterns we discussed before using the same example as before*

The UI implements both send/receive and request/response patterns. It sends a command which is received by the order service and handles the event generated by that command. The publish/subscribe pattern is implemented by the inventory and notification service by handling the events published by the order service.

3.1.7 Event-Driven Service Topologies

As we discussed before, event-driven services typically react to events; the name kind of gives it away, doesn't it? However, architectures composed exclusively of microservices that interact through events are rare. In the real world, often there is a mix between synchronous and asynchronous requests. As we discussed, event-driven indeed isn't a silver bullet, and even in an event-driven architecture, there are simple use cases that don't benefit from the added complexity of asynchronous interactions. This section will detail the ordinary interactions between services we often find and implement.

Typical CRUD (create, read, update, and delete) microservices have synchronous interactions. Users and other applications interact with them through an API to access their data. For example, if a service exposed a REST API, we could do an HTTP POST to create a given resource and an HTTP GET to obtain it, as pictured in Figure 3-9.

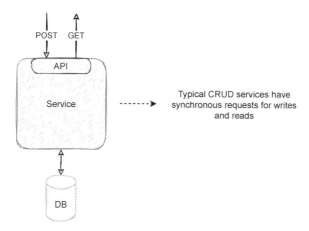

Figure 3-9. *We can request and change information synchronously from CRUD services*

An essential property of this topology is we obtain the response for our requests in a synchronous manner. If we create a resource, an order, for example, we immediately receive the response for the create request. If the service needs to validate the request to create the order, the service making the request obtains immediate feedback. Other asynchronous topologies we discuss next might need more complex ways to give feedback to the service issuing the request. This topology is straightforward but lacks the advantages of event-driven services; it should be applied to simple low-scale use cases. Simple domains with low amounts of data and fewer dependencies from other services typically benefit from using this approach.

CRUD services can also publish events, as depicted in Figure 3-10. We can still evolve typical synchronous services to publish events to allow other services to react to them. Adding publishing capabilities in existing CRUD services can be a way to include existing services in a new event-driven architecture.

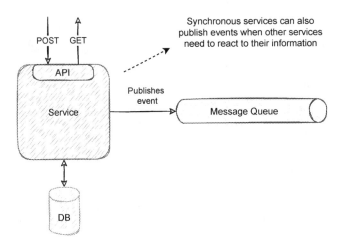

Figure 3-10. *CRUD services publishing events when their data changes*

By publishing the information to an event queue, we can benefit from the advantages of event streaming and share the data in the form of events to every other service that needs it. However, this topology and the one before suffer from the disadvantages we mentioned in Chapter 1. For example, suppose there are many services with synchronous APIs that call each other. In that case, we slowly but surely grow to a distributed monolith, where a failure in one service can cascade down to other services and affect the whole architecture.

As we mentioned in Subsection 3.1.2, commands are a type of message that request a given change to a service. Instead of receiving requests to change entities through a synchronous API like the examples we discussed before, we can receive through commands, as illustrated in Figure 3-11.

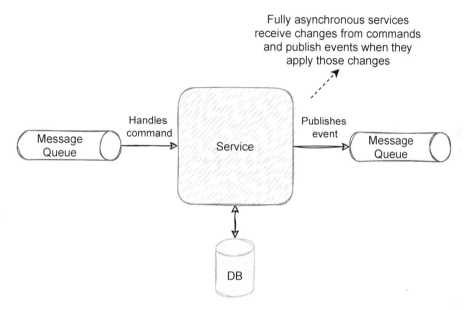

Figure 3-11. *Services can be fully asynchronous and receive changes in the form of commands. Both the input and output are asynchronous*

We send commands to a message queue, and like the example we discussed earlier about the order service, they request changes to a given entity. Once the changes are applied, the service publishes an event signaling those changes. This makes the service fully asynchronous and fully decoupled for other services. However, the fully asynchronous nature of the service can increase the complexity of different use cases that would be straightforward using a synchronous approach. For example, since we send each change in the form of a command to a message queue, there is no synchronous feedback to the user or system that triggered the request. If the command validation fails, giving feedback on why the verification failed can be tricky.

Services can also handle events and publish commands to other services, as illustrated in Figure 3-12. These services are typically called process managers or orchestrators. They react to information on different domains and instruct the services in its domain to react to those changes by sending commands. For example, in the order service, each order is an aggregate, and each command should only affect one aggregate

109

or entity. If a user changed its address on the user service, the order domain might need to reflect the change on all existing user's orders. To change each order, a process manager could react to the event and publish a command to each order.

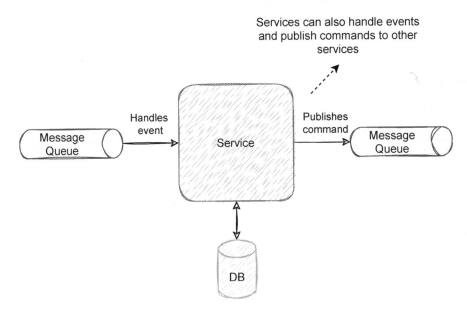

Figure 3-12. *Some services can handle events and publish commands to other services*

Instead of sending a command, this topology can also make a synchronous request to the target service depending on how the service exposes the functionality to change its resources.

The mix between these topologies and the synchronous and asynchronous interactions between the several services often raise difficult challenges in dealing with the eventual consistency associated with asynchronous services. Since some services might react to an event and facilitate APIs to expose their information, the request to obtain the information is synchronous, but the data is being changed asynchronously. The inherent eventual consistency can be troublesome to deal with, not only from a user perspective but also for other services consuming that information. How to deal with eventual consistency is further detailed in Chapter 5.

3.1.8 Common Event-Driven Pitfalls and Anti-patterns

Combining the patterns and topologies we just discussed sometimes originates in some common pitfalls. Most of them are very inconspicuous, and we might not notice they are there immediately, but they jeopardize the evolution of the architecture in the long run. In this subsection, we will discuss some pitfalls we often see people fall into.

Faking Synchronous Responses

As discussed in Chapter 1, an important consequence of event-driven architectures is the asynchronous nature they imbue in the systems. Often changes requested to the applications aren't reflected instantaneously, and feedback about the request often isn't returned in the same request flow. Often REST APIs, instead of returning the HTTP status codes of 200 (OK) or 201 (Created), can return 202 (Accepted). This status code means the system accepted the request; it was issued to be processed internally but wasn't yet processed. Often APIs convert requests to commands and send them to a queue; the response to that command is processed when the service handles that command. Since it is a queue, the time to respond can vary depending on the system's load; if there is a peak in load, the service might lag behind the number of messages being produced and might take a while to process it.

Since the response to the original request was accepted, retrieving the feedback to the issuing system or user might be problematic. For example, suppose you edit your billing address on an eCommerce platform, and after editing, the changes aren't reflected right away. In that case, it might be a bit annoying, but it probably isn't critical. However, in other use cases, it might be; if other services depend on that information, they might infer state based on stale information. In those cases, we might be tempted to fake synchronous responses by blocking the request and polling until the change is reflected.

Forging synchronous requests is an approach we often see, and although it gives a feel of being more consistent, it is very susceptible to issues when there is a higher load in the system. The minimal increase in message production might trigger timeouts in the blocked requests waiting for a response. Overall, it makes the system more brittle and susceptible to failure. If we use an event-driven approach, we should embrace the asynchronous nature and the eventual consistency they imply and avoid faking guarantees that no longer exist. Chapter 5 details strategies to deal with these issues.

Command Publishing

As we mentioned in Subsection 3.1.2, commands target a specific service and a specific domain. Sometimes we might feel the need to publish a command to several different services. This often implies that either the command has too much responsibility or there isn't a clear domain separation between the services. Services should react to events, to something that already happened in a domain, and they need to do something about it. Several different services shouldn't handle a request to change a given entity. They should react to each other rather than receiving the same order.

For example, if we bought a product in an eCommerce platform, it would trigger a command to create an order. Still, only the order service would handle that command; the inventory and notification service wouldn't know the command. Neither should they because the order creation request might be rejected. The only service responsible for managing the order domain is the order service. The other services should only react to things that already happened in that domain, like the order created event.

Passive-Aggressive Events

Events inform that something changed in some service. A common pitfall is to imbue an event with a hidden responsibility to do something in another service (Martin Fowler mentions this pitfall in this[8] article). Much like when my wife states that there are dirty dishes in the sink, she is stating the fact that there are dirty dishes in the kitchen, much like an event, but it has a hidden message behind it – that I really should do the dishes.

This pitfall often happens when an event from a service needs a given action to happen in another unrelated service. The change is typically modeled as a command, but the system that receives it needs other services to perform the action and publishes an event requesting that change. An event shouldn't request anything; it is a statement of a fact. To coordinate changes between several services, we should use different strategies. Although there is a gray area when designing events and guaranteeing we are not implementing passive-aggressive events, when we need to coordinate changes between several services, we should be concerned in ensuring the visibility and reliability of the flow of the messages and accomplishment of the overall process. To do that, we often need to implement a Saga or a process manager, which we will discuss further in Chapter 4.

---

[8] See Martin Fowler, "What do you mean by "Event-Driven"?", February 7, 2017, `https://martinfowler.com/articles/201701-event-driven.html`

3.2 Organizing Event-Driven Microservice Boundaries

Event-driven microservices are highly decoupled from each other, which enables changing a service without affecting other services. The ability to change and deploy changes independently is a pivotal characteristic to support a rapidly growing and evolving business. As the system grows, the complexity can hamper our efforts to achieve a highly evolutionary and decoupled architecture. Organizing and defining boundaries between the growing number of services becomes a main concern. This section will discuss the different approaches to defining microservice boundaries.

Chapter 1 discussed how event-driven architectures have a highly decoupled nature due to using events as a form of communication and as the source of truth. However, as the system grows and becomes more complex, we shouldn't take this characteristic for granted. Even when decoupled by a message queue, if we need to repeatedly add functionality that sprawls several services, they will often depend on each other's changes. This can easily lead to gridlock releases where several services need changes from other services to be released. They often need a strict order of releases and highlight complicated dependencies between a complex network of services. We can contain these dependencies if services have clear boundaries between them, much like the boundaries we create inside an application to separate the application logic and database logic.

There are several approaches to defining a microservice boundary. A good rule of thumb is code that changes together stays together. In Chapter 2, we deconstructed a monolith by using a domain-driven approach. We believe this is a sensible way to approach a boundary definition. Domains tend to be more stable than other types of approaches, and boundaries defined by having the company's domains in mind tend to accommodate changes without propagating them throughout the whole architecture. By drawing boundaries around a domain, it gives the space to evolve the domain and, at the same time, limit the impacts on other domains. They also tend to correlate well with the company's organizational composition; often teams are arranged around domain concepts, which translates well with an architecture with boundaries around those domains. Domain-driven design relates well with this kind of organization, and we deep dive into it in Section 3.3.

There are other approaches to organizing boundaries; you will often find that defining those boundaries and understanding where to fit new functionality are often a combination of those approaches. Keep in mind there isn't only one way to define something; a domain approach is a quite reasonable option, but it is important to understand it is not the only way, and often we benefit from combining more than one approach. In Chapter 2, we discussed we should have a strong reason to adopt an event-driven architecture, which can also play a role in this definition. Different reasons can drive different approaches and priorities.

3.2.1 Organizational Composition

Conway's law states that "Any organization that designs a system will inevitably produce a design whose structure is a copy of the organization's communication structure." If you look back at the architectures and organizational compositions of those architectures, you will probably find evidence of Conway's law even in awkward and funny examples. There was a company I worked with that had a boundary that, in the domain perspective, it made sense to be together with another existing boundary. No one could find a good name for it or to give a precise definition of why it was different from the existing one apart from small details. But why was it a distinct boundary? Well, it happened that the team that frequently changed it was in a completely different organizational structure than the teams from the existing boundary. The company's organizational composition actually influenced the technical boundaries.

It isn't necessarily wrong; in that context, teams inside the same organizational composition that owned services inside the same boundary were more autonomous and facilitated feature implementation. However, it is essential to understand its implications and use them to our advantage. That might mean shifting teams to different structures to achieve the desired architecture. The inverse will inadvertently happen; the way teams are composed will invariably influence the system's boundaries.

If we align this concept with the domain approach in the case of an eCommerce platform, we might have a composition of teams that work with order management, another for product management, etc. This organization will also allow those teams to specialize in the domain concepts of the services they work with, which benefits the overall modeling between the conceptual and technical domains.

3.2.2 Likelihood of Changes

An approach to design boundaries is to separate services into two groups: services that change and are likely to change often and services that don't. This separation allows for a boundary where most of the business innovation happens and another for services that don't and won't need frequent changes.

Conceptually, it makes sense to group services that are likely to change together. If our objective to adopt an event-driven microservice architecture is to optimize time to market, it makes sense to group those services and adopt different approaches for each boundary. However, in practice, it is hard to foresee which services will belong to each group. Historically, we can perceive which services were often changed and which ones currently aren't. But understanding how they will evolve in the future usually has a high degree of uncertainty. Also, changing one service that suddenly needs frequent changes from one boundary to another is often laborious. All the assumptions we made until now were that the service would hardly change; changing those assumptions can be problematic. Usually, new functionality ends up affecting services that supposedly don't change that often, leading to even higher time overhead.

We did experience some successful use cases when combining this approach with the domain approach. Typically inside a domain boundary, some services change more often than others, and we can benefit from having those identified and specific approaches to deal with them.

3.2.3 Type of Data

Some services have to deal with sensitive data like PII (personally identifiable information), PCI DSS (payment card industry data security standard), or PHI (protected health information). This kind of data often has additional regulations and requires audits from external parties. Implementing these requirements (like GDPR) can add a significant effort (as we discussed in Subsection 3.1.1), and we might benefit from limiting those changes to the services that actually handle that kind of data. Figure 3-13 illustrates several boundaries with different types of data.

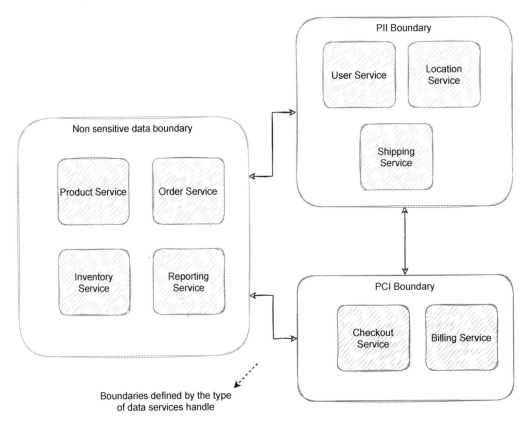

Figure 3-13. *Example of defining boundaries by the type of data existing in the services*

By having boundaries that handle the sensitive data and guaranteeing that the data only flows inside that boundary, we can focus the regulation's enforcement in a subset of the system. Some requirements, like the right to be forgotten and external audits to the system, can be hard to implement and manage. This type of organization enables to apply those requirements only to the services that need them. For example, inside the PII boundary, all services would have to apply the requirements, but the services in the non-sensitive data boundary wouldn't need to. This way, it is easier to manage and implement the requirements than addressing them in the whole architecture.

3.3 Brief and Practical Introduction to Domain-Driven Design and Bounded Contexts

Eric Evans first introduced DDD (domain-driven design) in his book[9] about this subject. It is an approach to design complex systems that provides a set of techniques to help us understand the application's domain and build it into a conceptual model. The complete details of these techniques and ideas are outside of this book's scope, but we will approach how they are important and how we can use them in designing boundaries between event-driven microservices.

One challenge developers always struggle with is to capture reality and model it into code. DDD can help us to design the domains that the business comprehends in our applications. Models and boundaries designed around the domain are likely to be more stable and translate the business's reality more accurately. It also facilitates the composition of the company allowing it to organize teams around those business concepts.

One key aspect of DDD is the focus on the domain. The company's business value is in its domain; by focusing on it, we are guaranteeing we are modeling what really matters or what differentiates the business. Any system has to model some kind of business value into code. Often the translation from the conceptual domain into code gets lost in translation. By having close communication between the conceptual and coded world and sharing the same language, we greatly reduce the area of failure. DDD focuses on exactly that, having a close communication with the domain experts and together developing a conceptual model of the domain. DDD also introduces a concept of a common language used by both business experts and developers (named as ubiquitous language) to reduce the risk of misunderstandings. Using the same names the business uses in the code, we reduce the risk of unclear requirements and business rules.

DDD enables us to reason with a complex, intricate domain to conceptually divide it, allowing several teams to work on it sustainably. Having said that, simple straightforward systems aren't likely to benefit much from some of the patterns typically used with DDD, much like we mentioned in Chapter 1 about event-driven microservice architectures. DDD provides the tools to model and maintain a complex, long-lasting system. If our project is small or short-lived, we won't probably benefit from it. But it might benefit from its mindset.

---

[9] See Eric Evans, "Domain-Driven Design: Tackling Complexity in the Heart of Software," August 20, 2003, www.amazon.com/Domain-Driven-Design-Tackling-Complexity-Software/dp/0321125215

Although the patterns associated with DDD like event sourcing or CQRS (we will detail these in Chapter 4) aren't a one-fits-all solution, the value we extract with DDD and the mentality shift it inspires are very important. We might end up with a small, simple system, but whichever system we are doing, having a clear understanding of the domain is pivotal to its success. Having a close communication with domain experts and having a clear understanding of the domain and how it maps to our implementations enable us to focus on the domain, where the real value is. A design approached this way enforces the importance of understanding and modeling the company's business value.

3.3.1 How We Can Apply It in Practice

Domain models are the core of the design. These models have detailed business knowledge and capture the domain knowledge from the domain experts. These models are converted to code and can scope the boundaries of that knowledge and verify its integrity. The teams designing the models have close communication with the domain experts, and they work together to develop these models. As the business evolves, so do the domain models.

By developing the domain models, we can understand the existing domain and its interactions. We lightly touched this subject in Chapter 2 when we discussed how to move from a monolith to an event-driven architecture. The exercise in understanding the monolith's existing domain is the same exercise to design the domain models, and we might end up with something similar to what we discussed in Chapter 2, illustrated in Figure 3-14.

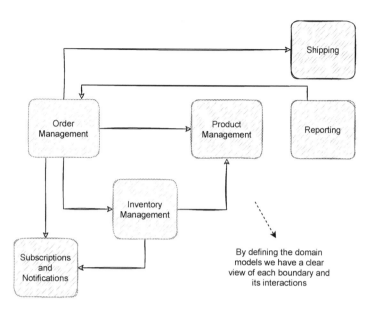

Figure 3-14. *The same domain models we discussed in Chapter 1. By defining them, we can have a clear understanding of each bounded context and its interactions*

When analyzing our existing eCommerce platform, we defined several different domains illustrated in Figure 3-14. Each of them is what DDD defines as a bounded context, and they usually represent a more extensive business domain concept. This domain concept often translates to a boundary and abstracts those domain details from the other bounded contexts. For example, the shipping bounded context might need to know the different shipping providers, but the order management bounded context doesn't or shouldn't.

Bounded contexts have one or more aggregates. There are many definitions of aggregate, but they often represent conceptually a domain unit inside the boundary. For example, in the order management bounded context, we could define the order aggregate, the product aggregate, etc. The aggregate models a domain concept, and an entity is an instantiation of that concept. We could define the order aggregate, and the specific order 231 is an entity.

Typically, services request changes to entities through commands, and changes are propagated through events. Aggregates can reject requests to changes and are used to maintain the consistency and to enforce the business rules related to that aggregate.

Aggregates can also be exposed to other bounded contexts or can be hidden depending on the domain. For example, the order management bounded context might have an order and product aggregate. It might make sense to expose the order aggregate in the order bounded context since it is the core concept in that bounded context. The product aggregate, however, might be needed just as a reference to another domain (the product bounded context), and since it is only an internal view of that boundary, it might not be exposed. Figure 3-15 illustrates an example of an aggregate composition in the order service.

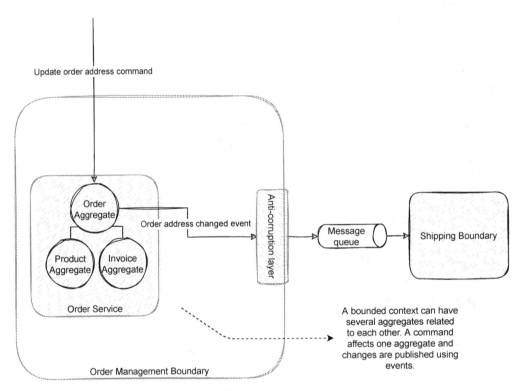

Figure 3-15. *Example of an aggregate composition for the order service. The order aggregate has two other associated aggregates*

We could define an order aggregate that relates to two other aggregates, the product and invoice aggregate. To change an order, we can issue a command to the order aggregate affecting a single entity (or a specific existing order). The command to change the order address can be rejected depending on the business rules the order service enforces.

We can communicate changes to aggregates to the other boundaries through events. Changing the order address triggers an order address changed event, which can be consumed by other boundaries to apply their own domain logic.

Each bounded context has its domain model. Since bounded contexts have to communicate with each other, it is essential to guarantee that the domain concepts from one bounded context don't leak into another. The anti-corruption layer enforces that all domain-specific logic and information remain inside the boundary.

A boundary can be implemented with a single service or can be composed of several different microservices. Figure 3-15 shows that the order service and the anti-corruption layer can be two different independent services or one single service. A piece of reasonable advice is to take the same approach we discussed in Chapter 2; first create arguably extensive services that represent a complete boundary. Later, if necessary, we can decompose that service into smaller parts. In more complex architectures, boundaries are composed of several services that work together to accomplish that domain's purpose and then communicate the changes to that domain to other boundaries that are also composed of several services. A reasonable approach is to do that incrementally; first we can understand the existing domain model, then create a single service to implement that bounded context, and then decompose that single more extensive service into smaller parts if needed.

Aggregates usually have a strong relation to concurrency and atomicity. Typically, changes to an entity are performed without concurrency or in single thread. That doesn't mean the service is single-threaded, though; the service can change multiple orders simultaneously as long as the changes are to different orders. If we change three different orders simultaneously, those changes can happen concurrently, but if we change three times the same order, those three changes typically occur sequentially. This concurrency management guarantees each aggregate's consistency while allowing parallel processing (how to handle concurrency will be discussed in Chapter 6).

The aggregate decomposition of a bounded context can be highly subjective. In Figure 3-14, we designed three aggregates, but we could quickly come up with a different design. As we will discuss in Section 3.4, aggregate design can have a considerable impact in the system and its performance. An arguably good approach is first to understand the domain conceptually and work closely with the domain experts to design a mental model you both agree with. Then map that model to the technical implementation and understand how the technical and performance implications influence the model.

3.4 Event-Driven Microservices: The Impact of Aggregate Size and Common Pitfalls

In Section 3.3, we discussed how to use DDD to understand and design an application's domain and boundaries. We discussed how the aggregate definition was a pivotal step in that design and that it can have a high impact on the whole system. This section will detail how it can affect the whole architecture's performance and how to avoid some common pitfalls.

We discussed that entities are an instantiation of an aggregate; for example, for the order aggregate, a possible entity could be the order with id 231 submitted by user John. We also discussed that aggregates have a strong relation with concurrency since each entity is changed transactionally (when someone is changing an entity, no other changes can occur simultaneously). Thus, deciding the correct granularity of the aggregate becomes pivotal and relates closed to the ability to guarantee consistency and performance in the system.

Let's illustrate this with an example; imagine we work with an eCommerce platform that sells beauty products. Each product can have several variants; for example, perfumes can have different bottle sizes, lipsticks can have different colors, etc. The stock is managed at the variant level; we could have in stock one small bottle of a given perfume and two large bottles. Products have a precise categorization, and the business often applies changes to categories of products. For example, from time to time, they might want every lipstick to have a given discount, or they might want to block the perfume category to ship to some countries due to the shipping laws of those countries, etc.

Typically, changes are applied to a single entity; changes that affect several entities or several aggregates often need the coordination of a Saga pattern or process managers (we discuss these patterns in Chapter 4). Once something is changed in a given entity, an event is published informing that change; thus, domain events usually have the same granularity of the aggregate definition.

There might be three different aggregates we could define: category, product, and variant. Using the variant as the aggregate would facilitate the stock changes and enable a high concurrency system to guarantee performance (since changes could be made to several variants in parallel). But it would also publish several smaller events; depending on the number of products and variants, this could mean a lot of stress on the message broker and the consuming services. While defining the category as the aggregate would guarantee the consistency of the larger discount and visibility changes and would publish larger individual events. But it could easily undermine the system's performance since each product in each category would be changed sequentially.

An arguably good first step is to define the aggregates conceptually, understanding the domain and designing it having in mind a real domain concept. But we shouldn't fall into the trap of creating using only the context of our service or boundary. For example, if we were in charge of developing the stock management service, a good aggregate would be the variant aggregate. The same could be said if we were in charge of designing the system to manage the product's categorization; it would certainly make sense to us to define the category as the aggregate.

However, a second good step is to understand who the consumers of those events are and the reality of those services and boundaries. What does their aggregate look like? Is it roughly the same as ours? Is it a larger domain concept or a smaller one? For example, let's say the service managing stock had a variant aggregate and published an event for each variant. The service applying the discount would need to know which variants have stock but had to apply the discount to a category of products. That could comprise several hundreds of products, each with several variants. The mismatch between the aggregates would mean that the discount system would have substantially more work to understand how each small change applied to their larger concept. Defining an aggregate as large as a category in the stock boundary might not make sense either. Still, perhaps if both boundaries adopt a product aggregate, they would benefit from the simpler communication between each other. Overall, understanding our consumers' needs and finding a compromise are often best for the overall architecture.

Defining the size of aggregates is always subjective. Changing it later on can also be a laborious task. However, when in doubt, rely on your domain experts' support and your understanding of the domain. Asking these questions often helps to decide:

- Does the aggregate translate to a real domain concept?

- How many events will we publish, and how granular are they? Can the message broker and the consuming services handle the load? Are we publishing an unnecessarily large quantity of events?

- How performant and scalable the system can be? If we grow to the millions of aggregates, does the system remain performant? Can we change several aggregates at the same time and scale seamlessly?

Sometimes you will find you got the aggregate size wrong. Often it is hard to foresee the load and usage of the system accurately. Don't be afraid to advance and change later on. Although these changes can be laborious, as we discussed in Chapter 1, the decoupled nature of event-driven services allows us to replace services reasonably easily. We will further discuss the impact of the event schema's size in Chapter 8.

3.5 Request-Driven vs. Event-Driven Services

In Subsection 3.1.5, we discussed several service topologies. When building a service in an event-driven architecture, the two main approaches are using a request-driven or event-driven service. Obviously, event-driven architectures are composed of event-driven services. However, most architectures aren't composed of only event-driven services. They arguably shouldn't be since the two approaches have different implications and aren't adequate for all use cases. In this section, we will discuss the two approaches and guidelines to which one to choose.

Event-driven architectures are characterized by using events as the source of truth. As we discussed in Chapter 1, this enables several powerful use cases, and we should follow this guideline throughout the architecture. Traditional microservices typically expose synchronous APIs and use them to provide access to their data. These kinds of services are simpler to use and to reason with, and often there are use cases where an event-driven approach to a microservice simply isn't the best way to go. Figure 3-16 illustrates the typical approaches of request-driven and event-driven services.

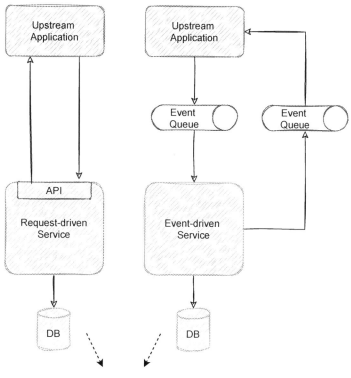

Request-driven services communicate using
synchronous requests while event-driven
services use event queues.

Figure 3-16. *Differences between the communication of typical request-driven
and event-driven services*

A request-driven service typically exposes a synchronous API like REST to expose
functionality to other applications. We can access data by issuing requests to the same
API. Functionality exposed by request-driven services is easy to reason with; it is similar
to a call to a local function we would do in the code, but instead of running in memory, it
does a remote network request.

Request-driven services have a place in event-driven architectures; not all use
cases are suitable for event-driven services. Most often than not, you will find and
work with both types of services in the microservice ecosystem. Event-driven services
introduce an asynchronous nature to the interaction between the applications. Some
use cases don't benefit from the additional complexity or cannot afford the eventual
consistency introduced by event-driven services. Stronger consistency guarantees are

hard (or impossible) to maintain in distributed event-driven microservices. If there is a use case for strong consistency, choosing a synchronous interaction in a request-driven service is often a better choice than using an event-driven one.

There are several strategies to deal with eventual consistency, and eventual consistency doesn't need to be slow (we further detail both points in Chapter 5). Still, there might be use cases where we simply can't afford any inconsistency whatsoever. Don't misunderstand me; we always need consistency, but it's relatively debatable whether we can maintain distributed strong consistency at scale (thus the rise of NoSQL databases).

We did come across some use cases where strong, consistent, and synchronous responses were needed in low-scale services. In these use cases, a synchronous request-driven approach is often a better choice due to the simplicity of accomplishing the use case. For example, if we have a frontend application that makes a couple of hundreds of requests per day to a service and needs a synchronous response, we probably wouldn't benefit much from the added complexity of asynchronous events between the two applications. We can also publish events in request-driven services to provide an event-driven approach to share their data.

However, we should avoid the pitfall of using a high quantity of request-driven services throughout the whole architecture. One important consequence is turning our microservice architecture into a distributed monolith. Frequent requests between the services often lead to high coupling between the services, which impacts new features and leads to complex dependencies. We also discussed in Chapter 1 how request-driven services are susceptible to cascading failures. A failure in one apparently not critical service can often bring the whole architecture down by cascading the failure through the complex network of synchronous requests. When the architecture starts to grow, it's often hard to understand the advantages of a complex network of request-driven services and a monolith.

Sharing data through synchronous APIs can be troublesome when services need a huge amount of data or frequent lookups. These kinds of requests often impact the service and limit their resources. Requesting a large chunk of a service's data can significantly impact the database, and doing so through regular paging often has bad performance. Those use cases really shine when streaming data through an event stream. As we discussed in Chapter 2, using event streams with event-driven services provides a very organic way to share the data without impacting the service that owns the data.

Be sure to focus on the event stream being the source of truth and the medium services share data. Using request-driven services in specific use cases makes sense, and we shouldn't be dogmatic on whether choosing only one type of approach.

3.6 Deciding When to Create a New Microservice or Add Functionality to an Existing One

Once we have an event-driven microservice architecture up and running, where to incorporate new functionality can be dubious. There are usually two options: either add new functionality to an existing service or create a new service. The decision often depends on the functionality being added and the existing architecture. There isn't a one-fits-all rule, but a few pointers can help us decide which one to choose.

We can use DDD to map the different bounded contexts in an existing system, but migrating existing functionality to new services by either creating a new service or adding it to an existing one can be subjective. For example, suppose a part of our system manages orders and deals with orders and order lines. In that case, an arguably clear decision is to maintain both of them in the same service due to the close relationship between the two entities. However, if we also manage stores and each store has stock, should we create a separate service for each concept or maintain both in the same service? And how about adding new functionality? If we received a requirement to add several complex pricing rules to our system, should we add those rules to the existing product system or create a separate system to manage those rules? The answer is subjective, and usually there isn't a right or wrong answer, just tradeoffs between the two solutions.

As discussed in Chapter 2, a sensible approach is to create coarse-grained services and then fine-grained services as needed. It's better to incrementally evolve and add complexity to the architecture than starting with several dozens of services early on. However, suppose our services begin to get too large and suffer from some of the limits of monoliths we discussed. In that case, it might be advisable to review the service and understand if it is handling too much responsibility. Either way, don't be afraid to try and adapt later; although it might lead to a lot of rework, the high decoupling of event-driven architectures allows us to swap services as long as we don't break the event contracts.

Here are some considerations we can keep in mind to help us decide. These points can help you sway in one solution or another, considering both can help you shift toward the best decision based on the system's characteristics you want to prioritize.

Some points that indicate we should add the functionality to an existing service:

- There is a very close relationship between the conceptual domain of the new functionality and an existing service. In the example we discussed about the order and order lines, they are very related domain concepts, and in many systems, it might make sense to keep them together. Typically, we want code that changes together to be together. So domains that are closely related and are likely to change together, keeping them in the same place might be a sensible decision.

- The new functionality will need to share another existing service's database. We discussed the disadvantages of sharing a database in Chapter 1. Handling schema changes between several services can make new functionality difficult to add and produce complicated lockstep releases. Also, different services that use the same database are keen to impact each other, for example, with a long-running transaction, which turns scaling each service into a challenge. If we need to add a new service that will need to share the same database as another one, it is a giant red flag, and we should avoid it at all costs. We can still create a new service if it needs a large amount of data from an existing service, but by consuming the event stream and creating an internal view of the data. Adding functionality to an existing service or using the event stream is almost always a better option than sharing a database.

- The anemic domain model[10] is a common object-oriented anti-pattern and a common pitfall in many services. When building a microservice architecture, you might find anemic domain services. These services are characterized by a simple sheath around the database that only writes or fetches information, lacking domain logic inside the service. Basically, it looks like a repository pattern with associated hardware. If the service lacks domain logic, odds are it is distributed somewhere else in the system. This characteristic can be a good sign to add functionality to that service and enrich it with

---

[10] More details in Martin Fowler, "AnemicDomainModel," November 25, 2003, `www.martinfowler.com/bliki/AnemicDomainModel.html`

domain value. It's not a rule though; some services aren't heavy on domain logic; they can perform more mundane tasks or are endowed with a more infrastructural nature.

Some points that indicate the functionality might belong in a new service:

- If we add functionality to a service that depends on multiple services, it might be a sign that this service has a lot of responsibility. In this case, we might benefit from creating a new service and even migrating some functionality from the existing service. The service can consume events from a myriad of different sources or request information from several services; either way, it might indicate we centralized a large quantity of logic in that service. Increasing its complexity might not be advisable and can be a sign we should separate some of that logic.

- Several different teams manage the existing service, and there is no clear ownership. An advantage of a microservice architecture is having autonomous teams who can deliver fast with minimal intervention from other teams. If we add functionality to a service already managed by several teams, it might be advisable to understand how we can divide the service and its responsibilities. Just this argument by itself might not be a strong enough reason to create a new service since we can manage this in other ways, but combined with others, it might form a strong argument.

- The new functionality requires a different technology stack. If we are adding a new functionality that we want to use a different technology stack or requires specific technology, adding it to an existing service can be challenging. Managing two different technology stacks in two different services makes the maintenance, release, and deployment a lot easier.

- When a new functionality has a very different usage pattern and needs to scale independently of any other service, it can be a good sign to separate it into a new service. Suppose we add functionality that will have several times of magnitude more usage than the current usage. In that case, it might mean we will need more resources for that functionality than the existing ones. Another use case is if the usage has seasonality associated with it; for example, every Friday has a large peak of usage. It might be effective to scale only that part of the system independently of the rest of the system. We can easily achieve that if the functionality is in a separate service.

It's fairly apparent where we should add most new functionality. However, from time to time, the question to create a new service or use an existing one arises. It is important to understand the implications and be able to build a strong argument. Each of these arguments alone might not mean much; the goal here is to give us the tools to build a strong, compelling case for either decision.

3.7 Summary

- Services can and should have the code organized in a tiered architecture. The clean architecture is a good example of an architecture we can use that promotes decoupling and enables easy maintenance.

- As the architecture grows to more fine-grained services, each service can translate to a different clean architecture's layer.

- Although we can use either durable or ephemeral message brokers, they accomplish different purposes. Event-driven architectures typically have high synergy with durable message brokers.

- Complying with some data security standards can be challenging in event-driven architectures. Crypto shredding is an option we can use to leverage those requirements.

- There are typically four types of entities in an event-driven architecture: commands, events, documents, and queries.

- Using documents or events can be debatable. When a system needs a large part of the entity's data, a document is often a reasonable choice. If a system needs the meaning and the inherent change behind the event, partial events are often a better choice.

- There are typically three types of message patterns we can use: send/receive, publish/subscribe, and request/response.

- Faking synchronous response, command publishing, and passive-aggressive events are three common pitfalls we should avoid while designing event-driven systems.

- To design a system's boundaries, we can use four approaches: organizational composition, likelihood of changes, type of data, and domain-driven design. Although a domain approach is a sensible option, we often benefit from combining more than one approach.

- We can use domain-driven design to understand the application's domain and build it into a conceptual model. Models and boundaries designed around the domain are likely to be more stable and translate the business's reality more accurately.

- The aggregate size can have high implications in the system's consistency management and performance. There are a few questions we can ask to help us design those aggregates.

- We can use both request-driven or event-driven services. Although event-driven is our go-to approach, we can benefit from request-driven services in specific use cases. We shouldn't be dogmatic about choosing only one type of approach.

- There are several characteristics we can go through to help us decide to either add new functionality in an existing service or a new one.

CHAPTER 4

Structural Patterns and Chaining Processes

This chapter covers:

- Understanding why strong consistency and transactions shouldn't be an option in distributed event-driven systems

- Why we should avoid two-phase commit and distributed transactions in distributed systems

- Using orchestration pattern to implement higher-level business processes

- Using choreography pattern as an alternative to orchestration

- Understanding CQRS (command query responsibility segregation) and event sourcing and applying it to an event-driven system

- Optimizing read queries by building multiple read models

- How to live with invisible domain flow and avoid the pitfall of a spaghetti architecture

As we start to learn computer science and software engineering, data consistency is a cornerstone to software development. Strong consistency and ACID guarantees are the very foundation of most applications. We are used to treating data as a single copy; when we write something, it is instantaneously available for every client to see. If a write fails, the data is always kept in a valid state and changes are roll backed. We use transactions to guarantee consistency across several tables, and often they are the foundation to fulfill complex business processes.

© Hugo Filipe Oliveira Rocha 2022
H. F. Oliveira Rocha, *Practical Event-Driven Microservices Architecture*,
https://doi.org/10.1007/978-1-4842-7468-2_4

In fact, this way of dealing with data is often wired into our minds. There's an awe-inspiring purity in a database schema under the third normal form.[1] The referential integrity and lack of duplication of a well-structured third normal form schema are a flimsy glimpse of an ideal platonic world. Data and consistency are precious, perishing the thought of having inconsistent or stale data returned to clients. Knowing the application will always fetch the latest state and every write will immediately be available is straightforward to understand, easy to reason with and facilitates developments. We are used to this bubble of safety and comfort ACID provides. And there's nothing wrong with it; actually in simple and small or medium-sized data applications (by medium-sized, I mean data that fits a single machine without overwhelming infrastructure costs), there's arguably little gain in adopting a distributed architecture as we discussed in Chapters 1 and 2.

However, for distributed or large data applications, it is a different reality. These strong consistency properties, easiness of joining information, and guarantees of transactions between disparate domains are often bastions of a dying order. As we walk toward a distributed architecture, we find we no longer live in that safety bubble a single database with ACID guarantees provides. We are faced with the challenges of how to manage processes that span several services with different databases.

In the previous chapters, we mentioned how guaranteeing strong consistency was a challenge in distributed architectures, but we never detailed why. Section 4.1 will discuss why guaranteeing a consistent business process that spans several domains might be challenging and why it is different from a typical single-process application.

We will approach how to manage a business process that needs the intervention of several different domains in Sections 4.2 and 4.3. These kinds of business processes are called Sagas, and in event-driven architectures, we can apply two types of solutions to handle these complicated business processes, either by orchestration or choreography. We will discuss how to apply both of these solutions in these two sections. Section 4.4 will discuss how we can combine both orchestration and choreography and how they can complement each other.

The distributed nature of event-driven architectures implies that the data is distributed throughout several independent services. Obtaining an aggregated view of data that spans several different services can be a challenge. Sections 4.5 and 4.6 will approach patterns to build denormalized views in event-driven architectures.

---

[1] Further details in "Third normal form," https://en.wikipedia.org/wiki/Third_normal_form

4.1 The Challenges of Transactional Consistency in Distributed Systems

Chapter 1 discussed the challenges of distributed event-driven architectures and the importance of an incremental adoption of event-driven services to deal with those challenges sustainably. One crucial consequence of deconstructing a single monolithic database into several smaller ones is the loss of the ability to guarantee consistency across several domains seamlessly.

Let's illustrate this with an example. If we have a single monolithic eCommerce platform, with a single monolithic database handling the user's orders, each order creation will change the relevant tables. Figure 4-1 illustrates this situation with a stock and order table.

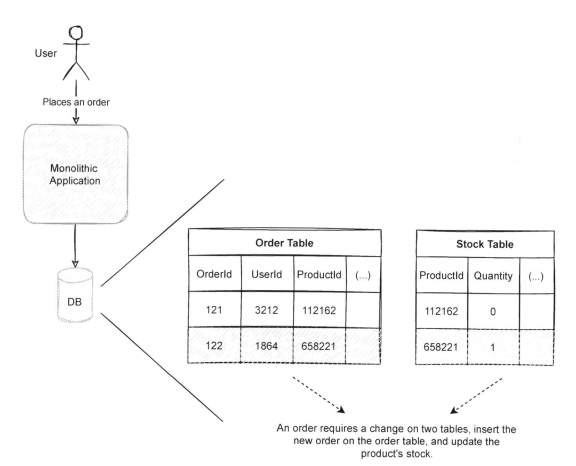

Figure 4-1. *The creation of the order inserts a line in the order table and updates the stock quantity in the stock table. Both changes can happen transactionally*

When the user requests a new order, the service inserts a new line in the order table, and the stock quantity is updated to reflect that user's order. Since both tables are inside the same database, we can use its ACID properties to guarantee that both changes happen simultaneously or don't happen at all, rejecting the order. Once the changes are made, they will also be immediately available to every client requesting them.

By moving to a distributed event-driven architecture, we would deconstruct the monolithic application into several services. We would also divide the monolithic database and distribute the data between them. Figure 4-2 illustrates how the same example could look like in an event-driven architecture.

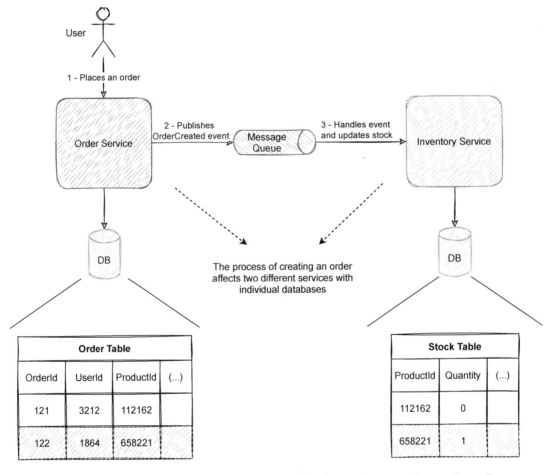

Figure 4-2. *To accomplish the order process, both services need to reflect the changes in their databases*

Since we separated the order and inventory domain into two distinct services, the order and inventory data aren't in the same database anymore. The segregation creates the challenge of how we can guarantee the strong consistency of fulfilling an order. The example only illustrates two services, but there might be processes that need the interaction of several different domains; for instance, if we needed to apply discounts, change the user information, etc., it might affect several distinct services. When creating an order with a single database, we could simply wrap a transaction around every table that needed changes, and we would be sure all changes would happen atomically. However, with a distributed architecture, we can't have the same guarantees. The alternatives to manage these kinds of issues come at the cost of added complexity as we will discuss in the following sections.

4.1.1 Why Move from a Monolithic Database in the First Place?

Besides the monolith's limitations, we discussed in Chapter 1, why forfeit the consistency guarantees provided by ACID anyway? In use cases that need strong consistency, we might just be better off by keeping that data together, even in a distributed microservice architecture. The strong consistency ACID provides can only be achieved by having data in the same place. Don't be dogmatic in adopting a distributed solution; if there is a critical use case for strong consistency, consider if it is feasible to maintain the data together and benefit from the properties associated with it. However, this is the exception; most use cases can live with weaker consistency guarantees distributed systems require; most of the time, they are good enough as long as the system is performant (we will further discuss this in Chapter 5).

In use cases that deal with vast amounts of data, we might need to forfeit the ACID properties anyway. The purity of the third normal form we discussed at the beginning of the chapter often doesn't have a place in the real world. Small and medium-sized data undoubtedly benefit from it, and in those situations, we often benefit from designing the database schema under those principles. But when faced with huge amounts of data, we quickly face its limitations. Often queries on database schemas designed under the third normal form need several joins between the different tables. I'm sure we all relate to debugging a given non-performant query with an obscene amount of joins in the past. A high number of joins between tables with millions of records requires excessive effort from the hardware. With increased usage, we quickly find we need better hardware. The only way to typically scale a relational ACID database is often vertically, which becomes very expensive very fast.

What were the traditional approaches to deal with this issue? We often add sharding and replicas to our databases – replicas that suffer from the replication lag the same way as event-driven architectures do but in systems that were not designed to do so. Often we need to rewrite or do dubious workarounds to afford the replication lag. To tackle slow queries, we denormalize data and optimize how data is persisted to enable high read performance. As we throw our referential integrity and lack of duplication out of the window, often against our inner values, which are chiseled in the properties of the third normal form, we say, "well just this time, this is the real world, sometimes we must forfeit these kinds of theoretical concepts."

I saw terrible implementations in the past due to a stubborn dogmatic approach to theoretical concepts, and I'm guessing at one time or another you saw it too. Sometimes in the real world, we need a pragmatic approach to the solutions we implement. But these kinds of solutions of "implementing as we go" often fail due to the lack of a deliberate long-term strategy. Instead of trying to fit performance and scalability into solutions that were not designed to fit them, and only when they become an issue, we should approach it as a property of the solution we create.

Deconstructing a monolithic database is a step in that direction. In event-driven architectures, besides having synergy with dividing an extensive database into smaller ones, the focus of the data is in the event stream, enabling the possibility to disseminate data without relying solely on the database infrastructure. We do gain complexity, and we might lose the stronger consistency properties ACID provides, but we won't constrict the business growth to a halt. If you don't see and don't ever foresee the database being a limitation, then you are probably better off not dividing it at all.

4.1.2 The Limitations of Distributed Transactions

When faced with the challenge of guaranteeing atomicity between two different databases, some people might be tempted to use distributed transactions. They provide a way to reason with a distributed system featuring several databases the same way we would with a single ACID database. Distributed transactions are often implemented with the X/Open XA standard,[2] which uses a two-phase commit to ensure the atomicity of all the transaction's changes. However, the two-phase commit protocol doesn't provide all ACID guarantees. It also has numerous failure modes that might need manual compensation and leave the data in an unexpected state. This subsection will detail how the two-phase commit protocol works and its limitations on a distributed system.

---

[2] Further details in "X/Open XA," https://en.wikipedia.org/wiki/X/Open_XA

The two-phase commit protocol typically uses two types of components: the transaction manager and the participants. The transaction managers coordinate with the participants the protocol's implementation for each transaction. Unsurprisingly, the protocol has two phases: the voting phase and the completion phase. In the voting phase, the transaction manager communicates with the participants to confirm that a given change can be made. Let's use the same example we discussed earlier in this section to illustrate this. Figure 4-3 depicts how this would play out with the stock and order tables.

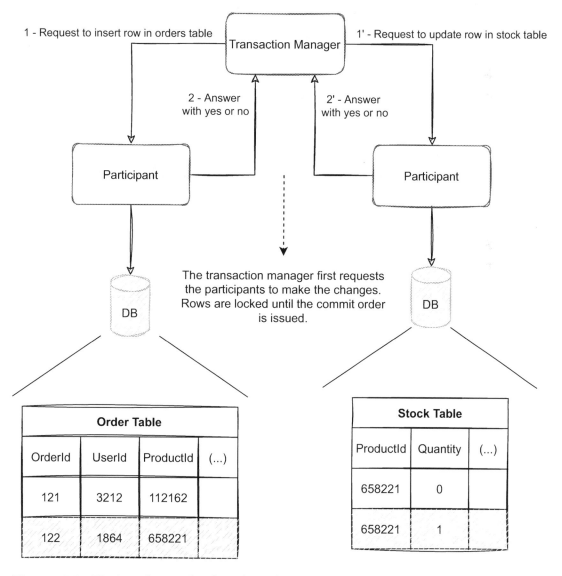

Figure 4-3. *Voting phase of a distributed transaction between the order and stock table*

The transaction manager requests the order and inventory database participants to insert the new order row and update the existing stock row, respectively. If one of them responds negatively, the transaction aborts. If both participants respond positively, then the transaction manager will advance to the completion phase.

In the completion phase, the transaction manager will request both participants to commit their changes, as illustrated in Figure 4-4. If a participant is unable to commit their changes for some reason, the transaction manager will have to request a rollback from all participants. A rollback will undo any changes that were made or release any locked resources. The transaction ends with all participants acknowledging the transaction manager's changes by successfully committing or roll backing the changes.

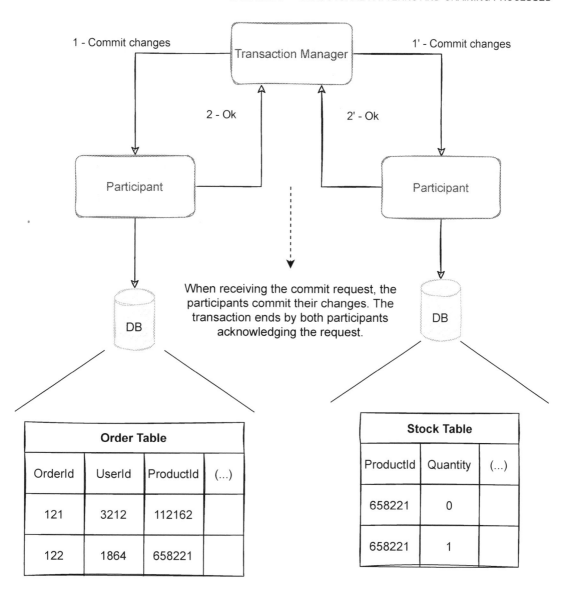

Figure 4-4. *Completion phase of the same distributed transaction between the order and stock table*

This protocol raises several complex issues and might leave the data in an unexpected state. Since two different processes handle both commit requests, they can happen at different times. So we don't have the ACID properties we discussed earlier anymore. A client can request the order information without the stock being updated, for example.

Also, since both operations occur separately, an arbitrary amount of time can pass between the voting and completion phases. Concurrent requests may try to change the same data while the transaction is running. For example, if someone submitted an order for the same product simultaneously, another process might try to change the stock line while the transaction is still running. To avoid concurrent changes, the participants often lock the resources until the transaction ends. That means while the transaction is occurring, every other request to access the same data will have to wait. We all know the associated performance problems with traditional transactions, but taking them to a distributed environment where they are susceptible to the network conditions and delays might severely impact the system. Two-phase commit protocol is suited for · fast operations; the longer they take, the longer the data is locked. The examples we discussed are with two participants, but the more participants involved, the longer the transaction takes.

Being susceptible to the network conditions also opens a wide range of new failure modes. Jepsen, a set of tests and analysis on distributed consistency on many popular databases, did an analysis[3] on Postgres which uses a special case of two-phase commit and highlighted some of these problems (there is also another interesting analysis on YugaByte DB[4] which uses a homegrown commit protocol based on two-phase commit highlighting similar problems). For example, in Figure 4-4, the participants have to acknowledge the commit to the transaction manager. If an acknowledgment is lost, for example, the participant suffered a network partition (more on network partitions in Chapter 5), the transaction fails. But the participant might already have committed the data and has no way to receive the rollback request, which can lead to unexpected results and produce an invalid state that must be solved manually.

Another issue with the two-phase commit protocol is the transaction manager. When several different services are involved in multiple transactions, the transaction manager acts as the coordinator between these different services. Event-driven architectures are naturally decoupled and enable us to build independent services; having a single component in charge of coordinating synchronous operations between the services is a step back in this mindset. Distributed transactions often raise more issues than the ones they solve. As we discussed in Subsection 4.1.1, if we really need the ACID properties for

---

[3] Full analysis in Jepsen, "Jepsen: Postgres," May 18, 2013, `https://aphyr.com/posts/282-jepsen-postgres`

[4] Full analysis in Kyle Kingsbury, "YugaByte DB 1.1.9," March 26, 2019, `https://jepsen.io/analyses/yugabyte-db-1.1.9`

a given use case, we are often better off by maintaining that data together in a database that affords ACID guarantees. But don't be tempted to see this is always the case; most often than not, we can live with weaker consistency guarantees, as we will discuss in Chapter 5.

4.1.3 Managing Multi-step Processes with Sagas

We discussed the limitations and why we shouldn't use distributed transactions, but what is the alternative? Business processes often span several different services. How can we maintain the consistency of those processes when multiple services are involved? This subsection will discuss how Sagas can be an alternative approach to distributed transactions and coordinating synchronous locks.

Sagas were first introduced in a paper[5] by Hector Garcaa-Molrna and Kenneth Salem, where they suggested the use of Sagas to manage long-living transactions. The paper argues the use of smaller short-lived transactions as an alternative to long-lived transactions. Instead of having a single transaction that lasts a considerable amount of time, we can have smaller ones for each step of the more extensive operation, minimizing the amount of data affected by locking.

Sagas are a sequence of individual operations to manage a long-running business process. In a distributed architecture, each of the Sagas' operations is carried out by a different service. In an event-driven architecture, the services typically are orchestrated or choreographed through events to achieve the larger business process. The business logic itself is located inside the services; each service will manage and validate its own domain. We define a compensating action for each step of the business process. Suppose a given service fails to perform the action due to technical or business reasons. In that case, the Saga's currently completed steps will execute the compensating action to leave the system in a stable state.

When used with DDD, Sagas manage operations across several aggregates between different bounded contexts. When an aggregate is affected by an event of a different domain, and we need to translate it to a command, it is often seen as a Saga. Operations that affected multiple aggregates are also commonly seen as a Saga. Although Sagas can be applied to reflect changes to multiple aggregates, the most common use case is to manage a long-lived business process between several bounded contexts.

---

[5] Full article in Hector Garcaa-Molrna and Kenneth Salem, "Sagas," December 1987, `www.cs.cornell.edu/andru/cs711/2002fa/reading/sagas.pdf`

Each operation of the Saga occurs separately and independently. This means the entire Saga isn't an ACID transaction nor enjoys its guarantees. As the Saga completes its steps, the changes each step applies are immediately available, even before the entire process finishes. Each step can have strong consistency guarantees and be inside the context of a transaction if the database in question supports ACID guarantees.

Sagas aren't strongly consistent as a whole, but they provide a way to understand and model a business process in a way we can act when something goes wrong. Each of the Sagas' steps can have a compensating action we can trigger if one of the following steps fails. This way, when a given step fails, we can maintain the consistency of the whole process. Let's illustrate with an example. Figure 4-5 depicts an example of an order submission process.

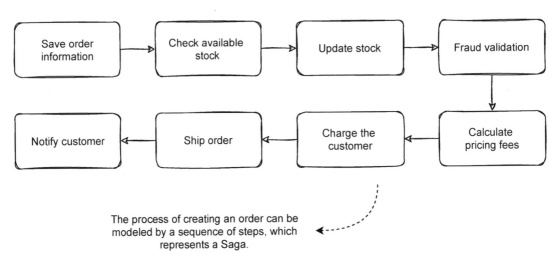

Figure 4-5. *An example of an order processing Saga*

Each step in the Saga might map to an action in a specific service or in different boundaries. For example, the order service might be responsible for saving the order information, but checking the available stock and updating it might be the responsibility of the inventory service.

In a monolithic approach, the example in Figure 4-5 could be implemented using a single transaction. If a step fails, the whole transaction would roll back and would maintain the consistency. Using a Saga, we must implement a compensating action for every relevant step. The rollback process has a workflow of its own depending on the stage that fails.

Figure 4-6 illustrates an example of a rollback in this workflow. Let's say the order the system was processing failed in the fraud validation step. The previous steps were already completed; for example, the stock has already changed.

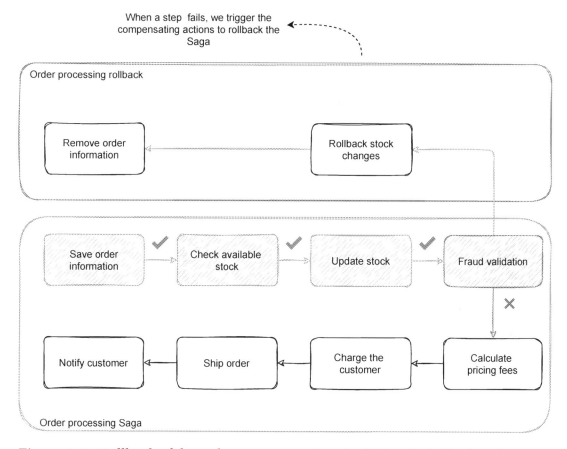

Figure 4-6. *Rollback of the order processing Saga by failing to do the fraud validation*

How can we roll back the process? To maintain the system's consistency, we would trigger the rollback process which would do a compensating action for every step that needs to. In this case, the fraud validation step's failure would trigger two compensating actions to undo the stock changes that happened on the third step and remove the order information that happened on the first step.

Stateless and idempotent actions, like the step to validate the available stock and calculate pricing fees, are more straightforward to handle since no state rollback is needed. The order we design the Saga's steps is also important. Depending on how we model the workflow, the rollback process might be more or less complicated. For example, if fraud validation was the first step, we wouldn't need to do any compensating action, and a rollback process wouldn't be needed. When modeling a Saga, a vital consideration is to think about the process and how we can minimize the chance of rollback and the number of compensating actions we need to do.

An important consideration is what kind of reason can make a step fail. If it fails due to domain validations or business rules, the compensating actions will suffice to put the system back in a reliable state. However, if steps can fail due to technical reasons, for example, if a given service is offline or unreachable, one can ask what we should do when the rollback process fails. For example, in Figure 4-6 after the fraud validation fails, what if the inventory service is unreachable or due to a network issue, or a failure reaching its database, or unable to perform the action due to a bug? We couldn't undo the stock changes done by the initial steps of the Saga.

Working with event-driven services and the natural decoupling and asynchronous nature they imbue in the systems provides a way to be more resilient to transient failures and enable us to build more failproof processes. Retrying the operation is easier, and even if the retries fail, the event is persisted in the event stream. If we need to reprocess a given action, we can retry the same event as long as the event handling is idempotent. In a synchronous process, the Saga might hang until a retry would work or might need ad hoc processes to retry the Saga. The asynchronous nature of the event streams naturally provides a way for the system to continue to respond without blocking while processing the workflow or cascading the failure to the other components. We will further discuss resilient message processing in Chapter 7.

4.2 Event-Driven Orchestration Pattern

In Section 4.1, we discussed how we could use Sagas to model a business process that needs the intervention of multiple independent services. Sagas usually come in two variants: orchestrated or choreographed. In this section, we will discuss how we can use orchestration to implement a business process.

Orchestration uses a primary component to manage the steps of the process. This component instructs the other services to start new steps in the process and triggers the start of compensation actions when needed. It works much like a supervisor that oversees the whole process and delegates the actions to subordinate services.

Let's use the same example about order processing we discussed in Section 4.1. Figure 4-7 illustrates how we could model that process with the orchestration pattern.

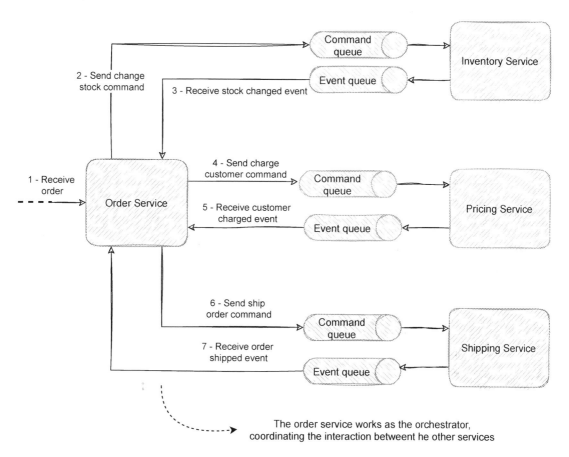

Figure 4-7. *The order process workflow implemented using an orchestration pattern*

In this example, the order service assumes the orchestrator role and coordinates changes between three other services: the inventory, pricing, and shipping service. In Section 4.1, we modeled the order processing Saga depicted in Figure 4-5. The first step of the workflow was receiving the order submission request. The order service would handle the request and coordinate with the other services to accomplish the process steps.

Instead of sending commands, this pattern could be implemented by sending an order created event to each service. But events aren't sent, they are published, and services react to them. If we want to change another service or domain, we should reflect that with a command rather than an event (as we detailed in Chapter 3). If we used an event, we would likely fall into the passive-aggressive events anti-pattern.

Notice that we also merged several steps into one operation (this wasn't just because it was simpler to draw the diagram, despite being a concern). Although we might conceptually model the order process with every step, we might want to merge some of them when implementing it. For example, if the check and update stock were two different operations, two orders for the same product at the same time might concurrently pass the validation. Since both operations belong to the inventory bounded context, we can implement them with one command.

The stock operations relate to each other, but what if we had other operations with the same challenge that we couldn't merge? If the order service had to validate the stock and then request it to change, it could lead to orders for products without stock. We could trigger an error and roll back the process by triggering the compensating actions, as discussed in Section 4.1, but that's a design solution for a technical problem. It is an option, but compensating actions are often better for undoing domain issues; for example, the customer doesn't have enough money to make the purchase. We explore eventual consistency and concurrency issues in Chapters 5 and 6.

The interaction between the services is fully asynchronous, and the process advances with the asynchronous handling of events from each participant service. The order service requests the stock changes; once they are processed, the inventory service publishes an event signaling those changes, which the order service uses to advance to the next step, requesting the pricing service to charge the customer in the same way. The same interaction occurs with other services until the order is fully processed.

A strong advantage of this pattern is the ability to easily monitor the process's status since only one service is responsible to manage it. It would be straightforward to understand each order's current step and result by looking only at the order service. It is also easy to reason with the logic of the order business process; we can quickly have a high-level vision of the process by only analyzing the order service.

The trap in this pattern is building the orchestrator to be an aggregator of all the process's logic. Code often has gravity; it pulls more code toward it. The more you add, the more it pulls. Stay with it and you likely end up with a monolith. These types of orchestrator services often become a quick solution to include new features, sometimes features that belong somewhere else.

Each service is responsible for maintaining its business rules and its domain's consistency. The decoupling provided by the queues promotes that, but it is important to include new developments in the appropriate domain. The order service only requests that changes be reflected in that domain and doesn't explicitly say what that domain should do. For example, it instructs the pricing service to charge the customer, but only the pricing domain knows the country's taxes, discounts applicable to the customer, and valid payment methods. Having a central piece to manage the workflow provides a tempting component to add logic that otherwise belongs to other domains.

A way to manage this is to use an approach similar to the one Cassandra uses to manage writes. Cassandra is a popular NoSQL database that uses a coordinator node concept instead of having the typical primary-secondary topology like SQL Server or MongoDB. Primary-secondary topologies require that all writes go through the primary. In Cassandra, any node can handle writes by coordinating the write to the node that holds the data.

We can use the same concept by having different services managing different business processes. It is understandable to include the order fulfillment process in the order service since the order's workflow is often closely related to the order domain. By following the same reasoning, we could include the update of the pricing fees business process in the pricing service, for example. Having a central agnostic orchestrator that handles every workflow or a large number of them is an anti-pattern and something we need to avoid. Falling in that anti-pattern will rapidly take us to a distributed monolith where we despair with both the disadvantages of monoliths and distributed systems.

If any of the services failed to process, the service would signal that failure sending an event. In that case, the order service would handle that event and trigger any corresponding compensating actions.

A synchronous process would wait for each service's response to complete the process. Even if we implemented a job style processing (having a job that checks the process's status from time to time), the orchestrator would have to poll the services to know when they finished the operation. The fully asynchronous nature of this process makes it easier to manage the load by distributing it to the dependent services, making it easier to scale the parts of the system that need scaling. The queues would also absorb the added scale; a load peak would only be reflected in the system by an increase in lag. The flow is also more organic since there is no pooling involved and the orchestrator manages the progress by reacting to the events being published by the services.

This pattern is an interesting solution to complex processes that need a central supervisor; however, we need to be aware to not fall into the pitfall of feeding the orchestrator beyond measure. Small and trivial business processes will hardly benefit from the orchestration. Often, not having central pieces that orchestrate logic helps to encourage the distribution of domain logic and the organic evolution of an event-driven architecture.

4.3 Event-Driven Choreography Pattern

In the last section, we discussed how we could use orchestration to model a complex business process. In this section, we will discuss choreography as an alternative to orchestration. We will detail how the example of the order processing we discussed before looks like using choreography.

When using choreography, the services involved react to each other to complete the sequence of steps. Rather than a central piece telling them what to do, like orchestration, the business process is autonomously coordinated; each service knows what to do once a service finishes its action. Instead of a supervisor delegating tasks to subordinate services, the services themselves know when to perform their tasks by reacting to the preceding service's events. This pattern's foundation is closer to the event-driven mindset than the previous one due to the organic flow of events without a commanding central piece.

Figure 4-8 illustrates the same order fulfillment process using a choreographed approach. There is no central component that manages the workflow of the events and oversees the process's progress. Instead, each service reacts to the changes happening in the ecosystem to accomplish its purpose.

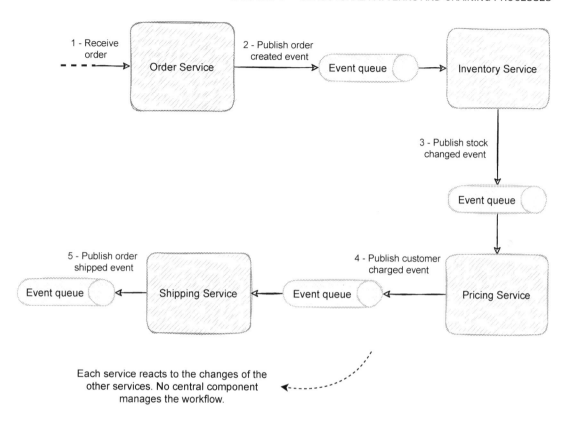

Figure 4-8. *The order process workflow implemented using a choreography pattern*

The order service after saving the information publishes an event announcing the order was created. The inventory service reacts to this event and changes the stock. Once the stock is altered, the pricing service reacts to the stock changed event to calculate the pricing fees and charge the customer. Finally, once the customer is charged, the pricing service publishes an event that the shipping service will use to ship the order and complete the process.

If something goes wrong and we need to roll back the process, an event from the service that failed to process would trigger the other services' compensating actions. For example, if the pricing service determines it is a fraudulent order, it would publish an event signaling the process's failure and the inventory and order service would react to it, triggering their own compensating actions.

This approach solves the issues we mentioned about logic being centralized in one place. Since there is no central orchestrator, the logic is naturally distributed throughout the services. Using orchestration, as we implement new functionality, one way or another, the team managing the orchestrator service ends up influencing the behavior of the other domains, often heavily biased on their own. Choreography often facilitates the evolution of the domains based on what is important for each one, without a central process manager's influence.

One of the caveats with this approach is we no longer have a straightforward way to understand the workflow. With orchestration, by analyzing only the orchestrator, we can follow every step of the workflow. With choreography, the workflow is embedded in the behavior of each service. The decoupling provided by the event queues also makes this process difficult. This is one main concern with event-driven architectures; the highly decoupled nature hinders the understanding of the event stream's high-level flows. We will detail strategies to tackle this later in this chapter.

The compensating actions might be harder to implement since each service will have to implement or react to each new step or change in the workflow. For example, if we added a new final step to manage the order returns in a new service, the other services would also need to react to that new domain's failures, if applicable. On the other hand, it promotes the mindset to reason with each domain independently; on an order return, how should the inventory domain react? It promotes the discussion on how that change affects each domain instead of delegating that responsibility to the orchestrator.

Another main concern with choreography is the ability to understand the current state of each Saga. With orchestration, if we needed to know in which step the order process was in, we would likely implement that feature in the orchestrator. Since it monitors every step and the overall workflow, it would be straightforward to know each order process step. With choreography, there is no prominent place to obtain each state. One solution is to listen to every event being published by each service and materialize them in an aggregated view, as illustrated in Figure 4-9.

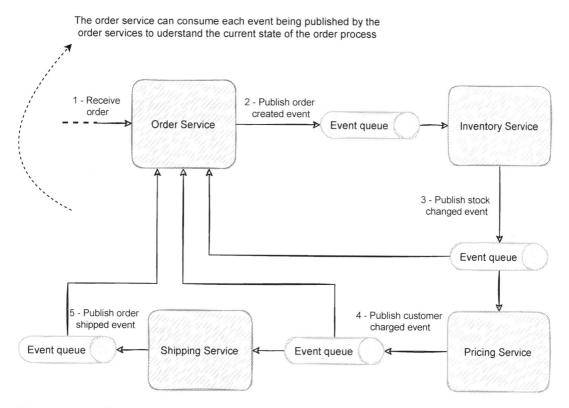

Figure 4-9. *The order service can listen to the other events to understand the current state of the order process*

The example shows the order service listening to every event but could be a different separate service to consume the events and materialize them into a view. The component handling the events and materializing the state will likely have to understand the higher-level workflow but doesn't manage it as an orchestrator does. Using this solution is still choreography but definitely has a halfway feel between the two approaches.

Simpler processes don't suffer as much with this solution's caveats. As the workflow grows more complex, the more challenging it is to deal with the drawbacks. Overall orchestration tends to be a common pattern in event-driven architectures, and it synergizes well with its mindset. The caveats can be tackled by the approaches we discuss further in this book. However, if we have a requirement that needs a central component to manage the process and keep its state, an orchestration approach might fit better.

4.4 Event-Driven Microservices: Orchestration, Choreography, or Both?

In Sections 4.2 and 4.3, we detailed how orchestration and choreography work and how we could apply them. But should we stick to just one approach? This section will discuss how typically they are implemented in an event-driven architecture and how they can coexist together.

In event-driven architectures, we typically use choreography since it naturally fits the event-driven mindset. We publish events to event streams and applications plug into those streams to access the data. One main benefit in adopting an event-driven architecture is the highly evolving nature and decoupled properties they provide. Typically, business processes have no central orchestrator. The lack of a central piece avoids the logic of being centralized in a single place and doesn't imperil those benefits.

When we continuously add functionality and new services to the architecture, an orchestrator typically grows more complex. As we add more people and more teams, we slowly start to struggle with the monolith's challenges in the orchestrator. Not having a central piece eases these issues and enables the domains to grow naturally. It gives the team's autonomy to decide what's best for their domain and deliver features autonomously without having to deal with a central shared piece.

An orchestrator outside the boundaries, coordinating the changes between them, will likely grow and potentially turn the boundary service's domain anemic. Having a different component in each boundary as the orchestrator for different business processes can help with this. Still, it also means different sources make changes to the entities, which can be hard to manage. Often orchestrators fall into the same difficulties traditional SOA with ESB usually fall. As you might recall, we discussed SOA with ESB in Chapter 1. Typically, ESBs are a place to centralize business logic and tend to grow as we add more and more features. Orchestrators are a great place to centralize that logic and have anemic satellite services.

Depending on the use case, choreography often tends to be the standard in event-driven architectures. As boundaries grow, it would likely be problematic to manage a central piece. However, it doesn't mean orchestration doesn't have a place in it. It is often useful to apply it in a more localized context, for example, inside a boundary. Figure 4-10 illustrates an example of this situation.

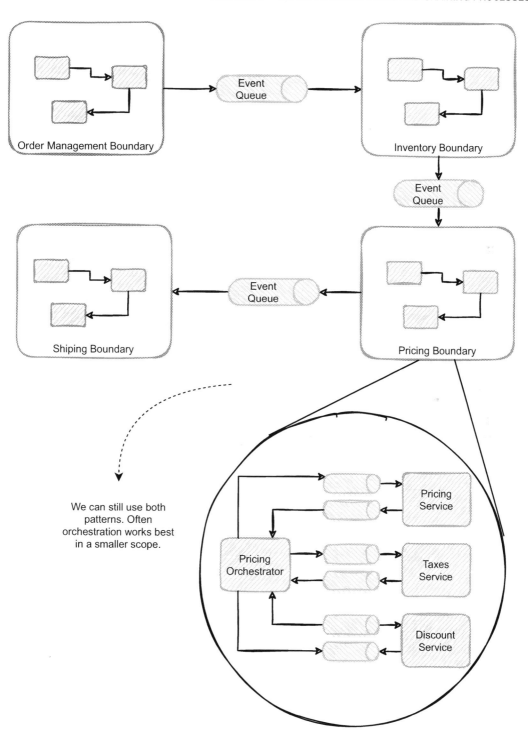

Figure 4-10. *Example of applying both patterns. We applied orchestration in a smaller scope*

Figure 4-10 illustrates the same example we discussed before, but instead of a single service, each bounded context is composed of several services. We use choreography between each boundary, but inside a boundary, we can apply orchestration, as illustrated in the pricing boundary. The more extensive higher-level process uses choreography, but to manage a smaller scope and more localized process, we could use orchestration like the pricing calculation.

This use case is just an example, but the main line of reasoning is to use choreography as default and in higher-level processes and apply orchestration on a limited scope. This approach allows a high decoupling between the services and enables the team's autonomy at the higher level where multiple teams are involved. And it uses orchestration on a smaller scope, where a small number of people are involved and have the autonomy to release features without impacting several areas.

4.5 Data Retrieval in Event-Driven Architectures and Associated Patterns

Until now, we described how event-driven architectures work, and we briefly mentioned queries as a common artifact of these architectures in Chapter 3. However, we didn't detail how to provide query functionality driven by events. Queries are a common requirement in most applications to provide data to the user or other services. CRUD-based services simply query the database and return the requested data synchronously. Event-driven architectures add a layer of complexity to the traditional approach since data is distributed throughout several services and likely eventually consistent. In this section, we will describe common patterns that synergize well with the event-driven approach.

Chapter 2 discussed how to move from a monolithic architecture to a distributed event-driven microservice architecture. We discussed how to split the monolith into several services and how to deconstruct the database; the data associated with each domain was moved to the respective service. When in a monolith and a monolithic database, all the data is centralized in the same place, and it is straightforward, from an implementation perspective, to obtain and join data. Typical monolithic platforms simply expose information through a synchronous API like REST or SOAP. This approach is arguably the most common and straightforward approach. It suffers, however, from all the scaling limitations we discussed in Chapter 1.

By deconstructing the monolith and its database, we are now faced with a challenge; how can we get an aggregated view of the data? We have a set of independent services, each owning its domain's data; each service will only be able to return information about its domain. For example, Figure 4-11 illustrates four different services; the UI needs to list a page with all the available products with their current stock and price.

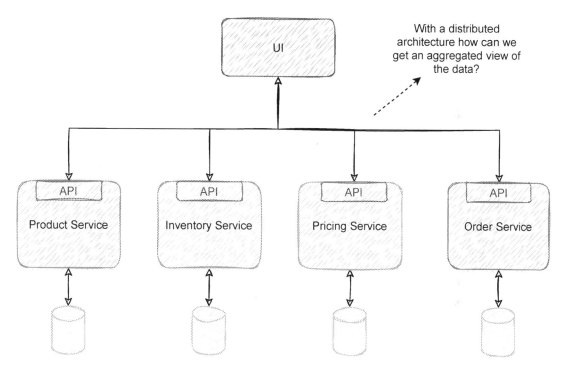

Figure 4-11. *Having a distributed architecture poses challenges on how to have a denormalized view of the data*

A possible approach to solve this challenge is to use the same strategy as illustrated in Figure 4-11. The UI application can fetch information from every service and merge and display it in a UI. This approach is usually called the API composition pattern, and it's probably the solution that first comes to our mind.

This kind of approach has severe limitations; as you can imagine when we deal with large amounts of data, this approach rapidly struggles. If we need to display a listing page with all the products, let's say with millions of products (although a lot less would likely suffice to make the application struggle), the UI would likely need to load several thousands of those items to memory. Imagine if the user needs to filter all products with stock and order them from the lowest to the highest price, a standard functionality in most eCommerce websites. The UI application to support such queries would likely have to fetch thousands of records from each service and filter them in memory to display accurate records with filtering, sorting, and paging. If several users did this simultaneously, the application would likely struggle with the performance overhead and the memory constraints.

API composition can be relevant for small data sets and can be a cheap solution for some use cases (although one can ask if we are using small data sets, why are we using a distributed architecture anyway?). Even for one product, it would mean three requests to different services. The additional requests can have a performance overhead in the UI and likely lead to poor user experience. Data at scale and complex searches require a different approach.

At the beginning of the chapter, we discussed how we needed to sacrifice the third normal form's values in the altar of performance and how we created denormalized models for specific querying requirements. Event-driven architectures with persisted event streaming provide a sustainable way to implement this. Since every event is readily available even after consumption, we can use those events to enrich a service's information.

Let's first look at a typical implementation of a synchronous query implementation. Figure 4-12 illustrates a service, the product service, exposing an API for consumers to use. Other applications can use that API to change the service's data or to retrieve information from the service.

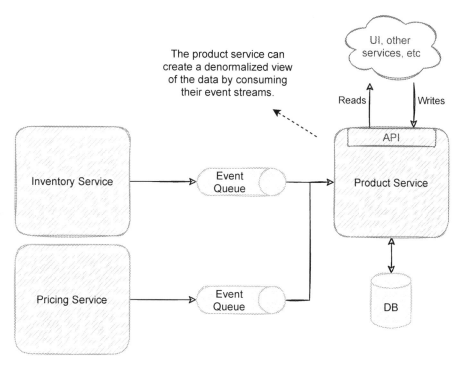

Figure 4-12. *The product service can build a denormalized view of the data by handling events from the other services*

In a distributed event-driven architecture, it isn't as straightforward since different services own different data. The example in Figure 4-12 handles events from an event queue to enrich its read model with additional data the service doesn't hold. For example, the product service might own all the data related to products, but the inventory information might be managed in a different service. Like a product listing page on a UI, queries to the product service might need the stock information for each product. The product service can enrich its information with stock information handling the events being published by the inventory service, thus the event queue.

Resuming the example we discussed in Figure 4-11, the product service can create a denormalized view of the data with all the information needed for the UI requirements by handling both inventory and pricing events. Filtering and sorting would actually be viable since there is a persistent denormalized model.

4.5.1 CQS, CQRS, and When to Use Them

An interesting pattern that usually has high synergy with this kind of approach, and is usually mentioned along with DDD, is CQRS (command query responsibility segregation). CQRS originated from CQS (command query separation), and people often are generally confused when distinguishing the two patterns; once you read this section, let's hope you're not one of them. This subsection will detail both patterns, what we can benefit from them, and how to apply them in the same product listing example we discussed before.

Bertrand Meyer formulated CQS in his book[6] *Object-Oriented Software Construction*. This principle states that methods can either be queries or commands but never both. Queries return a value but don't change state, and commands change state but don't return any value. Basically, asking doesn't hurt, and if you're not asking, don't tell.

CQRS originated from CQS and introduced a slight change; CQRS entities are split into two main concepts, commands and queries. Having a clear separation between the objects in code is handy because we can use queries at will; we are sure they don't change state. While with commands, we can be more careful about where to use them. It is also easier to find the code paths that change state and the ones that retrieve state. CQS can be a valuable approach to apply locally in specific services, the overall organization helps to reason better with the service, especially in APIs using protocols like REST where there are clear actions for retrieving (GET, HEAD, etc.) and changing (POST, PUT, PATCH, etc.) state. We can implement independent paths for reads and writes, which helps in the service's organization.

CQRS, however, is often associated to an architectural point of view instead of just locally in code. We can take it one step further and segregate commands and queries into different components. We can have two different services, one that only handles commands or changes in state and another that only handles queries that only retrieve data without changing it. Figure 4-13 illustrates how the example we discussed before with the product service would look like when applying CQRS.

---

[6] Book by Bertrand Meyer, "Object-Oriented Software Construction," March 21, 2000, www.amazon. com/gp/product/0136291554

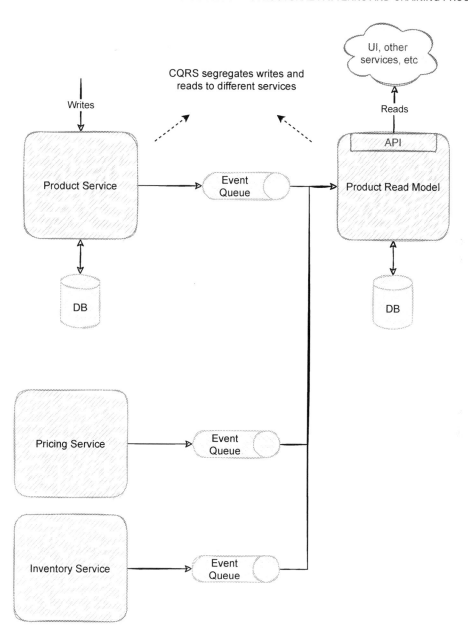

Figure 4-13. *When applying CQRS at an architectural level, we can have separate services for reads and writes*

When applying CQRS at an architectural level, we segregate the writes to one independent service and the reads to another independent service. The product service handles writes that can be done from an API or a command queue. The product read model handles reads and exposes the data through an API. The read model also handles the events from pricing and inventory service to enrich its model and be able to do the complex searches we mentioned earlier. But what do we benefit from this?

Having separate read and write models allows us to specialize each model for each purpose. The objects we return on reads, traditionally called DTOs (data transfer objects), are often modeled to the use case that needs it, for example, a UI. That model can be substantially different from the conceptual domain model, which is often modeled by the domain concept (the aggregate in DDD) and bearing in mind performance and transactional concerns. Often the query requirements end up influencing the domain model design negatively. Usually, it is also required mapping between the two, which can be more or less complex depending on the differences between them. Often having the same model for both ends up doing neither one well. Having a separate model for each, we remove a considerable part of that hassle.

Earlier in this chapter, we discussed the need to abandon the third normal form due to the data's denormalization. The third normal form minimizes data duplication which actually benefits writes. Since we have two separate models, we could apply the third normal form to the write side and denormalize the data on the read side.

Having two separate models with two different databases also allows us to optimize the model and the technology for each purpose. The write side could have data modeling optimized for writes, for example, event sourcing (we will detail event sourcing next) which is basically an append log enabling minimal locking with a technology optimized for writes. We can denormalize the model on the read side and use a technology built for fast complex searches (e.g., ElasticSearch).

New features and new query requirements can also be easier to implement. For example, if we need to launch a new UI with a different model and query needs, we would only change the read model service. That change wouldn't impact the service that handles the writes and has the domain logic.

Consistency can also be a factor with this approach. Usually, the write side has stronger consistency requirements due to the domain validations and the need to write consistent data to the database. The read side can often be more lenient to weaker consistency guarantees like eventual consistency. Besides this, most applications tend to exhibit a read-intensive behavior; the number of reads vastly surpasses the number of writes. Having separate services for each allows us to optimize and scale each side independently.

When to Use CQRS?

CQRS is not a silver bullet, nor should it be applied to every use case. It implies one more moving piece and increases the complexity of the solution. Having the writes separated from the reads with an event queue in between means the read side is also eventually consistent if it wasn't already. So when should we use CQRS?

Using CQRS has unsurprisingly similar motivations to adopting an event-driven architecture. Typically, simple and straightforward domains usually don't benefit much from it. There's little benefit in dividing something that's small and simple to begin with. Often domains that aren't close to the business core and don't have enough complexity or change too often don't benefit much from it.

A simple domain with a low scale that often doesn't change and needs strong consistency guarantees is a good candidate to not apply CQRS. I experienced simple services with small amounts of data where the teams applied CQRS and it only added confusion to both the architecture and to the business. Simple services often are better off with a traditional CRUD approach.

It's important when deciding to adopt CQRS to have a strong reason to do so. Some of the benefits we listed before can be arguably strong reasons, for example, if we have a service where the reads largely surpass the writes and we have the need to scale differentially. Having a conceptual write model substantially different from a complex read model might also be a good reason.

Using event-driven architectures, you will likely have some sort of CQRS or at least a denormalized model that aggregates information from different places. For example, the query needs in the example we discussed with the product service, we needed to merge data from various sources to provide meaningful searches to the business. When we need to build a similar read model, a good approach is to apply what we learn with CQRS, to understand if it makes sense to build it in a separate service and whether the benefits of CQRS are relevant for our use case. Figures 4-12 and 4-13 show two different approaches; we could ask some questions to help us understand if CQRS makes sense. For example, by merging everything in the same service, are we polluting the product domain model? Is the number of events from the other sources sufficiently disparate to justify independent scaling? Would the searches benefit from a different technology we are currently using in the product service?

These are just some questions we should ask ourselves when applying CQRS. Overall, it has high synergy with event-driven architectures, and it is valuable in some use cases. But we should always question if the benefits outweigh the complexity overhead.

4.5.2 The Different Flavors of CQRS

In the previous section, we discussed what CQRS is and how to apply it. We discussed its advantages and when we should use it. In the example we discussed, we created two different services with two distinct databases. This solution isn't the only way to apply CQRS, and there are some intermediate alternatives that we will discuss in this section.

CQRS is fundamentally about segregating the reads from the writes. In the example in Figure 4-13, we created one independent service for writes and another one for reads. This approach is the most flexible and the most complex. It makes a lot of sense in event-driven architectures because most of the drawbacks with that approach are already incorporated in the architecture. For example, eventual consistency is often a byproduct of most event-driven services and needs to be tackled consistently (no pun intended). The concurrency and ordering challenges of events, which might be hard to tackle in an architecture not oriented to them, are already a reality, and we likely already have strategies to address them.

However, it isn't the only approach. CQRS doesn't mandate we have a separate database for each service, for example. Figure 4-14 illustrates an alternative implementation of CQRS in the same example of the product service we discussed before.

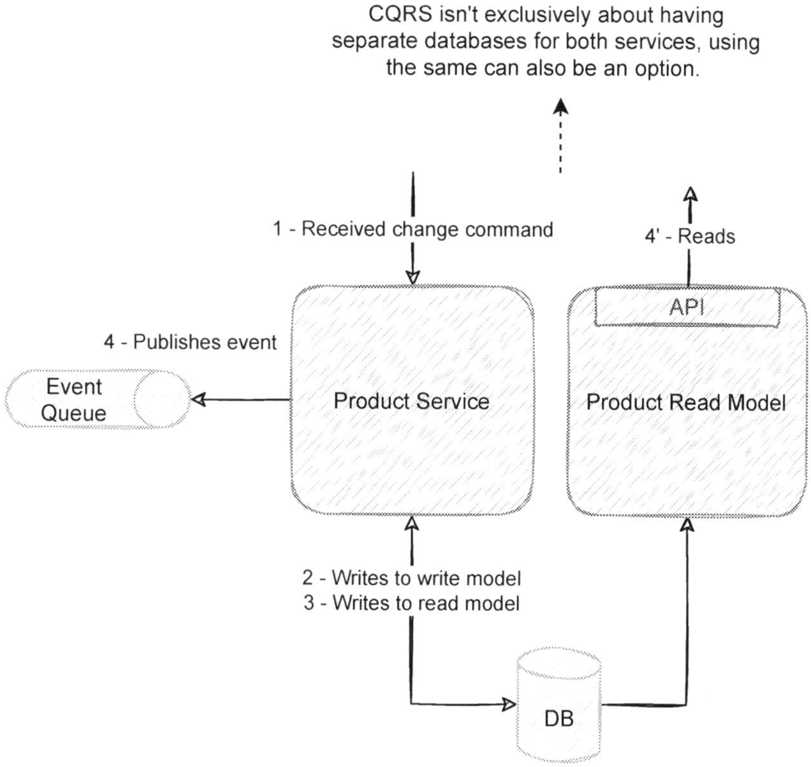

CQRS isn't exclusively about having
separate databases for both services, using
the same can also be an option.

1 - Received change command   4' - Reads

4 - Publishes event

Event
Queue

Product Service   Product Read Model

API

2 - Writes to write model
3 - Writes to read model

DB

Figure 4-14. *We can use different approaches to apply CQRS, with different tradeoffs*

Every time I see the same database shared by two independent services, I get post-traumatic stress flashbacks. But there are advantages to applying the pattern this way. A troublesome issue by having two separate databases is the associated eventual consistency. We will discuss strategies to deal with eventual consistency in Chapter 5, and as we discussed before, most querying needs tend to be lenient weaker consistency guarantees. The weaker consistency guarantees often hold especially true for UIs. Eventual consistency isn't new and wasn't introduced by events. Caches are a form of eventual consistency, and we apply it thoroughly. However, when another service needs to query an eventual consistency model and get stale data, it will do its business logic based on that stale data, leading to erroneous results.

For example, in Figure 4-13, there was a pricing service also listening to the events being published by the product service and had the need to ask for additional information from the read model API every time it received an event. If the product read model didn't yet process the same event the pricing service is processing, it would return stale data. The data returned to the pricing service wouldn't match the event the pricing service received.

With the approach depicted in Figure 4-14, we can update both the write and read model before publishing the event; this would solve the inconsistency between the event and the API response. With this approach, we can still scale the read and write side independently (although not the database). We do have to live with the same database in both services, which can be a challenge to manage schema changes. This approach might be a good option when there is a close relationship between the write and read model. If there is a situation where a read model listens to events from different sources (like Figure 4-13), we might benefit more from a more flexible option and more substantial segregation.

There are other options; we could not have two different services, having only one and having strict segregation of reads and writes only in code. On the other end of the spectrum, we can have a third service that handles writes to the read model (one service that writes to the write model, one that writes to the read model, and one that reads from the read model). In the last option, I seldom saw the benefits outweigh the drawbacks.

As with most solutions, it's all about the tradeoffs. The main goal is for you to have these tools in your toolbox and be able to decide accordingly – whether it's more fitting having a highly flexible highly complex solution or a less flexible less complex one or not using CQRS at all.

4.5.3 When and How to Use Event Sourcing

A typical pattern usually mentioned along with CQRS and DDD is event sourcing. Event sourcing is also an interesting pattern to apply in event-driven architectures since it has high synergy with the event-driven mindset. This subsection will detail event sourcing, its benefits, and how and when to apply it.

Let's look at the same example we discussed until now with the product service. When stored in a relational database, the product information would probably look similar to what's depicted in Figure 4-15.

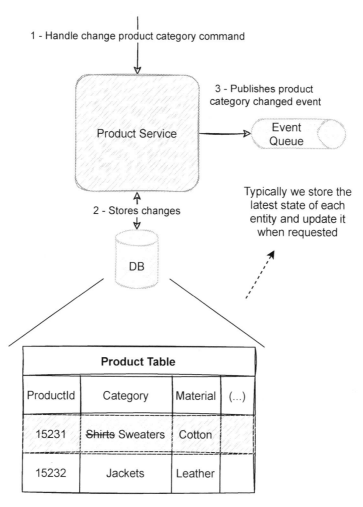

Figure 4-15. *Typical state storage in a relational database*

The product service handles a command to change an entity, in this example product 15231, changes the information in the database, and publishes an event signaling the product changed its category. The product table stores the latest information about each product. This is a common way to store data; we store the latest state and manipulate it when someone requests a change.

Event sourcing proposes an alternative way to store the entity's data. Instead of saving the latest state, an entity is the history of changes that generated that state. Conceptually the entity no longer is materialized with the most recent value of each property; instead, an entity is a stream of immutable events. If we apply all events of the stream, we can obtain the latest state.

For example, to store the product entity, instead of persisting each property's latest values, we would persist the events that signal each change. This is illustrated in Figure 4-16.

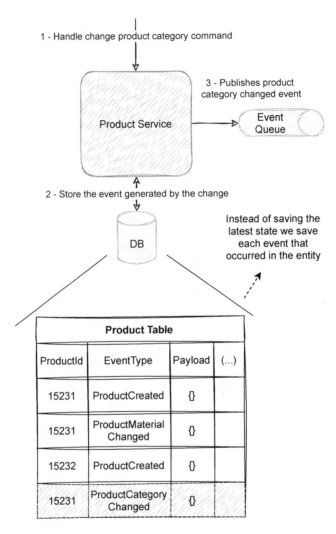

Figure 4-16. *Instead of saving the latest state of each product, we store the events generated by the change commands*

Instead of changing the product's category to the new one, the product service stores the category changed event that was generated by the change. The database stores the event type and the payload of the events. Instead of being a representation with the id, material, category, and so on, the products are the stream of events that occurred until now. The latest state of the product can be generated by applying all events in the stream.

At first sight, this sounds like a terrible idea, right? How are we supposed to query the data? For example, how can we obtain all products with category jackets? All we have persisted in the database is the history of events. To filter them, we would need to apply all events for each product to determine the latest state and then query.

That's one of the reasons event sourcing has high synergy with CQRS. As we discussed in Subsection 4.5.1, if we separate the write model from the read model, we can have substantially different models for each. We can use event sourcing on the write side and use the events to persist the latest state on the read side. By doing so, we can have an optimized model to query the data and an optimized model to write data.

As we discussed, events represent something that happened in the past and are immutable. The event stream basically functions as an append log. Write operations are often faster than update or delete operations; due to this, using event sourcing in the write model can often benefit from better performance.

An important consideration when building an event-driven architecture is to make events the source of truth. Event sourcing fully embodies this concept as events are the entities. The event stream can also provide a comprehensive history of the entities' state or be useful for debugging and auditing purposes. But the highest value is the ability to retain the original data and rebuild different views of the data for current and future use cases. We have the query requirements we need today, but we can rebuild different views of the data to future use cases by having the full history of the event stream.

If you are using a relational database, there is also a performance and conceptual gain in using event sourcing. There is an impedance mismatch (there's an article[7] by Scott Ambler further detailing this, and Greg Young explores this concept thoroughly in his CQRS documents[8]) between the OO (object-oriented) model and the relational world. How entities are modeled is substantially different between the two. This difference usually has performance impacts and additional complexity to reason with the models; complexity ORMs (object-relational mappers) tend to abstract. Using event sourcing simplifies these issues since the event is the same in both.

Figure 4-16 illustrates events being stored in the database and published in the event queue. With durable message brokers, we can further improve this topology by not having a database. Figure 4-17 illustrates this situation with the same example we used before.

---

[7] Full article in Scott Ambler, "The Object-Relational Impedance Mismatch," www.agiledata.org/essays/impedanceMismatch.html

[8] Full article in Greg Young, "CQRS Documents," https://cqrs.files.wordpress.com/2010/11/cqrs_documents.pdf

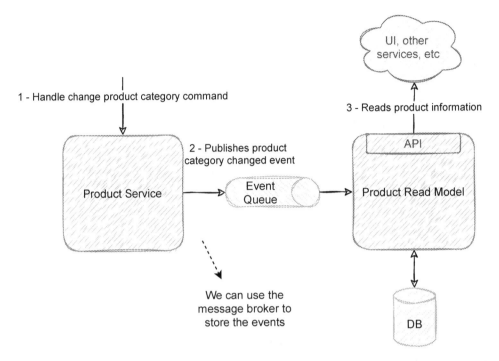

Figure 4-17. *The same example as before but using the event broker to store the events*

In the Figure 4-16 example, we had the events stored in the database and in the event queue. Notice in Figure 4-17 that the product service, which is responsible for handling the commands and applying the business logic, no longer stores the events in an internal database. Instead, it publishes the events to the message broker, and the events are stored there. This way, the events no longer are in two different places, benefiting from the infrastructural gains and the associated issues of guaranteeing both places are exactly the same. Also, storing and publishing events imply we need to ensure that both operations happen or fail together; otherwise, the system will become inconsistent. By only having one operation, this concern is greatly simplified. We also fully embrace a single event stream as the source of truth.

Storing events only in the message queue begs the question of whether we can fully trust a message broker to store the core business information. A few years ago, this kind of option would send a chill down my spine. But the rise of event streaming and the need to do it at a large scale certainly highlighted the concern and paved the way to do it reliably. Are durable message brokers a database? They certainly don't have the query capabilities we are used to with traditional databases, but they can afford at least as strong consistency guarantees as distributed databases. Martin Kleppmann has a very interesting keynote[9] about this subject with Kafka, which we recommend to further the topic.

In Figure 4-17, we also combined CQRS with event sourcing. This way, the product read model builds a denormalized projection of the product data optimized for querying. Using a persisted event stream in the write model, we can also rebuild the same or new models on the read model when needed.

4.5.4 Concerns and When to Use Event Sourcing

The main concern of event sourcing is the ability to query the data. This concern is mostly mitigated by using the read model and building projections to answer those querying needs. However, the read model is eventually consistent. When business logic requires to query the data, doing so in an eventually consistent read model can be hard to deal with. For example, if the product service had a business rule that only 25% of the products can have a price above 400$, it would have to validate that rule every time a product is created or its price changed. It would be hard or infeasible to do that query on the write model. We could query the read model, but the inherent eventual consistency could generate erroneous results. We further detail how to deal with eventual consistency in Chapter 5, but it always has a complexity increase.

Saving every single event of every single entity can also be impactful both cost-wise and performance-wise. This solution often requires retention strategies and the usage of snapshots. Although feasible and retention policies are probably already a concern on non-event sourced systems, snapshots require dedicated implementations and add to the system's overall complexity.

We don't need and shouldn't embrace event sourcing in every single service in the architecture. Usually, services with complex querying requirements might benefit from event sourcing and CQRS. Services that deal with core domain concepts and where the business might need to extract different projections from that information in the future also might be a good indicator. Having strong audit requirements is also a good fit since the event stream is the source of truth it can provide a detailed audit. Simple isolated services are likely not to be a good fit since they won't likely benefit from the associated complexity.

---

[9] Footnote available in Martin Kleppmann, "Is Kafka a Database?", October 17, 2018, www.confluent.io/kafka-summit-SF18/is-kafka-a-database/

In event-driven architectures with durable message brokers, we already face many of these concerns since we have persisted event streams. Using event sourcing is stepping up a notch to model our entities with event streams and fully embrace them as the source of truth.

4.5.5 Using Command Sourcing and Its Applicability

A very similar pattern related to event sourcing is command sourcing. Unsuspectingly, command sourcing uses the same approach event sourcing uses, but instead of persisting events, we persist commands. This subsection will discuss command sourcing and apply it in the same example we discussed previously.

In Subsection 4.5.3, we discussed how to apply event sourcing in the example with the product service. Using the same example, we could apply command sourcing by saving the commands reaching the service. Figure 4-18 illustrates how we could apply it.

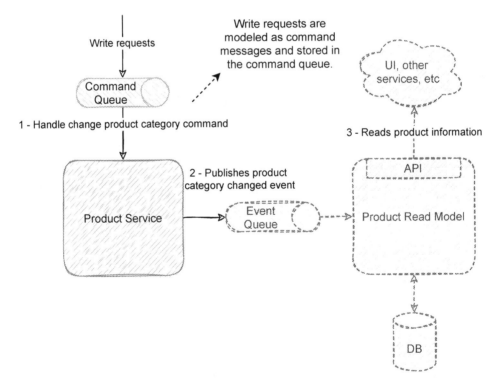

Figure 4-18. *Command sourcing applied to the same example with the product service*

Write requests are modeled as commands and sent to a command queue. The commands can be stored in the queue, as discussed previously with durable message brokers, or stored in the database. The product service consumes the commands from the queue and generates events. The events are published to an event queue and consumed by the read model where the data can be queried the same way we discussed before.

Command sourcing adds an additional layer of complexity and asynchronism to the flow. Write requests to the service can be refused if they fail the domain validations. If the request is synchronous, it is easy to return the feedback to the application issuing request. However, if it sits in a queue, it will be processed later. Returning feedback about validation errors might be troublesome. The concern is not because it is asynchronous, but the application will have to handle asynchronous feedback about failures to accept the commands and handle the regular events to understand when the request is applied. Although feasible, by handling the events and differentiating them, we might be walking very close to the line that separates a good solution from over engineering.

Command sourcing saves the user's original request before the application manipulates it, applies its logic, and transforms it into an event. It is often useful when the service receiving the commands has complex logic or intricate algorithms. Saving the original request allows us to regenerate the state if we introduce a bug in the service. It might also be useful if we want to try different versions of the algorithm and understand the results.

If there is an imperative reason to save the request precisely as the user submitted it, then command sourcing might be a good option. However, depending on the application needs more often than not, event sourcing is enough, and the complexity overhead doesn't pay off. In event-driven architectures, especially the parts using choreography, events are the glue that connects the different services throughout the flow. Commands are used less often in the places that we use commands; command sourcing can be a useful pattern; however, be aware of the complexity overhead and weigh whether it is worth it.

4.6 Building Multiple Read Models in Event-Driven Microservice Architectures

In Section 4.5, we discussed the difficulties of satisfying query requirements on data that is dispersed throughout several distributed microservices. We discussed that we could build a denormalized read model by handling events from different sources. This section will detail how to do it and how we can apply some of the concepts we discussed previously.

Let's use the practical example we worked with in Section 4.5. We have the requirement to list all products with stock and sort them by descending price. The relevant information is in three different services, the product, inventory, and pricing service. As we discussed, to be able to sustainably do that query, we could use an independent service to handle the events from each service and build a denormalized read model optimized for it. This situation is illustrated in Figure 4-19.

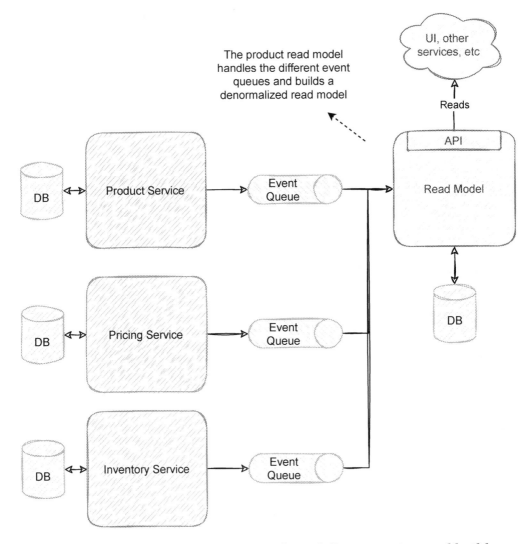

Figure 4-19. *A read model handles events from different services and builds a denormalized model*

In event-driven architectures, and often in microservice architectures also, these kinds of queries are often a common challenge (many of them similar to the ones raised when we discussed the API composition pattern). They are often solved by opting to build this denormalized read model. Event-driven architectures provide a way to do this by sharing information through events and offer a practical way to make the data readily available. The event streams provide a decoupled way to process data and transform it into something else, dedicated to a different purpose. They also do it in a continuous manner and in real time (as long as the subscriber is able to keep up with the throughput, which shouldn't be a problem since they are horizontally scalable). The associated decoupling of the services also guarantees that they don't impact each other by doing so.

But what kind of events would be best to build that denormalized view? As you'll recall, in Section 3.1, we discussed the differences between events and documents. Let's go through this practical example and discuss the tradeoffs.

As we discussed in Chapter 3, partial events are relevant when a service needs to react to that specific change. Read models typically have little or no business logic, as the business rules should be in the service that owns the domain and is the source of truth. We also discussed that documents are often relevant when the consumer uses most of the entity's data and is only interested in the most recent one. From this perspective, it would make sense to use documents to feed the read model. For example, Listing 4-1 illustrates a possible document the product service could publish.

Listing 4-1. ProductDocument schema definition

```
1    ProductDocument
2    {
3        Id: 152397,
4        Brand: "Nike",
5        Category: "Shirt",
6        Material: "Cotton",
7        Season: "Spring/Summer",
8        Sizes: ["XS", "S", "M", "L", "XL"],
9        Colors: ["Black", "Gray"],
10       CreatedAt: "2021-01-30T11:41:21.442Z"
11   }
```

If we had a partial event for each property, the read model would have to handle possibly six different events with different logic. A single document with all the information dramatically simplifies the effort to update the read model. It also reduced the number of events we have to publish and consume. For example, if the user edits several fields in one action, only one product document needs to be published, while if we had several partial events, we would need to publish one for each changed property.

An interesting solution is to combine this approach with Kafka's compacted topics. As we discussed in Chapter 3, when using compacted topics, Kafka removes older messages that share the same partition key. Figure 4-20 illustrates how this mechanic works.

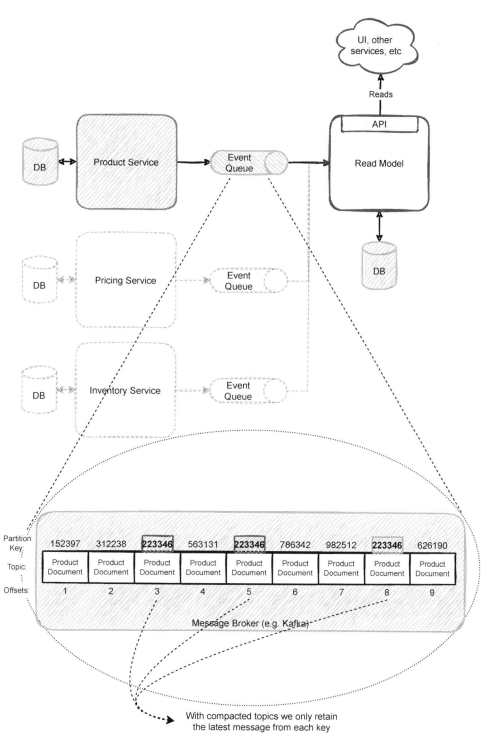

Figure 4-20. *Removal of older messages with Kafka compacted topics*

Notice that this is the same diagram we discussed earlier in Figure 4-19 but highlights the event queue's inner workings. We have a queue with only product documents, since we decided to publish just the document and don't use partial events. The numbers above the documents are the partition keys, which in this case translate to the product id, and the numbers below are the offsets. When the product service produces messages, it uses the product id as the partition key. Kafka internally uses this key to distribute the messages between different partitions (a concept similar to sharding, we will further detail how this works in Chapter 6).

When using compacted topics, Kafka removes the older messages with the same partition key. In the example in Figure 4-20, we have three documents with the same partition key (223346). The product service generated the three documents because the users changed the same product three times, so the product service published three documents informing each change. The two documents with offsets 3 and 5 are removed since they are older, and we only retain in the queue the latest one, with offset 8.

Compacted topics only remove older messages from repeated partition keys and always keep the most recent message per partition key. The product document we designed gives a comprehensive view of the product and its information. By combining both, the compacted topic acts as a product database but built in a way that is ready to be shared with other applications, and in a streaming fashion, new updates will be published as new documents at the end of the topic.

How could we build a similar denormalized model in a traditional microservice application using synchronous requests? Perhaps the read model would have to poll the product, pricing, and inventory service and fetch information about each product. This alternative would create a direct dependency between the read model and the other services, which would make it susceptible to cascading failures. It would also be less performant since the read model would have to request information even when no update was made. The time between editing information and being available in the read model (the inconsistency window) would be larger since it would be based on a specific interval rather than reacting to real-time changes. Scaling is also a challenge. The more requests we do to the services, the more the strain on the database; using this solution frequently might eventually impact the service responding to the requests, which begs the question of whether the solution is genuinely horizontally scalable.

Using an event queue and a streaming solution, we solve these problems in an organic way; changes are published and the services react to them. They are fully decoupled and don't need or impact each other directly. Adding more instances to the read model service, for example, would never impact the product service.

Rebuilding the model in case of an issue is also straightforward. Imagine if we introduce a bug in the read model service and the data is corrupted. If we need to rebuild the whole model, we can simply consume the topic from the beginning. Compacted topics retain the latest document from each product; by reading it from the beginning, we will consume the data from each product. There is no need for an ad hoc process or specific built application to migrate the data; neither is there the need for downtime. The code to rebuild the model is the same as the regular routine events. If we need to do it faster, we can add more service instances to consume the events more quickly during the rebuild.

If we receive a different search requirement from the business that our current model isn't optimized to fulfill, we can use the same strategy to generate the new model. Suppose we need to denormalize a different projection of the product data; we have the product information in the queue. In that case, we can use the same strategy to read it from the beginning and build that new projection.

Overall, this solution follows the same principles we have been discussing throughout this chapter; when data reaches a given scale, it often requires denormalized projections. Approaching the solution in an event-driven mindset provides us with the flexibility to build it according to the search requirements in a scalable and more reliable way.

4.7 The Pitfall of Microservice Spaghetti Architectures and How to Avoid It

In this chapter and the previous ones, we discussed how to transition to a microservice event-driven architecture, and we discussed how to build event-driven services and apply structural patterns. As we grow the microservice ecosystem by adding new functionality or creating more fine-grained services, the overall system's complexity continually increases. Besides all the challenges distributed architectures have, continuously adding more moving parts to the system can become hard to read and understand the overall picture. In this section, we will discuss this challenge, its impacts, and how to address it.

In a complex network of microservices, you often fail to find the correct flow. The same way we often struggle to understand the flow and logic of a single application's spaghetti code, a complex architecture can be even more challenging to read. When a business process spans several services, analyzing the code of several different services to understand the high-level flow can be a real detective's work.

Yuri Shkuro from Uber has a very interesting presentation[10] about tracing 2000+ services. The service network generated by Jaeger shows this difficulty and the associated complexity of such a high number of different components. Although the difficulty of understanding a complex web of distributed components is a drawback of distributed architectures and something we have to live with, we can take several actions that help us reason with that architecture more sustainably.

As discussed in Chapter 1, a drawback of monoliths is that they often have the right conditions to create spaghetti code without the right mindset and discipline in place. Microservices solve that since each service is physically separated from one another. In truth, they arguably delegate the challenge to a higher level, to the microservice organization and higher-level architecture. It certainly has many advantages; for example, it's easier for the teams working with the services to organize code and build new features. However, it's also easier for everyone to lose track of the overall flow and how the services impact each other, often creating complex corner cases. There are many resources and documented strategies to address spaghetti code. However, addressing spaghetti architectures often falls into a more dubious and more complex scope.

4.7.1 Domain Segregation and Clear Boundaries

In Chapter 3, we discussed DDD as a way to organize service boundaries. This organization can also be an excellent way to manage the microservice complexity. As we discussed in Chapter 3, services organized according to their domains are likely to be more stable than other types of organizations or not having one at all. They often prevent the impacts of new development to ripple through several components throughout the architecture.

---

[10] Presentation available in Yuri Shkuro, "Conquering Microservices Complexity @Uber with Distributed Tracing," September 4, 2019, `www.infoq.com/presentations/uber-microservices-distributed-tracing/`

Often in event-driven architectures, the domain's flow and the business processes are translated into the message flow between the several components. The highly evolutionary nature of these architectures also paves the way for them to change seamlessly. Losing track of the domain flow is easy, and understanding it is often tricky because it requires analyzing the message flow between several components.

Understanding the overall flow is often facilitated when services are clustered according to their domains. For example, in the practical example we discussed when detailing Sagas in Subsection 4.1.3, for fulfilling an order, we know we have to do a series of steps, for example, saving the order information, validating and updating stock, calculating pricing fees, etc. If services are organized using domain segregation, it's easier to map the business process flow to the services that implement it. Each service, or set of services, belongs to a bounded context related to a business concept. Even though there might be many services, each bounded context communicates to each other the same way the business process conceptually does, and the message flow advances the same way. This way, it's easier to reason with the architecture and the interactions between the services.

Another essential principle is to build clear boundaries across domains. One typically good practice in software engineering is to use dependency inversion (the D in SOLID[11]). It states that the code should depend upon abstractions rather than concrete implementations. Applying this to a high-level architecture, one boundary should access the other through the public interfaces, never by the internal service's implementations or endpoints.

You might recall when we discussed modular monoliths in Chapter 1. Modular monoliths are typically built by defining these boundaries and maintaining strict isolation between them. Shopify even built[12] a way to programmatically enforce these boundaries by validating code that doesn't access the public interfaces. It's easier to bypass these boundaries in a monolith since the code is centralized in a single solution.

However, in a complex microservice architecture, we can struggle with the same issue by having a chaotic network of dependencies between the services. Domain organization and strict boundaries mitigate this issue. Boundaries should be explicit on the endpoints they expose and clarify what functionalities are public and which

---

[11] See "SOLID," https://en.wikipedia.org/wiki/SOLID

[12] Full article in Kirsten Westeinde, "Deconstructing the Monolith: Designing Software that Maximizes Developer Productivity," February 21, 2019, https://shopify.engineering/deconstructing-monolith-designing-software-maximizes-developer-productivity

ones aren't (similar as they would be in a single code solution). This encapsulation helps contain the dependencies and lowers the likelihood of breaking contracts. A good approach is often guaranteeing the boundary has exclusive ownership of its domain's data and has clean dedicated endpoints that expose the boundaries' functionalities.

Overall, having domain segregation and enforcing the separation of concerns between bounded contexts can be useful in containing the architecture's complexity and a sustainable way to evolve the architecture without losing track of the high-level flow.

4.7.2 Context Maps

The patterns we discussed, like CQRS and event sourcing, aren't applicable in every use case, but DDD and its techniques have essential benefits that we can often use. DDD highlights the need to understand the system's domains and bounded contexts and their relationships. Its practices can often help us understand them even if we don't apply the more complex patterns like CQRS.

Context maps are typically mentioned in DDD, and they describe the existing bounded contexts, their relationships, and interactions in the form of a diagram or simply text. They can depict the higher-level relationships, dependencies, and flow of messages between the different bounded contexts. They are often similar to the diagrams we have been using throughout the book; an example is depicted in Figure 4-21.

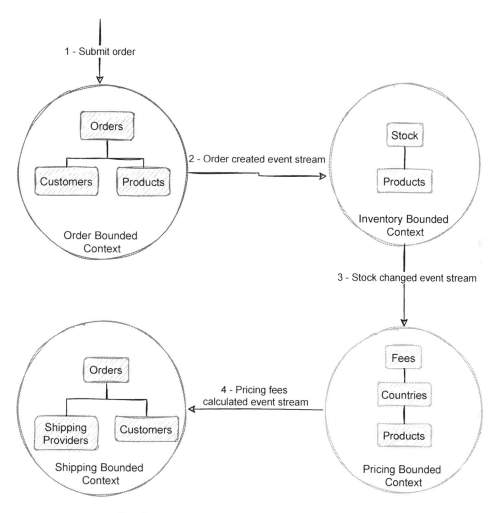

Figure 4-21. *Example of a possible context map for the eCommerce platform we have been discussing*

This example also details the entities in each bounded context. Also, an interesting note is the product entity, which is present in several bounded contexts but might have different information on each, depending on what is relevant. We can start by only drawing out the relations between the bounded contexts and later add more information like domains and entities. The details about relationships and their dependencies are often described in text or in a table that follows the diagram.

Context maps help to reason with the system, understand each boundary, and highlight where the boundaries share data. They also help to picture how the most important parts of the system relate to each other. In event-driven architectures, we can enrich the context map with the external event streams exposed and handled by the different bounded contexts. This approach can help provide a reference to reason and organize the architecture without losing track of the relationships between the services.

4.7.3 Distributed Tracing

In event-driven architectures, there is often no direct communication between services; this and the high decoupling between components can make the data flow hard to understand. Especially when using choreography, it is easy to lose the high-level flow of the events. Distributed tracing can be useful to tackle these challenges and help to map and understand these flows.

Distributed tracing collects and records services and operations that are in the scope of the events. That data can then be used to be searched and visualized. It can be a valuable method to reason with a distributed system, especially a highly decoupled one driven by events. It can also help to understand the relationships between the services.

Several tools can help us implement and record tracing. For example, we can use Zipkin along with Kafka's interceptor API[13] to record traces for every event produced and consumed. Another interesting example is using OpenTracing along with Jaeger.[14] OpenTracing can be used to add correlation data to the event's headers and use them in Jaeger to have a high-level visualization.

Distributed tracing can be a valuable tool to visualize how services interact, the flow of the data, and a high-level perception of how architecture evolved throughout time. We can use that high-level view provided by distributed tracing to organize and reason with the architecture in a more sustainable way. We can't improve what we don't measure; if we have that information and if the architecture has a chaotic network of dependencies, we can use that information to design a strategy to organize and make sense of the architecture's functionality.

---

[13] Interesting article on how to implement it in Jorge Quilcate, "The Importance of Distributed Tracing for Apache Kafka Based Applications," March 26, 2019, www.confluent.io/blog/importance-of-distributed-tracing-for-apache-kafka-based-applications/

[14] Interesting article on how to implement it in Aaron Burk, "Fault Tolerance in Distributed Systems: Tracing with Apache Kafka and Jaeger," July 24, 2019, www.confluent.io/blog/fault-tolerance-distributed-systems-tracing-with-apache-kafka-jaeger/

4.8 Summary

- Transactional consistency is a complex challenge in distributed systems. Distributed transactions and two-phase commit protocols are an alternative, but a very limited one often raising more issues than it solves.

- Sagas are a sequence of individual operations to manage a long-running process. We can use them to divide a long-running or traditional single database transaction into smaller ones, being more suitable for a distributed environment. Two common patterns of implementing Sagas are orchestration and choreography.

- Orchestration uses a primary component to manage the steps of the process. It is often valuable in complex processes that need a central supervisor.

- Services using choreography react to each other to complete the Saga's sequence of steps. Each service reacts to the changes happening in the ecosystem to accomplish its tasks. Choreography tends to be a typical pattern in event-driven architectures, and it synergizes well with its mindset.

- We can combine orchestration and choreography as we see fit. Choreography can be applied more commonly and in higher-level processes. We can use orchestration on a more limited scope and specific use cases.

- In event-driven architectures, having a set of independent services, each owning its domain's data, can pose a challenge to getting an aggregated view of the data. API composition can be a possible solution, albeit a very limited one.

- We can apply CQRS to segregate writes from reads. This segregation allows an optimized model and approach for each. CQRS isn't limited to segregating databases for reads and writes; there are other intermediate patterns that we can use.

- Event sourcing is a valuable pattern that synergizes well with event-driven architectures. It is important to understand the concerns and advantages of event sourcing as they might be useful in some use cases but also produce some complex limitations.

- Command sourcing relates to event sourcing and can also be a useful pattern when it is essential to save the requests exactly as the user submitted them. As with event sourcing, it is important to weigh its benefits and apply it only when it outweighs its concerns.

- Documents and Kafka's compacted topics can be a good approach to build several read models.

- Continuously adding more moving parts to the system can become hard to read and understand the overall picture. Domain segregation, clear boundaries, context maps, and distributed tracing can be valuable tools to tackle this challenge.

CHAPTER 5

How to Manage Eventual Consistency

This chapter covers:

- Why eventual consistency is a consequence of event-driven systems and its impact on the business and consumers

- Using event schema to avoid eventual consistency

- Applying domain boundaries to manage eventual consistency

- Using event versioning as a mean to react to inconsistent information

- Applying the end-to-end principle to guarantee a consistent flow

- Appearing consistent by maintaining a small inconsistency window

The funny thing about consistency in software engineering is that the meaning is not very consistent. Puns aside, the definition of consistency varies from context to context, and there are several levels of strong and weak consistency. Strong consistency is the consistency we are usually used to and provided by the traditional ACID (atomicity, consistency, isolation, and durability) properties. There are several degrees of weak consistency[1] that offer different levels of safety. Similar to what we would configure in a transaction isolation level, strong consistency would be the serializable level, while an example of weak consistency could be read uncommitted or read committed.

When dealing with distributed systems, there are several degrees of consistency, each with its peculiarities. I won't detail each of them since it's not in the scope of this

---

[1] Check this article by Jepsen which details the different degrees, "Consistency Models," https://jepsen.io/consistency

book's contents. Still, the duality between availability and strong consistency usually triggers a lively debate illustrated by the CAP theorem detailed in Section 5.1.

Typical monolithic applications enjoy the comfort of ACID properties and the traditional meaning of consistency. Transactional and relational databases usually treat data as a single copy; changes are atomic and instantaneous. If you change a record, you don't have to worry about any concurrent write since the operation is atomic. No one else can modify it simultaneously, and it will be available to anyone reading it instantaneously. When you read that record, you are guaranteed to read the last possible value.

These kinds of guarantees are typically available on monolithic applications. They simplify most developments and provide an easy solution to otherwise complex problems. This meaning of consistency is the foundation for many applications and is wired into our minds and our customers' minds while using the software. Looking back, this level of consistency is a warm fuzzy blanket on a dark cold night. When moving to an event-driven architecture, you most likely will need to leave that blanket behind and embrace the cold. Don't worry, the cold is always better than the heat of a SQL database CPU running at 100%.

Interactions between components in an event-driven architecture are often with asynchronous communications. Traditionally, communications between microservices are point-to-point synchronous communications. Often microservices expose APIs so other services can use their functionality and access their data. As exemplified in Figure 5-1, these APIs usually use synchronous communication like REST, and service 1 sends a request and obtains the response immediately. When using event-driven microservices, service 1 publishes an event which is handled by service 2, but no direct communication happens between the two services, and is always mediated through the event broker; the services don't know each other.

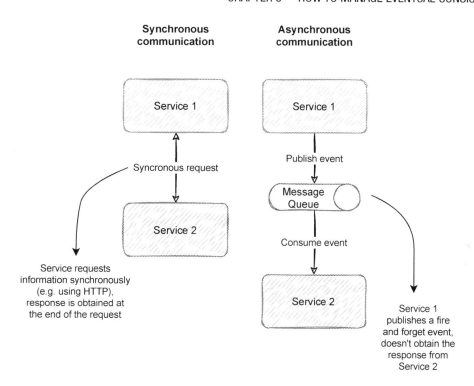

Figure 5-1. *Comparison between synchronous and asynchronous microservice communication*

It is often preached about the advantages of decoupling components through message queues; while this is undoubtedly useful, it also has the consequence of making the propagation of changes in the system asynchronous. The asynchronous decoupling produces what is usually named eventual consistency; reads on different parts of the system might return stale data, but given enough time, all reads will eventually return the same value. In event-driven architectures, all services processing events for a given entity will eventually converge to the same state as soon as they process those events. Eventual consistency is a specific form of weak consistency since it doesn't guarantee the stronger guarantees of ACID properties, for example. NoSQL databases have widely adopted eventual consistency as a means to enable high scalability and provide availability guarantees that are hard (or impossible) to achieve with strong consistency models in a distributed environment. Section 5.1 will further detail this topic and its relation to the CAP theorem.

Having components that possibly return stale values impacts the system's users and has an even higher impact on other services that depend on that information. When a service's domain logic depends on information from an eventually consistent read model, it might produce erroneous results due to the stale information. It is fundamental to know how to handle eventual consistency to leverage these impacts.

This chapter provides several techniques to deal with and leverage eventual consistency in an event-driven architecture. In Section 5.2, you will learn how event schema design can avoid eventual consistency. The impacts of event schema design are further detailed in Chapter 8.

In Section 5.3, you will learn to use domain boundaries to contain the impacts of eventual consistency. This relates to the choreography pattern described in Chapter 4. Section 5.4 will detail how to use event versioning to detect stale information and use compensation strategies to deal with eventual consistency.

The end-to-end principle can guarantee consistency in the end-to-end flow while allowing eventual consistency on the system's smaller components. This will be detailed in Section 5.5 and include a real-world example of its use. Section 5.6 will weigh eventual consistency with small inconsistency windows and show how real-world uses of NoSQL databases can apply it in production. You will learn how the same strategy can be applied to event-driven architectures.

5.1 The Impacts of Eventual Consistency and the Need for Alignment with the Business

In this section, you will learn the impacts of eventual consistency and understand that not every component needs or should be eventually consistent. There's no magic solution to eventual consistency, just ways to leverage it. It should be a conscious decision to adopt it and needs alignment with the system's business owners. There is also the need for a deliberate strategy to deal with your system's future consumers and should be clear to them that the service might return stale data. This section will also detail and illustrate the impact of eventual consistency and teach you to weigh the tradeoffs.

Let's illustrate eventual consistency with an example. Figure 5-2 depicts a user buying a product on an eCommerce platform based on a single application. At the moment of the purchase, the system would need to validate the available stock and create the order. The subscription service would also need to validate the remaining stock and notify interested parties if the product has just one stock unit left.

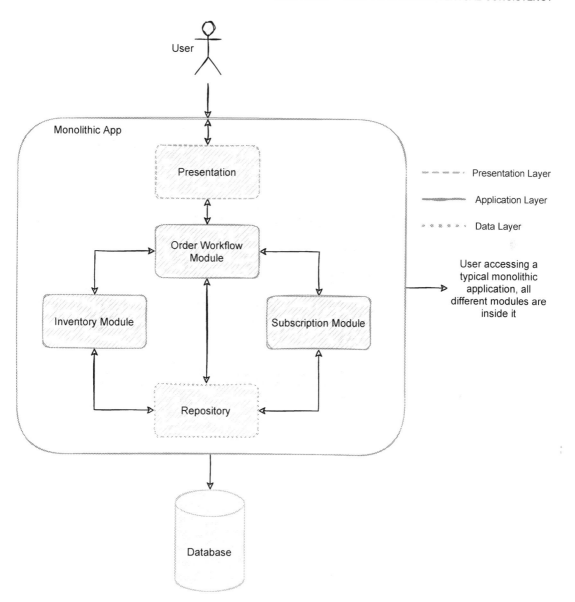

Figure 5-2. *Monolithic application with several different modules*

Since there is only one application, each operation is synchronous. The logic and the domain flow of the order are sequential inside that application. The database changes can occur atomically, and the information about, for example, the product's stock on the platform will be updated when the user orders the product. The new stock will be instantly visible to every user on the platform.

Now let's see the same example as before but with each module with an independent event-driven microservice as pictured in Figure 5-3. The order service would create the order and then publish an event informing about the operation. Inventory service would then handle that event and update the stock for that product. Since these two operations are asynchronous between the moment the user created the order and the moment the service updated the stock, there could be another order for the same product. Since the stock model wasn't up to date yet, the user could view and order stock for that product. The stale data and the concurrency of the orders would produce a duplicate order for stock that might not be available.

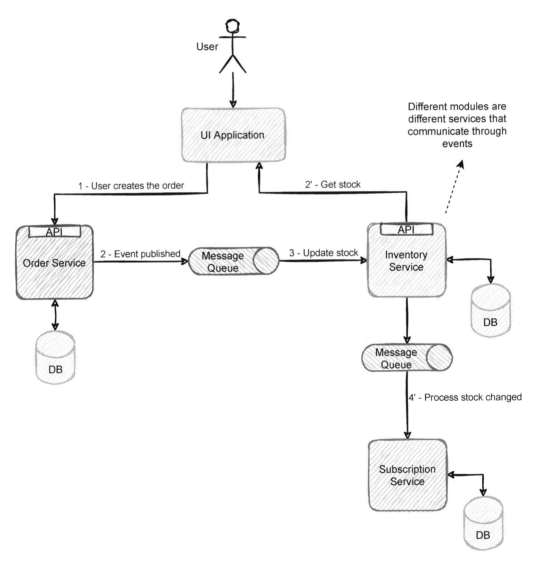

Figure 5-3. *Event-driven approach to the same application*

Distributed systems like event-driven architectures have two core properties[2]: safety and liveliness. These two properties provide the foundation to understand why eventual consistency is a challenge.

5.1.1 Safety

The safety property guarantees that no "bad things" happen in the system. Bad things are situations that could make the data invalid or to have a state that was never on the system (e.g., concurrency issues inside the system, possibility of deadlocks, unordered operations, etc.). Typical eventual consistency has no safety properties; however, in an event-driven system, we can avoid most of these issues. How to solve them is explored in Chapters 6, 7, and 8. An important consideration is while the system is inside the inconsistency window (the time between an update occurs and the change propagates throughout the system), the state returned can be invalid, which might be an issue depending on the use case. This chapter discusses possible solutions for these issues. If we model events to be small, the partial state of the entity we build through them might be temporarily invalid. For example, if you change your profile's full address and the system processing it sends partial events for the street name and the city, the built model might have the new street name and the old city temporarily. Chapter 8 explores this subject in greater detail.

5.1.2 Liveliness

The liveliness property guarantees that "good things" happen in the system. In this context, the most important consequence is higher availability. Availability is one of the most useful advantages of event-driven microservices as they endow the system with higher resilience, enabling for higher percentages of the service's availability.

The first most obvious consequence is for the users of the system. Changes by the system's users might take time to propagate to every service in the ecosystem, impacting the tools. I'm guessing you probably used an application that after doing an update took a few refreshes of the page to see those changes reflected. Although it is a dubious user experience and mildly infuriating, it might be acceptable to live with depending on the

---

[2] These two properties were first described in this article by Bowen Alpern and Fred B. Schneider, "Defining Liveness," October 7, 1985

business. There might also be the case that it is better not to be available than displaying stale information. The most crucial property in this situation is the length of the inconsistency window; if it is small enough, it won't be noticeable, and as far as users are concerned, fast eventually consistency is strong consistency as explored in Section 5.6. There are also ways to design UIs to be more compatible with asynchronous systems, as will be discussed in Chapter 9.

When there is business-critical functionality built on top of eventual consistency, you need to weigh whether forfeiting consistency in favor of availability is acceptable to the business. There might be use cases where not accessing the data is preferable to base decisions on stale information. We saw this firsthand on a system that managed an eCommerce platform products' visibility. The business had several agreements with brands to not allow certain categories of products to be available in specific regions. The punctual delays in the UIs due to peaks in load made the business completely stop using that feature to manage it in more error-prone manual alternatives because they simply couldn't trust the system. This example highlights the need to understand the functionality's criticality and to weigh if another solution is preferable.

The issue also gains a different magnitude in synchronous HTTP calls between services. The example in Figure 5-3 illustrates this issue; the UI application does an HTTP call to the inventory service API to obtain the stock after creating the order to validate if there is just only one stock unit left to notify customers. The stock returned by the inventory service might not be up to date since both the subscription service and inventory service are processing it. The stale data might result in two possible faults if the subscription service processes the order created event faster than the inventory service:

- The stock quantity is two, resulting in no notification sent since it wasn't the last stock unit.

- The stock quantity is one, resulting in the service sending a repeated notification for a stock quantity no longer available.

When a service has domain logic that depends on synchronous data from a different service, this issue will always have a chance to happen even if the inconsistency window is small. A peak in the service load might cause it to lag, producing stale responses for every dependent service.

In this case, living with eventual consistency won't be enough, and we require more deliberate strategies that are discussed further in the next chapters.

5.1.3 The CAP Theorem in the Real World

This subsection will detail further the impacts of eventual consistency and how they relate to the CAP theorem. Eventual consistency has been highly debated in the context of the CAP theorem as a means to justify its presence on event-driven architectures. By learning its meaning and real-world impacts on real production databases that deal with the same challenges, you will be able to understand the tradeoffs between availability and consistency, as pictured in Figure 5-4.

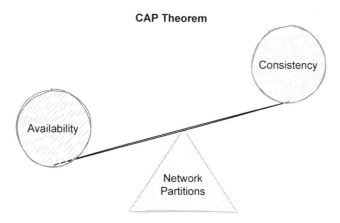

Figure 5-4. *CAP theorem and the duality between consistency and availability*

Distributed databases with high-availability requirements typically provide several copies of the original data in different nodes in geographically separated locations. This feature allows the system to maintain the data's integrity even when a node is lost and enjoy lower network latency for clients close to those geographical locations. However, the system has to copy the data to different nodes; the replication doesn't occur instantaneously and might produce inconsistent results across other nodes; one update that happened in one node might not yet be available for a read on a different node. Maintaining a consistent response from several nodes is even more hampered by network faults, typically known as network partitions. When a network partition occurs (due to, for example, failure in a hardware component), it can split the cluster's nodes into smaller groups that cannot communicate with each other; changes in one group's data will be invisible to the other and vice versa. The question arises on what strategy to choose, to either wait out the fault in the network and thus be unavailable or return a possible less consistent version of the data allowing the system to respond to requests.

This dilemma is illustrated by the CAP theorem, which appeared in 2000 by a keynote[3] presented by Dr. Eric Brewer and greatly influenced how engineers design distributed storage systems since that time. It laid the foundations for many NoSQL databases that appeared and evolved since then and contributed to the general acceptance of weak consistency models. The reasoning behind adopting an AP (available and tolerant to network partitions) data store is very similar to the logic to adopt an asynchronous event-driven solution and lays out the fundamentals of why eventual consistency is needed. Also, the properties raised by the CAP theorem are unavoidable in any distributed system.

The CAP theorem is based on three properties: consistency, availability, and tolerance of network partitions. It states that a distributed system can either be available or consistent in the presence of network partitions. It is not possible to choose two properties out of the three since network partitions are inevitable on a distributed system; instead, you have to decide whether availability or consistency prevails. Let's dig down on those three properties:

- Consistency: The word consistency is broad and usually is the source of misunderstandings; in the scope of the CAP theorem, it means linearizability (differs from the consistency in ACID[4]). It guarantees that any single operation like a read or write on an entity occurs in real time, similar to what would happen if there was just one copy of the data. For example, if there are two updates on an object after one node returns the latest update, all nodes must return that update as well. It seems simple but in the context of distributed computing is a challenging problem to solve.

- Availability: The system is available 100% of the time, in the scope of network partitions. An important detail of this definition is that there is no limit to latency.[5] A response is considered available even if it takes several days to return, for theoretical purposes is fitting, but for a realistic view of the real world is counter-intuitive.

---

[3] See Dr. Eric A. Brewer, "Towards Robust Distributed Systems," July 19, 2000, `https://people.eecs.berkeley.edu/~brewer/cs262b-2004/PODC-keynote.pdf`

[4] Further details in "CAP Twelve Years Later: How the "Rules" Have Changed," May 30, 2012, `www.infoq.com/articles/cap-twelve-years-later-how-the-rules-have-changed/`

[5] See Martin Kleppmann, "A Critique of the CAP Theorem," September 18, 2015, `https://arxiv.org/pdf/1509.05393.pdf`

- Tolerance to network partitions: A network partition occurs when the connectivity between two nodes gets interrupted and are unable to communicate. Network partitions can happen due to various reasons like failures in network hardware.

This definition splits distributed systems into two groups AP or CP, by either choosing availability or consistency. Due to the demanding availability requirements of Internet applications, we often see AP distributed systems as a necessary consequence of the high volume of current applications' data. AP systems typically use eventual consistency as a means to be both available and tolerant to network partitions. Eventual consistency is also a natural consequence of the asynchronous nature of event-driven systems and nowadays is an accepted characteristic of most event-driven solutions. But should it be so lightly accepted?

The CAP theorem's availability isn't the operational availability we are used to but limited to the scope of network-related problems. Usually, we define availability as the ability of a system to respond to requests successfully. In the CAP theorem, the definition is more blurred than that. It refers to the availability of the theorem's algorithm[6] that is closely related to faults in the network. That means 100% availability in the CAP context doesn't guarantee 100% overall availability. Several failures can jeopardize the system's availability besides network-related problems like wrong configurations, bugs on the application code, limited resources, etc. But what does that mean in real use cases? Google revealed that its Google Spanner database of all the incidents occurred only 7.6% were due to the network, and more than half were due to human-related[7] issues like misconfigurations.

In practice, the difference in availability between CP and AP systems isn't as significant as we are led to believe; both systems can guarantee availability levels in the 99.999%; for example, Facebook's HBase[8] CP system also reached similar levels of availability.

---

[6] See Martin Kleppmann, "A Critique of the CAP Theorem," September 18, 2015, https://arxiv.org/pdf/1509.05393.pdf

[7] Full article in Eric Brewer, "Spanner, TrueTime & The CAP Theorem," February 14, 2017, https://static.googleusercontent.com/media/research.google.com/en//pubs/archive/45855.pdf

[8] Full article in Rishit Shroff and Zelaine Fong, "HydraBase – The evolution of HBase@Facebook," June 5, 2014, https://engineering.fb.com/2014/06/05/core-data/hydrabase-the-evolution-of-hbase-facebook/

The limited meaning of the CAP theorem's availability raises the question of whether it supports a sufficiently compelling case to adopt AP systems at the expense of consistency. This question has been raised more and more[9] often due to the impacts of the loss of consistency in solution design.

It is undeniable that network partitions are an unavoidable concern[10] and have a considerable effect in any distributed system; however, we should question if it is reason enough to blindly embrace weaker consistency models like eventual consistency.

Traditional monolith applications typically enjoyed ACID guarantees that we took for granted. Consistency was the very foundation of software and was imbued in our way of thinking and interacting with a system or database. Arguably, consistency should be handled at the database level; not doing so is pushing the responsibility and a significant increment of complexity to every client using that system. The question of whether to adopt a CP or AP system and the impact of availability in the CAP theorem's scope illustrates the same ramifications whether we should apply an event-driven architecture to a given system. The inherent asynchronous nature of event-driven systems can and most likely will produce eventually consistent models. This nature will push the complexity to handle inconsistent results to every client using that system similarly as AP systems do. It impacts the users and other applications that interact with the system since they will have to manage the possibility of inconsistent responses leading to complex and intricate solutions to dubious user experiences or convoluted business processes. Before turning business functionality eventually consistent, we should question whether the business can effectively live with it. Either way, there are approaches we can take to minimize its impact, as we will discuss in this chapter.

---

[9] See Robert Yokota, "Don't settle for eventual consistency," February 17, 2017, https://yokota.blog/2017/02/17/dont-settle-for-eventual-consistency/#fn-517-10, and Ben Darnell, "The Limits of the CAP Theorem," June 27, 2017, www.cockroachlabs.com/blog/limits-of-the-cap-theorem/

[10] Further details in "The network is reliable," June 2, 2013, https://aphyr.com/posts/288-the-network-is-reliable&ved=2ahUKEwjY7sjEvKfsAhVOcBQKHf78AxIQFjAEegQIAxAB&usg=AOvVaw3159NbJwFhJotfpzh8iCBR&cshid=1602245361376

5.2 Using Event Schema in Event-Driven Microservices to Leverage Eventual Consistency

In this section, you will learn how event schema can avoid eventual consistency on downstream consumers of events. Adapting event schema to your consumers' needs and real use cases is often more useful than following a strict guideline on how to design event schema. This section will illustrate with an example and discuss two different approaches to schema design.

In Section 5.1, we used an example of a user buying a product on an eCommerce platform. Let's drill down on the inventory and subscription service. Since most inventory management systems require audit on stock movements, they are often a typical use case to apply event sourcing. As discussed in Chapter 4, event sourcing can be paired with CQRS to allow more flexible reads. Figure 5-5 depicts inventory service with CQRS and its relation to the subscription service.

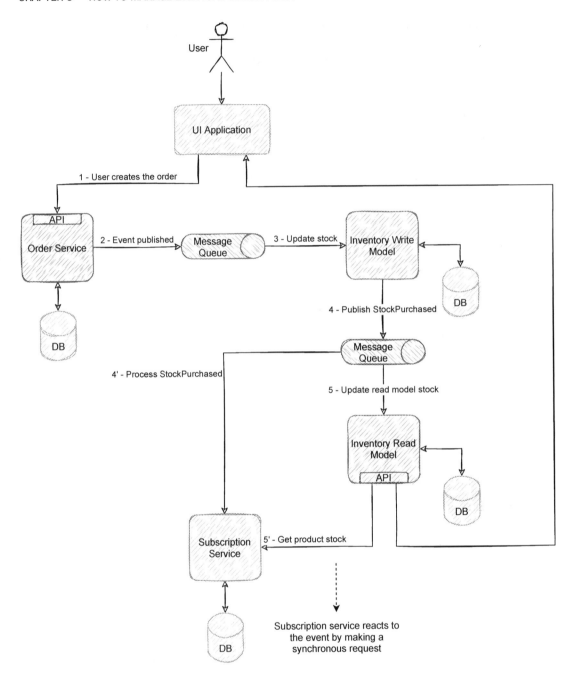

Figure 5-5. *Event-driven approach mixing a synchronous request*

Having the read and write model decoupled by a message queue makes the read model eventually consistent. The system will apply changes in the stock first to the write model, which is also the owner of the inventory domain logic. If the change complies with the domain rules, the service will apply the change, and an event will be published, signaling the change in stock. All interested parties can consume that event and do what their domain needs to do with that information.

A common best practice is to design events to be small and fine-grained. Fine-grained events have many advantages; performance-wise, it's faster to handle small events than large ones, serialization and deserialization are quicker and lightweight, and they have less impact on the message broker. It is also a common best practice to design events to reflect the user's intent when using a DDD approach (domain-driven design; refer to Chapter 3 for more details). This way, the events and commands will have domain value and highlight the business flow throughout the architecture.

Applying these concepts to the example of Figure 5-3, we would model the stock changed event to be small and fine-grained and reflect the user's intent. Typically, stock changes occur at the product's stock-keeping unit level; for example, if the user was buying a shirt, it would be of a given size like XS. A possible event for this situation would look like Listing 5-1.

Listing 5-1. StockPurchased event

```
1    StockPurchased    #A
2    {
3        ProductId: 15251212,
4        Size: "XS",
5        Quantity: 1
6    }
```
#A Stock purchased event with minimal information

This event reflects the intent of the user; the user bought one product of size XS. It also is fine-grained and only has minimal information needed. Usually, these kinds of events are the easiest to publish due to all the required information being available in the publishing service at the moment of the change; the service has no additional effort to create the event.

Let's now discuss how the subscription service would consume this event. The subscription service needs to alert every user that subscribed to the alert of the product's last available stock unit. As seen earlier, the event only provides the quantity that the user bought of that size. And here lies the challenge of the subscription service domain logic; from that event, the service has no way to know the total quantity of the product.

A product has several sizes, for example, they can range from XXS to XXL; the event's quantity is only referring to that specific size. The event also only provides the quantity that the user bought, not the size's current quantity.

A developer who needs to implement this functionality in the subscription service would probably fetch the current stock quantity for that product through the inventory service API. But since the inventory service read model is eventually consistent, it might return stale data. Since the inventory read model and the subscription service are consuming the same event in parallel, they will consume it at different rates. The event the subscription service is consuming might not be reflected in the read model at the time of the request. When the inventory read model returns stale data, the subscription service will incur in one of the two faults described in Section 5.1.

This logic is in line with the reasoning of NoSQL databases adopting eventual consistency and delegating the complexity of achieving strong consistency to the applications that use them explained in Subsection 5.1. In this case, the choice of fine-grained schema on inventory service delegates the complexity of handling stale information to the consumers. If we deal with this only on subscription service, it will add significant complexity to the service to solve a purely technical and not business-related issue.

Most resources advise to create small fine-coursed events, mostly due to performance and other considerations. However, in the real world, what most teams find out is as the microservice ecosystem grows, so this concern becomes more pressing. One highly beneficial approach is to approach it by designing event schema with consumers' needs in mind.

Going back to the inventory and subscription service example as seen in Figure 5-3, since inventory service has the stock information for all sizes, it would be arguably easy to send an event with additional details, illustrated in Listing 5-2.

Listing 5-2. StockPurchased event denormalized

```
1    StockPurchased   #A
2    {
3        ProductId: 15251212,
4        Size: "XS",
5        Quantity: 1,
6        ProductCurrentQuantity: 5,
7        ProductSizes:[
```

```
8               {
9                   Size: "S",
10                  Quantity: 3
11              },
12              {
13                  Size: "M",
14                  Quantity: 2
15              },
16          ]
17  }
```

#A Stock purchased event with information adapted to the consumer needs

The property indicating the product's current stock information for every size would greatly ease the implementation in subscription service because it would be able to know the product's total stock instead of a single size. Instead of requesting the current stock information from an eventually consistent model, the service would process its domain logic by relying solely on the event's data. Besides removing a great deal of complexity from the subscription service, this approach also gives it a performance boost since it avoids the need for a network request.

Adding additional information to the event is a good strategy when the information is available but depends on the inventory service design. The aggregate size becomes a pivotal decision in this situation:

- If we design the aggregate in the inventory service to be the product, it would be trivial to obtain the total product's stock.

- If we design the aggregate in the inventory service to be the product's size, it would require a more complex solution. Since the product stock comprises each size's stock information, we would require interaction between several aggregates. To obtain this information, we would need to apply a more complicated solution like a process manager. We further detail this topic in Chapter 8.

Adapting the event schema to consumer applications' needs can be one of the most powerful patterns you can use to avoid eventual consistency. It easily contains the complexity of the architecture and the applications while retaining the advantages of event-driven systems.

The full implications and additional alternatives to event schema are also discussed further in Chapter 8.

5.3 Applying Microservice Domain Boundaries to Leverage Eventual Consistency

In this section, you will learn to contain the impact of eventual consistency by segregating the services into domain boundaries. Bounded contexts are a core concept in DDD and you can use the same rationale to an event-driven architecture, especially when the system starts to have a high number of components. Using a boundary organization enhances the autonomy of the teams working in those components and can contain the impact of eventually consistent models. This section will detail how domain segregation can control that impact, illustrating it with an example.

In the last section, you learned how to solve the challenge of fetching stale data from an eventually consistent read model by adapting the event schema. We can use additional options to solve the need to fetch additional data; using the same example we used before with a user buying a product on an eCommerce platform, we can simply have the subscription service consume an event after the read model is updated. By changing the sequence of consumers between the services, we guarantee that the model is up to date with the event's information, illustrated in Figure 5-6.

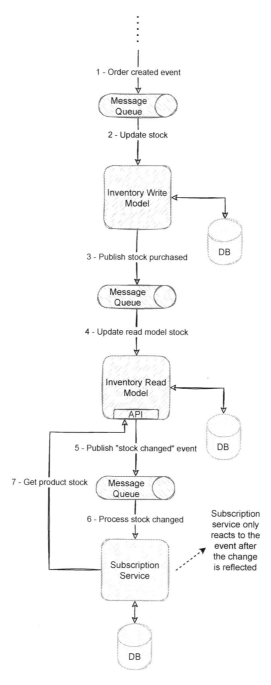

Figure 5-6. *Subscription service processing the change only after it is reflected on inventory read model*

This approach also solves possible inconsistency issues by informing the user too early if the subscription service would notify the user with a link to the product. If the user accesses it while inside the inconsistency window, the user would see incorrect stock. Changing the sequence of components, the subscription service would only notify the user when the data is updated.

However, this solution has some pitfalls:

- It is fairly debatable whether a read model should send an event. If we look at it in purely DDD terms, only a change in an aggregate should trigger an event; in this case, the only event that should be published would be from the write model that is the owner of the domain. It is arguably justifiable if it is not an event just a notification that the read model is up to date. However, it usually is a sign that something is out of place (in this case, we should avoid the synchronous call).

- You should use this approach sparingly and inside a specific context. Using it often will rapidly increase the complexity of the overall architecture and the flow of the information. The architecture should have clear boundaries and manage these issues inside each boundary. The data should flow between the boundaries and not have a tangled flow between the read models and the domain owners.

- The overall time to reflect the change throughout the system will increase.

In DDD, a bounded context is the contextual relationship of a specific domain model. It usually represents a subset of the domain of the overall system with its individual domain model. It's also segregated from other bounded contexts with clear boundaries between them. Although the bounded context refers exclusively to the domain model, in a microservice event-driven architecture, one bounded context can span various individual components. For example, when applying CQRS, we can have one component responsible for the write model and another component responsible for the read model. They both use and represent the same domain, so the two components are part of the same bounded context.

In a growing microservice architecture, it's important to understand the system's bounded contexts and which services belong to each one of them. Having clear domain boundaries between slices of the system will facilitate the evolution of the business. The decoupling between boundaries is the stepping stone to the seamless business evolution and limiting the technical impacts of that evolution. We detailed DDD and domain boundaries on an event-driven architecture in Chapter 3.

An alternative solution for this problem could be defining two separate boundaries, one for the inventory domain and another for the subscription domain. This separation has high synergy with a DDD approach, forcing you to understand the business and think about what kind of boundaries make sense and where to draw the boundaries. The business process is the flow between all needed domain boundaries. This is similar to the event choreography pattern detailed in Chapter 4. The anti-corruption layers guarantee that concepts from a given domain don't leak to another domain. Chapter 3 details this concept. We illustrate this solution in Figure 5-7.

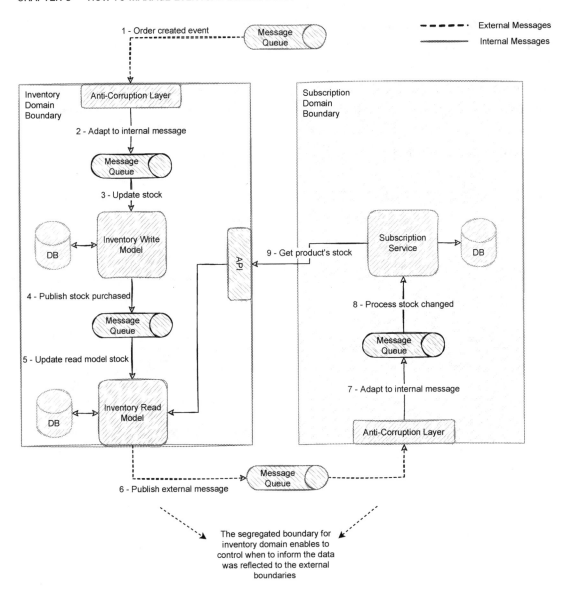

Figure 5-7. *Applying domain boundaries to the same use case*

This solution is a more structured way to evolve the domains without losing track of the overall flow. The order created event is forwarded inside the boundary by the anti-corruption layer that adapts the event to keep only the needed information for that boundary. Inside the boundary, the inventory services will process the event accordingly with their logic. The write model will change the aggregate's stock and publish an internal event. The read model will use the internal event to update its information and publish an external event only when the data is reflected in the read model.

The complexity inside the inventory boundary is abstracted from external boundaries, like the subscription boundary, and can evolve as needed without impacting other boundaries.

Each domain can change; we can add or remove more components, but the business process's overall flow will remain the same. We also deal with eventual consistency inside the boundary; changes that happen are notified to external consumers only when all the services inside the boundary processed it. This feature contains eventual consistency for external consumers; this way, we can guarantee the change the consumer is reacting to is already propagated inside the domain.

5.4 Handling Eventual Consistency Delays with Event Versioning

In this section, you will learn how to use event versioning to understand delayed responses and possible actions to mitigate its impacts. The most direct approach to eventual consistency is simply to try the operation later when it is no longer eventual. This solution is very straightforward and would probably be the most obvious alternative to deal with temporarily stale data. However, it has two not so obvious caveats: knowing the data is not up to date and when you should use it. We will illustrate this solution with an example and discuss possible approaches to avoid these caveats.

There is a fascinating article[11] named "The Tail at Scale" from Jeffrey Dean and Luiz André Barroso detailing how Google managed to obtain 99.9% latency SLA on some of their services by optimizing the slowest requests on the 95th percentile. Distributed systems typically have latency fluctuations beyond the scope of the service. In a perfect world, we would avoid those fluctuations entirely, but these fluctuations are unavoidable in a complex distributed system, much like the fault-tolerant techniques we often employ. The article details several tail-tolerant methods to minimize or mask the impact of these temporary latency spikes. Some of them rely on retrying requests to the replicas when the original request takes longer than a specified time. The retrying strategy has a higher resource consumption due to the additional requests, which, the article explains, can be as low as just 2% with the right approach.

---

[11] Full article in Jeffrey Dean and Luiz André Barroso, "The Tail at Scale," February 2013, `https://cacm.acm.org/magazines/2013/2/160173-the-tail-at-scale/fulltext`

We can draw an analogy from this article to retrying strategies in an event-driven architecture. Event-driven services should keep up with the message load and not lag behind the changes that occur in the system (as discussed in Section 5.7). However, the services will likely lag eventually one time or another due to unforeseen peaks in load, but that should be the exception rather than the rule; it should be the curve's tail. If this is in fact the case, we can argue that we can opt for an optimistic approach; we can assume there isn't eventual consistency. When a request fetches stale data, it can react to it with a retry.

Using the same example with the inventory and subscription service, when requesting the information to the inventory service if the data is stale, the service should make an additional request after a predefined amount of time. However, this assumes that the inventory service is faster and is usually up to date; the retry would be the exception.

The first caveat is how to know the data is stale. To solve that, we can use event versioning; each event should have a version (it is also essential to manage idempotency detailed in Chapter 7) that identifies the entity's version. In DDD terms, it could be the aggregate version; for every change that happens on the aggregate, the service increments the version. It can also be a timestamp, which is more practical, although not sequential. This version should also be available on the API; the subscription service, when making the request, would compare both versions; if the version of the event were higher than the version of the API, the service would need to retry the request. This means the service didn't reflect the change in the event on the read model yet.

Retrying the requests is the most straightforward strategy you can do but is also riskier. We often hear how retrying strategies can improve resilience, however, more often than not it sets the system up for failure. We can apply it only in less critical components or as a quick bandage. The consequence is that the service is considerably more susceptible to its dependencies' load peaks. The implementation should have a circuit breaker and a backoff strategy. Used throughout, the architecture will make the system brittle and vulnerable to cascading failures. Retrying is the symptom of the lack of a more sustainable approach; we should use it wisely and sparingly.

There is also the issue of what to do when all retries fail. I saw some services that simply failed the message processing or delegated the failure to a business process, like a manual operation. Although they might be acceptable in some contexts (e.g., some less critical use cases like logging), I find these kinds of approaches disheartening and half-hearted. There are some compensation alternatives like scheduling the handling of the failure to a later date; ultimately, consistency is well, eventual, so at some point in time, the lag will clear.

Ordering is also an important consideration; retries make sense when message consumption is associative, commutative, and idempotent. Otherwise, the service might not be able to retry with consistent results. For more details, refer to Chapter 6.

Event versioning isn't a definite solution on its own, just a tool that we can use to manage delays. We should apply it as a tactical solution for an urgent matter; more often than not, we require a more sustainable and reliable solution like the others mentioned in this chapter.

5.5 Saving State in Event-Driven Microservices to Avoid Eventual Consistency

In this section, you will learn how to prevent eventual consistency by storing state external to the service. Typically, microservices are faced with eventual consistency due to the hybrid nature of most real-world architectures. Some services react to events, and others make synchronous calls depending on the use case. By storing state, we can spare the synchronous call, avoiding dealing with an eventually consistent model.

Using the same example with the inventory and subscription service. depicted in Figure 5-5, the issue with eventual consistency rises due to the synchronous call between the subscription service and the inventory read model. To avoid doing the synchronous call, we could store the product's stock internally in the subscription service. When the subscription service needs the stock information for all product sizes, it could fetch it locally, as in Figure 5-8.

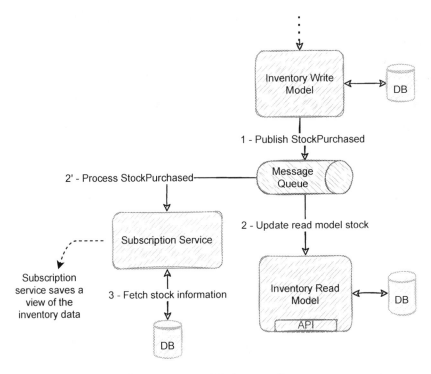

Figure 5-8. *Storing external state to avoid the synchronous request*

This approach is the most adherent to the event-driven mindset. By removing the synchronous request, the service becomes entirely decoupled from the dependency. It becomes more resilient since it won't be affected if the inventory read model is unavailable. Performance-wise is also better since fetching the database's data is often faster than a remote network call. Similarly to the solution adapting event schema, the subscription service is only dependent on the upstream inventory events.

However, the subscription service must maintain and internally store all the inventory information. When there is a large amount of data, storing it will impact the infrastructure and its costs. The subscription service will also need to maintain that data up to date, which has a considerable development overhead than just requesting the inventory read model data.

This approach gives precedence to the service's autonomy and performance. It is a useful alternative to solve this kind of challenge; however, we must avoid the pitfall of applying it blindly in every use case. Otherwise, several copies of the service's data will spread throughout the architecture, becoming hard to manage and maintain. We discuss further the tradeoffs of using events to provide state transfer in Chapter 8.

5.5.1 Buffering State As an Alternative to Persistence

We discussed how storing state could avoid the dependency of synchronous requests to an eventually consistent model. We also discussed the drawbacks of storing that data. An alternative to persisting the state is buffering it to memory. Storing every external state a service needs as an internal view of that state can be difficult to manage, to initialize, and to maintain up to date. An alternative to persisting the state is to load it in memory. There are two strategies to achieve this:

- A predefined buffering window: The service keeps in memory all events that arrive inside that window's timespan. This strategy is relevant when a use case applies a batch of operations to the same or related entities in a small time frame, for example, bulk actions or uploads of information. If the service needs the data from the entity it is processing or a related entity, it can load directly from that buffer. This strategy's success is directly related to the timespan's size and the likelihood of the entity changing in that timespan. There's always the chance the service doesn't find the needed entity in memory and might have to fall back to a request, thus being limited to specific use cases. This strategy is also useful in data-intensive applications that write to data stores. Usually, a bulk change is faster than several single changes; the buffer can help cluster changes and update them on a single operation.

- Loading the full state: The service can load all the dependent states to memory. This solution implies all the event streams are available on the event broker. The service can read all the information from the beginning of the topic and keep it in memory. Other events would keep the in-memory view up to date. This strategy is only relevant to small data sets that aren't expected to grow in the future. For example, if the subscription service would alert users only for products in the "shoes" category, it might need the product's category information. Assuming there won't be more than a few hundred categories in the platform, the service could load them to memory and use that view when needed. The service needs to load all the information on startup, which can be too cumbersome in large data sets.

Figure 5-9 illustrates this solution applied to the same example using the subscription and inventory service. The subscription service loads the events in memory and, instead of making the synchronous request to the inventory read model, uses that information. This way, the service can decide whether it is the last stock unit left and if it should alert the user.

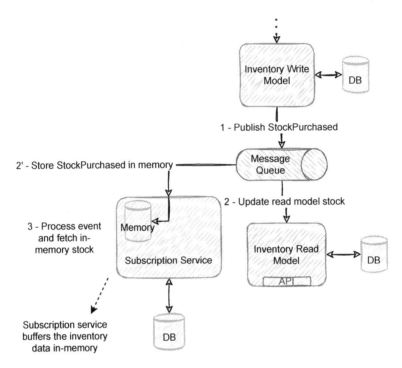

Figure 5-9. *Subscription service saves the stock event stream in memory*

However, this alternative depends on whether the subscription service has all the information of all sizes in memory. In this case, a buffering window would only be an adequate choice if the system changes all sizes simultaneously; otherwise, most likely the service won't have all the information needed. If we read the event stream and load all stock information to memory, we would address that problem. However, it would only make sense if the stock information isn't excessive; otherwise, we risk occupying a significant percentage of the service's memory.

By keeping the information in memory, the service doesn't need to request the information or persist it in a data store, making it easier to manage and contain costs. However, this is only relevant for small data sets; use cases with or more than hundreds of thousands of entities are better off by either persisting the information in a database or using another alternative. This alternative is also the most performant since all information is in memory; it is faster than fetching it from the database or doing a remote request.

5.6 Tackling Eventual Consistency with the End-to-End Argument: A Real-World Use Case

In this section, you will learn how to reduce the impact of smaller, eventually consistent parts of the system by guaranteeing the end-to-end flow's correctness. You will learn what the end-to-end argument is and how we can use it in an event-driven architecture. We will illustrate its application by using an example of an eCommerce platform.

Until now we discussed a retail eCommerce platform that sells products to a general audience. When buying a product on that platform, the user creates an order which is processed by the order management boundary. To complete the full order workflow, several other boundaries would have to handle the event and process accordingly to their own domain; for example, the order boundary would publish an event signaling an order was created that would be consumed by the pricing boundary to apply the relevant taxes on the order, then the inventory would update the stock information, and so on. The product boundary would aggregate all the product information and provide read models to search on several product properties. By accessing the UI application, the user would be able to request information from these read models. Figure 5-10 illustrates this example.

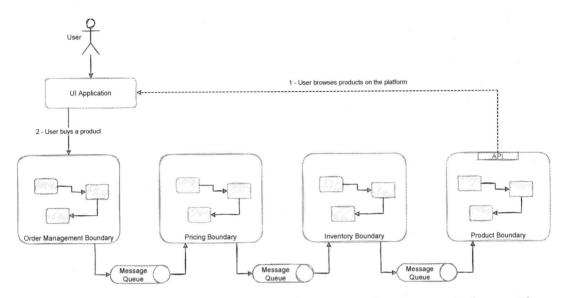

Figure 5-10. *User browses and buys a product on an eCommerce platform with several event-driven domain boundaries*

By reaping all the benefits event-driven provides, the product read models are eventually consistent. When the user browses the platform's product catalog, it might see inaccurate information due to the data's eventually consistent nature. The users might even try to buy products that don't have stock anymore because the upstream services are still processing them. We can take several approaches; an interesting approach in this situation is the end-to-end argument.

The end-to-end argument was first articulated in an exciting paper[12] by Saltzer, Reed, and Clark in the context of computer networking design. In it, they described how strong guarantees at low levels of the system might be hard to implement and have a negligible impact by providing them at that low level. The reliability guarantees could be implemented in the end-to-end flow rather than in smaller, low-level components. Doing so opens the opportunity for those smaller components to have more straightforward and more performant approaches by forfeiting those stronger guarantees.

In the paper, the authors describe the use case of a file transfer. There are several intermediate components between the transmitting and receiving computer to transfer one file between two computers. Each of those components can be the victim of several

---

[12] Full paper in J.H. Saltzer, D.P. Reed, and D.D. Clark, "End-to-end arguments in system design," May/June 1998, https://web.mit.edu/Saltzer/www/publications/endtoend/endtoend.pdf

types of faults like system crashes or network faults. One can argue that to achieve a careful file transfer, we need to guarantee each component's resilience and endow each component with retry strategies and duplicate copies to ensure it is fault-proof. However, providing those kinds of guarantees to each component will significantly harm those components' performance and complexity. Besides, guaranteeing the fault tolerance in one component doesn't ensure the end-to-end file transfer success. Thus, the implementation overhead of being exceptionally reliable in a single component does not reduce the end-to-end functionality burden to guarantee reliability.

To solve the issue for the use case in Figure 5-10, we could try to force the product boundary to be strongly consistent and provide consistent results. Every time any change occurred in the system, it would have to be reflected instantaneously on the product boundary. That strategy would also mean complex interactions and forfeiting decoupling between every other boundary and the product boundary. It would likely mean every other component of the workflow would have to guarantee consistency across boundaries, so each one provides consistent results all around. In a distributed system, this situation would mean sacrificing performance, availability, and the ability to scale seamlessly. It would also significantly increase the complexity of each component.

The end-to-end argument draws a compelling proposition that is applicable in a distributed microservice event-driven architecture. Instead of increasing each component's complexity substantially, we could loosen the constraints on intermediate components of the flow as long as we guarantee the end-to-end flow's consistency. In this concrete example, illustrated in Figure 5-11, we could maintain the decoupling between boundaries and keep the product boundary eventual consistent as long as at the moment of the purchase, the system would have a way to guarantee the information's consistency, for example, the product having stock.

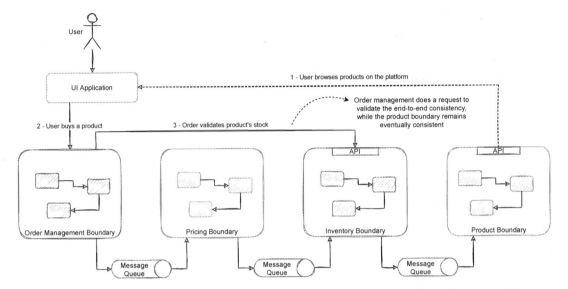

Figure 5-11. *End-to-end validation of the product's stock*

The order management system would validate the conditions of the order before advancing with the flow. This example is the typical situation where you are browsing items on a website and, although the UI displayed that item as having stock, the checkout might fail because the UI wasn't up to date anymore. This way, the component responsible for aggregating information from several different sources the UI needs (product information, stock, price, descriptions, etc.) can enjoy the decoupling and performance boost for not guaranteeing strong consistency, as long as there is an end-to-end process that ensures the business rule is satisfied.

5.7 For Most Use Cases, It's Not Eventual If Nobody Notices

In this section, we will put eventual consistency into perspective and understand how the business can coexist with it without considerable impact. We will discuss eventual consistency in NoSQL databases and detail how we can apply the same reasoning to event-driven systems.

As we discussed in Subsection 5.1, eventual consistency provides no safety guarantees. The very meaning of eventual is daunting; it states that sometime in the future the system will return a consistent result, but it doesn't say when. It is hard for a business to come to terms with such a vague notion of something so pivotal as consistency. It is also hard to manage the users' expectations; an ordinary user expects changes to be instantaneous. It doesn't expect them to take an indefinite amount of time to be reflected throughout the system, and surely explaining the CAP theorem to them isn't the solution. Considering this, it might sound odd how NoSQL databases adopted eventual consistency and why it is widely deployed to production.

In NoSQL databases, it is observed that in practice, with real-world use cases, eventual consistency looks like strong consistency. Some studies show that the inconsistency window in eventually consistent databases is small and can often be neglected. For example, one study[13] found that about 98% of requests have an inconsistency window between zero and one millisecond when within a single availability zone for Cassandra. For MongoDB, the same study shows an inconsistency window of 5ms or less in 96% of requests. Another study[14] showed that out of the curve requests, Cassandra's inconsistency window was almost always less than 200ms.

As we discussed in Subsection 5.1, it is fairly debatable if we should settle for eventual consistency in databases. But the fact they are widely adopted, and we can see eventual consistency as good enough for many use cases, raises the question of why. It is because, in practice, the inconsistency windows in these use cases are small. So small most often are deemed insignificant.

Eventual consistency is a consequence of event-driven systems. The best way to deal with it is by designing the system to be fast and guaranteeing the inconsistency windows are small. As proven by eventually consistent databases, if eventual consistency is fast enough, it appears strongly consistent, having a neglectable impact. Eventual consistency doesn't need to be slow; if it is fast enough to appear strongly consistent, as far as users and developers are concerned, it isn't eventually consistent.

What does it mean to be fast on an event-driven microservice? We need to build two fundamental characteristics from the ground up: the ability to scale and meaningful metrics. As discussed in Chapter 1, we design microservices to be autonomously developed and individually deployed. Also, they should be horizontally scalable. By providing these characteristics on an event-driven microservice, we can scale it on demand to face unforeseen peaks in load. We need meaningful metrics to react to

---

[13] Full paper in David Bermbach, Liang Zhao, and Sherif Sakr, "Towards Comprehensive Measurement of Consistency Guarantees for Cloud-Hosted Data Storage Services," August 2013, www.researchgate.net/figure/Distribution-of-Inconsistency-Windows-in-MongoDB_fig5_259540354

[14] Full paper in "Toward a Principled Framework for Benchmarking Consistency," October 2012, www.usenix.org/system/files/conference/hotdep12/hotdep12-final17.pdf

the system's delay and use them to deploy new instances. One important metric is the number of messages waiting to be processed; if it is large, likely the inconsistency window also is. The best way to guarantee this happens seamlessly is to have an autoscale system in place and use it to react to unforeseen load peaks. When a metric, for example, the consumer lag, is above a given threshold, new instances will be deployed. We will work through a practical example in Subsection 5.7.1.

If we guarantee the size of inconsistency windows isn't a concern; we can reduce the impact of eventual consistency with the best approach possible, by living with it.

5.7.1 Event-Driven Autoscaling Use Case with Prometheus and Kafka

In the last section, we discussed the importance of having a small inconsistency window to reduce the impact of eventual consistency. We also discussed how an autoscale system could help achieve this. In this section, we will explain how we could implement an autoscale system using Prometheus, Kubernetes, and Kafka.

In the example in Figure 5-5, the subscription service uses stock events to understand if the product has only one stock unit left in order to alert users. If the team managing the product's stock does a massive stock import, it is very likely that the subscription service lags behind the unexpected load of messages. If we have a system in place to monitor the subscription service consumer lag (e.g., Prometheus and Kafka Exporter), we could react to the delay by deploying new service instances. We can make the detection and deployment of new instances automatic (e.g., Kubernetes and HPA). In Figure 5-12, we illustrate this example.

Relevant technologies mentioned in Figure 5-12:

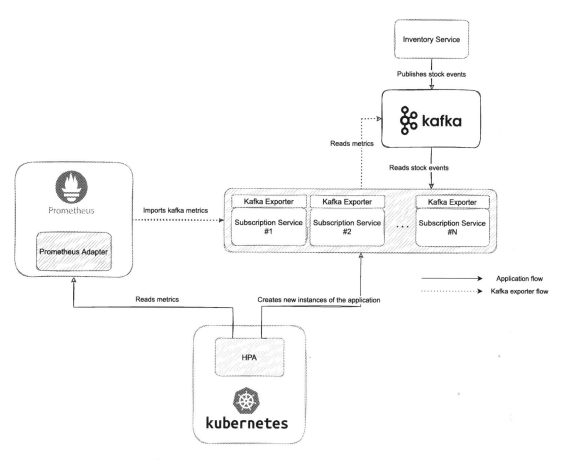

Figure 5-12. *Autoscaling subscription service example with Kubernetes, Prometheus, and Kafka*

- Kubernetes: A platform for managing containerized services. This example will use it to read the relevant metrics for scaling and horizontally scale the application with new instances.

  - HPA (horizontal pod autoscaler): Used by Kubernetes; automatically scales the number of instances of the application.

- Prometheus: Systems monitoring and alerting toolkit. This example will use it to import Kafka's metrics and make them available to HPA.

- Kafka: An event streaming platform; can be used to publish and subscribe to streams of events. We will use it as the event broker where the service reads and publishes messages.

- Kafka Exporter: Application to extract metrics from Kafka (e.g., topics and consumer lag) and expose them.

In the example, Kafka Exporter reads metrics from Kafka and exposes them to Prometheus. The most relevant metric in this example is the consumer lag; we want to deploy additional instances of the subscription service when the lag goes above a given threshold. Prometheus creates custom metrics for Kubernetes; we used Prometheus in this case because it is a powerful monitoring tool that can be combined with several other metric capabilities and exposes simple functionality to configure custom metrics. HPA will use the custom metrics exposed by Prometheus to add additional instances of subscription service when needed.

Subscription service lag will increase when inventory service publishes an unforeseen load of messages. When the lag reaches the specified threshold, the HPA will deploy additional subscription service instances to consume the lag faster. When below the threshold, it will remove the additional instances. Since there isn't a throughput higher than expected and we dealt with the load peak, there is no need to oversize the service. So the HPA will automatically deallocate the resources, guaranteeing the additional cost for the other resources occurs only on the peak. This use case is one example of how we can use autoscaling to maintain the system fast and guarantee that the services don't lag behind the changes the users do on the system.

5.8 Discussing the Tradeoffs of Typical Eventual Consistency Handling Strategies

In this section, we will discuss the tradeoffs of each solution we discussed until now and quickly sum up their advantages and limitations. This quick sum up will make it easier for you to weigh the tradeoffs when applying to a given use case.

In this chapter, we discussed several patterns of dealing with eventual consistency in several different use cases. Each of them has advantages and limitations, summed up in Table 5-1. The use cases you will find in real life sometimes will be easy to understand which one is the most adequate for that situation; some use cases won't be so easy. Most of the time, several solutions can be applied to a use case making it hard to know which one to apply. Most of the time, there isn't a perfect fit; it is about weighing the tradeoffs and making the best decision with the information we have.

Table 5-1. *Tradeoffs of the different patterns*

Pattern	Advantages	Limitations
Denormalized event schema	Straightforward to implement Higher decoupling Better performance due to the removal of the external request Scaling is more linear due to the removal of a dependency	Larger events have a performance hit on the broker and producing and consuming messages (although much lesser than the external request) The information has to be available on the upstream service; otherwise, it will significantly increase the complexity Events might lose their meaning if they become too generic
Saving state	Future use cases might benefit from the local data Higher decoupling Better performance due to the external request removal Scaling is more linear due to the dependency removal More resiliency due to the dependency removal	Increase in storage cost Development and maintenance overhead Applied throughout the architecture, data will be copied several times; substantial changes to the source system schema might impact several services
Applying domain boundaries	None or little developments needed, just a clear strategy Often comes for free if boundaries was a concern since the beginning	Overall time to process the flow will increase Without boundaries and a clear strategy to manage the flow, it will soon become complex and hard to track
Event versioning	Straightforward to implement Useful when in need of an easy fast solution to an incident or urgent requirement	Doesn't solve the eventual consistency; it's just a band-aid Without compensation actions might fail with load peaks With compensation actions substantially increases the application complexity Impacts performance

(*continued*)

Table 5-1. (*continued*)

Pattern	Advantages	Limitations
End-to-end argument	Easy to implement Gives the tools for intermediate components of the flow to be flexible about their consistency guarantees Better performance on the overall flow	It is often needed a synchronous way to validate the business rule

5.9 Summary

- Eventual consistency can impact the business, and we need to weigh the tradeoffs between using an event-driven or a synchronous approach.

- The tradeoffs between availability and consistency illustrated by the CAP theorem are significant when designing event-driven solutions, although the CAP theorem itself has limits.

- We can adapt the schema of events to avoid synchronous calls to eventually consistent read models, thus avoiding processing stale data.

- We can organize and structure our services so that downstream services don't need to deal with eventual consistency, having in mind the flow of the business process.

- Event version and entity versioning are essential to understand if the service is processing stale data. Retries can be an alternative to deal with delays, although we often need a more sustainable approach.

- Saving a view of the external information can avoid the need to request synchronous information from eventual consistent read models. We can further optimize this by keeping the information in memory for small data sets.

- With the end-to-end argument, instead of increasing each component's complexity substantially, we could loosen the constraints on intermediate components of the flow as long as we guarantee the end-to-end flow's consistency.

- Eventual consistency doesn't need to be slow; if it is fast enough to appear strongly consistent, as far as users and developers are concerned, it isn't eventually consistent.

CHAPTER 6

Dealing with Concurrency and Out-of-Order Messages

This chapter covers:

- Why tackling concurrency in a monolithic application is different than tackling it in a distributed microservice architecture

- The impacts of concurrency in distributed event-driven services

- The differences between pessimistic and optimistic concurrency and when to use each

- How to apply pessimistic and optimistic concurrency strategies

- Using event versioning to handle out-of-order messages

- Applying end-to-end partitioning to avoid concurrency and out-of-order messages

- How to avoid hotspotting as a consequence of routing events

In Greek mythology, when Zeus sent Pandora to earth to be married, he wanted to punish the human race for accepting fire from Prometheus. Pandora, oblivious of his real intent, gratefully accepted his wedding gift, a mysterious jar that Zeus warned never to open. Pandora, who was created to be curious, couldn't resist the desire to open the jar. When she finally did open it, all the world's greatest evils and life's most devious afflictions flew from that jar and cursed the world: envy, pain, hatred, war, event consumption concurrency, and unordered messages. However, Pandora was able to close the jar before the last thing flew out, the thing that killed message partitioning.

© Hugo Filipe Oliveira Rocha 2022
H. F. Oliveira Rocha, *Practical Event-Driven Microservices Architecture*,
https://doi.org/10.1007/978-1-4842-7468-2_6

Mythology apart, concurrency is often a dreaded topic, an obscure concern banished to a scarce number of use cases and to those unlucky enough to need to face it. Reasoning with code that runs in parallel is challenging and often requires a trained mind. Concurrency issues can occur when two threads or services use the same resource or change the same state simultaneously (typically referred to as race conditions). Race conditions are often hard to understand, replicate, and tackle consistently.

Usually, race conditions are very challenging to pin down due to happening very sparingly. I'm sure you came across the argument "well, this will probably never happen" a time or another. There are probably race conditions on the software used today due to never being detected or the user just ignoring it and restarting the app or refreshing the page. However, when you move to a high-throughput, high-availability ecosystem with hundreds of changes per minute, that "probably never" becomes "almost certain." For example, I had a team struggling with a bug that occurred once every one million calls; the service consumed approximately one hundred messages per second, which means it happened on average nine times per day. Now I can't even tell you how hard it was to reproduce locally. If I had to design an experience to prove Murphy's law, event-driven systems would likely be a viable candidate. The "everything that can go wrong will go wrong" plays an essential role in these situations. Event-driven services usually handle enormous loads turning near impossible chances into very likely, which many of the issues are related to parallel message processing. These issues must be dealt with upfront and must be tackled in the solution design with deliberate strategies. This chapter works through those strategies and explains how you can apply them to event-driven services.

We often use and work with sequential programs and applications without the need to worry about concurrency. In truth, without the performance requirements and relevant scale, concurrency is mostly unnecessary. Concurrency is performance; we use concurrent execution to increase throughput or reduce execution times, often to use all available physical resources and turn the system as fast as it can be. Performance often only becomes a concern with the relevant scale. Some applications might avoid concurrency issues; however, in event-driven architectures, they are an omnipresent concern.

Performance aside, concurrency can also become a concern with parallel requests to the same resource, for example, two users buying the same product at the same time. Monolithic applications traditionally tackle this issue with the traditional ways to deal with concurrency, like locking resources. We also often deal with this at the database level, for example, with transactions.

Messages are consumed in parallel and, most likely, by several instances of the same service. Each service needs to maintain a valid state while processing multiple events that access the same resources simultaneously. Processing multiple messages that access the same entities across different instances raises a different problem than we usually face in monolithic applications.

Concurrency is often a primary concern in event-driven services due to the scale and the performance requirements. The way we handle concurrency needs to have the lowest performance impact it possibly can. Event-driven services are also horizontally scalable; the services that can extensively use the available physical resources and provide satisfying performance have better scaling properties. Having both acceptable performance and linear scaling is essential in managing eventual consistency and increasing demand.

As we discussed at the beginning of this chapter, Pandora closed the box right before the last thing came out. In the original mythology, it was the thing that killed hope. We distorted the story and said the last thing to fly from the box was the thing that killed message partitioning, which, as you will see in Section 6.6, is the equivalent of hope in event-driven architectures.

6.1 Why Is Concurrency Different in a Monolith from an Event-Driven Architecture?

There are many ways to deal with concurrency in traditional single-process applications. However, it's a substantially different challenge dealing with concurrency in a distributed architecture. It is essential to understand this difference when dealing with event-driven services; not being aware of the parallel event processing consequences can trigger some difficult corner cases and intricate bugs. This section will detail the differences between managing concurrency in a single-process application, like a monolith, and managing it in an event-driven service.

As discussed in Chapter 1, monoliths are single-process applications where all applications' functionality is deployed together. Often, all the application requests go through the same single application. In this type of application, we can use the standard strategies to deal with concurrency. Let's illustrate this with an example.

Let's say we are buying a product on an eCommerce platform. When we submit a new order, the application has to save the order information and check the available stock for the item we just requested. The product can have stock in several different warehouses. For example, if we were buying a shirt with size M, we could have a US warehouse with one stock unit, another one in the UK with one stock unit, and another one in Japan with five stock units. To minimize the order's shipping costs, the application would have to retrieve the available stock from every warehouse and apply a routing algorithm to understand which warehouse to retrieve the stock. Once it figured out which warehouse to use, it would decrease the stock and ship the order. Figure 6-1 illustrates this example.

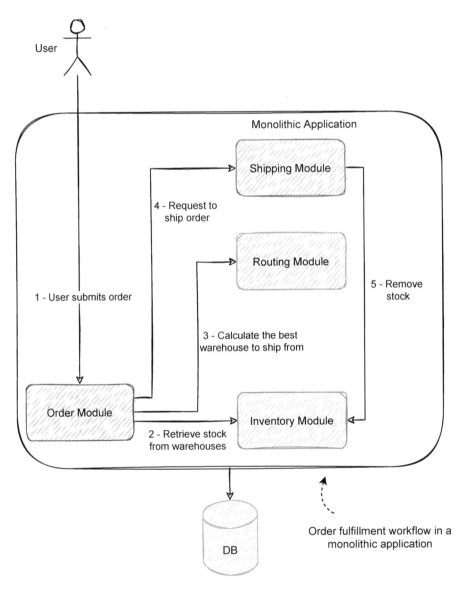

Figure 6-1. *Example of an order fulfillment flow in a monolith*

The order fulfillment process follows the flow we just discussed:

1. The user submits an order which the order module receives.

2. The order module requests the stock information from every warehouse from the inventory module and validates if there is enough stock to fulfill the order.

3. The order module requests the routing module to calculate the best warehouse for that customer's address and the available warehouses.

4. When the routing module calculates the best warehouse, the order module requests the shipping module to ship the order.

5. The shipping module (could also be the order module if we were following the orchestrator pattern) requests the stock changes to the inventory module and ships the order.

Hopefully, our eCommerce platform doesn't have one user at a time using it; that would mean it had only minimal success, although it would make things a lot easier. A random number of users would be browsing and submitting their own orders. Let's say another user submitted an order for the same item we were buying simultaneously. The application would receive and process both orders in parallel. Unfortunately, both orders are from the United States, and the product we are buying has only one stock unit left in the closest warehouse. With the preceding process in place, the system would fulfill which order?

If we are unlucky enough, and we are always unlucky enough in production, it could be both orders. Imagine if two orders go through the workflow in parallel, the order module would retrieve the stock and request the routing module to calculate the best warehouse to retrieve the stock. Let's say there is one stock unit available in the US warehouse and one stock available in the UK warehouse. If the users placed both orders in the United States, the routing module would likely answer that the best warehouse for both orders was the warehouse in the United States. When advancing, both orders would retrieve stock from the same warehouse. Since only one stock unit is available, one order would either advance for an unexisting stock unit or would fail, depending on the implementation. Despite the fact, there might still be stock available to fulfill that order in other warehouses.

In a single-process application, it is easier to manage this issue, and there are several strategies we can use. We can use a pessimistic approach and lock the order processing for each product (or product size, depending if the products vary by size). If we receive a second order for a product we are already processing, it will have to wait for the processing of the first order to finish. An important detail is to lock per product; we can still process different products in parallel; we just avoid processing the same product simultaneously. This detail ensures the application retains some of the performance and isn't severely impacted.

Alternatively, we could use an optimistic approach and assume there is no concurrency. The workflow would normally run without any lock or validation. In the last step, the shipping module could detect if no stock was available and request the routing algorithm to run again with the latest stock, retriggering the process.

We could also partition our requests so that the application never processes orders for the same product simultaneously. This way, it is possible to build highly concurrent, highly scalable systems without the need for locks or retries; we solve concurrency by architecture rather than implementation. We won't go into much detail on how to achieve this now, but we will work through a practical example at the end of the chapter and detail this concept.

How is concurrency different in event-driven services? In fact, some of these strategies are still applicable in event-driven services, at least in some use cases. Others can't be applied due to the distributed and horizontally scalable nature of the services. Let's work through an example to illustrate this. Figure 6-2 shows the order created event consumption workflow in the inventory service.

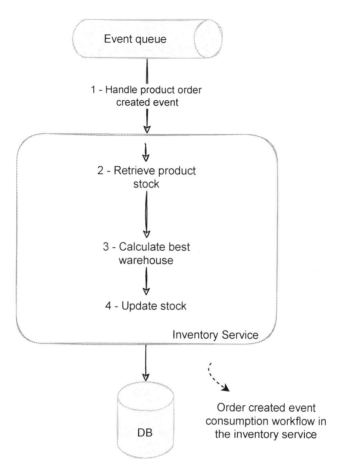

Figure 6-2. *Consumption of the order created event for a given product inside the inventory service*

The inventory service needs to change the stock for each order submitted to the system. To do that, it handles order created events from an event queue. For each event, the service has to retrieve the current product's available stock from all warehouses, calculate the best warehouse to satisfy the order, and update the product's stock in that warehouse.

In this example, we can have a concurrency issue the same way we did in the last example with the monolithic application. For example, if we receive two events for orders created for the same product simultaneously, the service will fetch the product's stock for both orders and calculate the best warehouse. If the warehouse is the same, the service will try to retrieve stock from the same warehouse simultaneously, potentially originating a concurrency issue if there isn't enough stock.

For some services, it might be sufficient to work in a single thread and completely avoid concurrency issues; however, this isn't the most frequent use case. As we discussed at the beginning of the chapter, we design event-driven services to be horizontally scalable and respond promptly to varying load or usage needs. We often adopt event-driven architectures to have systems that have these characteristics. The need to scale and deal with increasing amounts of requests usually means we need performant services. Single-threaded services won't likely cut it; as we discussed, concurrency is performance.

We can horizontally scale single-threaded services, but we would likely need a much higher number of services than we would need when using concurrency and parallelism. Even when hosted in cloud providers, single-threaded services won't probably use all the available physical resources. Depending on what the services do, they often only use a modest percentage of the CPU and memory, even on lower-tier machines. As you might guess, this isn't cost-effective, and we aren't making the best usage of the resources we have available. Also, by being single-threaded, we can't tune the service to make the most of the available resources. When using parallelism, we can adjust the number of services, and the degree of parallelism in each service to optimize the minimum number of machines (or containers) needed with the max usage of physical resources, optimizing the cost and performance metrics accordingly.

The example pictured in Figure 6-2, and the concurrency issue it can produce, has the same nature as the one we discussed when using a single-process application, illustrated in Figure 6-1. In what way an event-driven service is different from the situation we discussed before? Having multiple instances of the same service can add an additional layer of complexity when tackling concurrency. Figure 6-3 illustrates this situation.

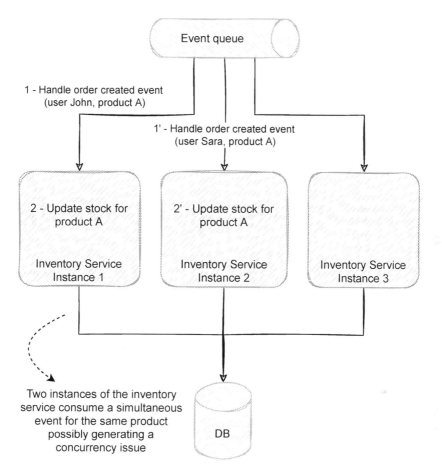

Figure 6-3. *Multiple instances of the inventory service consuming events in parallel*

Figure 6-3 illustrates three instances of the inventory service. All three instances process events independently from each other. They can also be processing multiple events in parallel inside each instance, so we have two parallelism degrees, inside each instance and between instances. In this example, the service receives two order created events simultaneously for the same product (product A), one for user John and one for user Sara.

Inside a service's instance, we can use the same strategies we would use in a single-process application like a monolith. But they don't guarantee we won't have concurrency because other instances might be simultaneously processing concurrent changes. For example, if we locked product A in instance 1, the lock would only work on that instance; instance 2 would have no knowledge of it due to being a separate independent process.

To an inexperienced developer, this kind of concurrency problem might seem far-fetched and unlikely. To be fair, some of these problems have a minimal chance of happening. How likely is it to have two different users buying the same variant of a product with the limited stock at the exact same time? Often it comes down to windows of a few milliseconds. Is it worth it to solve a problem with such low chances of happening, even if it happens occasionally? There are solutions to problems that are more costly than living with the bug happening once or twice per year.

In the end, it's all about scale. We discussed in Chapter 1 how event-driven architectures could be the answer for challenging scalability problems and might be best applied when an existing application struggles with a given scale. When we are consuming dozens, hundreds, or thousands of events per second, it's not about how it likely won't happen. It will, several times per hour or minute.

It's not just about saying our solution is performant and horizontally scalable, it's also about saying that it is consistent and trustworthy at scale. No matter how much scale the business will need in the future, this kind of issue won't happen no matter how much load you throw at it. We can't take concurrency lightly, and we need deliberate and sustainable strategies to tackle it from the ground up.

6.2 Pessimistic vs. Optimistic Concurrency, When and When Not to Use

Traditionally, there are two types of strategies to deal with concurrency, pessimistic and optimistic. In fact, I propose a third, which is avoiding concurrency altogether, handling concurrency by design as opposed to handling concurrency by implementation. This section will detail what differentiates pessimistic and optimistic concurrency, when to use each, and how the architecture and data model design can avoid concurrency altogether.

Pessimistic and optimistic concurrency is the difference between apologizing and asking permission.[1] Pessimistic strategies request access to the resource and will only act based on the response, while optimistic strategies assume they have access to the resource, and when they don't, they apologize by acting accordingly.

---

[1] Full article exploring this concept in Maurice Herlihy, "Apologizing Versus Asking Permission: Optimistic Concurrency Control for Abstract Data Types," March 1990, `www.researchgate.net/publication/234778080_Apologizing_Versus_Asking_Permission_Optimistic_Concurrency_Control_for_Abstract_Data_Types`

Let's illustrate this with the example we discussed in the last section. In Figure 6-2, we discussed how the inventory service had to fetch the stock, calculate the best warehouse, and update the stock for that warehouse. We could take a pessimistic approach by locking the product's stock quantity during the operation. Or we could assume there is no concurrency, calculate the best warehouse, and try to update the stock. If the stock changed in the meantime, we could fail or retry the operation.

Pessimistic concurrency strategies lock the resource upfront. The services request access to the resource; if it is available, the application locks it, and it becomes unavailable for every other access that might happen until the application frees the resource. Suppose the resource is unavailable (another consumer or thread already has a lock on it). In that case, the access will fail, and the application will either wait to release the lock or fail the operation.

Optimistic concurrency strategies assume there is no concurrency and act when concurrency occurs. Typically, there is no locking involved; the flow of the application runs without synchronization. When the application is about to persist the changes, it validates if anything has changed since the start of the operation. If it did, the application aborts or retries the operation.

6.2.1 Pessimistic vs. Optimistic Approaches

A pessimistic approach is the easiest to reason with since once the application acquires the lock, we can reason with the program's flow in a single-threaded mindset. This attribute dramatically eases the way we understand and develop the service's logic. However, it might have a considerable impact on performance. Since we are locking a resource and preventing other requests from accessing it, the higher the number of requests for the same resource, the higher the time it will take the application to respond.

An optimistic approach typically doesn't involve any kind of locking and doesn't block the application. The lack of locks, under certain circumstances, can lead to much higher performance; under the right conditions (we will detail them next), it will behave as no concurrency prevention strategy is in place. However, every time a write collision is detected, it has to retry the operation, which can be costly. Also, reasoning with concurrent code while developing the service's logic is more complex and can easily introduce bugs without a constant concern on concurrency issues. Retries must also be idempotent, a common concern in event-driven services, which we will detail in Chapter 7.

Retrying the operation is often more expensive than acquiring and maintaining a lock. For example, in the situation we discussed earlier, using a pessimistic approach and locking the inventory service's execution will affect performance. But retrying the operation when the service detects conflicts implies the service has to fetch the stock, calculate the best warehouse, and try to save the information again. If this happens frequently enough, it will likely be slower than restricting the resource's access through locking. Imagine if we have ten concurrent users trying to buy the same product, in an optimistic approach, one of the ten would succeed, but the other nine would fail and would have to retry. On the next retry, some would likely fail and would have to retry again. In these situations, it would be best to lock the resource upfront and mediate the access.

Optimistic strategies are only cost-effective if the chances of the operation succeeding are sufficiently high. A good rule to follow is to use a pessimistic approach when there is a high chance of conflicting requests and use an optimistic approach when the chances are low. If it is very likely that a request conflicts, we restrict access to the resource, which guarantees orderly access and prevents consecutive retries. In use cases where it is still possible but unlikely for the requests to conflict, we can use an optimistic approach and enjoy the same performance as if we have no mechanism to prevent concurrency to begin with, unless for the unlikely requests that cause concurrency. Using a pessimistic approach in an environment with low chances of concurrency may severely impact the performance for a small percentage of occurrences; thus, the cost-benefit ratio is smaller.

6.2.2 Solving Concurrency by Implementation and by Design

For example, suppose our eCommerce platform has a small quantity of highly sought-after products with thousands of active users, and the chances of several users ordering the same product simultaneously are high. In that case, we might benefit more from using a pessimistic approach. On the other hand, suppose products are expected to be on sale for a more extended period, like a real estate selling platform, where houses are on sale for considerable periods with a handful of users actually requesting to buy the house. In that case, an optimistic approach might be best.

As with most solutions, it isn't a black and white kind of choice. We can use both approaches or combine them as we see fit. There might be use cases in the architecture, or even in a specific service, that benefit from applying a pessimistic approach in one place and an optimistic one in another.

Often, the hard part is not about deciding which kind of approach is more beneficial but rather how long it stands to the varying needs through time. Different systems and applications exhibit different patterns of usage. The likelihood of concurrency and the conflict patterns often change over time; a highly concurrent use case might be so during a limited window of time. For example, our real estate platform might have low concurrency patterns, unless for sporadic, once-in-a-lifetime deal houses that have a vast demand and attract hundreds of users at the same time. It's complex to have a strategy that varies not by use case but by specific timespans.

To deal with these cases, concurrency is best solved by design rather than implementation. In the specific case of event-driven services, routing messages and using end-to-end partitioning is the best approach as it avoids concurrency as a whole in a performant and transparent way. However, as we discussed before, event-driven architectures often aren't composed of only event-driven services. Sometimes, in the real world, we need to combine both asynchronous and synchronous functionalities. In those use cases, we might need to use the traditional optimistic or pessimistic strategies, but they are the exception rather than the rule.

Solving concurrency by design isn't always possible or practical. As we will detail in Section 6.6, it also has several limitations that might not apply to every use case. Handling concurrency by design relies on being able to design the system in a way concurrency is impossible. In event-driven architectures, it is often based on event routing. Routing events isn't always possible in various use cases, for example, when we don't have a suitable routing key or integrate from external systems. In those situations, solving concurrency by implementation is preferable. Concurrency by implementation is also simpler to reason with since it's similar to the traditional concurrency handling approaches. In the following sections, we will approach by implementation strategies first since they will exercise your thought process toward concurrency issues, are easier to grasp, and are valuable tools for you to have in your toolbox when by architecture strategies are impractical.

Data modeling also plays a part in concurrency; the way we model the data can impact the performance and how we deal with concurrency. In Chapter 3, we discussed aggregates' size and how changes to the same aggregate shouldn't be done in parallel when we detailed DDD. The aggregate size also impacts how concurrent a system is, thus affecting the system's performance. For example, let's say our platform sells clothes, and we can choose to design the aggregate to reflect either a product or a product's size (like an XS). If we choose the product granularity, we can process different products simultaneously, and if we choose the size granularity, we can process different sizes, even from the same product, simultaneously. The smaller aggregate size has higher throughput but also has all the implications in the consumers that we discussed in Chapter 5 and will further detail in Chapter 8.

Finally, the strategies to handle concurrency we discuss in this chapter are in the scope of several distributed instances of the same service (e.g., several inventory service instances). You might ask how to solve concurrency across different services (e.g., between the order and inventory service). These strategies (except end-to-end partitioning, as you will see) aren't effective across different services. Although we can use them, one service shouldn't lock another; they are self-sufficient and should be able to scale independently. To manage concurrency across different services, we should use a higher-level approach, like a Saga, as discussed in Chapter 4.

6.3 Using Optimistic Concurrency

Section 6.2 discussed how optimistic and pessimistic concurrency prevention strategies work and when to apply them. But how do we use them in practice? In this section, you will learn how to apply optimistic concurrency as we work through a practical example.

Let's look at the same example we discussed in Section 6.2 involving the inventory service. When processing an order created event, the service has to retrieve the product stock, calculate the best warehouse, and remove the stock for that product in the corresponding warehouse. Figure 6-4 illustrates this process when the service processes two order events for the same product.

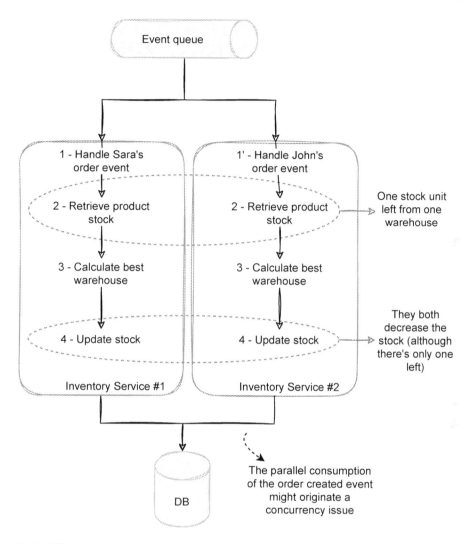

Figure 6-4. *The inventory service consuming two order created events, from two different users, for the same product*

Two instances of the service process simultaneously one order created event each: one from Sara and one from John. Both ordered the same product, which has only one stock unit left in one warehouse. If the fourth step that updates the stock only decreases the quantity, the product will end up with negative stock. An immediate solution could be to add an additional step before updating the stock to check whether there was still enough stock to perform the operation. Nonetheless, we would only decrease the chances of having concurrency issues and wouldn't remove it entirely. As we discussed, even if the chances are small, the scale and number of events the service processes will make an unlikely incident certain. Even if we currently have low scale, we leave the chances for it to happen in the future when the scale and throughput increase.

How could we solve it using an optimistic approach? As we discussed in Section 6.2, optimistic prevention strategies assume there is no concurrency and act when concurrency is detected. In this case, when the service is updating the stock, it would only apply the change if the stock for that product wasn't changed since we fetched it in step 2. If it was, the service wouldn't decrease the stock and would, for example, retry the operation.

Let's work through this solution if the service was using SQL Server, for example. The inventory database would save the stock information in a table containing information about the product, warehouse, and stock quantity. Listing 6-1 illustrates an example schema of this table.

Listing 6-1. Stock table schema and possible updates

```
1    -- Create table stock
2    CREATE TABLE Stock #A
3    (
4        ProductId int,
5        WarehouseId int,
6        Quantity int,
7        LatestChangeTimestamp bigint, #B
8        primary key (ProductId, WarehouseId)
9    )
10
11   UPDATE Stock SET Quantity = Quantity - ? WHERE ProductId = ? AND
     WarehouseId = ? #C
12   UPDATE Stock SET Quantity = ? WHERE ProductId = ? AND WarehouseId = ? #D
```
#A Stock table definition
#B Unix timestamp column
#C Update stock by decreasing the current quantity from the ordered amount
#D Update stock by setting the quantity to the calculated value by the service

After fetching the stock and calculating the warehouse, the inventory service would update the quantity column in this table. It could do it in two ways, by choosing one of the two updates in Listing 6-1. If the service updated the stock using the first, the stock quantity could turn negative (1-1 and then 0-1). If it used the last, both operations would succeed by setting the stock to zero, although there was only one quantity available.

With an optimistic approach, we need to know if the data changed when doing the second update. We could do that using the LatestChangeTimestamp column. Every time the stock quantity changes, that column is also updated with the timestamp of the change. In step 2 of Figure 6-4, the service fetches the current stock along with the timestamp of the last update. In step 4, the service only changes the stock if the timestamp is still the same. It could use an update operation similar to the one illustrated in Listing 6-2.

Listing 6-2. Optimistic update operation

```
1    UPDATE Stock SET Quantity = ?

3    WHERE ProductId = ?
4    AND WarehouseId = ?
5    AND LatestChangeTimestamp = ? #A
#A Version clause
```

With the condition using the LatestChangeTimestamp, the update will only apply if the timestamp is still the same; otherwise, it won't find and consequently won't affect any row. We used the timestamp, but it could be an incremental version or another field that made sense. The Unix timestamp is a straightforward property to use as a version since we easily generate it from a timestamp; it's an integer and always increases. After the operation, if no rows were affected, then the record was the target of concurrency, and we could retry the operation. In this case, the last order wouldn't be fulfilled due to lack of stock.

Optimistic approaches like we detailed here are very simple and straightforward to use. They don't rely on a specific technology or external dependency. If we understand the mechanism, we can apply it regardless of the technology. When concurrency is an issue, this can be a simple and performant solution.

In this example, we used SQL Server, but it can be applied in most database technologies. In fact, this strategy is used under the hood by many technologies. For example, ElasticSearch has a way to manage concurrency using a sequence number[2] (the same version or timestamp we discussed) to address concurrency in a very similar way we detailed here. Cassandra has the concept of lightweight transactions[3] that is very similar to the mechanism we just discussed. The concept of optimistic locking[4] is also discussed in the context of Cassandra, which uses the same similar approach. NEventStore,[5] a popular event sourcing framework, which can be used with the persistence engine for MongoDB, uses the same concept to manage concurrent changes to the same aggregate. EntityFramework also has an optimistic concurrency management approach[6] similar to what we discussed.

This approach's simplicity and flexibility makes it a viable solution to have in our toolbox and apply it where we see fit. As we discussed in Section 6.2, optimistic concurrency shines in environments with low chances of concurrency. Environments with operations that are likely to conflict and how they benefit from pessimistic approaches are detailed next.

6.4 Using Pessimistic Concurrency

Pessimistic concurrency prevention strategies are usually the standard way to deal with concurrency. They are easier to reason with since they guarantee no other operation happens simultaneously. This section will discuss how to use a pessimistic approach to handle concurrency. We will work through a practical example similar to the one we discussed when detailing optimistic concurrency in Section 6.3.

---

[2] Full technical reference in Elastic.co, "Optimistic concurrency control," www.elastic.co/guide/
en/elasticsearch/reference/current/optimistic-concurrency-control.html

[3] Full technical reference in Datastax.com, "Using lightweight transactions,"
https://docs.datastax.com/en/cql-oss/3.3/cql/cql_using/useInsertLWT.html

[4] More details in Sandeep Yarabarla, "Learning Apache Cassandra - Second Edition,"
April 2017, https://learning.oreilly.com/library/view/learning-apache-
cassandra/9781787127296/5e5991cb-eb1e-4459-9114-1d86e974e927.xhtml

[5] GitHub project and details here: https://github.com/NEventStore/NEventStore

[6] Full technical reference in "Handling Concurrency Conflicts (EF6)," October 23,
https://docs.microsoft.com/en-us/ef/ef6/saving/concurrency

Let's use the same example illustrated in Figure 6-4. Two instances of the inventory service fetch, manipulate, and update the stock quantity for the same product. In a single-process application (e.g., if we had only one instance of the inventory service), the typical approach would be locking a resource while the service is processing that call. But since an in-memory lock would only work for the local instance, it isn't the right approach when we have two or more service instances.

6.4.1 Distributed Locks in Event-Driven Microservices

A similar approach we could use is a distributed lock. A distributed lock works the same way a local lock would (like a mutex) but relies on an external dependency to manage the lock across several instances. Figure 6-5 illustrates this approach in the same example we discussed before.

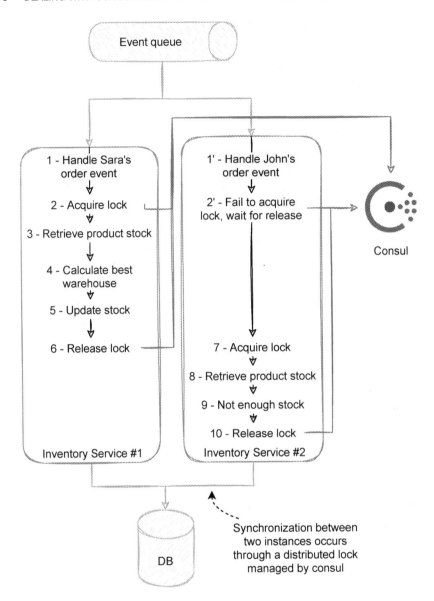

Figure 6-5. *A distributed lock applied to the same example with the inventory service*

The first instance handling Sara's event acquires the lock successfully. Then it proceeds to process the event by fetching the stock. The second instance receives John's order and tries to obtain the same lock. Since the first instance already acquired it, the service will block until it is released. Meanwhile, in the first instance, Sara's order is fully processed and removes the only stock unit left from the product. The first instance advances to the last step and releases the lock. By releasing the lock, the second instance starts to process John's order and fetches the stock. Since Sara's order already removed the stock, the second instance will reject the order.

Let's deep dive into how this situation could work in the code. Listing 6-3 illustrates how we could implement the lock logic in the inventory service.

Listing 6-3. Acquiring and releasing lock in inventory service

```
1    public async Task Consume(
2            CancellationToken cancellationToken,
3            OrderCreatedEvent orderCreatedEvent)
4        {
5            // Generate lock key based on product id
6            var lockKey = orderCreatedEvent.ProductId.ToString(); #A
7
8            // Create consult client and lock
10           var distributedLock = consulClient.CreateLock(lockKey);
11
12           try
13           {
14               // Acquire lock for that product
15               await distributedLock.Acquire(cancellationToken); #B
16
17               // Fetch product's stock
18               var stockList = await this.stockRepository
19                   .GetStockAsync(orderCreatedEvent.ProductId);
20
21               // Calculate best warehouse for that order
22               var bestWarehouseId = this.routingService
23                   .CalculateBestWarehouse(stockList, orderCreatedEvent.
                       OrderId);
24
25               // Change stock for that warehouse
26               await this.stockRepository
27                   .UpdateStockAsync(
28                       orderCreatedEvent.ProductId,
29                       bestWarehouseId,
```

```
30                        orderCreatedEvent.Quantity);
31              }
32              catch (Exception)
33              {
34                  // Any exception occurring during the execution of the
                        process
35                  // is handled here
36              }
37
38              // Release the lock
39              await distributedLock.Release(cancellationToken); #C
40          }
```

#A Generate lock key
#B Acquire lock based on the generated key
#C Release the lock once the operation finishes

The way we create and release the lock is very similar to how it would work in a local, in-memory lock using a mutex or a lock statement. Instead of managing the lock locally, the service relies on an external dependency to manage the synchronization, in this case, Consul. The statements using the distributedLock are requests to Consul. In the distributedLock.Acquire method, the instance requests to acquire the lock; if it succeeds, it will advance with the remaining operations. If the lock is already in use by another instance, it will block until it is freed. The instance releases the lock and makes it available for other instances once the service completes the event processing, with the distributedLock.Release method.

An important point is how we generate the lock key. In this example, the lock key is the product id, illustrated by the lockKey variable. Instead of generating a different one on each event, we could choose a static key, for example, "InventoryServiceKey." That would mean the service would try to lock the event consumption independent of the event's contents for every event. This way, the service would act as a single thread service, and the service's performance would deteriorate significantly. We also wouldn't gain much from blocking the consumption for every event since concurrency issues might occur for processing simultaneous changes for the same product, not across different products.

Using the lock key as the product id guarantees only one instance is processing one product simultaneously, but different products are processed concurrently. It is an important detail since it dramatically benefits the service's performance. This detail also relates to what we discussed in Chapters 3 and 4 about the aggregate size. If the aggregate scope is considerably large, it will negatively affect the service's performance since it limits the ability to have higher levels of concurrent changes.

We used Consul to manage the lock, but there are other options. ZooKeeper, a popular tool to provide distributed synchronization and configurations, is another viable option. Kafka in the past used ZooKeeper to manage information about the cluster, topics, and partitions across nodes. It also can provide fully distributed locks that are globally synchronous.[7] Redis can also be an option, and there are several implementations of distributed locks with Redis.[8] Martin Kleppmann also has an interesting article[9] about fencing locks approach with Redis, which is worth checking if you want more details about the implementation and its impacts.

You might recall when we discussed the Jepsen tests in the previous chapters and their usefulness in validating distributed systems' safety. In fact, the Jepsen tests found issues with Consul in the past,[10] for example, and although they are surpassed and Consul fully complies[11] with the Jepsen tests, they raise an interesting concern on how our distributed services might interact with an external lock management system. In fact, what would happen if the service crashes, is unavailable, or suffers a network partition? In that case, Consul would free the lock, but that instance of the service might still change information concurrently with other instances.

Kyle Kingsbury has a fascinating talk[12] about distributed databases that highlight many of these problems and the associated limitations of distributed locks. Distributed locks might be useful in some use cases and, as we discussed, can be a straightforward way to apply a pessimistic approach to concurrency. However, they also suffer from

---

[7] Referenced in ZooKeeper documentation in "ZooKeeper Recipes and Solutions," `https://zookeeper.apache.org/doc/r3.5.5/recipes.html#sc_recipes_Locks`

[8] Further details in Redis.io, "Distributed locks with Redis," `https://redis.io/topics/distlock`

[9] Full article in Martin Kleppmann, "How to do distributed locking," February 8, 2016, `https://martin.kleppmann.com/2016/02/08/how-to-do-distributed-locking.html`

[10] Further details in aphyr.com, "Jepsen: etcd and Consul," June 9, 2014, `https://aphyr.com/posts/316-jepsen-etcd-and-consul`

[11] Full analysis in consul.io, `www.consul.io/docs/architecture/jepsen`

[12] Full talk in Kyle Kingsbury, "GOTO 2018 Jepsen 9: A Fsyncing Feeling," May 8, 2018, `www.youtube.com/watch?v=tRcOO9VgzBO&t=1526s`

problematic limitations and can lead the service to process invalid states. Techniques to handle inconsistency and transient errors can help, like event idempotency and versioning, which will be detailed in Chapter 7. They also introduce an additional dependency of a third-party tool to manage locks. Distributed locks can be useful when used sparingly and in specific use cases where locking is a must. However, in most use cases, other alternatives are more straightforward and less impactful.

6.4.2 Database Transactions As a Concurrency Approach in Distributed Microservices

Perhaps the most common way and what first comes to mind as a solution to deal with concurrency issues is the use of transactions. In fact, they can be a very straightforward and performant way to solve some concurrency issues. When we horizontally scale a service and add more instances, they all share the same database. We can use it as a point of synchronization between all instances, and transactions are easy to reason with to most developers due to their widespread usage. We are excluding here the distributed transactions and the two-phase commit protocol we discussed in Chapter 4.

How could we solve the concurrency issues we detailed with the inventory service in Figure 6-5? We could open a transaction when fetching the stock, calculate the best warehouse, and commit the transaction when updating it. This way, the database guarantees no other instance changes the same information while the transaction is running. Often we hear the issues of transactions and the performance impacts they have; however, more often than not, it's more a theoretical concern than a practical one. Transactions are a very optimized tool that can achieve fantastic performance even in high-throughput systems. Relational databases are often associated with monolithic databases (as we discussed in Chapters 4 and 5), but they are as valid as any other database when applied in a specific service if that service benefits from using it.

Some databases also enable locking and unlocking the service based on a given resource specified by the application. One example of this is the sp_getapplock[13] from SQL Server, which can act as a distributed lock much like what we discussed with Consul. We observed some success with some use cases using this approach. Still, there are more sustainable and straightforward ways to deal with concurrency than using the database as a distributed lock.

Although useful and straightforward, transactions can be troublesome with long-running operations and severely affect the system's performance. The example we discussed was relatively simple, but imagine if calculating the best warehouse involved more complex operations or communication with external systems. The transaction might lock data for an unfeasible amount of time.

Also, the transaction management in this kind of system tends to leak toward the application or domain logic. In practice, how could we replace the lock for a transaction? One of the easiest ways is to wrap the operations in a TransactionScope (in C#). If we exchanged database technologies, would that code live unchanged as it was supposed to? Likely it wouldn't. To be fair, we don't change database technologies often, if ever. However, it hints at how easily the database's transactional logic spreads to the domain and application logic, which can make the code difficult to maintain.

Transactions are also limited to the technologies that support them. Many NoSQL databases don't support transactions. Overall, if we are using a database that uses transactions, it can be a simple way to deal with concurrency issues and a quick fix to some pressing issues. Still, as we saw when discussing distributed locks, a better solution is to avoid concurrency altogether, as we will also discuss at the end of the chapter.

6.5 Dealing with Out-of-Order Events

A related concept that can also derive from concurrency is out-of-order events. Until now, when we discussed the service consumption from an event stream, we always assumed the events in the stream were in order. However, this isn't always the case; services can consume unordered events due to several reasons. This section will discuss how events can become unordered and how we can deal with and mitigate their impacts.

---

[13] Further details in Microsoft documentation, March 14, 2017, `https://docs.` `microsoft.com/en-us/sql/relational-databases/system-stored-procedures/` `sp-getapplock-transact-sql?view=sql-server-ver15`

Why does event ordering matter? Let's illustrate with an example. Let's say we have a product service that has an aggregated view of the product's information and exposes that information to other services. It also handles stock events from the inventory service and saves the product and stock information locally in a denormalized read model. The inventory service publishes stock changed events every time a product's stock changes. For example, a given product has three stock units, and the users buy it two times. The inventory service will publish one stock changed event with remaining stock quantity two for the first purchase and a stock changed event with remaining stock quantity one for the second one. The product service handles those events and updates the product stock to quantity two and then to quantity one similar to what we discussed in Figure 6-5.

But what if the two events arrive in an incorrect order? If the earliest event (the stock changed to quantity two) arrives after the latest (the stock changed with quantity one), the product service will update the stock to quantity two, which doesn't reflect the product's real quantity.

6.5.1 How Can Events Lose Their Order?

Incorrect ordering can happen due to several reasons. Multiple publishers for the same queue can also have a desynchronized clock. Clock synchronization across machines is typically done with the NTP (network time protocol); the considerations about this protocol and how it achieves clock synchronization across machines are beyond the scope of this book; however, the median for most providers is in the millisecond range or under. For most use cases, this synchronization is enough and provides satisfactory results.

Besides clock synchronization issues, the event stream might not be in the correct order in the first place. Ordering issues can also be related to the message broker technology we are using. For example, individual consumers using RabbitMQ can observe out-of-order messages when multiple subscribers requeue messages.[14] Network partitions can also cause ordering issues depending on the broker's configurations.

Resilience strategies can also impact ordering. For example, depending on the way retries are implemented, the order can be lost when retrying a message. We often discussed the ability to replay an event stream to rebuild a view of the data. In a way, expected or not, it jeopardizes message ordering since we will start to consume older messages.

---

[14] Further details in RabbitMQ documentation, "Broker Semantics," `www.rabbitmq.com/semantics.html`

Concurrency can, and often will, play a factor in ordering events. Even if events are published and stored in order in the event stream, two instances of the same service (or even two threads of the same service) concurrently consuming the messages can unorder them due to different processing rates. Figure 6-6 illustrates this example.

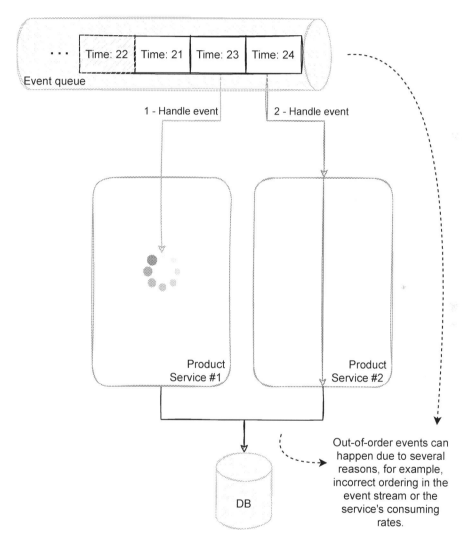

Figure 6-6. *Two instances of the same service consuming from a queue with out-of-order events and different consumption rates*

Two events might have different operations depending on the event's processing logic. Even if the two events have the exact same operations, the associated data will likely be different, which implies different times in fetching and handling that data. Two instances, or even two threads, will execute the same operations at slightly different rates (due to the associated data and even due to the underlying hardware and operating system characteristics). Consuming both events concurrently is enough for one consumer to occasionally handle a concurrent older event faster than a more recent one.

6.5.2 Solving Out-of-Order Events with Versioning

Since events can lose their order due to several factors, what can we do to prevent invalid states? One way is using event versioning. Events reflect a change that happened to an entity. Conceptually, the event's version is the version of the entity at the time of the change. For example, if our entity is a product, a product created event could have version 1; if someone changed the product's category, it would publish an event with version 2; and so on.

The concept of a sequential version per entity relates to the DDD aggregate concept. The entities are related to the aggregates we define in the domain. Every time an entity changes, the version increases. Each version represents the state of the entity at that given moment in time. Events can use the same version and relate to the state change that triggered the event.

However, managing a sequential, unique, and incremental version can be tricky[15] in distributed systems. Twitter Snowflake,[16] for example, highlights the challenge of generating unique ids in a distributed database like Cassandra. Consistently generating these ids can also have performance impacts in heavy workloads. A timestamp, or using the number of milliseconds since the epoch, for example, can be a valid alternative. This way, each service can easily generate a version always higher than the previous, although not sequential.

---

[15] Further details in João Reis, "Unique Integer Generation in Distributed Systems," September 20, 2018, `www.farfetchtechblog.com/en/blog/post/unique-integer-generation-in-distributed-systems/`

[16] Further details in Twitter blog, Ryan King, "Announcing Snowflake," June 1, 2010, `https://blog.twitter.com/engineering/en_us/a/2010/announcing-snowflake.html`

A sequential version can be relevant in partial events where the event doesn't have the entity's full information. For example, if the inventory service published stock in events and stock out events, a service building the product's stock couldn't skip any version. Otherwise, the stock wouldn't add up to the correct value. In those use cases, services often need to consume every event in the stream in the exact order (can't skip versions). When a service exhibits this behavior, it can be harder to reason with and is often less resilient, as we will discuss in Chapter 7.

The way we design events can also have an impact on the importance of order. We would need to consume every stock in and stock out in the stream to have the latest stock quantity (this has other implications; for example, we would need to allow negative stock at least temporarily). But notice that a stock in and stock out event, contrary to a stock change, aren't idempotent, which is an important property to have, as we will discuss in Chapter 7.

Event versioning provides a way to understand if the event the service is processing is older or more recent than our internal state. In the example we discussed with the inventory service in Figure 6-6, when consuming the event with version 21, we could detect that the current version of the product's stock is 22. Then we could decide on what to do.

Some business processes might benefit from still processing the event or all events that arrive late within a given window. For example, if we needed to send a notification every time a product has one last stock unit, the ordering wouldn't be that relevant and we might want to process every event despite the order the events arrive. However, in this example where we are updating the current stock for each product, we are only interested in the latest state, so we could ignore older events.

Notice that even with event versioning and validating the version on each event, we wouldn't absolutely guarantee that we wouldn't process older versions. Two services could be processing sequential versions concurrently and process the most recent version faster than the older one. We would still have to combine this with one concurrency prevention strategy we discussed before.

Versioning events is always relevant, and, either by using an aggregate version or a timestamp, it is useful for consumers to use. It is important to manage idempotency and out-of-order events on the consumer side. We can also delegate the responsibility to order events to the event broker by routing messages to specific partitions, as we will discuss in Section 6.6.

6.6 Using End-to-End Message Partitioning to Handle Concurrency and Guarantee Message Ordering

Until now, we discussed solutions to ordering and concurrency using by implementation strategies. We discussed patterns we can apply to solve the concurrency and ordering issues. A better and more sustainable approach is to avoid concurrency and ordering issues altogether, solving concurrency by design. This section will work through a similar example to the ones we discussed in this chapter and detail the inner workings of a message stream and how we can partition messages to avoid concurrency altogether.

Let's work through the same example we discussed before with the inventory service handling multiple order created events. Instead of just focusing only on the inventory service, let's look at the flow since the order service. Figure 6-7 illustrates this flow.

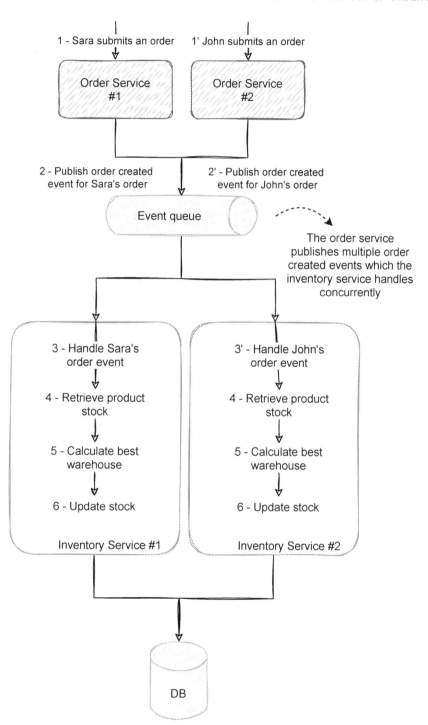

Figure 6-7. *Multiple instances of the order service process multiple orders. The inventory service handles concurrently the events for those orders*

The order service, such as the inventory service, can be scaled horizontally and can have multiple instances; in Figure 6-7, each of them has two. Each instance of the order service handles multiple order requests; in this case, Sara and John both submit an order. The order service handles the requests and publishes events signaling the order was created and is ready to follow the order fulfillment flow. The inventory service handles those events and changes the stock according to those orders. Since both John and Sara ordered the same product, which only has one stock unit left, processing both orders simultaneously can produce a concurrency issue the same way we discussed before.

How can we solve this by partitioning messages? To understand this concept, it's important to understand how the message broker works internally. To illustrate this, let's look at Kafka and detail how it arranges messages.

6.6.1 Real-World Example of Event-Driven Message Routing Using Kafka

In the example in Figure 6-7, the order service produces events to an event queue; in Kafka, it's called a topic. The inventory service subscribes to that topic and consumes the events. Events are stored durably and remain available after consumption (as we discussed in Chapter 3). The order service has multiple producers (since there are several instances of the order service) and has multiple consumers, in this case, the various inventory service instances.

In this case, the only consumer is the inventory service, but there could be other services also with multiple instances reading from the topic. The anatomy of a Kafka topic and its interactions with different services is illustrated in Figure 6-8.

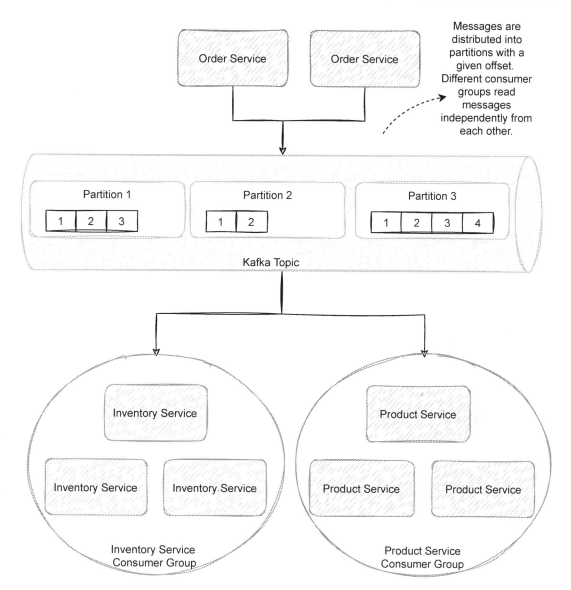

Figure 6-8. *Detail of a Kafka topic and its interactions with other services*

The order service publishes messages to the Kafka topic. Kafka distributes those messages to different partitions. Partitions enable good scalability since they allow producers to write data, and consumers to read, to multiple nodes at the same time. Partitions are also crucial for high availability; partitions can be replicated across several machines to guarantee fault tolerance.

Topics are basically a distributed append log; when services publish a message, the broker appends it to the end of the stream. Each message has an offset which represents the message position in the stream for each partition. For example, if a given partition has ten messages, when a producer writes a new one at the end of the stream, it will have offset 11.

Consumers read from the topic and consume messages from the different partitions. Messages are distributed to service instances with the same consumer group, and each consumer group acts as a single consumer. The example depicted in Figure 6-8 shows three instances of the inventory service and three instances of the product service. Instances of the same services have the same consumer group; different services have different consumer groups. For example, each of the three instances of the inventory service consumes different messages; they advance in the stream as a group; thus, different instances with the same consumer group never receive the same messages. Different consumer groups will consume from the stream independently and concurrently. For example, the message with offset 1 will be delivered to inventory service's instance 1 and product service instance 2, but never to more than one service instance within the same consumer group. Figure 6-9 illustrates the offsets of the two services.

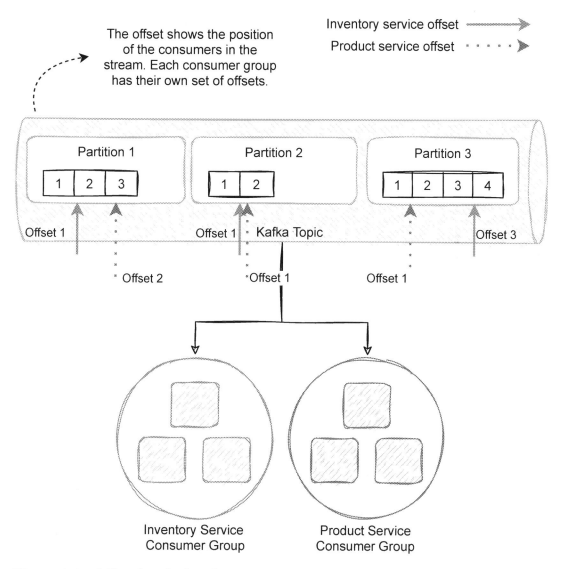

Figure 6-9. *Offset detail of each consumer group for both services*

The arrows in Figure 6-9 illustrate the consumer's position in the stream. In fact, in Kafka, consumers are cheap; you can reason as if they were a pointer in the event stream – opposed to ephemeral message brokers, where consumers often require an additional effort by the broker and often struggle if consumers start to pile up messages in the queues. As illustrated in Figure 6-9, consumers only advance in the stream, and messages remain in the topic and aren't removed. If a new service needed to consume from the stream, it would have the messages available. If the inventory service needs to rebuild its state, it could merely set its offset to zero and reread the stream.

The topic's number of partitions is an essential factor to the scalability and performance of the system. Kafka assigns a number of partitions to each consumer. For example, if a topic has six partitions and the inventory service has three instances, it will likely be assigned two partitions to each inventory service instance. In the example in Figure 6-9, we have three partitions to three service instances; each instance will likely have one partition. However, what if we decided to further horizontally scale the inventory service by adding one more instance? Although one consumer can consume messages from several partitions, each partition is consumed by exactly one consumer. So if we add another instance to the inventory service, there would be no partition to assign it to; hence, the new instance wouldn't have any load whatsoever. We wouldn't be able to scale the service further.

We can change the number of partitions after the topic is created, but adding partitions doesn't change the partitioning of the existing data, which might be troublesome to the consumers as we will see in the next section. The number of partitions limits our ability to scale; an arguably reasonable decision when creating a topic is to plan beforehand the scalability needs of the topic and create it with a larger number of partitions than it currently needs. This planning will give space to scale the service in the future.

Kafka has two pivotal characteristics that can help to deal with out-of-order events and concurrency. In a partition, Kafka guarantees events are read in the same order they were written. This guarantees ordering on the broker side; events can still lose the order on the consumer side, as we discussed in Section 6.5. It is essential to notice that Kafka only guarantees ordering inside a partition. A topic has several partitions, so ordering is not guaranteed across partitions and throughout the whole topic. However, when publishing, we are also able to define the event's routing key. The broker ensures it delivers events with the same routing key to the same partition. This property is a fundamental characteristic we can use to avoid concurrency and out-of-order messages as we will detail in the next section.

6.6.2 The Relevance of Message Routing and Partitioning in Event-Driven Microservices

At the beginning of the section, in the example in Figure 6-7, we discussed how the inventory service could have a concurrency issue by simultaneously processing the order service's events. The concurrency issue occurs because two instances of the inventory service process order for the same product at the same time; in this case, both John and Sara ordered the same product. John's order was processed by one instance and Sara's order by another instance.

But how would this example play out if we defined a routing key in the order service? Every message with the same key will be routed to the same partition by specifying a routing key. As we discussed, each partition has exactly one consumer. If we use the product id as the routing key, every order for the same product would be routed to the same partition and consequently to the same consumer instance. Figure 6-10 illustrates this flow.

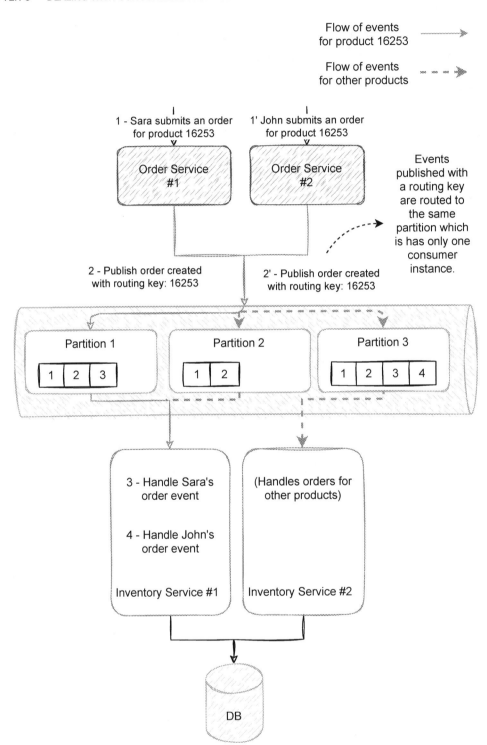

Figure 6-10. *Flow of the order events when published with a routing key*

John and Sara are both trying to buy product 16253, which only has one stock unit left. The order service publishes events using the product id as the routing key, in this case, 16253. Since both events have the same partition key, they are both routed to the same partition, in this case, partition 1. Each partition has only one consumer; inventory service instance 1 is handling events from partition 1, so this instance will assuredly receive both events. The instance will also receive the events by the order they were published since ordering is guaranteed in the same partition.

Looking just at this example, we might think the other service's instances won't receive any load, but they will continue to receive events, just not for that product id. The other instances are still processing other products with other ids. This strategy guarantees every event with the same partition key will be processed by the same instance, but every instance will continue to process events for the partitions assigned to them; hence, they will continue to process other products. We can reason as if we assigned a range of products to each instance; events from products inside the range will be processed only by the corresponding instance.

Using this strategy, we just transformed the distributed concurrency issue into a local one. Is this sufficient to eliminate concurrency and ordering issues altogether? Each service instance will likely have parallelism, so concurrency issues can still occur inside each instance. For example, we might receive John's and Sara's order in the correct order and in one instance, but two threads might process the events concurrently inside the instance. However, this way, there isn't the need to synchronize the several instances through the database or a distributed lock manager. By routing messages, we avoid distributed concurrency issues and only deal with local ones, where the traditional mechanisms to deal with concurrency are relevant.

6.6.3 Using End-to-End Partitioning to Handle Concurrency and Ordering

Distributed synchronization is complex and is often the root of complicated issues and corner cases. It isn't arguably suited to the distributed event-driven mindset since it creates strong dependencies between the instances. Partitioning messages is one way to avoid distributed synchronization through architecture design. However, as we discussed, even in a local scope, concurrency is still an issue. Solving concurrency by implementation often implies complicated developments and is often hard to reason with and to maintain. This subsection will take one step further the partitioning approach and detail how we can avoid concurrency altogether.

To handle concurrency in the service's local scope, we can use the traditional approaches like an in-memory lock or one of the techniques we discussed in Sections 6.3 and 6.4. However, an arguably good way to handle concurrency by design is to follow the same approach we discussed when we detailed the broker's event routing. Following this approach, we can route the events we receive in the service to specific paths. Figure 6-11 illustrates this situation.

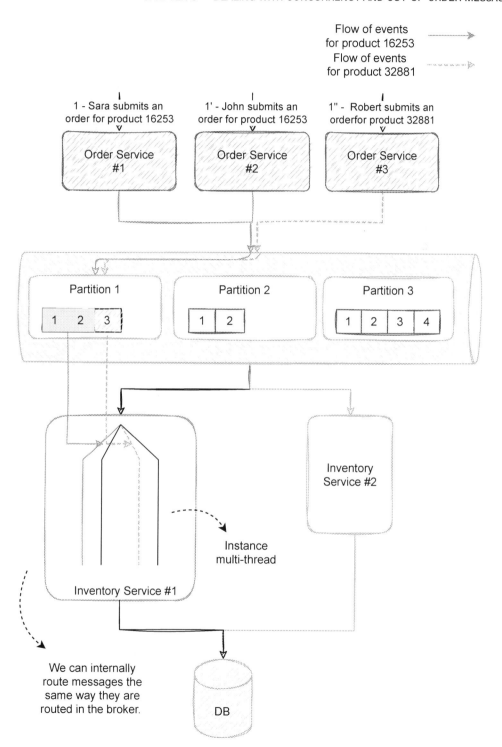

Figure 6-11. *Flow of the events from the producer to the consumer using end-to-end partitioning*

Inside instance 1 of inventory service, we detailed several thread paths that correspond to the service's parallelism. In this case, the service processes four events in parallel. Figure 6-11 highlights two paths, the path for the two events of orders for the same product (with id 16253) with the solid line and the path for a third order for the product with id 32881 with a dashed line. The three instances of the order service publish the three events using the product id as the partition key. The broker routes the events to partition 1, which is assigned to the first inventory service instance. The inventory service can handle the three events concurrently since the parallelism degree can process four events simultaneously.

However, when handling the events, we can route them to specific thread paths based on a routing key. We can forward the events with the same key to the same thread so we can process them sequentially. By handling them in a single-threaded manner, there are no concurrency issues. The service itself is multi-thread since the other threads will process different ranges of routing keys. For example, events with product id 32881 will be processed simultaneously with events with product id 16253 (as illustrated in the diagram), but the two events for id 16253 will be processed sequentially; the second will only start to be consumed when the first finishes. We can route the messages using the same routing key the broker uses or even the partition number, as long as the number of partitions is higher than the number of parallelism of all instances.

If we guarantee the order service publishes events in order, we also avoid ordering issues. The broker ensures that inside a partition, the order is maintained; if we have the same consideration when assigning messages in-memory threads, we maintain the end-to-end ordering.

With end-to-end partitioning, we can achieve greater performance by enabling parallelism inside and outside of the service and tune the parallelism to take the most out of the physical resources while completely avoiding concurrency and ordering issues. It also avoids the dependency of an external dependency, locks of any sort and retries. This approach has high synergy with the event-driven mindset; reasoning with the service is always in the context of the event flow. It is an exceptionally simple way to use an event-driven mindset to completely remove ordering and concurrency concerns without performance overhead. Developments can be implemented in a no concurrency context which greatly reduces the complexity and allows developers to focus on the business logic rather than technical concerns.

6.6.4 Limitations of End-to-End Partitioning in Event-Driven Microservices

As we discussed, end-to-end partitioning entirely avoids concurrency and guarantees ordering. In a fully event-driven architecture, it can be an excellent approach to apply consistently across services, but it does have some limitations in some use cases. It also has some inconspicuous caveats that are easy to miss. This subsection will discuss those limitations and propose possible solutions.

Hotspotting

The event broker uses the partition key to route events to one partition; hence, every event with the same key will be routed to the same partition. You might imagine what happens if a large percentage of the entire set of events has the same key; the data distribution will be largely unbalanced.

For example, in the use case we discussed until now, we used the product id as the partition key. But imagine we needed to guarantee concurrency across product categories, and we didn't want to process products simultaneously with the same category. We could use the category id as the partition key. Let's say most of our product catalog is composed of clothing, while the other categories, like shoes and accessories, represent a considerable small fraction of the entire catalog. By this design, most of our events would have the clothing category id. Since every event with the same id would be routed to the same partition, the partition with the clothing products would be fairly larger than the remaining partitions.

This unbalance between the partitions is called hotspotting. As you might recall from the previous sections, the number of partitions is pivotal to performance and scalability concerns. In this case, a large percentage of our data would be assigned to a single partition which only has one consumer by the broker's design. This unbalance also means a single instance would handle a large portion of our events, which will undoubtedly degrade the system's performance. It also limits the ability to scale since no more consumers can be assigned to that partition. When the number of messages is extensively large, the broker might also struggle with it; Kafka, for example, has to fit one partition in a single machine. If we have a considerably large number of messages, it might be impracticable or costly to fit them in one machine, and the broker might struggle to deal with it properly.

In our example, we used the product id as a routing key; it is natural that some products are more sought-after than others and thus have more orders. Having more orders also means more events with the same key. However, with a large number of products, the number of messages in the partitions will eventually even out; products with less orders will compensate for the ones that have more.

Two important considerations when choosing a partition key are the key's granularity and diversity. The partition key needs to be granular enough to accommodate for an even distribution across partitions. It also needs to have enough diversity (several times greater than the number of partitions) and sufficient different values to enable adequate routing options.

There might be use cases where an adequate routing key is not available (as we discussed with the category's example), but this is often the exception. Event-driven systems often imply a large scale, which, despite all its challenges, provides adequate data diversity to enable suitable routing keys. However, be mindful when choosing a routing key.

Momentary Hotspots

We often think of solutions in their clean and platonic state. If we receive three events and have three partitions, the broker will route one event to each partition. Balanced, as all things should be. However, in the real world, things are messy, unpredictable, and often chaotic. Solutions might not behave as we expect they would all of the time.

Although most of the time predictable, traffic can be erratic and unpredictable patterns might occur from time to time. For example, in the example we discussed in this section, we published order events and used the product id as the partition key. Most of the time, traffic might be somewhat stable. However, imagine we drop a highly sought-after product in our platform, which users order intensively. This will temporarily generate a large amount of events with the same routing key, creating a momentary hotspot.

The performance of the system might drop while this is occurring if the load is sufficiently disparate. This is often a rare event and one that the system might afford. However, we should understand its implications and understand if there are relevant consequences for the business. We should also design our systems not to produce momentary hotspots often. For example, we should avoid recovery processes that unload an impactful number of events with the same key.

The Mix of Event-Driven and Synchronous APIs

An apparent limitation of the end-to-end partitioning approach is when the service needs to handle events and process synchronous requests through an API. Although this kind of services might be the exception in an event-driven architecture, they are relatively common and might make the end-to-end partitioning approach inviable. This use case is illustrated in Figure 6-12. We should avoid these kinds of configurations and preferentially use a fully event-driven approach or a synchronous API; having both can be particularly challenging, especially when we need to prevent concurrency and ordering issues. Having said that, in the real world, we might find this kind of approach. In this topology, we can't directly apply end-to-end partitioning since routing and mixing synchronous requests with events might be unsuitable.

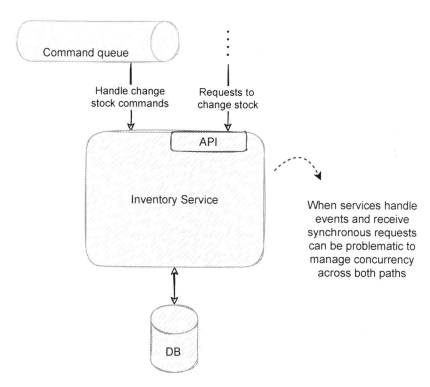

Figure 6-12. *Service handling events and processing synchronous requests*

One possible approach is to convert the synchronous request into a command and publish it to the queue. For example, the inventory service would receive a POST request to change stock, but instead of synchronously satisfying the request, it would send a command to the command queue. This way, we would have only one entry point, and it would be possible to route the commands accordingly. However, this approach might not be viable if the API needs to respond synchronously. If this is the case, we can still apply a pessimistic or optimistic concurrency prevention strategy to manage both scenarios.

6.7 Summary

- Handling concurrency in a single application has different implications than handling it in a distributed architecture. The traditional strategies to prevent concurrency are often unsuitable for distributed event-driven services.

- We can solve concurrency by implementation or by design. Implementation strategies often involve either optimistic or pessimistic approaches. The end-to-end partitioning pattern can be an effective way to handle concurrency by design in event-driven systems.

- Optimistic concurrency prevention strategies shine in environments with low chances of concurrency. They don't involve locking and often require retrying the process when concurrency is detected.

- Pessimistic concurrency prevention strategies are suited to environments with high chances of concurrency; they lock a given resource and block access. They often rely on an external dependency to manage the synchronization.

- We can achieve pessimistic concurrency with distributed locks by resorting to an external tool like Consul or ZooKeeper. Instead, we can also use some database technologies or use transactions.

- Out-of-order events can be troublesome and jeopardize the consistency of the system. We can use event versioning to tackle ordering issues.

- End-to-end partition is a way to solve both concurrency and ordering issues by architecture design. In event-driven architectures, it's arguably our go-to solution to solve these issues. It can be a clean, performant strategy to handle ordering and concurrency.

- Hotspotting can be an impactful consequence of routing events. We should be mindful of this issue when defining the partition key and design the routing strategy accordingly.

CHAPTER 7

Achieving Resilience and Event Processing Reliability in Event-Driven Microservices

This chapter covers:

- Understanding common failures in distributed microservice architectures

- How event-driven architectures can provide more reliable processes

- Understanding the impacts of the several message delivery semantics and how to apply each of them to event-driven services

- Maintaining correctness when saving state and publishing events

- What we can use from ACID 2.0 and apply to event processing

- How to avoid message leak

- Applying common resilience patterns in event-driven services

- How to repair state in event-driven services

- Using the bulkhead pattern to contain failures

H. F. Oliveira Rocha, *Practical Event-Driven Microservices Architecture*,
https://doi.org/10.1007/978-1-4842-7468-2_7

The Banqiao Dam is a major dam in China. After its construction, it suffered from some construction and engineering errors, which were repaired and made the dam undergo a significant redesign. After the new design, it was dubbed the "iron dam" and considered unbreakable. In 1975, typhoon Nina affected the nearby location, and although the hurricane-force winds are arguably the most infamous characteristic of typhoons, another unsung consequence of tropical cyclones is torrential rains. Typhoon Nina stopped moving due to a cold front, which made it pour down torrential rain on the same location for three days. That location was the region of the Banqiao Dam. The immense quantity of water eventually compromised the dam's integrity and led to a catastrophic failure. Seven hundred million cubic meters of water flowed through the surrounding areas. The destruction of the dam triggered a domino effect which provoked the collapse of other 61 dams throughout the region. The dam failure triggered a chain reaction that caused the third deadliest flood in world history.

An unavoidable challenge of typical microservice architectures is dealing with cascading failures, which resembles this particular episode of the Banqiao Dam. Sometimes one nonessential and somewhat isolated service can bring the whole architecture down due to the chain of synchronous requests between components. The failure of that inconspicuous service is propagated across the complex network of synchronous calls, eventually spreading the failure to critical components that stop vital business processes.

Event-driven architectures are naturally resilient to these issues due to their asynchronous nature. The event queues between the services are a natural barrier to load peaks and limit direct dependencies between services. One failure in a single service isn't propagated across the architecture; instead, it often affects only that service, endowing the architecture with higher resilience.

However, as with most things in software engineering, it's about tradeoffs and deciding what's best on a given use case. As we discussed in Chapter 1, event-driven architectures have their own set of limitations and challenges. One of them is to perceive events as the source of truth. Events aren't simple signals anymore; they carry meaning and are as paramount to the system as databases in traditional applications. Consistency in an event stream is pivotal and as necessary as consistency in a database. Failing a database write in a monolithic application when a customer saves information is as critical as not publishing an event in an event-driven architecture.

Guaranteeing a coherent approach is pivotal to achieve consistency across the architecture. As discussed in Chapter 5, microservice architectures' distributed nature forces us to look at consistency differently. This different view on consistency often translates into relying on a different set of properties we can apply to event-driven architectures. The state can become invalid due to issues with new releases. In these situations, event-driven services provide a unique and powerful way to recover data by rewinding the event stream to repair state. Resilience also relates to the system's availability and how it deals with its dependencies; patterns like the bulkhead pattern can help provide stability when dependencies fail, which we will discuss in this chapter.

7.1 Common Failures in Microservice Architectures and How They Relate to Event-Driven Architectures

While we are building functionality, we often focus on the solution's design, its reusability, and cleanness. Thinking about how it can go wrong, it's often unnatural, like throwing mud into a pristine masterpiece. We are often inclined to assume things for granted, the database, the event broker, the network, etc. Things are bound to go wrong; in production, nothing is taken for granted. Our applications' success is directly related to its ability to mitigate the impact of the failure. This section will discuss common failures in distributed microservice architectures and how relevant they are in an event-driven architecture.

Let's analyze a typical topology of the services we discussed until now. A regular service has its own physical resources, might have a database, and communicates with an event broker. It communicates to several types of external dependencies through different protocols. Figure 7-1 illustrates this topology.

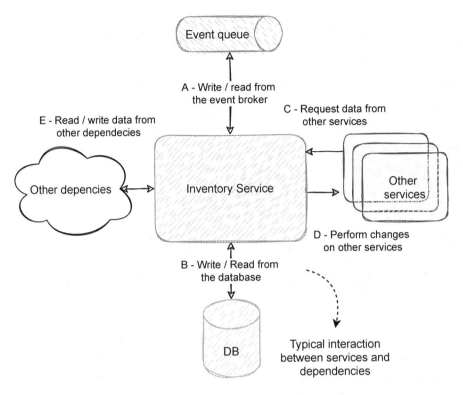

Figure 7-1. *Typical service topology and common dependencies*

Event-driven services typically interact with the message broker, either by reading or writing events or both (A). They might need to store some data by writing and reading data from a database (B). Although more sparingly, services might synchronously request data from other services through, for example, an HTTP request (C). They also might change data on other services through synchronous requests (D). Besides other services, they might have different dependencies, for example, a distributed cache like Redis (E).

Each of these interactions can fail due to several reasons. The broker might face a catastrophic failure and be unreachable. The same can happen to each of the other services or the database. The service itself can suffer a catastrophic failure due to issues in the underlying hardware. Even if both the service and its dependencies are healthy, the communication between them can fail. We typically write software with unmentioned assumptions like our trust in the network's reliability (illustrated in the fallacies of distributed computing).[1] The network can fail, and it will fail eventually like every other dependency we mention in Figure 7-1. As we said in Chapter 6, with enough scale and time, unlikely and far-fetched problems become certain.

Infrastructure components and hardware can fail due to their physical components, although they only affect the applications on rare and isolated occasions. However, network issues like virtual hosts' failure or connectivity issues, like network partitions and similar, are more frequent. Besides physical components failing, maintenance operations can introduce instability; I'm sure we all relate to some kind of patch or upgrade gone wrong. Sparingly the very update of the operating system running the services and upgrading versions can introduce issues, and, of course, human errors while operating these infrastructure components. Other teams operate other services in the architecture; new releases can introduce bugs or make the service unavailable.

Direct dependencies, like synchronous requests, overall increase the likelihood of the system's instability. In the use case of Figure 7-1, we depict an inventory service; other services might request data from it, like the order service to fetch the current product's stock. The inventory service might depend on other services, for example, a location service to fetch the warehouses' addresses. The location service itself might depend on other services. Each of those services has its own dependencies, which can all fail and will fail eventually. The overall system's availability is often translated into the combined availability of all services, which is lower and harder to manage. This kind of cascading failure, which we will detail next, is a common failure mode in microservice architectures that event-driven services can mitigate.

7.1.1 Cascading Failures and Event-Driven Services

The services and their dependencies can fail due to many reasons. This failure can make the service unavailable and fail requests. A local failure has limited impact, depending on the service's business function. However, as we discussed with the Banqiao Dam, when that failure triggers a cascading failure to other services in the architecture, the impact grows exponentially and can bring the whole system to a halt. This subsection will work through a practical example of typical microservice architecture and how it would play out in an event-driven architecture.

---

[1] Further details in "Fallacies of distributed computing," https://en.wikipedia.org/wiki/Fallacies_of_distributed_computing

In typical microservice architectures, communication between services is synchronous, through, for example, HTTP requests. This kind of architecture is prone to develop a complex network of synchronous requests. You might recall the example we mentioned when detailing distributed tracing in Chapter 4, how Uber traces 1000 microservices[2] and its complex network. In the network, there are large nodes that several services depend upon; if one of these becomes unavailable, it will likely affect the whole architecture. But it can also be the other way around; less critical and more isolated services might cascade issues to other more essential services and aggravate the problem. Let's detail how a cascading failure could affect an eCommerce workflow similar to the ones we discussed until now in a microservice architecture.

---

[2] Full presentation by Yuri Shkuro, September 9, 2019, "Conquering Microservices Complexity @Uber with Distributed Tracing," `www.infoq.com/presentations/uber-microservices-distributed-tracing/`

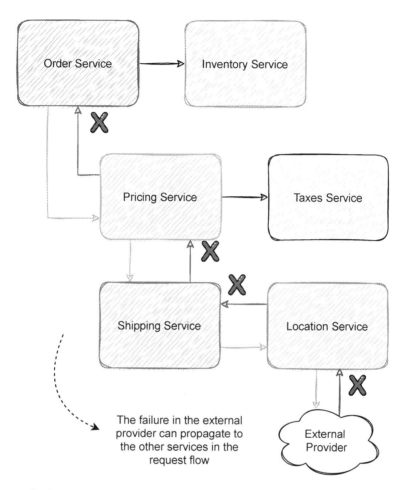

Figure 7-2. *A failure in an external provider cascade to the other upstream services*

The order fulfillment flow requests the pricing service to calculate the fees for each order it receives. The pricing service depends on the shipping service to process the shipping and address information, which depends on the location service, which manages more generic information about geographic and country locations. The location service also depends on an external provider to fetch the country's information. In the example, the location service fails to fetch data from the external provider. By failing to fetch the information, it will also fail to respond successfully to the shipping service. The failure is cascaded to the other upstream services, eventually failing the order fulfillment process. In this case, a relatively isolated issue, and not very relevant business-wise, ends up affecting the main order fulfillment flow.

In this case, it was an external provider that failed. But it could happen to any of the other service's dependencies we discussed earlier. For example, the database could also fail, and although the database becoming unavailable is relatively uncommon, a load peak can make the database struggle due to limited physical resources. In these cases, a peculiar phenomenon often occurs. A common approach to deal with failing requests is to retry the request. As the service struggling with the excessive load starts to fail some requests, the requesting services also increase their throughput due to the retry strategy. A particular situation where I've experienced this was when a service became unavailable due to connectivity issues. Once the team solved those issues and the service started to recover, the additional retry throughput of every dependency fully occupied the service's resources and crashed the service again due to an overwhelming load. This issue highlighted the need for appropriate coping strategies like backoff retries and circuit breakers (further discussed in the next sections).

Unexpected load affecting services with modest resources is also a common reason for cascading failures. Imagine if, with the same example of Figure 7-2, the platform had a higher usage due to a sales season. The order service would likely have a peak in usage, which often translates into higher numbers of requests to the downstream services. If the order service received a peak in orders, it would likely request more information from the pricing service to fulfill those orders. The pricing service would likely translate that load peak to the shipping service and the shipping service to the location service. The order, pricing, and shipping service would likely have ample resources due to their criticality. Their importance is also obvious in the order fulfillment flow. However, if the location service is outside of the critical radar and has a modest impact, it will likely have modest resources to be cost-effective. This way, the excess of requests can impact the service, deteriorating its response time or even making it unavailable, which would likely cascade to the upstream services.

The load peak can even occur due to other operations happening in the architecture. For example, imagine the taxes service needed to update all the system's taxes and temporarily request information from the location service. The bulk operation and the added load might impact the location service in the same way, cascading the failure to the critical order fulfillment flow. A complex network of synchronous requests is often very susceptible to these kinds of issues. When an apparently innocuous operation in one end of the system ends up impacting the other end, or the whole system, it might make us wonder if a distributed microservice architecture is any better than a monolithic application. In fact, when we suffer from these kinds of challenges, we are closer to a distributed monolith than a real decoupled and horizontally scalable architecture.

Event-driven architectures are still susceptible to these kinds of issues; synchronous requests are often a reality in most architectures. However, an event-driven approach offers a way to mitigate the impact of cascading failures naturally. How would the previous failure affect an event-driven architecture? Figure 7-3 illustrates the same use case.

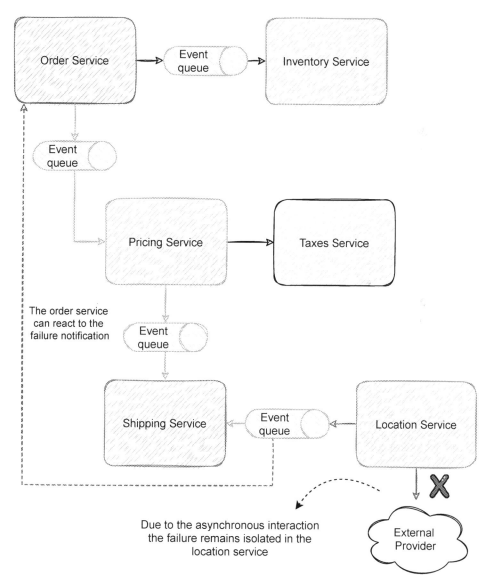

Figure 7-3. *The same failure in the external provider remains isolated in the location service due to the decoupling provided by the event queues*

The failure in the external provider and the requests by the location service remain isolated in that service. The decoupling provided by the event queue mitigates the cascading effect of the failure. Let's say the shipping service used the location service to retrieve additional information about the geographical details of each country. Using the event queue and building an internal state with that information (in a similar way that we discussed in Section 4.6 about building multiple read models), the service becomes autonomous and avoids the direct dependency. There is still an impact; new changes to those geographical locations aren't updated while the location service is unavailable since no new events reach the shipping service. However, the impact is significantly smaller than stopping the whole order fulfillment flow.

7.1.2 Load Balancing and Rate Limiters in Event-Driven Services

The previous subsection mentioned how additional load to synchronous microservices could trigger cascading failures. A strategy to typically manage additional load and load peaks is the use of load balancers. Rate limiters can also be a valuable strategy to guarantee the service keeps responding to some requests while denying others. This subsection will detail this concept in a typical microservice architecture and how it relates to event-driven architectures.

As we discussed, a service can fail due to a myriad of reasons. In production, we should always have more than one instance per service to guarantee high availability. If one instance fails, becomes unresponsive, or has connectivity issues, the remaining ones can satisfy requests while the struggling instance is recovering. Microservice architectures typically accomplish this with load balancers. Load balancers keep track of the responsiveness of the service and route traffic accordingly. If one instance has issues, the load balancer routes the unavailable instance's traffic to the other healthy instances. Figure 7-4 illustrates the order service requesting information from the inventory service through a load balancer.

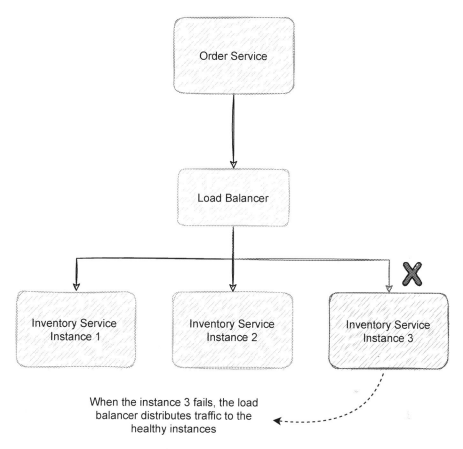

Figure 7-4. *The order service requests stock information through a load balancer*

When the inventory service instance 3 becomes unavailable, the load balancer routes the instance's traffic to the other healthy instances. Having three instances of the service provides higher availability. For the inventory service to be completely unavailable, all three instances would have to fail simultaneously, which is much more unlikely than one instance failing. Load balancers can also understand if the service response time is degrading instead of only reacting if the instance is unavailable.

Load balancers are usually relevant to instances that use synchronous requests. In event-driven services, the load balancing is generally managed by the event broker. The broker knows each instance's state and distributes messages to each one, as illustrated in Figure 7-5.

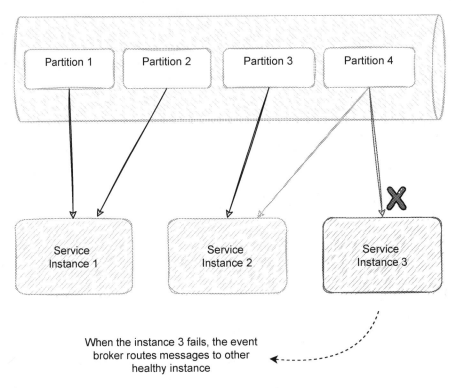

Figure 7-5. *Load balancing through a message broker*

You might recall when we detailed the anatomy of a Kafka topic in Chapter 6, a topic in the message broker can be divided into several partitions, and each partition is assigned to one consumer. In this case, instance 3 becomes unavailable; the broker can detect that the instance is down and reassigns the partition to another instance. The event broker can act as a load balancer without an external tool to manage it; the event consumption enables the balancing to occur more naturally. If it was a temporary failure, for example, the service loses connection to the broker temporarily, the broker will reassign a partition to the recovered instance when the service becomes available again.

A common reason for service failures is unexpected load peaks or large amounts of requests. DDoS (distributed denial of service attack) is often accounted for by the exterior architecture's security layers against external attacks. However, a similar common issue is excessive requests by internal services, a sort of internal DDoS attack but unintentional. Typical microservices often establish and enforce rate limits to guarantee the reliability of the service.

However, rate limiters typically imply rejecting some requests; when they surpass a specified threshold, the service denies a part of the requests. There are different strategies the service can apply besides blindly refusing a portion of the requests. It can prioritize critical business traffic or prioritize pivotal clients. However, it implies failing a segment of the requests and informing clients the request was refused (through an HTTP status code 429 – too many requests, for example). Upon receiving this response, the clients should adapt and moderate the number of requests. This strategy is known as backpressure and is applicable depending on the use case; rejecting requests is often (or always) not ideal. Applying backpressure also pushes the complexity to the clients; they need the rejected requests, so it often forces clients to use ad hoc retry-later strategies.

These kinds of approaches often seem like a workaround; we have a synchronous process that can't handle the required throughput, so we refuse requests, which forces the clients to apply a semi-synchronous approach by retrying the request later. Fully embracing an asynchronous approach is often more resilient and transparent. Rate limiters are arguably irrelevant in event-driven systems. If the service is receiving a higher throughput than it can handle, the impact is to build up lag (an increase in the number of messages to process) rather than failing. The broker naturally queues higher throughput than the service can handle. The queue piles up events to be processed later rather than pushing that responsibility to the clients. This strategy is far more resilient and avoids rejecting or failing requests. The services' horizontal scalability also provides the opportunity to increase or decrease the number of instances (even automatically) to guarantee that the lag doesn't grow to troublesome values since it can impact the eventual consistency, as discussed in Chapter 5.

The services that expose synhronous requests benefit from having a deliberate load balancing and rate limit strategy in place. However, for fully event-driven services, load balancing and rate limits are naturally imbued in how event streams work and don't need an ad hoc or external dependency to manage it, unlike typical microservices. This characteristic enables the system to be more resilient and adapt to varying throughput needs or unexpected unavailability situations.

7.2 Understanding Message Delivery Semantics

Until now, we described the interactions with the event broker as atomic and one-time operations. However, as you might imagine, it's not that simple. As we discussed in the previous section, services and other components can fail, and it can impact the overall system's availability and the reliability of the message communication. Services, and the broker itself, can fail and become unavailable while publishing and consuming messages. This section will detail how these failures can affect message consumption and production.

Let's work through a simple publish/subscribe example. Figure 7-6 illustrates a common use case of the examples we discussed in the previous chapters; the order service publishes an event to the message broker and the inventory service consumes it.

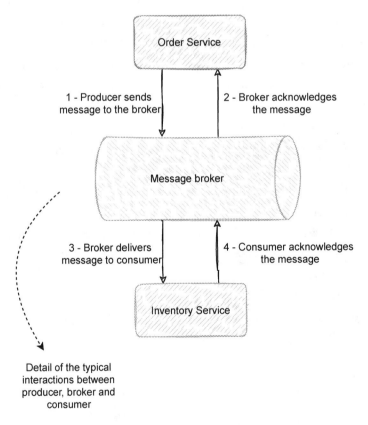

Figure 7-6. *Detail of the interactions with the message broker*

As depicted in the example, when the order service publishes an event, there are usually two steps associated with it: the transmission of the message from the order service to the broker and the broker's acknowledgment of the message reception. On the consumer side, it works similarly; the inventory service receives the message from the message broker and acknowledges it.

Each of these steps can fail and can originate different consistency issues:

1. The broker, or the connection between the order service and the broker, can be unavailable. The order service will fail to publish the message to the broker.

2. After receiving the message, the broker can lose the connection with the order service, or the service can crash, failing to acknowledge the message's reception.

3. The inventory service, or the connection between the inventory service and the broker, can be unavailable. The broker will fail to deliver the message to the consumer.

4. The consumer, in this case the inventory service, can fail to acknowledge the reception and processing of the message to the broker.

If the order service failed to deliver the message to the broker, it would likely retry the message since each of these failures can be, and often are, transient. Even on a prolonged outage, arriving requests would need to be retried sooner or later. Retrying step 1 wouldn't likely impact the stream consistency since no message arrived at the broker yet.

However, what if step 2 failed? The message arrived at the broker, the broker persisted it internally, but when it acknowledged the message, the order service crashed, or the network became temporarily unavailable. When the service recovered, it wouldn't have a way to know if the message publication failed or the acknowledgment failed. It would likely retry the message publication, but in this case, the message had already arrived at the broker; the order service just didn't know it had. The publication retry would generate a duplicate message on the broker.

A similar situation can happen on the consumer side. After receiving the message, the inventory service can crash or lose connection to the broker. If so, it has no way to confirm the message reception. In case of a crash, it would likely reprocess the last messages it was processing, leading to duplicate message consumption.

Depending on the behavior of the producer and the consumer, we can have different message delivery semantics:

- At-most-once delivery: Messages might fail to be delivered but won't be delivered more than once. For example, in Figure 7-6, if the order service publishes a message but the message broker has an internal error persisting the message and returns an error, the message might not have been processed by the broker. With at-most-once semantics, the order service when faced with this error won't retry the operation. Meaning messages will never be duplicated, but not all messages will reach the consumers. We avoid duplicate messages, but we also accept that we can lose messages.

- At-least-once delivery: Messages will always be delivered but might be delivered more than once. In the same use case we discussed before, if the order service didn't receive an acknowledgment from the broker, it could retry the operation. The broker already received the message and only failed to acknowledge it. By retrying, we would end up publishing a duplicate message. Thus, we guarantee messages are always delivered but might be more than once.

- Exactly-once delivery: Messages will always be delivered to the consumers without duplicates. In this case, the order service might receive an error, and even by retrying the operation, the message would arrive only once to the inventory service. Exactly-once is the most desirable delivery semantic but is also exceptionally hard to guarantee in a distributed system.

Table 7-1 resumes the impacts of each delivery semantic.

Table 7-1. *Recap of the characteristics of the different delivery semantics*

Delivery Semantic	Pros	Cons
At-most-once	No message duplication High performance Practical to implement	Might lose messages in failure scenarios
At-least-once	Guaranteed delivery Practical to implement	Might have message duplication in failure scenarios Performance hit
Exactly-once	No message duplication Guaranteed delivery	Exceptionally hard to guarantee and implement

These kinds of problems are related to the two generals' problem.[3] The challenges of coordinating several distributed components through an unreliable network make it exceptionally hard to achieve a strategy with strong consistency, like implementing exactly-once delivery semantics.

At-most-once delivery is often associated with higher performance due to the lack of verifications (waiting for timeouts, for example) or retries. However, it also means we might lose messages from time to time. For example, when deploying a new version of a service or application, the service might be processing messages; with this approach, you might lose some messages because of the processing interruption when the service or application stops for the deploy. Losing messages, more often than not, is not acceptable, especially in streams with business-critical data where history is important. However, it might be valuable to less critical and high-load use cases. For example, like telemetry data, if new recent data is published frequently and there is no value in the history, some use cases might afford losing messages in failure scenarios.

At-least-once delivery often has a performance hit, but it usually isn't very significant; after all, failures happen but don't happen that often. It states that messages will always be delivered but might have duplicates. Duplicate messages, depending on the implementation, can generate erroneous results or duplicate work.

Exactly-once delivery is exceptionally hard to guarantee in a distributed system. Even if we only focus on the interaction between the producer and the message broker, in order to guarantee exactly-once delivery, we likely need the coordination between our services and the message broker. Not all message brokers expose this functionality; some

---

[3] Check "Two Generals' Problem," https://en.wikipedia.org/wiki/Two_Generals%27_Problem

do, as we will discuss next with Kafka. Typically, end-to-end exactly-once semantics is only possible when all components in the flow participate in the coordination. Even with brokers that enable it, they usually do so in the message production and consumption. In use cases where consumers depend on external dependencies to process the event (like a database or an external service), it is extraordinarily hard to extend these guarantees to those dependencies. Exactly-once delivery provides the ideal guarantees but is often impractical.

Where does that leave us then? Two out of the three delivery semantics might leave us with incorrect or missing data, and the last one is exceptionally hard to achieve. It really depends on the use case, and we can't give you a one-fits-all rule, but here are some arguably practical pointers to help you decide. Exactly-once is excellent if the message broker supports it, doesn't have a considerable performance hit associated with it, and we don't need an overly complex solution to support it. At-most-once is suitable for use cases where you can afford to lose messages (data that is refreshed often, for example, the telemetry data we discussed). However, losing data is a terrifying thought and not viable in many scenarios.

If we rely on exactly-once semantics, we might implement event consumption with stronger assumptions that we likely need and make the system less flexible. For example, it might be harder to recover from a wrong state introduced by a bug (i.e., retries and event replays might become impracticable). At-least-once is arguably the most flexible and standard solution. Achieving at-least-once delivery can be straightforward, and by designing the event consumption to be idempotent (more on this in Section 7.4), we can avoid incorrect states if duplicates are found. We might have duplicate work, but it likely won't be significant if we process a handful of messages twice in a range of thousands or millions of events. Designing for idempotency makes the overall system more resilient and flexible (rewinding the event stream can be a valid approach, for example).

7.2.1 Exactly-Once Delivery Semantics in Kafka

Kafka introduced exactly-once semantics in the 0.11 release. It achieves exactly-once by implementing message idempotency with a sequence number similar to TCP and combining transactions across different topics. The throughput performance hit is arguably low, only 3% comparing with at-least-once and 20% comparing with at-most-once.[4]

For systems that explicitly need exactly-once is a good alternative with arguably low impact. Implementing exactly once with Kafka is mostly configuration and straightforward.[5] It has the caveat we discussed before when the consumption has the dependency of an external system; we need additional coordination to effectively achieve exactly-once semantics,[6] which can be troublesome or impossible in some use cases.

However, as we discussed, we might benefit from designing for at-least-once and following ACID 2.0 (more on this in Section 7.4) to guarantee reliability and resilience. We imbue the message processing with additional flexibility, and we aren't tied down to more strict message processing guarantees.

7.3 Avoiding Inconsistencies When Saving State and Publishing Events in Event-Driven Microservices

Event-driven services usually react to events and apply their own domain logic, usually generating a different state in the domain's entities. They often need to save state and publish an event reflecting that change. We discussed the importance of the event stream's consistency and how we use it as a medium to share state across the organization. When we save state and publish an event, we are doing two different operations where any can fail. If one fails, we end up with an event stream that doesn't reflect the service's internal state. This section will discuss approaches to avoid this inconsistency, work through a use case, and discuss the possible solutions.

---

[4] Full details in this article by Neha Narkhede, June 30, 2017, "Exactly-Once Semantics Are Possible: Here's How Kafka Does It," `www.confluent.io/blog/exactly-once-semantics-are-possible-heres-how-apache-kafka-does-it/`

[5] Full walkthrough in "How to maintain message ordering and no message duplication," `https://kafka-tutorials.confluent.io/message-ordering/kafka.html`

[6] Full documentation in `https://kafka.apache.org/documentation/#semantics`

Most stateful services handle requests made to them by saving some sort of state. For example, Figure 7-7 illustrates the order service handling order submission requests.

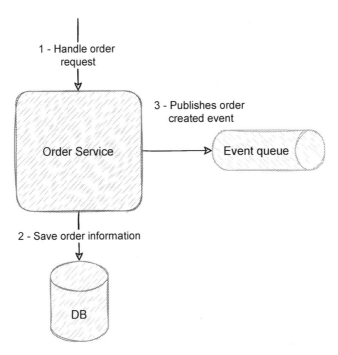

Figure 7-7. *The order service handles order requests by saving state and publishing an event*

The service saves the order information in the database and then publishes an event informing the ecosystem that an order was created. The challenge of having two steps in the order fulfillment process (saving state and publishing an event) is guaranteeing the atomicity of both operations. If the service faced an issue saving the information in the database, it would fail the request but wouldn't compromise the coherency between the database and the event stream. The failure is troublesome and needs to be addressed but wouldn't generate inconsistent states. However, if the service saved the new order but failed to publish an event, the event stream would diverge from the database. The stream would no longer represent the actual state of the orders and would be inconsistent.

This situation poses an additional complexity to the system's recovery. The service's connectivity to the message broker would need to be addressed, but that alone wouldn't be enough to return the system to a valid state. While the event broker, or the service's connection, was unavailable, the service already saved the order information to the database, but the service didn't publish the related events. Failing the request might not be admissible since the changes were already persisted. The event stream is the source of data for every other service depending on the order information. If the event stream is inconsistent, we propagate the issue to the whole ecosystem.

This issue is especially relevant for a choreography pattern we discussed in Chapter 4. Suppose the order fulfillment process depends on a series of choreographed steps. In that case, one service failing to inform it has finished processing the order, and without other mechanisms in place, it might stall the following operations.

7.3.1 Event Stream As the Only Source of Truth

As we discussed, event-driven also relates to the change of mindset in having a database as the source of truth and changing it to an event stream. In light of that, we could use the event stream as the primary source of information as opposed to the database. What does that mean to the example we discussed? We could publish the event and then update the current state by reacting to the same event. Figure 7-8 illustrates this situation.

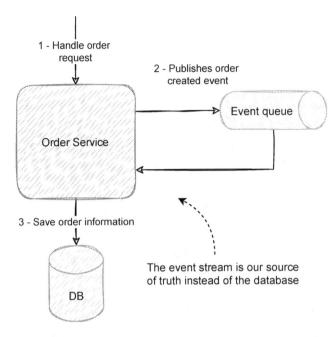

Figure 7-8. *By saving state only when reacting to events, we turn the event stream into the source of truth*

The order information is only saved by reacting to the order created event. This way, we guarantee the event stream is the source of truth; the current state is derived from the same stream. If the update to the database fails, we shouldn't acknowledge the processing of the event. Successful processing requires handling the event and updating the state (we will detail how to accomplish this in Section 7.5).

This use case is very similar to the event sourcing and CQRS pattern we discussed in Chapter 4. The event queue effectively acts as an event sourcing store if the events are durably retained indefinitely. The event stream is also the system's write model, while the database is the read model. We could further segregate the responsibilities if we fully apply the CQRS pattern and detach writes and reads into separate services. Figure 7-9 illustrates this segregation.

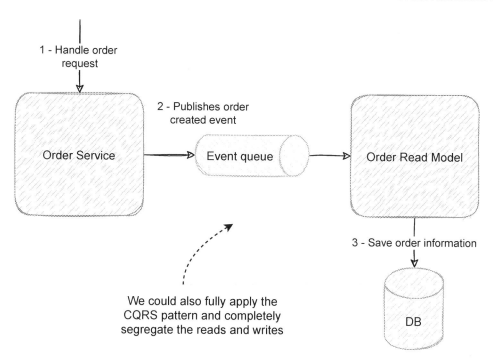

Figure 7-9. *The same example but with fully segregated writes and reads*

The order service receives orders and publishes events, while the order read model reacts to those events and updates each order's current state. The order service has the responsibility to publish events and the order read model to update the state in the database. This way, we can handle each failure separately and in a resilient way.

Although this solution aligns closely with the event-driven mindset, it has some associated caveats. This approach is a good solution as long as the service involved is a stateless stream processor, that is, it doesn't rely on a local state to apply its domain logic. If it does, it will depend on an eventual consistent store, and we risk performing domain validations against stale data. For example, in Figure 7-7, if the order service received a change to an order and needed to fetch the current order, there could be events in the queue that weren't yet applied against the read model.

Event sourcing typically loads all events from an aggregate (in this case, the order) and applies them sequentially, generating the latest state. However, most message brokers don't have this type of querying functionality. Unless we use the database as a queue, although not unheard of,[7] other technologies are arguably more suited to do so. It often comes down to reading the whole queue and filtering the correct entity (or order id) with durable message brokers. Although this is possible, it is highly impractical and resource-consuming for large quantities of events. It's often discussed whether Kafka, for example, can be used as an event sourcing store. There is an interesting article[8] on how to achieve this with Kafka Streams and state stores; with it, we can avoid the challenge of consuming the whole topic.[9] However, we might also run into the eventual consistency issue we mentioned. The services should apply domain logic and validations against the source of truth; if we can't retrieve the current entity's event stream, it can be troublesome to guarantee the correctness of the domain logic.

7.3.2 Outbox Pattern in Event-Driven Microservices

The outbox pattern is a standard solution when it's necessary to fetch state, apply domain logic, update the state first, and then publish an event. It typically involves two sets of updates, one for the entity's data and another for an outbox event table. The operation's atomicity is usually guaranteed with a transaction wrapping both operations, although we will also explore an alternative for non-transactional databases.

In the example we discussed involving the order service, let's say we save the order information in an order table. To apply this pattern, we would also create an outbox table that saves the events to be published. When receiving an order submission, the order service would insert the new order into the order table and the event into the outbox table. Figure 7-10 illustrates the two order service tables.

---

[7] Detailed example in this article by Microsoft, 2012, "Exploring CQRS and Event Sourcing," `http://download.microsoft.com/download/e/a/8/ea8c6e1f-01d8-43ba-992b-35cfcaa4fae3/cqrs_journey_guide.pdf`

[8] Full article by Adam Warski, March 13, 2018, "Event Sourcing Using Apache Kafka," `www.confluent.io/blog/event-sourcing-using-apache-kafka/`

[9] Further details on why Kafka isn't suitable for event sourcing in this article by Jesper Hammarbäck, August 18, 2020, "Apache Kafka Is Not for Event Sourcing," `https://dzone.com/articles/apache-kafka-is-not-for-event-sourcing`

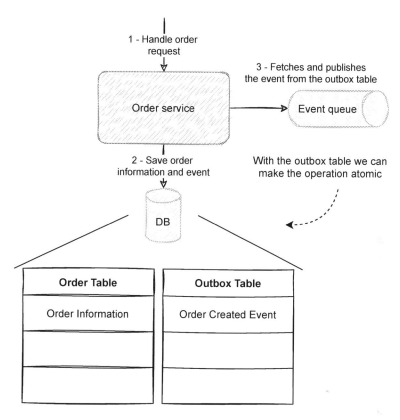

Figure 7-10. *The outbox pattern uses an outbox table to make the operation atomic*

When receiving an order submission request, the order service saves the order information in the order table and the event in the outbox table. Since both operations occur in the same database, we can use a transaction to make them atomic; they either fail or succeed together. An asynchronous process inside the order service can fetch events from the outbox table and publish them to the message broker. If the service saves the information in the database and fails to publish the event, it will still be saved in the outbox table. When the connection recovers, the process can fetch and publish events that failed. Once the events are published, the service can delete them from the table.

If the service crashed, there might be events in the outbox table that weren't published because the service might stop between saving the information in the database and publishing the events. When starting, the service can fetch the events and publish them to the broker. To fetch the outbox table's events, we can implement an ad hoc process that polls the table. An arguably better solution is to do so only when a failure occurs, and the service starts. During regular operation, the service can save and publish directly without waiting for the polling process; this avoids delaying the process by the poll interval.

Instead of implementing an ad hoc polling process, we can use CDC (change data capture), as we discussed in Chapter 2. For example, Kafka supports this out of the box if we use a connector with debezium.[10] It can detect changes in the database and publish the messages to Kafka directly.

This pattern guarantees the reliability of the process by relying on the ACID properties of transactional databases. However, what if we use a database that doesn't support transactions across different tables? A possible solution is to guarantee the database writes are idempotent (applying the operation several times always produces the same result; we will detail this in Section 7.4) and not acknowledge the successful processing of the message until both writes succeed.

Let's say when saving the information in the order table, the operation is an upsert; that is, saving two times the same order produces the same result and doesn't fail due to a duplicate key error, for example. If the service saved the order information and then was unable to write to the outbox table (e.g., the service crashed), there would be an inconsistency; the service changed state but didn't publish an event reflecting that change. However, the service didn't acknowledge the command creating the order either. When the service recovered, it would process the same command again and write to both tables. Since the first operation is idempotent, it wouldn't effectively change anything, and the remaining operations would resume and publish the missing event. We will further detail these strategies in Sections 7.4 and 7.5.

7.3.3 Transactions and Compensating Actions to Avoid Inconsistencies in Event-Driven Microservices

The first option that likely comes to mind to solve this kind of consistency issue is to use transactions. If we are using a database that supports them, one possible solution to avoid this problem is to wrap the whole operation in a transaction. The service would open a transaction, write to the database (the save state step we discussed in

---

[10] Further details on how to implement in this article by Rod Shokrian, October 1, 2019, "Event-Driven Architecture and the Outbox Pattern," `https://medium.com/engineering-varo/event-driven-architecture-and-the-outbox-pattern-569e6fba7216`

the beginning of the section), publish the event, and commit the transaction. If the publishing fails, so will the transaction. However, we can't forget the database and the event stream are two separate components. An important detail is that we can publish the event, and then the transaction can fail to commit. The connection to the database can fail transiently or be unavailable after publishing. In that situation, we would have inconsistency, but the other way around, the event stream could have changes that were persisted by the service.

When the event publishing fails, instead of using transactions, we could undo the changes that were persisted in the database. We could have a series of compensating actions that reverted what was done before the event publishing. Compensating actions are also applicable to databases that don't support transactions. However, they suffer from a similar limitation; if the compensating actions fail, we end up with an inconsistent state.

Although still having a chance to fail, transactional and compensating actions significantly reduce the likelihood of leaving an inconsistent state. Saving state without publishing an event and vice versa only happens if the connectivity to both the database and the message broker fails at the same time. In Chapter 6, we discussed how unlikely events are almost inevitable with enough scale. If that scenario can happen, then it will certainly happen eventually.

However, we should also have a pragmatic view of problems and solutions. If the chance of an issue occurring is remote enough, it might not be worth the effort of a flawless solution; we might be able to live with some issues if their impact isn't relevant enough. This kind of reasoning sends a chill upon my spine, and if you dealt with production systems for long enough, it probably sends a chill upon your spine too. I wouldn't advise following this line of reasoning as a standard, obviously, but we also need to be pragmatic and choose the right tradeoffs. Transactions and compensating actions might be a viable solution in that scope; they are often familiar and straightforward to implement when a more sustainable approach is impractical.

7.4 Applying ACID 2.0 As a Resilience Strategy in Event-Driven Microservices

Failure in distributed systems is given for granted as a variable we must incorporate and account for in our solutions. Typical resilience strategies incorporate retrying strategies in some way. Retrying techniques are also applicable in event-driven services; when processing a message if a service's dependency or the service itself fails, a common resilience strategy is to retry the message consumption. Consuming a message that was already consumed in the past can be troublesome depending on the service design. This section will discuss how to apply the concepts of ACID 2.0 (associativity, commutativity, idempotence, and distributed) in event processing and use them to achieve fault tolerance.

Consuming repeated messages can become a common use case, for example, if we need to replay the event stream to repair data that was corrupted due to a bug. Retrying is fairly helpful when transient failures occur; in fact, transient failures are typically more common than outages that span a considerable amount of time. However, if the proper measures aren't in place, doing the same operation more than once can generate erroneous results.

Imagine if we have a service that manages the product's inventory and publishes events for stock changes. The product service stores information of all the product catalog, including stock. To update the stock information, it handles the stock events published by the inventory service. Figure 7-11 illustrates this example.

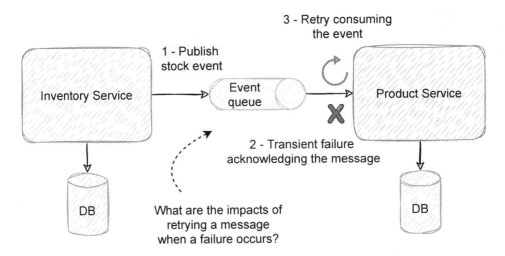

Figure 7-11. *The product service retrying a stock event after a transient failure acknowledging the message*

The example illustrates the product service facing a transient error acknowledging the event processing when consuming an event from the inventory service. On the first attempt, the product service can retrieve the event and write the changes to the database but fails to acknowledge the successful processing to the event broker. As a resilience strategy, the product service retries to consume the same event. The retry process will consume the same event and process it from the beginning. On the second attempt, the service can acknowledge and successfully process the event. However, the service wrote the stock changes to the database twice, producing a wrong value for the product's stock depending on how the product service consumes the event. For example, if the inventory service published a stock out event signaling the product stock was decreased, it would subtract the stock twice.

As we discussed in Section 7.2, exactly-once semantics is often complex to guarantee. To assure every message is processed, we often rely on at-least-once message delivery semantics. A service may receive repeated messages due to the message broker's failures or the upstream services, thus the at-least-once semantic. Under those circumstances, services should be able to receive and generate valid states with duplicated messages.

Event processing often benefits from understanding a set of principles about maintaining distributed consistency captured by the CALM[11] theorem. CALM (consistency as logical monotonicity) states that systems which process a progressive set of facts without changing what already happened are safe to run on an eventually consistent store. This concept closely relates to the event-driven approach; events reflect the evolving state of the entities and represent a fact that already happened which shouldn't be changed. ACID 2.0 (associativity, commutativity, idempotence, and distributed[12]) embodies a set of design patterns closely related to the CALM theorem. By applying these properties to distributed systems, we can achieve distributed consistency and logical monotonicity.[13]

---

[11] Full article by Peter Alvaro, Neil Conway, Joseph M. Hellerstein, and William R. Marczak, January 9–12, 2011, "Consistency Analysis in Bloom: a CALM and Collected Approach," https://people.ucsc.edu/~palvaro/cidr11.pdf

[12] Very interesting article by Pat Helland and Dave Campbell, June 7–10, 2009, "Building on Quicksand," https://database.cs.wisc.edu/cidr/cidr2009/Paper_133.pdf

[13] Full article by Peter Bailis and Ali Ghodsi, April 9, 2013, "Eventual Consistency Today: Limitations, Extensions, and Beyond," https://queue.acm.org/detail.cfm?id=2462076

Chapter 5 discussed the impacts of distributed systems in traditional consistency and the difficulties of maintaining regular atomic consistency under the CAP theorem. The clever acronym behind ACID 2.0 raises the challenge of reflecting on a new kind of consistency under distributed systems, opposed to the traditional ACID in relational databases. ACID 2.0 is based on three main properties, associativity, commutativity, and idempotence, which happen in a distributed system (the D in ACID 2.0).

Associativity and commutativity translate the system's ability to perform out-of-order operations, which translates to the ability to tolerate unordered events in an event-driven system. Idempotence is the ability of a system to perform the same operation multiple times and obtain the same outcome. In event-driven systems, it translates to the ability to process the same event multiple times and obtain the same result.

How can we apply the ACID 2.0 properties to event processing? One possible approach is related to the event schema and how events are designed. In the example we discussed before, the stock out event (an event signaling the user removed or bought stock; basically the stock for this item was decreased by a quantity) isn't idempotent. If we process the same stock out event multiple times, the service will decrease the stock by the number of times it processes it, producing a different result each time. Instead of publishing a stock out event, the inventory service could publish a stock changed event that informs the product's current stock quantity. Listing 7-1 illustrates an example of both events.

Listing 7-1. StockOut vs. StockChanged event

```
StockOut
{
    ProductId: 15251212,
    Size: "XS",
    Quantity: 1
}

StockChanged
{
    ProductId: 15251212,
    Size: "XS",
    CurrentQuantity: 5
}
```

The events have similar information, but the stock out event represents a removal of stock quantity from an item. The stock changed event signals the current stock of the product. If the product service consumes the same stock changed event multiple times, it will always produce the same result; it will constantly update the product's stock to the same quantity. We changed the event schema to be idempotent. We also made the retry operation safe. However, we also changed the event's meaning; a stock changed event has typically less domain value than a stock out event. If the user is buying a stock unit and decreases the stock, the stock out event reflects clearly the intent of the user; a stock changed event doesn't translate it as plainly. Nevertheless, it is essential to adapt to our consumers' needs, and in this case, the stock changed event is arguably the most reasonable choice (we will further discuss event schema design in Chapter 8).

A critical consideration also related to the event schema is the fact that the stock out events are order agnostic. We just need to process them once; it doesn't matter in which order (not taking into account negative stock validations). If the service publishes a stock changed, the order matters; we only want the latest quantity, thus the newest stock changed event. We can manage the order with event versioning as we discussed in Chapter 6. In this case, as with most decisions, it's about weighing the tradeoffs and choosing a set of properties above others. Order is often easy to manage; idempotency is more challenging and provides strong resilience properties, being more useful in similar situations.

However, changing the event schema isn't always possible. An alternative is to make the event consumption idempotent. In Chapter 6, we discussed how to use event versioning to handle unordered messages. We can use a similar strategy to guarantee the processing is idempotent. For example, if we only process each event version once, we can turn the event handling idempotent. In the stock out event example, if we store the versions we already processed, we can ignore it when receiving a repeated event. This way, consuming the same event multiple times has no impact. We can also achieve the same result by ignoring repeated changes by the id or the event's date, depending on the event.

When duplicated events can generate invalid results and we don't enjoy ordered, exactly-once guarantees, we may need to reason how we can turn the event consumption idempotent and order agnostic. Event schema or event versioning can be the solution; sometimes we can change the way we are consuming the events and make it idempotent; sometimes it can even be solved as a business process. One of the main takeaways we should interiorize is comprehending the impact of repeated events and establishing a strategy to make the consumption idempotent.

7.5 Avoiding Message Leak in Event-Driven Microservices

An inconspicuous detail we can often miss is how to guarantee messages aren't lost in the presence of errors. Message leak occurs when the service acknowledges an event as successful and then fails to process it due to an error; the service might lose that event without the correct approach. When processing messages, the standard way to retrieve messages from the message broker is to acknowledge them promptly. Although efficient and straightforward, when faced with unexpected failures, it can generate message leaks. This section will work through an example illustrating this situation and how we can address it.

You might recall when we detailed the interactions between the services and the message broker in Section 7.2 (Figure 7-6) and discussed how the consumers acknowledge the event's processing after retrieving them from the broker. Figure 7-12 illustrates this situation with the pricing service.

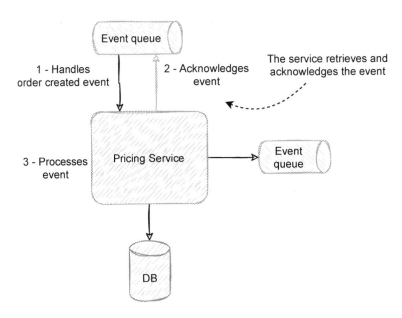

Figure 7-12. *Example of an auto acknowledge interaction*

The service retrieves an order created event from the message broker, acknowledges the event, and then proceeds to carry out the operations to process the event. This implementation is often the standard way to interact with message brokers; for example,

Kafka has an auto-commit consumer configuration, which by default is enabled, which periodically and automatically commits offsets upon message reception. In RabbitMQ, you can choose between automatic and manual acknowledgments in the consumer (manual acknowledgments are the default).

This detail is essential because if the service crashes or one of the dependencies fails, we already acknowledged the message, the broker already marked it as consumed. In Kafka, the offset was already committed; in RabbitMQ, the broker already removed the message from the queue; etc. The service acknowledges the message to the broker, but it is still processing it in memory. Any issue that makes the service lose the message from memory will leak that message. This issue can happen if the services crash, or, depending on the deployment process, it may happen by deploying a new version. This means we might lose messages every time the service crashes or even when we deploy the service.

A more suitable approach is only to acknowledge the message after the processing is completed. The service retrieves the message; does all the processing it needs to, in this case, the pricing logic related to the order; and acknowledges the message. The service might have parallelism and process multiple messages but will only acknowledge each one after completing all operations involved in the event's processing. This way, if the service crashes, it will reprocess the events it was processing before it crashed instead of losing them.

Imagine the pricing service also publishes an event signaling the prices calculated for each order. These two approaches mark the difference between at-least-once and at-most-once semantics in the pricing service event publishing. If the service acknowledges the order event immediately, the service might crash before sending the pricing event but will never send repeated events. However, if the service acknowledges the order event after publishing the pricing event, it might send it twice. If the service crashes after the event publishing, it will reprocess the same event sending a duplicate event. Depending on the message delivery semantics we need, we can automatically or manually acknowledge messages. However, to not lose messages, acknowledgments should be manual.

7.5.1 Poison Events

There is a subtle difference between not losing events and ignoring events with corrupted or unexpected information. There might be events the service fails to process due to unforeseen data or failing validations. In those cases, should we ignore the event? If the service can't process the event due to failing validations, it might make sense to ignore it, but there can also be the case the service is failing to process events due to a bug or unexpected data.

We can fix the service and replay or change the offset to reprocess those events in those cases. Having a dead letter queue[14] is also an option. When failing to process an event, we can publish it to a queue that only has failed events and resume regular work. Then an ad hoc process or a specific consumer can process or requeue the events. Uber has an article explaining how they implemented this with Kafka.[15] Dead letter queues might make sense when a large number of events have been published after the failing events since it might require reprocessing many events that already succeeded. However, with durable message brokers, since the events are persisted and still available, moving back the offset and reprocessing when possible is often a more simple solution.

7.6 Applying Common Resilience Patterns in Event-Driven Microservices

As we discussed at the beginning of the chapter, event-driven services might have a set of external dependencies. Each dependency or the network connection between the service and the dependency might fail. When a failure of this type occurs, there is a set of traditional approaches we can adopt. This section will detail these strategies and work through a practical example of applying them to event-driven services.

Event-driven services enjoy a higher level of decoupling and independence that avoids cascading errors to the upstream services. However, the service itself might face unexpected errors from its dependencies. The impact of those failures is often limited to the service's scope; for example, a read model might still respond to requests even

---

[14] Article on how to implement it by Robin Moffatt, March 13, 2019, "Kafka Connect Deep Dive – Error Handling and Dead Letter Queues," www.confluent.io/blog/kafka-connect-deep-dive-error-handling-dead-letter-queues/

[15] Full article by Ning Xia, February 16, 2018, "Building Reliable Reprocessing and Dead Letter Queues with Apache Kafka," https://eng.uber.com/reliable-reprocessing/

though an upstream service is failing. Data will become stale since the service is no longer processing updates, but the event-driven architecture's nature allows the system to respond. It is often far more valuable to have the platform continue to respond even though a part of the system is unavailable.

Even though the scope is often smaller, the services have their own role and pivotal business value. The service dependencies might fail, and the service should be reliable enough to maintain correct operation and recover as soon as possible. We should also maximize availability and be resilient when facing a failure in a local dependency.

7.6.1 Retries As a Resilience Approach in Event-Driven Microservices

Retries are the standard approach to deal with transient errors. You likely implemented some kind of retry mechanism when accessing an external service or dependency. In fact, the constant presence of transient and network errors highlights the usefulness of retries. A request might fail from time to time due to numerous reasons; retrying the request is often better than a manual process to recover data.

In event-driven services, we can apply a retry strategy in different operations of the processing flow. As illustrated in Figure 7-13, we can use a retry strategy while accessing external dependencies like other services or the database or applying a retry strategy to the event consumption itself.

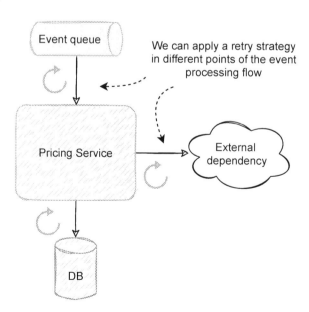

Figure 7-13. *The retry strategy can be applied in different scopes*

Applying retry strategies to external dependencies is often more useful when dealing with transient issues. We can also have retries at the event consumption level; when consuming, we can retry the whole event processing flow if an error occurs. This kind of retries is often more helpful when dealing with eventual consistency, optimistic concurrency, or invalid domain logic where we need to perform all the operations in the flow again.

There is a fascinating article[16] detailing how Google achieved 99.9% latency SLA on some of their services by using retry strategies (we also mentioned this article in Chapter 5). Retries have higher resource consumption since the service has to make another request; however, as the article details, with the right approach, it can be significantly small (only 2% in the article use case) and significantly improve reliability and availability. Retries are often related to timeouts; when defining and triggering a timeout, we can retry the request. An arguably good approach discussed in the article is understanding the typical latency and specifying timeouts for the 95th-percentile expected latency before canceling and retrying the request.

As discussed with cascading failures, retries can be troublesome by adding additional load to an already struggling service. A common approach is to use retries with exponential backoff and a maximum limit. The retry strategy should always have a maximum number of retries to avoid more significant impacts or halting consumption. Imagine the service receives an event with unexpected data; if we indefinitely retry the consumption, the service will indefinitely try to process the event, impacting the throughput. Retries should also only be performed against conditions that are likely to succeed by repeating a request. We should be able to filter the conditions that will always fail.

Exponential backoff retries are also useful to limit the impact of the additional load on dependencies. We can successively make additional requests but separated by an exponentially increasing time interval between the requests. We can also increment a random value (also known as jitter) to randomize the time interval. The jitter helps to avoid accidental choreographed load peaks across different services.

We can also have different strategies when all retries fail. We might have dependencies critical for the service's logic or others that we might be able to continue processing, although with some degradation. For example, if the connection to the database fails, it might impact all types of events consumed by the service. However, if the caching mechanism fails, we might still process events without cache, but perhaps

---

[16] Fascinating article by Jeffrey Dean and Luiz André Barroso, February 2013, "The Tail at Scale," https://cacm.acm.org/magazines/2013/2/160173-the-tail-at-scale/fulltext

with reduced throughput. When a critical component fails, an arguably good approach is to apply a circuit breaker (we will detail circuit breakers next) and not acknowledge the messages that failed (as discussed in Section 7.5). This way, the service won't try to process additional messages and reprocess the messages that failed once the service recovers.

7.6.2 Circuit Breakers in Event-Driven Microservices

Retries are great for transient failures or short-timed unavailability. However, providing resilience while facing more extended outages (a failure that persists after several retries) might require different approaches. Retrying an operation that is unlikely to succeed might be pointless or aggravate an already difficult situation. Instead, the application should avoid frequent requests and handle the failure in the most suitable way possible. The circuit breaker pattern can be a safety net to prevent the service from making excessive requests. This subsection will detail how the pattern works and how we can apply it to event-driven services.

Event-driven services can have external dependencies, like the database or a distributed cache. For example, suppose we have a pricing service responsible for calculating the order's price according to country and discount rules. In that case, it could have a dependency on a distributed cache like Redis. Transient connection issues to Redis can be handled using retries, but we might benefit from applying a circuit breaker pattern to deal with longer outages. This example is illustrated in Figure 7-14.

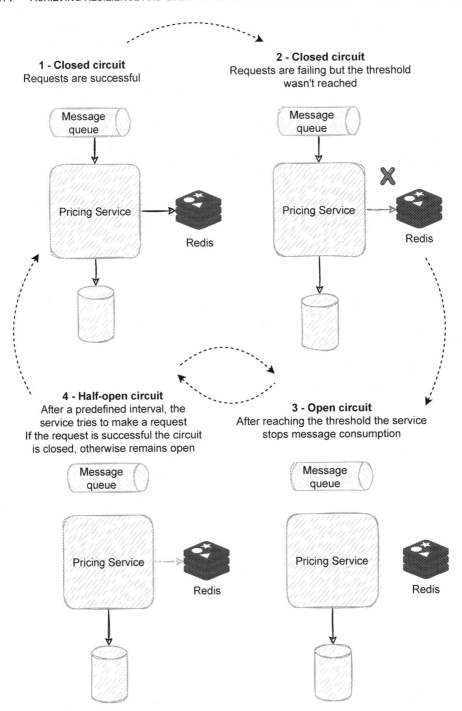

Figure 7-14. *The different states of a circuit breaker pattern applied to an event-driven service*

The pricing service reacts to order events and uses Redis and the database to process its domain logic. While in normal working mode, the circuit is considered closed; external requests are successful and events are processed. The concept of opened and closed circuits originates from actual electrical circuit breakers. They were electrical switches designed to interrupt current flow when faced with an issue; thus, when in a closed state, the current flows, and in an open state, the current stops. The pattern uses the same concept: when the service is processing normally, the circuit breaker is closed, and when faced with an issue, the circuit breaker opens and stops the processing flow.

If the pricing service has an issue reaching Redis, the requests will start to fail. When the number of failed requests goes above a defined threshold, the circuit breaker opens. In this case, it stops message consumption and consequently the requests to Redis. When in this state, the circuit breaker is considered opened. However, the service can't remain in this state forever; from time to time, the service will try to reach Redis. While the requests fail, the circuit will stay in the open state. When the requests finally succeed, it will close the circuit and resume message consumption.

One of the advantages of reacting to events in a queue is the service won't lose data or fail requests. The upstream services will continue to publish events; once the service recovers and resumes message consumption, it can process the events queued during the outage. The service can lag behind the latest changes happening in the ecosystem and might pile up work; however, it's better than failing or losing those requests. If the number of messages is significantly high, we can horizontally scale by adding more instances to reduce the lag faster and remove them when the lag clears.

Circuit breakers also open the opportunity to create a more resilient service by providing the possibility to choose a suitable fallback when applicable. In this case, instead of stopping event consumption, we can replace the external dependency with a fallback. For example, while facing a Redis outage, the service can fall back to an in-memory cache; it might not be as efficient as a distributed one but might be enough for the service to cope with regular demand while the outage recovers.

7.7 Recovering Data and Repairing State in Event-Driven Microservices

The previous sections discussed how to guarantee messages are sent and processed reliably. We also discussed how not to lose events and to ensure every event received is processed. With these approaches, we provide tools to control failures and avoid data repair processes. However, data can still be corrupted, or the services can generate an undesirable state (due to a bug, for example). This section will discuss how we can use durable event brokers to recover data and repair the service's state.

Let's work through a practical example similar to the ones we discussed in the previous sections. The pricing service handles order created events from a queue, processes the charges, generates an internal state in a database, and publishes an event informing the order's charges. We released new functionality that changes the way taxes are calculated, and, unfortunately, we introduced a bug. We quickly noticed the issue due to our comprehensive monitoring and alarmistic and rolled back the release. This situation is illustrated in Figure 7-15.

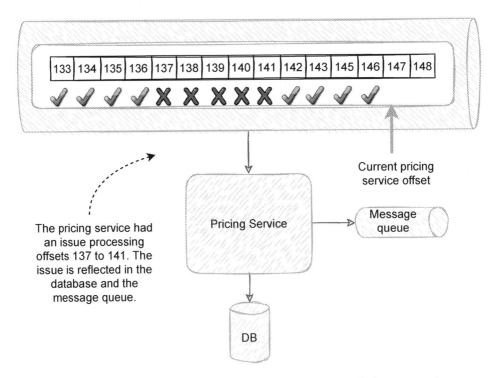

Figure 7-15. *The pricing service generated invalid state while processing a set of events*

314

However, the pricing service ran with an invalid version against a set of events. The service stored the state generated by those events, and it is safe to assume part of our data is corrupted. This situation has an additional aggravating factor; since the charges were wrong, the events the service published are also impacted, which might also affect the downstream services.

In a traditional monolithic application, a possible solution would be to identify the affected orders and run an ad hoc process to recover them by running a database script. In that case, it might be somewhat straightforward since all data is in a single database, and we can correct everything in a single operation, even though it's often an error-prone process. In a synchronous microservice architecture, it might be more challenging; a database script wouldn't likely suffice since the pricing service's dependencies wouldn't be affected (in a synchronous architecture, the event queue would be replaced by a direct request to the service that needs the pricing data). The alternative could be running an ad hoc process to call the service to repair the affected orders. Identifying the orders with an invalid state can also be challenging if there aren't the querying capabilities to do so or there is an overwhelming number of orders.

In an event-driven service, an arguably straightforward solution is to change the service's offset to the offset before the bug was introduced. In the case of Figure 7-15, we could change the pricing service's offset from 147 to 137, and the service would reprocess the affected events (from 137 to 141), and the state would be repaired. The drawback is events from offset 142 to 146 would be reprocessed even though they were successful, hence the importance of idempotence we discussed in Section 7.4.

The service already published invalid events, and if we are not using documents, they should remain as is. As you might recall from Chapter 3, documents have the entity's complete state, and the event broker only retains the latest ones (as we discussed with Kafka compacted topics). It might seem odd, but events represent facts that happened in the past; if charges were effectively wrong, then the event history should reflect that fact. To repair the state, by going back in the offset, the service will publish new events with the correct information, thus repairing the downstream services that will react to those events. As we discussed before, the service only publishes an event if the state changed. In this case, the service would only publish events related to the invalid orders that the service corrected. Although the service reprocesses the already successful orders, it won't change any state, reflecting in no new events, and thus won't affect the downstream services with additional load.

We mentioned the wrong events should remain as is, except for documents. In those use cases, the queue doesn't retain the history but rather the newest state. Since we would publish a new document with the correct information, the service would also correct the data in the document queue since the broker would only retain the latest documents. The invalid ones would be older and thus would be purged by the broker.

If we apply the other strategies we discussed in this chapter, this approach is likely limited to bugs and similar issues since outages are already accounted for. However, even if we don't have those strategies in place, this solution can be a valuable approach to recovering from leaked events or random outages.

Notice that this approach doesn't involve any ad hoc manual process or specific developments to recover the state. We use the same flow the service uses to process regular events; we just rewind the event queue and reprocess. The beauty of having a durable event queue, besides being able to derive value from history and generating new views of the data, is having all the tools needed to recover state sustainably.

7.8 Bulkhead Pattern in Event-Driven Microservices

Bulkheads are usually employed in ships as a means to contain failures. They separate the ship into several isolated partitions; if the hull takes damage and one section is compromised, the bulkheads guarantee the failure doesn't spread to the rest of the ship. A ship can still sail with some flooded partitions; the bulkheads avoid an otherwise catastrophic failure. This section will discuss how we can apply a similar concept to an event-driven architecture.

 On a side note, the Titanic had bulkheads, but they didn't prevent the ship from sinking. Titanic's bulkheads didn't go full length due to mainly not hindering the passenger's comfort and movement throughout the ship. Since they weren't tall enough, the bulkheads didn't contain the water in the damaged partitions, the software engineering equivalent of marking resilience developments as "nice to have" in planning meetings.

 Anyhow, how do bulkheads apply to event-driven services? Let's use the same example with the pricing service. The service handles order created events, processes the charges for each order, and saves state in a database. Let's say we also have a taxes service in charge of managing changes in taxes across every country. We discussed why each service should have its own database; however, the database cluster can have multiple databases. For example, if we use MongoDB, we might want to group several domain-related databases in the same cluster. Perhaps more theoretical references might refer to this as an anti-pattern, and truth be told, the ideal situation is to have complete segregated database clusters for each service. However, this is often not the case due to practical and monetary reasons, and it isn't due to solid reasons. Although often oblivious to us, a solution that has a considerable cost to maintain, even though with excellent performance and scalability properties, isn't a very good solution. After all, we are building the tools for a business to strive.

When the taxes change, they produce a bulk operation in the taxes service, which is very database heavy. The additional load starves the cluster's resources and might impact both the taxes and pricing service, as illustrated in Figure 7-16.

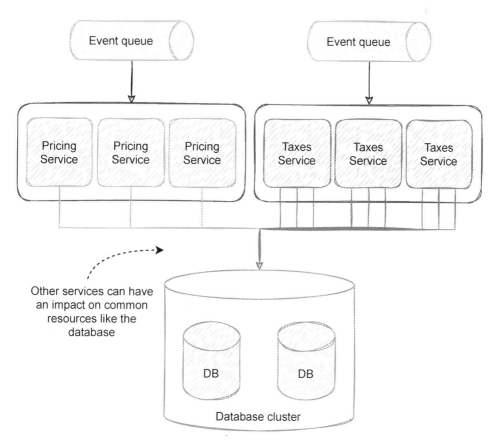

Figure 7-16. *The taxes service produces additional load on the database cluster due to a bulk operation*

In order to mitigate the impact done by the taxes service, we could apply the bulkhead pattern by adjusting the parallelism degree in the taxes service. We discussed in Chapter 6 we might have several instances of a service, and each service instance has parallelism to optimize physical resources. By decreasing the parallelism degree, we would also reduce the impact the service has on the database cluster. If the service has several instances, we can also reduce their number. The parallelism degree and the number of instances are essential parameters we should include in our solutions from the ground up to adjust the service performance and mitigate this kind of impact.

Obviously, the taxes service will process slower, but a bulk action might be more permissible to be processed slower than the charges applied to each order. The bulkhead pattern is about containing failure; the service might process slower, but it won't propagate the issue to the pricing service or other processes running in the taxes service. In this case, as a more sustainable solution, we could upscale the database or separate it into different clusters in order to avoid the impact, as we discussed before. However, it might not justify the cost and might be more reasonable and cost-effective to say a bulk operation might take a while to finish with modest parallelism. We can apply this approach to any kind of dependency, a distributed cache, or a synchronous request to another service. When using synchronous requests to other services, the bulkhead pattern might be an arguably good solution since those services might be susceptible to cascading failures. A bulkhead approach in the upstream services might quickly avoid widespread impacts.

7.8.1 Priority Queues

Another way to manage the impact of the unexpected load is to segregate operations into different queues. In the previous example, the taxes service received a bulk operation which might reflect an abnormal message arrival rate. Since, typically, a bulk operation has lower priority than the changes happening in real time in the ecosystem, we could delegate them to a lower priority queue.

By having segregated queues, we can allocate different resources to each queue. The queue with the regular everyday changes might have a higher degree of parallelism than the queue handling bulk operations. This way, we can adjust each queue's parallelism degree to guarantee there is no lag in the higher priority queues. The lower priority queues get processed at a sustainable rate without affecting the service's dependencies and resources. The assumption is the service might lag in the low priority queue, which should be alright since the changes don't need to be processed in real time. We can delegate longer-running processes to low priority queues and significant business changes to higher priority ones.

7.9 Conclusion

How all the patterns we discussed throughout the chapter are applied to the service's dependencies? Figure 7-17 illustrates how these patterns relate to the initial discussion of a typical service topology and its dependencies (Figure 7-1).

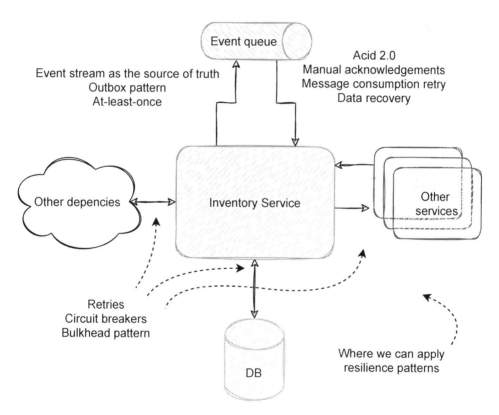

Figure 7-17. *How the patterns discussed throughout the chapter relate to the service's dependencies*

In typical external dependencies like other services, distributed caches, the database, etc., it's often relevant to use retries, circuit breakers, and the bulkhead pattern. When publishing messages, we can use the event stream as the source of truth, the outbox pattern, and publish in at-least-once semantics. We can consume messages according to

ACID 2.0, do manual acknowledgments/commits, retry the message consumption, and use the data recovery strategy.

If we apply the patterns we discussed in this chapter, we can guarantee we process events reliably and without leaks. We also guarantee the safety of the service's dependencies and ways to regulate traffic and load.

7.10 Summary

- Services have several dependencies, and each one of them can fail due to a number of reasons. We need to guarantee these failures don't affect the reliability and the correctness of the service.

- Event-driven services are less likely to suffer from cascading failures due to their decoupled nature.

- Load balancing and rate limiting are often already incorporated in the design of event-driven services due to their interaction with the event broker.

- Event delivery can have three different semantics: at-least-once, at-most-once, and exactly-once. Exactly-once is the most useful and the hardest to guarantee. At-most-once loses messages but typically enjoys higher performance. At-least-once might generate repeated work, but it's straightforward to achieve and ensures no messages are lost.

- The service's state must reflect the event stream. We can achieve this by making the event stream the source of truth, with the outbox pattern, or using transactions and compensating actions.

- Applying ACID 2.0 properties to message consumption can provide higher resilience and flexibility, especially when associated with retrying strategies.

- Manual acknowledgments or commits can guarantee messages aren't lost in a failure scenario.

- Retries and circuit breakers are common resilience patterns we can apply to make the service more resilient and regulate throughput to external dependencies. We can combine circuit breakers with fallbacks to make the service resilient to common failures.

- Rewinding the event stream can be a powerful tool to recover data.

- The bulkhead pattern can contain the proliferation of local failures. Priority queues can also be a viable option to regulate traffic with different urgency without overwhelming the service's resources.

CHAPTER 8

Choosing the Correct Event Schema Design in Event-Driven Microservices

This chapter covers:

- Model events using event storming

- Using and understanding which information benefits from being transferred in event headers

- Designing small events and their impacts

- Designing large and denormalized events and their impacts

- Understanding the importance of involving consumers in the event schema design

- Avoiding breaking changes and how to evolve event schema

© Hugo Filipe Oliveira Rocha 2022
H. F. Oliveira Rocha, *Practical Event-Driven Microservices Architecture*,
https://doi.org/10.1007/978-1-4842-7468-2_8

Darwin once said it isn't the stronger or most intelligent species that survive but the most adaptable. Events are much like it; there isn't a one-fits-all rule to design events; they often need to be adapted to each use case and have the requirements of the consuming application in mind. Events are the essence of every event-driven architecture; as we discussed in the previous chapters, they are a meaningful and sustainable way to share data throughout the company. They represent the business's very history retaining its value and exposing it in a decoupled and scalable way. Exposing data in a streaming and scalable medium provides the foundation for powerful use cases. Events are the blood flow in an event-driven architecture; designing the correct event schema for each use case becomes a key design consideration.

We discussed the advantages of having durable event brokers and retaining the history of events. It's a powerful concept, until you have to insert a breaking change in the event schema, and then history seems a lot less valuable compared to the challenge of handling multiple event schemas. This chapter will also discuss how to approach schema changes and work through a use case illustrating how we can approach schema evolution.

Designing events is often a gray area; there are standard best practices, but following them blindly can severely impact the architecture and produce complicated workarounds. Understanding the implications of the different design approaches, weighing the tradeoffs, and making deliberate decisions is fundamental to achieve a maintainable and scalable solution. This chapter will discuss these tradeoffs and work through a use case using different approaches explaining the advantages and downsides. Although it won't give you a silver bullet to always design the correct schema, it will provide you with the considerations to make sustained decisions and choose the appropriate implications for each use case.

8.1 Event Storming and Event-Driven Microservices

Event storming is a technique to model complex business processes that has high synergy with event-driven architectures. It shares some of the DDD concepts, but it's focused on a timeline of events that we can often directly translate to code. The full implementation of event storming is out of this book's scope, and it's fully addressed in Alberto Brandolini's book,[1] its original creator. This section will give you the foundations for exploring it further and why event storming can be relevant in modeling an event-driven architecture and its events.

---

[1] Book by Alberto Brandolini, "Event Storming," www.eventstorming.com/book/

Event storming is a tool to gain a higher level of understanding of a complex domain and promote shared understanding around the domain's business processes. It involves modeling a business process as a flow of events represented by stickies on a whiteboard. The technical and business experts use different colored stickers to model the sequence of domain events, commands, components, external systems, and questions in a business process. In a relatively short session, around one hour, a rather complex business process can be modeled, as long as the right people are in the room and the appropriate mediation is provided. Further sessions can be scheduled to dive down on unclear subjects or to further detail higher-level flows.

It's also about gathering the right people in the same room and doing temporal modeling of the business process. Instead of focusing on a structure like typical modeling approaches (like UML, sequence diagrams, etc.), focuses on mapping the timeline of successive events that happen in the process. It can be highly beneficial as a tool for collective learning and modeling the whole end-to-end process. It also helps identify possible early gaps, blockers, misunderstandings, and gray areas that might become a problem later in the project.

So, how can we apply it? The crucial point about event storming is the presence of the right people in the event storming session. There should be elements of the development team and the domain experts. If we don't have the correct people in the session, we should postpone it and guarantee everyone is present. Once we gather all relevant people and clearly define the session's objective (e.g., event map the order fulfillment process), we should ask the participants to model the process with events. Events are represented by orange stickies and should be placed on a large open area. A large area is important; we want the participants to map the process and not discuss it fruitlessly without physical support. A cramped space to put the stickies limits the thought process; discussions without physical support often have no real conclusions or action points; we want to avoid that. Then the participants should map the process as a sequence of events. Figure 8-1 illustrates the sequence of events in an order fulfillment flow.

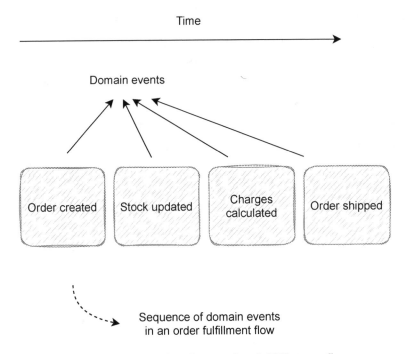

Figure 8-1. *Domain events example of an order fulfillment flow*

The most valuable first step is to model the business process as a sequence of domain events. The sequence by itself vastly increases the knowledge of the process of everyone in the session. An arguably good first interaction is to have the moderator ask the participants an event of the business process and write it down, which typically helps break the ice and kick off the activity. Domain events are a business occurrence that is relevant for the business experts. Domain experts can explain the process according to these events as they flow in a timeline. Presenting the business process with this mindset provides a valuable framework for storytelling and is easy for anyone, even without a technical background, to understand. An important moderation tip is to let the domain experts map the events, and the developers explore their meaning instead of developers guiding the thought process.

Once you have the main flow of domain events, you can add the other typical elements of an event storming session:

- Domain events, which we just discussed (typically represented by orange stickies)

- User commands, a user action (typically represented by blue stickies)

- Questions, risks, assumptions, and concerns, which we use to signal possible gaps or parts of the process that need further analysis (typically represented by pink stickies)

- Persona/actor, who initiated the action (typically represented by yellow stickies)

- External systems, events from an external system (typically represented by light blue/cyan stickies)

- Data, data consultation to make a decision or a read model (typically represented by light green stickies)

I find that typically it's best to map the domain event sequence and then iterate on adding detail about the other types of artifacts. Eventually, it can evolve to something similar to Figure 8-2.

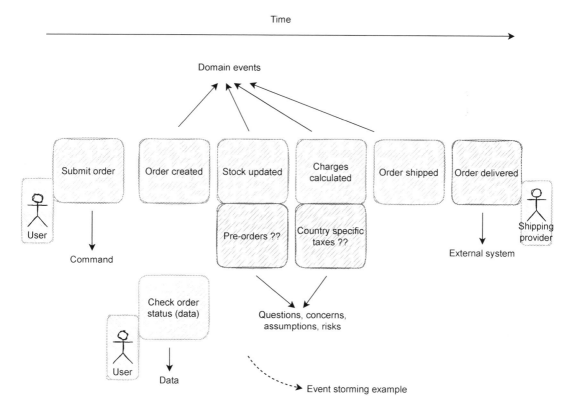

Figure 8-2. *Event storming example of an order fulfillment flow with additional artifacts*

An important detail is the question/pink stickies; if the participants get stuck discussing a subject, write it on one of those stickies. It promotes everyone's collaboration, and if the discussion takes too long, we can mark it and move on. Also, following the typical diverge, explore, and converge approach can be beneficial. You want the participants to discuss the overall process and the sequence of events (diverge and explore). Next, try to make sense of the confusion and group everyone to organize the event flow (converge).

This process promotes active collaboration to discover the right thing to do. In large microservice architectures, developers tend to implement projects focused on a single or few services, and it is easy to lose the whole picture of the end-to-end process. It is also easy to do what they are told, which might not be the right thing. Event storming greatly benefits the dissemination of knowledge and clarifies the main objective of the project.

One thing DDD often mentions is the domain expert. In fact, in large organizations, there isn't one domain expert; typically, there are knowledge silos. In each silo, there is one or a few domain experts specialized in that silo; there is hardly anyone with knowledge of all silos. Event storming shines in these environments where we can bring each domain expert to the session. Each person in the session individually might not know everything, but everyone's combined knowledge provides to be exceptionally insightful. It also provides a platform for group validation, much like a code review to a process modeling done by domain experts.

Event storming has high synergy with event-driven architectures since the domain events often map to the technical domain events, and what better way to design those events than with the domain experts' input? It also highlights some beneficial architectural decisions. For example, in Figure 8-2, we have an order created domain event and a check order status data model; this might directly translate to a CQRS pattern. It often proves to be a smooth translation from the model to the actual implementation.

For further details and moderation guidelines, we highly recommend Alberto Brandolini's book; he also has a great talk at a NewCrafts conference worth checking out.[2] Paul Rayner also has a fascinating talk with several moderation tips and detailing event storming concepts.[3]

---

[2] Talk in NewCrafts Conferences, Alberto Brandolini, "Introducing EventStorming," June 9, 2015, https://vimeo.com/130202708

[3] Talk in Saturn 2017, Paul Rayner, "EventStorming: Collaborative Learning for Complex Domains," May 31, 2017, www.youtube.com/watch?v=vf6x0i2d9VE

8.1.1 What Are the Limitations of Event Storming?

Event storming might not be suitable for simple and straightforward domains. For example, if a domain can be clearly expressed by a CRUD implementation, modeling it by events might not be adequate. However, much like DDD, the understanding and knowledge acquired by the exercise are often extremely valuable.

In more extensive processes and domains with intricate interactions, moderation becomes especially relevant. Experienced moderation can be hard to find and might be a challenge for people trying out event storming[4] for the first time. The book *Game Storming* can help with some frameworks.

One challenge is often having the right people in the session; the domain experts are often hard to pin down. The presence of the right domain experts is usually a do or break requirement; we need the right people in the session to be productive. It also becomes an issue with distributed teams; having people physically in the same room produces a unique atmosphere and promotes a different type of collaboration than having people collaborating remotely. You might still benefit from the exercise, but it might not be as valuable.

8.2 Event Schema: Headers and Envelopes

The event's payload is obviously the pivotal part of the event. However, an often overlooked detail is the event's headers. In some use cases, the event benefits from having some generic properties available in the headers or the event's envelope. This section will discuss the advantages and drawbacks of having an envelope and will work through a use case illustrating which information can be relevant to add to an envelope or headers.

There is some information relevant for every event, independent of their content or origin. This type of generic information or metadata can be shared using a generic structure like an event's headers or an envelope, as illustrated in Figure 8-3. Having standardized properties across the organization can help generic processes or utilities (like tracing) without digging down to the event's payload. It also provides better segregation; the event's payload will only have the information related to the occurrence and the domain, while we can segregate infrastructure information with a more abstract nature to an isolated structure.

---

[4] Book by Dave Gray, Sunni Brown, and James Macanufo, "Gamestorming: A Playbook for Innovators, Rulebreakers, and Changemakers," August 17, 2010, www.amazon.com/Gamestorming-Playbook-Innovators-Rulebreakers-Changemakers/dp/0596804172

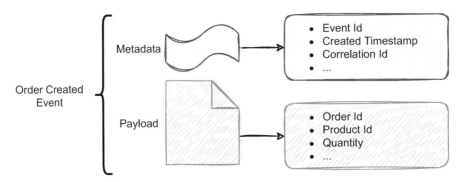

Figure 8-3. *Segregation of the event's metadata and payload*

The metadata provides contextual information about the event, while the payload provides the event's information. It's similar to an HTTP request; the body of the request carries the request's payload, and the HTTP headers have more contextual information about the request. The event's metadata can be transferred using an envelope or through message headers. A message envelope is like a wrapper around or inside the event's payload with a standard structure common to all events. Most message brokers also support message headers, and much like HTTP headers, they are often modeled in a key-value approach with the flexibility to define custom values.

8.2.1 Headers vs. Envelopes in Event Schema

There are typically two approaches to implement event envelopes, either by a composed or flat structure. A flat structure adds the information next to the event's payload, with a property containing all metadata information. The composed structure is more popular and resembles an actual envelope; the envelope is a wrapper with contextual information and an abstract payload. Listing 8-1 illustrates the two types of envelopes applied to an order created event.

Listing 8-1. Composed vs. flat envelope structure

```
1    Composed OrderCreatedEvent
2    {
3        Metadata:
4        {
5        EventId: 1231,
6        Timestamp: "2021-01-30T11:41:21.442Z"
```

```
 7          },
 8          Payload:
 9          {
10              OrderId: 3621,
11              ProductId: 2184,
12              Quantity: 2,
13              UserId: 164
14          }
15    }
16
17    Flat OrderCreatedEvent
18    {
19          Metadata: [{"EventId": 1231}, { "Timestamp":
              "2021-01-30T11:41:21.442Z"}],
20          OrderId: 3621,
21          ProductId: 2184,
22          Quantity: 2,
23          UserId: 164
24    }
```

Every event with a flat structure has a property specific to the event's metadata. While the composed structure segregates it at a higher level, the event has two root fields: one for the metadata and one for the payload. The metadata in the composed field can also be a generic array of dynamic properties, although there are advantages of defining static metadata fields. For example, if we define a standard envelope for the company, we can enforce specific fields like the correlation id or the user id for audit purposes. It also incites collaboration on the envelope definition (although this can be an advantage or drawback depending on the company).

However, the envelope tends to get in the way of the event and sometimes can be challenging to deal with. It introduces extra information to serialize and deserialize having a performance hit; also changes in the envelope tend to be difficult to manage. If changing an event's schema requires a lot of communication and alignment, imagine changing the envelope's schema when all events share the same envelope. Also it can become hard to simultaneously handle sources that use envelopes and sources that don't use envelopes, often leading to additional code overhead. There is an interesting Confluent article[5] further exploring the different envelopes worth checking out.

Headers often tend to ease this process; we can share common contextual information in event headers and typically offer better segregation of concepts; the payload has the event and the headers have the metadata. Headers are a common feature in most brokers, and since they are dynamic and optional, they make different use cases easier to handle. To guarantee coherence across services, most use cases might benefit from a common definition with the custom headers and the ones the company wants to implement. However, it is harder to enforce the presence of specific headers; if a requirement requires the absolute presence of given information across all services, then an envelope might help to enforce that requirement. It depends on the use case, but overall, using headers tends to be a more flexible and less intrusive approach.

8.2.2 Relevant Contextual Information in Events

Envelopes and headers are great for sharing common contextual information. But what kind of information is relevant to use as metadata or contextual data? It heavily depends on the use case, and you might even find it helpful to define specific custom headers only relevant for your domain or business. However, there's often common information useful for most use cases; this subsection will detail some common use cases of contextual information. This way, you can reason whether it makes sense for your use case and which kind of information is typically sent in the metadata.

HTTP has a reasonably detailed definition in terms of requests, responses, and even common headers. This definition provides interoperability across systems, companies, and services. Having a clear contract to adhere to and some assumptions on how the system works facilitates communication and developments. Events, being the medium for communication across companies, especially in event-driven architectures, could arguably benefit from a similar definition. CloudEvents[6] is an approach giving this definition and provides a specification for describing event data. It provides some examples of mandatory and optional contextual attributes. Here are some examples typically relevant to most use cases:

---

[5] Full article by Alexei Zenin, "How to Choose Between Strict and Dynamic Schemas," November 9, 2020, `www.confluent.io/blog/spring-kafka-protobuf-part-1-event-data-modeling/`

[6] Project in GitHub, `https://github.com/cloudevents/spec/blob/master/spec.md`

- Id: The event's id. Having an event id is often useful for debugging, tracing, and even managing idempotency (like we mentioned in Chapter 6). It has to be unique per event; generating a unique incremental id can be troublesome; using a UUID (universally unique identifier) can be helpful.

- Correlation id: An id associating different operations together. For example, when we discussed the choreography pattern, several services choreographed to fulfill an order. The order service created the order, the inventory service managed the order's stock, the pricing service calculated the fees, etc. Each service would publish an event; having a correlation id across all services is a way to quickly obtain all operations in the scope of a single order.

- Source: The service and operation that published the event. Especially relevant when different processes in a single service can generate an event.

- Version: The aggregate's version. Often valuable for managing idempotency and for debugging purposes.

- Timestamp: The date when the event occurred. Also relevant for debugging and tracing purposes. It can be helpful to manage concurrency when a version is absent.

- Priority: The importance of the event. We can assign events to different streams with different priorities (as we discussed in Chapter 6).

- User id: Id of the user that triggered the event. Often useful for auditing and debugging purposes.

8.3 Town Crier Events Pattern

Several questions can arise when designing event schema. A common design question is how much information the event should have and how large it should be. An often discussed best practice is to design events to be small and carry only the information about the change that triggered it. Following this approach usually produces town crier events (also known as event notifications[7]). The term comes from real town criers, who typically inform people of important announcements by shouting them in the streets. In medieval England, most people couldn't read newspapers; town criers were an essential way of communicating news. The town crier shouted the central part of the announcement, and an additional note was usually posted at the local inn in case anyone would like to have more information. Town crier events follow a similar approach; events are published with minimal details, and the subscribing services can request additional information about the change to the producing service. This section will discuss this approach to design event schema and illustrate it with a use case using an order submission process.

Let's work through a similar example to the ones we discussed in the previous chapters. The order service manages the orders of an eCommerce platform. Users submit orders and can edit their information as long as the order doesn't reach a given state. In this case, the user changed the street door number of the order's address. Listing 8-2 illustrates a possible event reflecting this change using only minimal information.

Listing 8-2. Example of an OrderStreetNumberChanged event

```
1    OrderStreetNumberChanged
2    {
3        OrderId: 3621,
4        AddressStreetNumber: 21
5    }
```

Keeping the event schema small and single-purpose is excellent for the overall system. Small events are easy to process and are faster in terms of serialization and deserialization. They also usually have less impact on the message broker and the service's resources. An often good approach aligned with the DDD mindset is to

---

[7] Article by Martin Fowler, "What do you mean by "Event-Driven"?", February 7, 2017, https://martinfowler.com/articles/201701-event-driven.html

design events according to the user's intent. In this case, think of it in designing an OrderUpdated vs. OrderStreetNumberChanged; the first we don't know which was the exact intent of the user, and the latter represents cleanly the intent of changing only the address street number. Designing events this way captures the business value of the process and imbues events with domain value. The event stream will cleanly capture the user's intent and the flow of the business process. The domain itself doesn't sit solely on the service's logic but in the event stream as well. Retaining this domain value can be highly beneficial as an audit or when rebuilding different views of the data according to business needs. However, depending on the use case, this minimal design might also pose some challenges to the consumers.

The event has only the essential information related to the change, the id of the order that the user changed and the new street number. Let's say the inventory service handles order events to reflect stock changes and calculates the best warehouse to satisfy the order. Every time the order address changes, it has to recalculate the best warehouse and reflect the changes in the product's stock. The routing algorithm to calculate the best warehouse to satisfy the order is based on its full address. In this case, this event schema design poses a challenge to the inventory service. The service needs the complete address to calculate the best warehouse, but the event only has the new address street number. When handling a partial event, the inventory service would have to request the whole order's address from the order service, as illustrated in Figure 8-4.

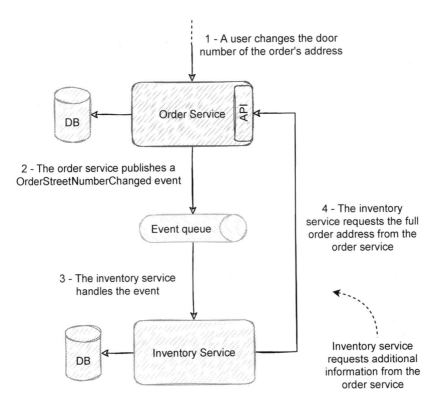

1 - A user changes the door number of the order's address

2 - The order service publishes a OrderStreetNumberChanged event

4 - The inventory service requests the full order address from the order service

3 - The inventory service handles the event

Inventory service requests additional information from the order service

Figure 8-4. *The interaction between the order and inventory service with a town crier event*

The additional remote request to fetch the remaining address information has the impacts we discussed in the previous chapters. The inventory service now has a synchronous dependency on the order service, being susceptible to cascading failures. If the order service has an issue, the inventory service might be directly affected instead of just processing the events asynchronously. Scaling might also become an issue; if we need to horizontally scale the inventory service by adding more instances, it will trigger additional requests to the order service, which might need to be scaled as well. This topology is closer to the distributed monolith we discussed before. Consuming the event might also need additional complexity if the order service's read model is eventually consistent. For example, suppose the order service applies a CQRS pattern and asynchronously updates a read model API that the inventory service uses. In that case, the information in the API might not be up to date with the event. Ideally, we want the consumers to be able to process events without recurring to external dependencies.

Partial and small events are usually helpful when consumers need to react to the specific change that triggers the event. For example, the order service could publish an OrderUpdated event every time the user changed anything in an order. Still, in this case, the only thing the inventory service cares about is the address. If the inventory service were consuming an OrderUpdated, it would have to understand what changed; any data in the order could have changed, not only the address. It would likely need to store some metadata of the order's address to understand the address changed and not something else in the order data to react accordingly. In this situation, an arguably better option would be to publish an OrderAddressChanged instead of an OrderUpdated or OrderStreetNumberChanged.

Town crier events are relevant when consumers need to react to the domain process that triggered the change. Designing them according to that change is a good approach, but we need to be aware to make the event sufficiently relevant for the consumers to rely on it without depending on synchronous dependencies.

8.4 Bee Events Pattern

An alternative to requesting additional data upon handling an event with minimal information is to keep an internal state about the event's entity. This approach produces an interesting effect where the event's state is persisted across several services. It is in many ways similar to the effect bees have on flower pollination. Pollination is the transfer of pollen grains between flowers by animal activity that generates fertilization. Pollination isn't carried deliberately by bees, it is the unplanned consequence of the bee's travels. Pollen sticks to the bee's body, and it is spread from one blossom to another as the bee moves. Bee events (also known as event-carried state transfer[8]) are fairly similar; consumers handle events and persist the event's data locally, actively spreading the event's state across several services, even though that might not be the producing system's intent. This section will work through an example with bee events and detail the impacts on overall architecture and consumers.

In Figure 8-4, we discussed a practical use case using the order service. Upon receiving the OrderStreetNumberChanged event, the inventory service made a synchronous request to the order service to fetch the additional address information.

---

[8] Article by Martin Fowler, "What do you mean by "Event-Driven"?", February 7, 2017, https://martinfowler.com/articles/201701-event-driven.html

In order to avoid the synchronous request's limitations we discussed before, the inventory service could save the address of each order internally. With each partial event published by the order service, the inventory service would update each order's address internally. The OrderCreated event would update the address for that order, the OrderStreetNameChanged would update the street name, the OrderStreetNumberChanged the street number, etc. This way, the inventory service could fetch the complete address from its local database to calculate the best warehouse to satisfy the order.

This solution preserves the decoupling properties of event-driven services. The services depend only on their resources to do their business logic without relying on external dependencies, effectively avoiding the drawbacks of synchronous requests. It also has a performance boost since fetching information from a local database is typically faster than a remote request. Storing a view of the order information also provides the opportunity to materialize it in the most beneficial way for the service. Each service would only store the relevant information for its use case in the granularity that it needed. One obvious consequence is the order information will be scattered across several services, as illustrated in Figure 8-5.

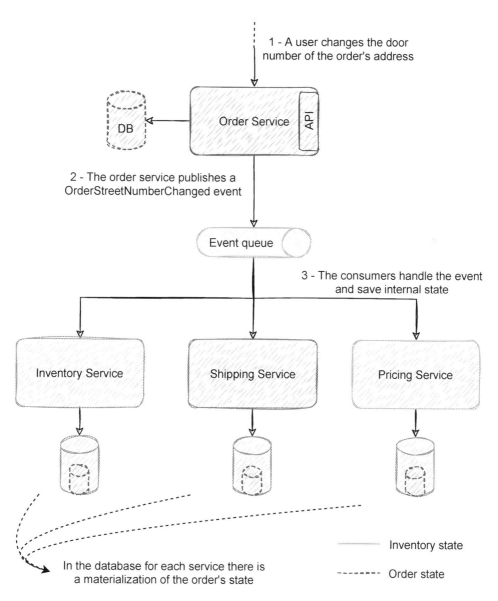

Figure 8-5. *Several services persisting a view of the order information*

In this case, the inventory, shipping, and pricing service need the order address to calculate the stock changes, ship the order, and calculate the country's taxes, respectively. To access the order's full address, they save it internally and keep it updated by applying each new event to their internal state. Bee events end up transferring the order state to each consumer.

Having the order state distributed across all consuming services has an impact on the service's resources; it will require additional database space, although currently disk space isn't as concerning as it used to be. The real challenge can be initializing and maintaining the data accurately. In traditional applications, this could be troublesome; however, as we discussed in Chapter 7, a new service could initialize the order state by reading the event stream from the start; new events would both trigger the business logic and update the order metadata. A bug in the order service might affect the other services' metadata, but guaranteeing the event stream is the source of truth; fixes are also published to the stream, which will automatically heal the consumer's state.

There are more complicated situations where the order service has to do a substantial restructuring of its internal schema, which can end up affecting other services. These situations can be troublesome to manage and end up needing the coordination of several teams. To avoid complex challenges, we need to guarantee each domain is segregated and has clear boundaries. The order state in the inventory service should be relevant only to the inventory service and not a copy of the order service. Anti-corruption layers should guarantee that only the relevant information exists in each boundary. Clear segregation should avoid internal schema changes in the order service to propagate to other services. If consumers rely solely on the event contracts, the order service can incrementally migrate its schema along with the event contracts (we will further discuss schema evolution in Section 8.6).

The impact of having a small event schema can be solved with this approach. It is more aligned with the event-driven mindset than requesting the information with a remote request. Although usually requesting data through a remote request is easier and faster development-wise, this solution tends to be more sustainable when applied frequently. It preserves the services' domain segregation and fosters more resilient properties.

8.5 The Event Schema Goldilocks Principle

In Sections 8.4 and 8.5, we discussed how a small event schema can be beneficial to each service but can impact the overall architecture. We could easily argue if it was worth designing a small event schema if it affects the architecture in a way that makes the consuming services request or store a view of the data. This section will discuss a different approach by finding a middle ground between large and small event schema.

The Goldilocks principle[9] also applies to event schema; we should avoid large events and small events can be challenging to consume, but in some use cases, the event schema size can be just right. Let's continue with the example we discussed in Sections 8.3 and 8.4; using town crier or bee events solves the challenge of consuming a partial event. In event-driven architectures, teams typically have ownership of different services usually related to their domain (as discussed in Chapter 4). Different teams might maintain the order service and the inventory service, and it is easy for the team managing the order service to design events most beneficial to their context, in this case for publishing. Publishing small events is often easier and more straightforward from the producer perspective; as we discussed, the issue is in the consumer. An often ignored and essential consideration while designing event schema is always having consumers' needs and use cases in mind. Involving current and future consumers in the discussion can avoid intricate solutions. For example, instead of the order service publishing an OrderStreetNumberChanged event, it could publish an OrderAddressChangedEvent as illustrated in Listing 8-3.

Listing 8-3. Example of an OrderAddressChanged event

```
1     OrderAddressChanged
2     {
3         OrderId: 3621,
4         StreetName: "Palm Avenue",
5         StreetNumber: 21,
6         State: "FL",
7         City: "Tampa",
8         Postal: 33619,
9     }
```

Instead of publishing only the information that changed, for example, the street number, the order service could publish the order's full address, even though the only information the user changed was the street number. Designing a more comprehensive event adapted to the consumer's needs can be advisable in most use cases. In this example, the inventory service would avoid any external dependency or additional internal state, as pictured in Figure 8-6.

---

[9] Wikipedia page at https://en.wikipedia.org/wiki/Goldilocks_principle

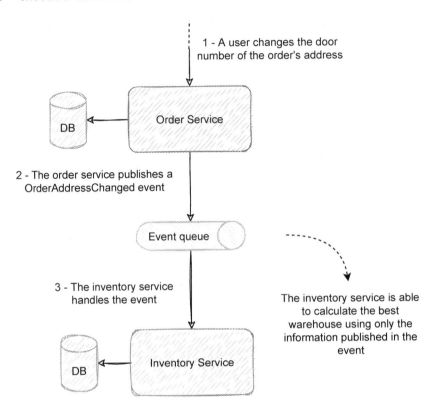

Figure 8-6. *The consumer is able to apply its domain logic using only the event's information*

This way, the inventory service would be able to calculate the best warehouse using only the event's information, avoiding the complexity overhead of the other solutions. Depending on the use case, it might be harder to enrich the event with additional information on the producing side, and it can be highly beneficial on the consumer side.

The caveat is to not add too much information to the event, especially information not in the service's scope or domain. If the inventory service needs the country's geographical position, which is another service domain, adding that information in the order event would be inadvisable. Large events might also reflect that the service has too much responsibility and might need to review its boundaries.

The event might also lose its domain meaning; an OrderAddressChange carries less domain value than an OrderStreetNumberChanged since it's no longer clear which field the user changed. If consumers need to react specifically to changes in the street number, the latter is typically more advisable than the first.

As a consumer, you might not be able to request changes to the existing events. For example, if they come from an external tool or a legacy application or the additional information requires breaking changes, it might not be practical to adapt them to the consumer needs. In those situations, you might have to follow one of the town crier or bee events patterns. An arguably sound reasoning would be to give precedence to bee events and avoid direct dependencies between services. As a faster, more tactical approach, town crier events might be more advisable since they are typically quicker to implement but avoid applying it frequently.

Finding a middle ground or the Goldilocks sweet zone might be tricky and require a more profound knowledge of the overall architecture, thus the importance of involving the consumers. We often argue if the solution will survive the test of time and try to do futurology of possible use cases. Still, sometimes a more pragmatic approach of the current use cases might wield better results than optimizing the solution for use cases that might never happen. Try to follow an incremental approach, involve the existing consumers and design for those use cases, and then iterate on the most appropriate design.

8.6 Denormalized Event Schema

As the microservice architecture becomes more complex and services become more fine-grained, you might encounter the challenge of needing the information of several event streams. Handling several event streams can be a challenge due to the difficulty of managing concurrency and consistency of the different data sources. This section will discuss how we can overcome this challenge by denormalizing the event schema.

Data being distributed across different components is a consequence of moving to a microservice architecture. As we discussed, this has several advantages but also proves to be one of the most difficult challenges of distributed architectures. Although many use cases adapt well to this distributed nature, some use cases don't. Instead, they need a more comprehensive and aggregated view of the information. Providing an aggregated and denormalized view can prove extremely difficult without complicated solutions or falling into the trap of building a monolithic service. Also, the strategies we discuss in Chapter 6 are extremely useful to solve concurrency and ordering; however, they require the consumption of a single event stream. If a service consumes data from different services, the various events can have different granularities and routing keys.

For example, the shipping service is in charge of shipping orders from a warehouse to the user's address after the payment is processed. The service would likely need to consume events from three different services: the order, inventory, and product service. The service would require a denormalized view of order with the information of the products, stock, and warehouses to process each order. This example is illustrated in Figure 8-7.

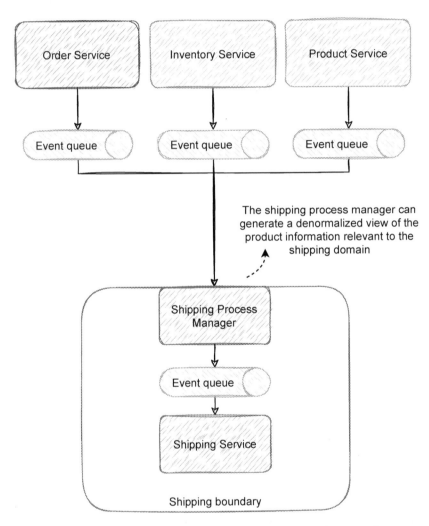

Figure 8-7. *A process manager can make a denormalized view of an entity relevant for a boundary*

To build an aggregated view of the order, we can use a process manager to join the information from the different streams in a larger denormalized schema. The order service events would only contain information about the order, the inventory events about the stock, and the product events about the products. The process manager would be responsible for merging each order's information into a larger event relevant to the shipping domain logic.

We mentioned before how each boundary could have a view of the entities of other boundaries with only part of the information relevant to that boundary. However, the inverse is also true; the view of an entity can also be larger. The order entity in the shipping boundary is larger and more comprehensive than the remaining services, reflecting in larger denormalized event schemas.

The process manager acts as an anti-corruption layer and enriches the order data. This way, the shipping service that owns the shipping domain logic can process the orders without dealing with the complexity of merging several event streams. The internal order event stream in the shipping boundary also effectively reflects the view of the order inside the shipping boundary and might be useful for other services, such as a read model.

The caveat is guaranteeing the process manager doesn't accrue extensive responsibility. The process manager is in charge of adapting and merging information and creating a denormalized view of the events; it shouldn't have substantial domain logic if any. Using denormalized event schema often produces larger events which have the challenges we discussed in Section 8.3. Still, the advantage of applying event routing and dealing with concurrency and order by design often surpasses the impacts of larger events.

8.7 Schema Evolution in Event-Driven Microservices

Event schema is as essential as API contracts and often as difficult to change. Inserting a breaking change on an API can be highly complex and require the alignment of all consumers. The same applies to event schema, although there are some strategies we can follow to ease that transition. This section will discuss which kinds of changes are safe to do on event schema and detail those strategies working through some practical use cases.

Event schema changes through time; we might need to add new information or descope old one in light of new use cases. The changes to the event schema can have larger or lesser impacts depending on the change's nature. More often than not, we can't simply change schema and consumers at the exact same time. Changes to the event schema are prolonged during a period where services adapt to the new changes. It is also vital that anyone changing event schema is aware of the impacts. Enforcing compatibility rules is also a good approach to avoid accidental or unforeseen impacts. Some serialization systems, like Avro,[10] can implement these rules and make them transparent across producers and consumers and avoid harsher changes in the schema.[11] There are typically four compatibility types when evolving schema: backward, forward, full, and no compatibility.

8.7.1 Backward Compatibility

Consumers can read events produced with an old schema with the new schema. It allows consumers to read events with both old and new schema. Let's illustrate an example of a backward compatibility change with the event in Listing 8-4.

Listing 8-4. Order created event example

```
1    OrderCreatedEvent
2    {
3        OrderId: 15251212,
4        ProductId: 1147421,
5        Address: "9980 Rock Maple Street",
6        Quantity: 1,
7        OrderedAt: "2021-01-23T18:25:43.511Z",
8        UserId: 12168,
9        UserName: "John Allan"
10   }
```

Let's say we create a new service to manage the user information and no longer want to publish the user's name in the order events. Removing the UserName field would be a

---

[10] Avro home page in http://avro.apache.org/

[11] Article in confluent documentation, "Schema Evolution and Compatibility," https://docs.confluent.io/platform/current/schema-registry/avro.html

backward compatible change. Consumers that have already updated to the new schema (the OrderCreatedEvent without the UserName) would be able to consume events with an old schema (event with a UserName field); they would ignore the old field.

Backward compatible changes can be especially useful when producers and consumers design a new schema and make it available before the functionality. The event schema is available; consumers can update to the new schema even though the producers are still publishing events with the old one. Once the functionality is available, the service can publish the new schema since the consumers were already updated.

It also might be helpful when replaying events from a stream with an old event schema. If the event schema evolved to different versions and wasn't upscaled (old events converted to the latest schema), backward compatible changes allow consumers to reprocess old event streams if needed.

8.7.2 Forward Compatibility

Consumers can read events produced with the new schema with an old schema. Even though consumers didn't update to the new schema, they can still receive events with the new schema.

For example, in Listing 8-4, if we needed to add a country field in the event, it would be a forward compatible change. In most situations, consumers with the old schema (without the country field) would be able to consume events with the new field; they can simply ignore it.

Forward compatibility is especially relevant when producers develop new features and publish events with the new schema, and consumers will be updated in the future. Since this is frequently how new features are implemented, guaranteeing forward compatibility is often incredibly useful to manage new developments.

8.7.3 Full Compatibility

Full compatibility is the combination of backward and forward compatibility. Consumers can read new events with old schema and old events with new schema. Since full compatibility requires the ability to define a default value for removing or adding new fields, it is only supported by some message formats. The JSON format, for example, doesn't support fully compatible changes, unlike Protobuf and Avro, for instance, which support optional fields.

Imagine if we wanted to add a description field in the event in Listing 8-4. It is a forward compatible change, but it isn't backward compatible since consumers with a new schema wouldn't know what to fill in the description field when receiving old events without that field. However, if we were able to define a default description when the description isn't present, that would make the change fully compatible. The same can be said for non-forward changes when we remove a field.

8.7.4 No Compatibility

There might be changes that aren't in any way compatible. Some updates to the schema change it in a way they are utterly incompatible for consumers with a different version. For example, if we changed the UserId in Listing 8-4 to an UUID, it would be an incompatible change. Consumers with the new schema wouldn't be able to handle old events, and consumers with the old schema wouldn't be able to handle new events.

Incompatible changes can be hard to manage since, with a typical topology, consumers and producers would have to update the schema simultaneously. In a distributed architecture, this is often impossible. Since each service is independent and has segregated deployment procedures, coordinating a simultaneous change is exceptionally challenging.

8.7.5 Managing Changes

Forward, backward, and full compatible types are illustrated in Figure 8-8. These compatibility types with careful coordination support the incremental evolution of the schema. If we support any of these three compatibility types, we can manage schema evolution without substantial changes, just coordination.

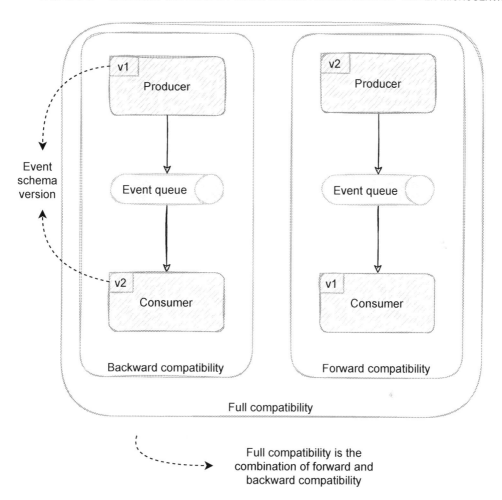

Figure 8-8. *Backward, forward, and full compatibility types*

But what about cases where we need more structural and non-compatible changes? For example, in Listing 8-4, how could we change the address field from a string to a structured object containing the address data in segregated fields? Listing 8-5 exemplifies the new event schema.

Listing 8-5. Order created event example

```
1    OrderCreatedEvent
2    {
3        OrderId: 15251212,
4        ProductId: 1147421,
5        Address:
```

```
 6      {
 7            "StreetName": "Rock Maple Street",
 8            "StreetNumber": 12,
 9            "City": "Orlando",
10            "State": "FL",
11            "Country": "USA",
12      }
13      Quantity: 1,
14      OrderedAt: "2021-01-23T18:25:43.511Z",
15      UserId: 12168,
16      UserName: "John Allan"
17  }
```

The change in the address field type is an example of an incompatible change; the only way to apply it to the event is to change consumers and producers simultaneously. However, changing both consumers and producers is likely risky and impossible or impractical. Instead of applying the change in a single transition, we can divide it into two steps: transforming the incompatible change into a forward compatible change and then into a backward compatible change.

We can add the new address structure along with the existing one. Adding a new field is a forward compatible change; consumers with the old schema can still process this event. Publishing events with the new field allows consumers to adapt to the new structure sequentially. We might have several different applications consuming our events; each of them will have different priorities and roadmaps; by exposing a new field, we give the flexibility to each consumer to change to the new structure in the correct timing. Once all consumers adjust to the new format, we can remove the old address field being a backward compatible change.

A reasonable approach is to define a max period to maintain the old field and let consumers adapt. Having a period instead of doing the change in a single moment is easier to manage; we let consumers adjust to the new data incrementally. If anything goes wrong, they can roll back to the old field, being also a safer and more resilient approach.

8.7.6 Event Stream Versioning

Applying the incremental evolution we discussed before can be a good approach. Still, it might not be practical when we need to do a substantial redesign of the event schema or discontinue an event and replace it with a new one. In those situations, we need a more sustainable approach to manage schema evolution. This subsection will detail how event versioning can be a relevant approach to those situations.

Migrating schema can be risky, even traumatic when not managed correctly. As with most developments we deploy to live, we want to avoid big bang releases. We want to guarantee changes are incremental, and when they go wrong, we can roll back to the previous version. One way to safeguard these guarantees is to use stream versioning. Each event schema version is published to one stream; when we need to evolve the schema and create a new version, we create a new stream with the new schema. Figure 8-9 illustrates an example of this approach.

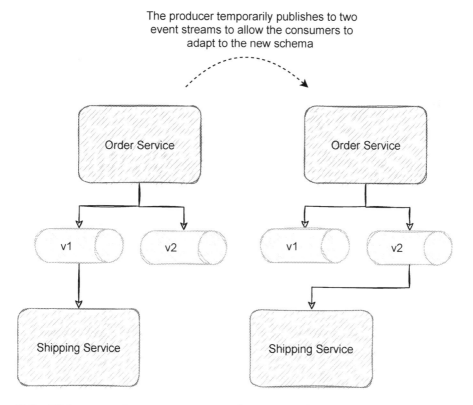

Figure 8-9. *Using one stream per event schema version*

The order service evolves the schema of an event from version 1 to 2. Initially, it starts to publish the version 2 events to a separate stream while also maintaining the version 1 stream. The consumers, in this case the shipping service, can make the required changes to adapt to the new schema. Once all consumers use the new event schema, the order service can descope the old schema and only use the latest one. The order service should also republish all the existing events in the old schema stream to the new one in order to guarantee the event history and that the new stream has all relevant data.

This approach allows the consumers to gradually move to the new stream without a big bang release. If anything goes wrong, they can also roll back the consumption to the old stream. Publishing to two streams has the disadvantage of guaranteeing every event is published to both streams or none; we have to ensure both are consistent and have the same data. To do so, we can use one of the strategies we discussed in Chapter 7. Kafka also supports transactions when publishing events to two streams[12] simultaneously.

8.7.7 Using a Downscaler/Upscaler When Evolving Event Schema

Profound changes in the event schema are often associated with a change in a domain concept or leaving some kind of legacy representation we no longer want to support. Using stream versioning has the disadvantage of the service in charge of the domain having to maintain the logic to generate the old event schema until all consumers adapt to the new one, which can take a considerable amount of time. An alternative to this approach is to segregate the legacy logic into a separate component commonly known as a downscaler. This subsection will work through the same use case in Figure 8-9 but with a downscaler approach.

Sometimes it can be challenging to maintain the old schema when we do substantial changes. For example, imagine if we moved the logic that managed the user's address to a service that manages users. We would need to remove the address information from the event in Listing 8-5. Publishing events with the old schema would require maintaining (or fetching) the address information from that service. It wouldn't be beneficial to the order service to maintain that logic until all consumers adapt to the

---

[12] Article by Apurva Mehta and Jason Gustafson, "Transactions in Apache Kafka," November 17, 2017, www.confluent.io/blog/transactions-apache-kafka/

new paradigm. In order to maintain the responsibility of the order service focused on managing the orders, we could delegate the legacy logic to a different component, a downscaler. Figure 8-10 illustrates the same example but with a downscaler.

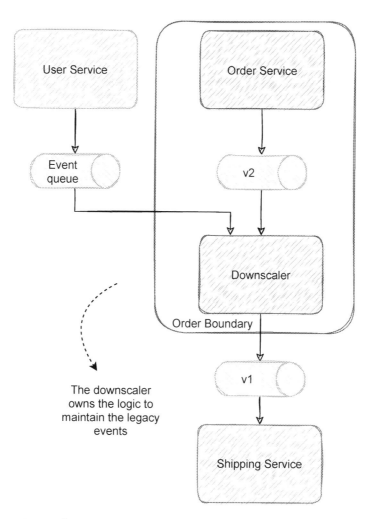

Figure 8-10. *Using a downscaler to segregate the logic to maintain the events with the old schema*

The downscaler uses the information from the new order events and the user events to maintain the old order events. This pattern has the advantage of keeping the order service (the owner of the domain) clean and focused only on the vision we have for the domain, without the additional complexity of dealing with legacy events. Once all the consumers use the new version, we can discontinue the downscaler. The downscaler only has the responsibility to maintain the old schema and is only relevant while they are needed. This approach is an example of leveraging the high decoupling nature of event-driven architectures and the flexibility of microservices to segregate legacy logic to contained services. Once the old logic is no longer needed, we only discontinue the service; we don't have to change anything in the order service. It can evolve freely without waiting for the consumers to adapt. The inverse (adapting an old version schema to a newer version) is also possible with the same approach using an upscaler.

This pattern is relevant when consumers are expected to take a considerable amount of time to adapt to the new schema. Otherwise, it might not be worth the effort of creating and releasing an individual service. We also don't need to create a separate component; the downscaler can be a separate module on the order service as long as we can maintain it decoupled from the surrounding logic. The pivotal point is when we want to discontinue the logic, it should be straightforward and not affect the main service logic.

8.8 Summary

- Event storming can be a valuable strategy to model your business process according to the flow of events. It provides a collaborative way to obtain a higher level of understanding of the domains and temporal business flow. The event storming session's output events are also valuable to design the service's domain events and technical schema.

- There is common information relevant to most events, like the correlation id or version. These generic properties are often best shared with a generic structure like an envelope or event headers.

- Consumers handling town crier events are notified of changes in an upstream domain. The service requests additional information when the event schema doesn't have all the required data. Partial and small events are usually useful when consumers need to react to the specific change that triggers the event. But when the consumer needs to request additional information through synchronous requests, other options are typically more beneficial.

- Consumers handling bee events keep an internal state about the event's entity. It is more aligned with the event-driven mindset than requesting the information through a remote request but has the disadvantage of spreading the event's state across several services.

- Having the consumer's needs and use cases in mind is a pivotal concern to design event schema. It can significantly simplify the architecture and avoid complicated solutions on the consumer's side.

- Consumers should be able to make the decisions they need using only the information in their domain and the event's information. This approach will contain the dependencies between each service and enable a truly decoupled scalable architecture.

- We can use a process manager to denormalize event schema and enrich events with additional information to simplify consumers.

- There are four compatibility types: forward, backward, full, and no compatibility. Forward, backward, and full are useful to evolve the schema incrementally without substantial changes in the ecosystem. The no compatibility type requires more complex solutions.

- To manage more profound and structural changes in event schema, we can use stream versioning or a downscaler/upscaler.

CHAPTER 9

How to Leverage the User Interface in Event-Driven Microservice Architectures

This chapter covers:

- Using an aggregating layer with API composition to build information for the UI

- Applying UI composition both by modules, pages, and sections to interact with distributed data

- Using backends for frontends to provide a denormalized view of the data

- How task-based UIs can be relevant to manage the asynchronicity of event-driven architectures

- Using event-driven APIs to support responsive UIs

As we build a fully segregated, highly scalable, top-of-the-line microservice architecture platform, we tend to forget who's at the end, using the functionality, often a user interface. You might have heard of the three-mile island incident in Pennsylvania in 1979, where a nuclear power station's reactor partially melted and caused a radiation leak that led to the evacuation of thousands. It is the most significant incident of commercial nuclear power plant history of the United States. Even though there were no injuries, it had the potential to make the whole area uninhabitable for

H. F. Oliveira Rocha, *Practical Event-Driven Microservices Architecture*, https://doi.org/10.1007/978-1-4842-7468-2_9

the foreseeable future. The entire chain of events that caused the incident originated in a misunderstanding in a UI. The nuclear reactor primary system's relief valve became stuck and stayed open for an extended period after a failing close command, allowing large quantities of nuclear reactor coolant to escape. The lack of coolant led to the reactor meltdown. Why didn't the operators close the valve manually? A light in the interface lit up when the valve was open and went out when the valve was closed. But the light went out when the system sent the signal to close the valve, not when the valve was physically closed. So, the computer sent the signal, the light went out, but the valve didn't actually close, which led to the operators not noticing the valve was open. If you work around event-driven services and eventual consistency for enough time, this type of issue feels too familiar. There is a difference between informing the user that an action was done and waiting to signal the change only after it took place.

Not all of us have the sole mission to build a microservice platform; some of us have the pristine purpose of delighting users with aweing interfaces. Although I would take the challenge of handling eventual consistency over aligning every element in a reactive web page every day, there is an eye-watering wonder in watching a complex architecture do its work through a UI perspective.

Microservices add a layer of complexity to traditional UI approaches; fetching information becomes a non-trivial task due to the high data fragmentation. Some use cases might need an aggregated view of data from different domains. When each domain is isolated by a segregated service with an independent database, retrieving an aggregated view of the data across domains can be exceptionally challenging. The platform exposed by the microservice architecture should be agnostic of the user interface since a myriad of clients can access it; there can be desktop users, mobile users, even outside interactions with APIs. The platform should support those use cases. However, being abstract enough for the different use cases often brings challenges on how to answer specific use cases with acceptable performance.

This chapter will work through some examples of how we can overcome these challenges and explore some approaches to implement communication with the user interfaces. Although some of them can be tackled by the UI layer, they might be inappropriate for more complex, data-intensive use cases. Event-driven architectures are built in a way where we can easily share, transform, and build different views of data accommodated for more complex use cases. Events are also aligned with the reactive nature of UIs; building a bridge between the two can be exceptionally valuable, as we will discuss at the end of the chapter.

9.1 Using an Aggregating Layer to Build a UI in a Distributed Microservice Architecture

In a typical monolithic application, the backend could feed the UI with aggregated information in a trivial way since all data often sits in the same database. As we segregate each domain and distribute the domain's data into separate services with independent databases, fetching information from different domains can be cumbersome. This section will approach the use of an aggregating layer to facilitate the fetch of data in the UI and discuss the impacts of API composition.

Let's say we have a UI for an eCommerce platform that displays the product listing, the user's current order information, and the recommendations for similar products that the user bought recently. Ideally, we want to retrieve all data from the backend in a single request and display it in the interface. However, different parts of the data will likely sit in different domains and different services. Figure 9-1 illustrates this example.

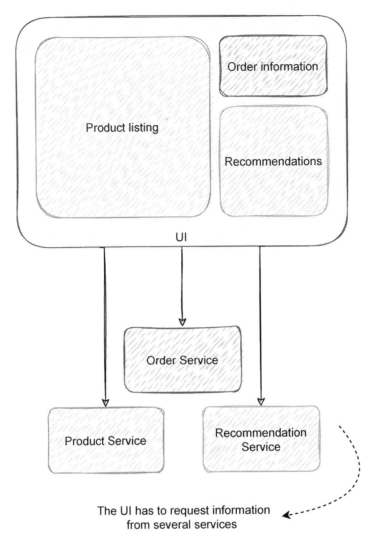

Figure 9-1. *A UI fetching different information from several services*

The filtering and aggregation logic would also be centralized in the single frontend application and in one deployable unit. This kind of approach usually suffers from the drawbacks of monoliths we discussed in Chapter 1. Releasing new functionality when several teams have ownership of the same application might be challenging to manage.

Also, the UI has to make three separate requests to fill a single screen. The excess of requests can be troublesome due to mobile users' network speed and bandwidth limitations, for example. The data fetched from the microservices might not be adapted to the needs of the UI, for example, the product service might return all the product information even though the UI might only need the product name.

A typical approach we can use to improve this situation is to use an aggregating layer between the microservices and the UI. Instead of the UI requesting information from each microservice and aggregating it, it would request the information from the aggregating layer, as illustrated in Figure 9-2.

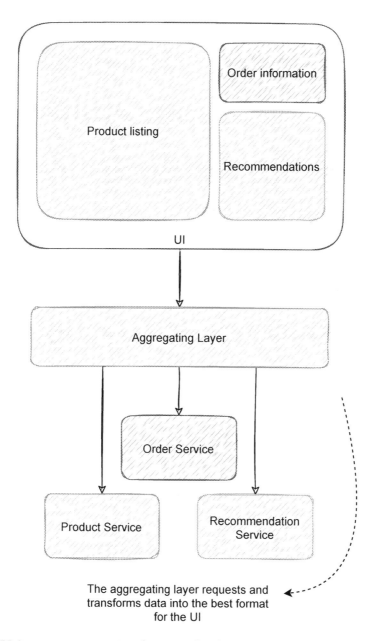

Figure 9-2. *Using an aggregating layer to fetch and transform data for the UI*

The aggregating layer has the logic to fetch, join, and transform data in the best format for the UI. This way, instead of making three separate requests, the UI makes one that returns only the required information. By decreasing the number of requests and the size of the data requested by the UI, we optimize the request's response time and the required bandwidth.

Although we optimized the requests for the UI, this generic component in charge of orchestrating the requests to the microservices might become a monolith in its own right. As we add more microservices and the different types of UIs keep growing, so does the aggregating layer. As the UI supports various use cases, user experiences, and devices, managing all the different requirements in a single application can be challenging. This kind of segregating layer between the internal microservice platform and the outside clients tends to grow and become a bottleneck to delivery.

These two patterns, a single frontend application and using an aggregation layer, are typically best for small applications with full-stack teams that develop both the UI and the platform. As with monoliths, it's often beneficial to resort to these patterns while the application is simple and doesn't support many requirements. As the application grows, the more challenging it is to manage.

9.2 Backends for Frontends (BFFs)

An aggregating layer can be challenging to manage as the application grows and incorporates more use cases and different user experiences. Chapter 1 discussed how a monolith could become a constricting knot to business growth; an aggregating layer can suffer from the same drawbacks. Since it is a piece that glues the frontend and backend together, it has a pivotal role in the continuous delivery of value. For example, if we need to add more product information to a product listing, we might not only need to change the product listing UI and the product service but also the aggregating layer. If every other UI needs to do the same, all deliveries touch the aggregating layer, potentially becoming a bottleneck. This section will discuss backends for frontends as a way to solve that challenge.

The functionalities we expose on our microservice platform are often designed to be generic and agnostic of the use case. For example, our platform might expose several REST endpoints with conceptual resources for the external applications to interact with, like order, product, stock, etc. In fact, the functionalities supported by the microservices are focused on their domain and usually exposed as a generic concept any interface can interact with. For example, we might design the order service in light of the order fulfillment business flow and expose it according to that design, which might or might not be aligned with the needs of the UIs. This mismatch is not necessarily a bad thing; the microservice platform should follow the domain concepts and expose more conceptual functionalities since it can be used by a myriad of use cases, ranging from graphical user interfaces to integrations with external systems. However, the mismatch between the platform functionalities and the needs of the UIs needs to be addressed somewhere. As we discussed, an aggregating layer could be an option; however, it can quickly become bloated and struggle to keep up with each different use case.

That's where backends for frontends come in. Instead of grouping every use case in a single application or delegating that responsibility to the UI, individual backends support the functionalities for specific UIs. For example, the product listing UI we discussed in Section 9.1 could be supported by a specific backend built for that use case. Other UIs like the order details UI and mobile interfaces would be supported each by its own backend, as illustrated in Figure 9-3.

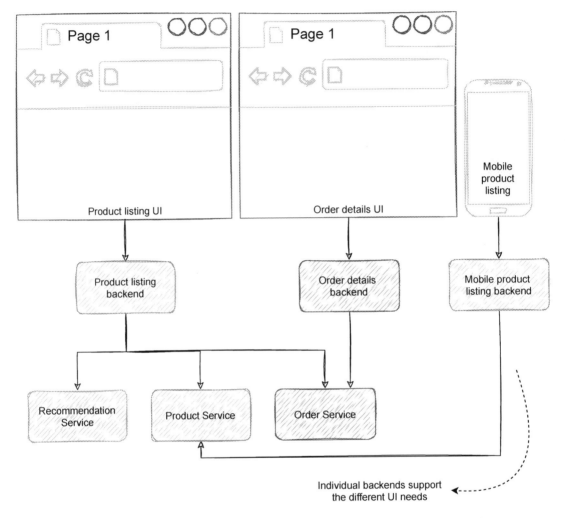

Figure 9-3. *Each of the different UIs is supported by a backend built for that use case*

In the example, we have a product listing and an order details UI hosted on a web browser and a product listing on a mobile device. Each of the three use cases is supported by its own backend, tailored for that purpose. There's usually concern about avoiding coupling the microservice platform design to the needs of the UI applications. For example, the order management platform functionalities should be agnostic of the order management application UI design. If another UI or even an integration with an external system decides to use the platform's functionalities, it should do so without further developments. Backends for frontends can fill that gap and adapt the requirements of the UI and platform without the concern of coupling to specific UI needs, since they are built for that purpose.

The example raises the question of how granular we should go on the design of the backend. For example, do we really need two product listing backends? Well, a reasonably good approach is to understand the use case and how the user interacts with the application. The web UI would have information about recommendations and the order details; however, we might not display all of those sections in a mobile UI due to size and bandwidth constraints. The mobile UI would also likely show fewer products than a web UI would, and perhaps with a different interface (the way we go through the products could be different; on a web UI, we could use paging, while in a mobile, scrolling could be more appropriate). Those might be strong reasons to have an independent backend for each. The organization of the teams is also an important factor. If the same team develops both the web and mobile UI, it might be reasonable to have only one backend. As with microservices, having a backend accruing too much responsibility and several teams working on it can be good indicators to build a finer-grained one.

When there are separated teams for backend and frontend, BFFs can bring benefits to abstract the downstream platform functionalities and provide higher segregation of responsibilities. BFFs might not benefit simple applications where all functionality can be centralized in a single layer without dependencies, since they add complexity to the overall architecture. A reasonable approach is to use them when there is a complex logic to aggregate several services and a high diversity of use cases and frontend technologies.

BFFs still have limitations in larger data sets with more comprehensive search requirements. Saving state in BFFs, which is not unheard of with Redis and other technologies, might not be the best approach to a backend dedicated to serving a UI. BFFs and the patterns we discussed in Section 9.1 both rely on API composition, which can be hard to manage in certain use cases. Section 9.4 will detail these limitations and discuss an approach to solve them in event-driven architectures.

9.3 UI Decomposition Pattern in Microservice Architectures

As we discussed, one way to fetch information for a UI is to request data from the microservices. We can further optimize the requests by using an aggregating layer that fetches, joins, and shapes data to the UI needs. However, as our UI grows and requirements evolve, so do the responsibilities of the UI. The UI application can grow and suffer from the same limitations of monoliths. This section will discuss how we can decompose a single UI application into smaller parts.

When UIs are responsible for a limited array of responsibilities and are simple and straightforward, we might benefit from using a single UI application. Like backend monoliths, a small team working in a single application might benefit from having a single application rather than dealing with the complexity of managing several smaller ones. However, as the application grows and accrues more responsibility, the developing teams also grow. Boundaries might become faded, releases become more complex and less common, and teams spend increasing amounts of time coordinating developments.

A pattern that arose to answer those difficulties is micro frontends. It relies on segregating the UI into smaller independently developed and deployed applications. Different teams own different micro frontends. It also provides the opportunity to have full-stack teams that own a smaller domain in the architecture and can implement both the UI and platform functionalities. Full-stack teams often can deliver value more consistently than having different teams for the backend and frontend and manage dependencies between the two. However, this approach requires the right company's context and ability to do so; but it might be more flexible delivery-wise than segregated platform and UI teams. Micro frontends can typically be implemented by application decomposition, page decomposition, and section decomposition, which are detailed by the following sections.

9.3.1 UI Application Decomposition Pattern

Application decomposition relates to segregating different purposes to different applications. It can be a valid approach when decomposing a single larger UI application into smaller ones. A comprehensive UI might aggregate several distinct responsibilities, which might benefit from having a segregated codebase, different team ownership and release cycle. It shares the same mindset of deconstructing a monolith into microservices; building smaller UI applications with a clear purpose for a set of domains can promote domain segregation. It can also be a catalyst for smaller teams to build functionality from top to bottom, from the microservices to the UI, as we discussed before.

Clearly independent domains, use cases, and even user groups gathered in the same application can be signals that the UI application has too much responsibility and might benefit from segregation. For example, an eCommerce management application might benefit from having a segregated order fulfillment application and a customer management application, as illustrated in Figure 9-4.

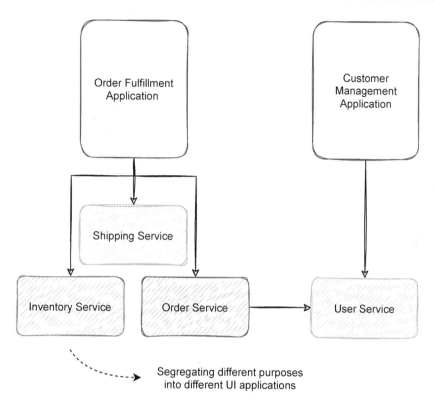

Figure 9-4. *Using different applications for different purposes and business flows*

In this example, the order fulfillment flow and the customer management application have two different purposes and business flows. Situations like this might benefit from dividing applications and building micro frontends for each use case. Ideally, each application would map to a single microservice; however, it can be hard to achieve as microservices get more fine-grained. The customer management application is a good choice for this approach; the team that develops the user service can also build the customer management application. The order fulfillment application, since it comprises more significant responsibilities and concepts, might depend on several services; in those cases, we might benefit from finer-grained segregation like the following two patterns, page and section decomposition.

9.3.2 UI Page Decomposition Pattern

Page decomposition decomposes the application into a more fine-grained level by each page. We can look at an application by having different pages. For example, an order fulfillment application might have the functionality to manage stock, oversee the flow of the order, request order shipments, organize shipping providers, etc. Each functionality might be supported by a different set of pages, as illustrated in Figure 9-5.

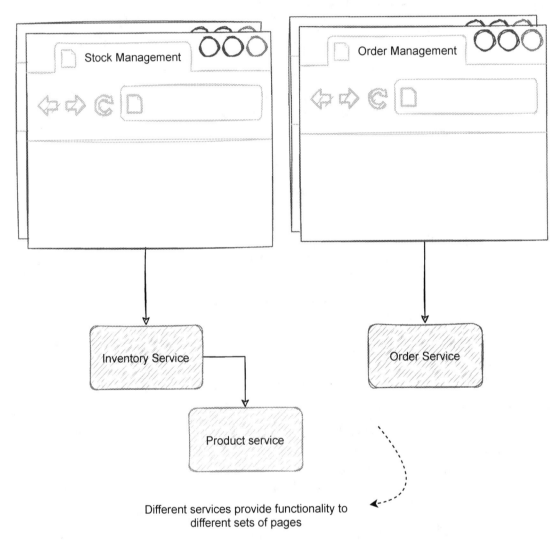

Figure 9-5. *Different use cases are supported by different pages, which relate to segregated services*

The functionality to manage stock is supported by the inventory and product service; the order management pages are supported by the order service. In this case, the inventory service might depend on the product service to support the full functionality of the stock management pages, since the stock by itself might not mean much and might need to be enriched in the product information. However, this dependency doesn't need to be a direct synchronous dependency; the inventory service can build a custom view of the product data using the product event stream to support the UI.

The main advantage of this approach is not having the UI or an intermediate layer to request and aggregate data from several sources. The decomposition by page helps to have finer-grained segregation inside the same application, which might help to segregate responsibilities and boundaries. It also often translates more cleanly to the service platform. If we have pages for stock management, they will most likely rely on the inventory service, order fulfillment on the order service, shipping on the shipping service, and so on.

Page segregation often has a good translation to the Web; the navigation will be page-based which is aligned with the nature of the Web and has further synergy if different services are involved for each page. SPAs (single-page applications) became popular as a way to design applications to fit in a single page. SPAs have several advantages; for example, most resources (like scripts, CSS, HTML, etc.) are loaded one time which often makes the application faster. However, they can quickly become bloated for more complex applications; navigation often involves scripting. Multi-paged applications, on the other hand, often lead to simple developments; to navigate, we simply go to a different location on a separate page without the complex logic SPAs often have. Although they might not map so cleanly for mobile applications, they can be a good choice for more comprehensive applications on the Web.

9.3.3 UI Section Decomposition Pattern

There are use cases that might translate cleanly to a page and a microservice. A stock management page, for instance, might be a reasonable use case to apply it. However, there might be use cases where the entire page functionality might rely on several different services. This kind of aggregated view becomes an increasing concern as we build more fine-grained services. Another similar, more fine-grained approach we can take is to segregate the UI by sections.

The example we discussed in Figure 9-1 had a UI that had a product listing, current order information, and recommendations for relevant products. Each section of the page has a reasonably segregated functionality which translates to different services, thus the need to aggregate results from various services on the UI or an intermediate layer. A different approach could be to compose the UI into different micro frontends for each section, which have their source in different services, as illustrated in Figure 9-6.

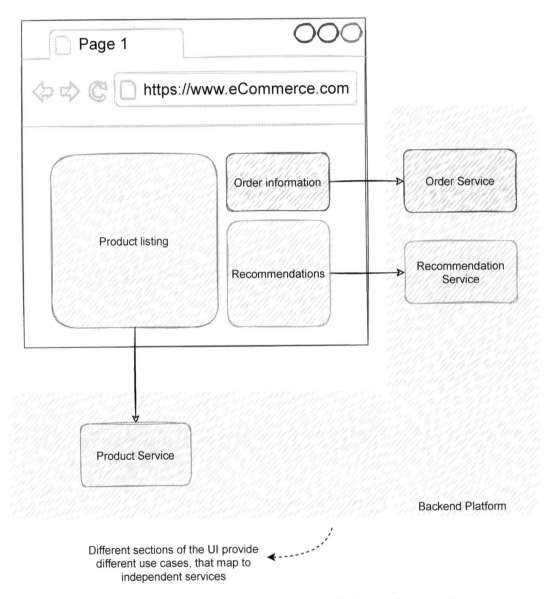

Figure 9-6. *Relationship of different UI sections to independent services*

Each section uses functionality provided by different services; for example, to list the product information, the product listing frontend can rely solely on the product service. We might still need to do three separate requests to provide the UI's full functionality. Still, having segregated sections for each use case, we can adapt to show only a subset of the sections on UIs more sensible to bandwidth limitations (like mobile), depending on the page's use case.

An important consideration is the ability to build independent sections backed by independent micro frontends. Each section can be individually deployed, meaning we can implement new functionality on the recommendation section and deploy it without changing the product listing and order information section. There's still the need of a UI to stitch the sections together; however, the main functionality is supported by the section's frontend. This flexibility to segregate into different frontends facilitates the collaboration of different teams to the same UI, which could be hard to do with an application or page decomposition.

It also promotes the build of full-stack teams; the product listing and the product service could be developed by the same team and deliver value independently. The ability to have a team with autonomy to deliver new features from top to bottom often facilitates delivery and makes delivering value faster and more straightforward for the business.

When we can segregate use cases into different pages, a page decomposition can be more beneficial. With page decomposition, we can avoid the complexity of composing and supporting the communication of different sections. Section decomposition can be a valuable approach in complex and more comprehensive single page UIs that provide a wide range of features. It can be a good approach to segregate responsibilities and provide a scalable way for different teams to contribute to the same UI.

9.4 The Limitations of API Composition

Section 9.1 discussed how the UI or an aggregating layer fetched information from the microservice platform using synchronous requests. Aggregating data from several microservices can be a valid approach when the data is small and is centralized in a small number of services. For example, to build a UI to provide the details of an order, we would likely need a couple of requests to the order and product service. On the other hand, large sets of data and requirements to aggregate data from different sources can be troublesome to deal with. Fetching and aggregating information from different sources is usually referred to as the API composition pattern. As you might recall, we briefly discuss API composition in Chapter 4; this section will further detail and work through a use case detailing the limitations of this approach and when it is most helpful.

In the example we discussed in the beginning of the chapter in Figure 9-1, different areas of the UI use different information. In that situation, it might be manageable since each section doesn't have a strong relation to the other ones. The product listing doesn't have a strong relationship with the recommendation and order section, for example. But aggregating data from different sources can be extensively limiting when a single component has to merge the information and provide it in the same section. For example, the listing page would likely have to provide a more aggregated view of the product catalog with information relevant from different domains. An example of a UI with this functionality is illustrated in Figure 9-7.

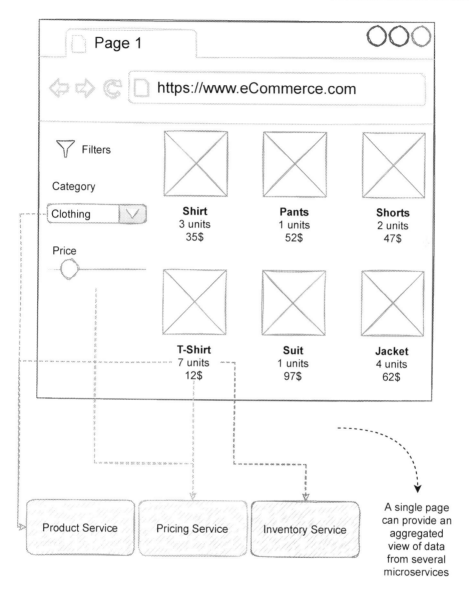

Figure 9-7. *Example of a product listing page providing information from different sources*

The product listing page provides information about the product description, current available stock, and price of the item for the user's country. It also allows the user to filter products by category and define a price range. These kinds of requirements are fairly simple use cases; in a real situation, a more comprehensive list of filters would likely be available along with sorting capabilities.

Using API composition, the application would request the information from each individual service, which in simple use cases might be straightforward. However, when there is a need to do more comprehensive operations on the data across several services, it becomes extensively challenging or even prohibiting in data-intensive use cases. In this example, the listing page displays six products; it might be affordable to request the six products from the product service and the price and stock quantity from the pricing and inventory service; it would likely only take three requests. What if we apply a category filter? It would be similar; we apply the filter in the request to the product service and fetch the results information from the other services. However, what if we filter by category and use a price range, for example, all clothing items with a price lower than 50$? We would need to apply the category filter to the product service and the price filter to the pricing service. If we request the six clothing products from the product service and then fetch the price, only a subset of them might be lower than 50$. We would need to make a series of subsequent requests until we find a set of products that oblige all criteria; the number of needed requests can quickly become infeasible. Imagine now we only want to display products with stock; we would need to fetch results from the three services that oblige to all filters. If we add sorting, it gets even trickier.

Eventually, more comprehensive searches are required by the business. Using API composition in these use cases with considerable quantities of data will require overwhelming requests by the UI or the aggregating layer, often leading to poor performance. Perhaps we can afford making a few requests to fetch information, but when there are hundreds of thousands of entities in each service, it becomes unacceptable to fetch all data from the downstream services and join it in memory. It also would have a considerable impact on the resources of the component aggregating the responses. Imagine if the products that fulfill the results aren't on the first pages, the component would have to fetch page by page, keep the results, join them with the responses of the other services (which might also be at the end of the result list), and select the ones that comply with the filters. If hundreds of users made the same request, it would definitely impact the component's memory and CPU. ElasticSearch actually works in a similar way[1] and warns about the impacts of deep paging, which might bring down nodes due to lack of memory. By applying this strategy to complex requirements, we would likely suffer from similar limitations.

---

[1] Article in ElasticSearch documentation, "Paginate search results," `www.elastic.co/guide/en/elasticsearch/reference/current/paginate-search-results.htm`

Some requirements might need an aggregated view of the data to support more comprehensive ways to look at the information. Event-driven architectures are designed in a way that supports data sharing efficiently. We could continuously build an optimized view of the data by handling the different event streams, as illustrated in Figure 9-8.

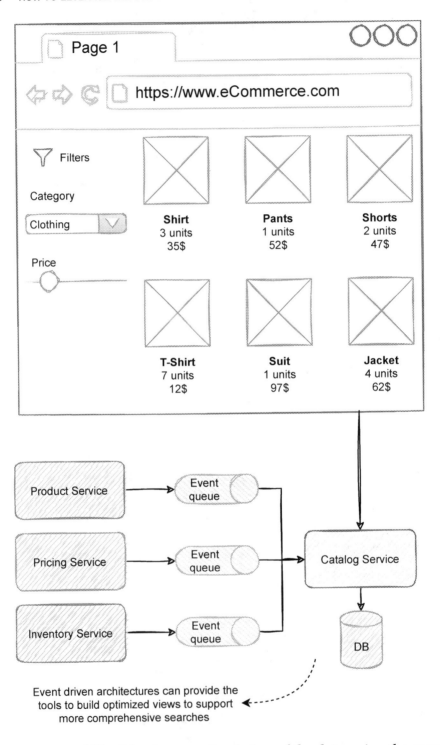

Figure 9-8. *We could build a denormalized view of the data using the event streams of each service*

This approach is very similar to the CQRS pattern. Each service acts as the write model and owns the rules and logic of each domain, while the catalog service simply builds a denormalized view of the information of each service. This view is optimized to the searching requirements and is able to support a more comprehensive view of the data. An essential consideration in this approach is guaranteeing the domain logic exclusively relies on the respective service; for example, the pricing domain logic can't exist in the catalog service, solely in the pricing service. The catalog service should only handle the information relevant to the use case it is supporting. For example, the discount rate might be relevant information, but if there isn't any use case to support it, then the catalog service should ignore it (using an anti-corruption layer, for example).

An important pitfall is to transform the catalog service into a monolith in its own right. If more fine-grained services start to appear, we might feel the need to increasingly add functionality and different kinds of searches to the catalog service. It really depends on the use case, but following the same approach of BFFs, using a model per use case or user experience might be a sensible approach. If the service has too much responsibility, we should consider splitting it.

Another important concern is the ownership of the service. Ideally, the same team would be able develop the UI and own this component to allow the implementation of new functionalities without dependencies on other teams. Developing the backend functionalities based on the event streams and the UI, features tend to be delivered faster. However, depending on the organization might be hard to find the skills to develop both components.

API composition is still valid; for example, a UI that displays the user's order details might only need a couple of requests to the downstream services to retrieve the required information, and we would hardly benefit from having a dedicated service to build a denormalized view. However, it has limitations; if you find API composition has enough performance to support the use case, it usually is the easiest and most straightforward solution. In use cases that require a more comprehensive view and filtering, building a dedicated model might be a reasonable approach to guarantee acceptable performance.

9.5 Task-Based UIs

Until now, we discussed the difficulties we can find when adapting the backend functionalities to the frontend UI requirements and the patterns we can use to overcome those challenges. However, we haven't detailed how the UI could actually look like. Although UI design and the concepts of UI user experience are beyond the concepts of this book, event-driven architectures introduce different challenges in the way users interact with the application and the overall system. A reasonable understanding of those challenges and a deliberate approach to UI design can substantially smooth the interaction users have with the platform. This section will discuss how task-based UIs can help ease that interaction and provide a smooth transition to an event-driven, domain-oriented architecture.

Traditional UIs are typically CRUD-based. We open a UI, the application fetches the current state, we change the data in some forms and submit the changes, and the application persists the new state in the database. For example, imagine we had an application to create products for an eCommerce platform, we could have a UI with several forms to submit the product's information, for example, the brand, category, price, stock units, etc. Once we filled in the required fields, we could submit the product data, as illustrated in Figure 9-9.

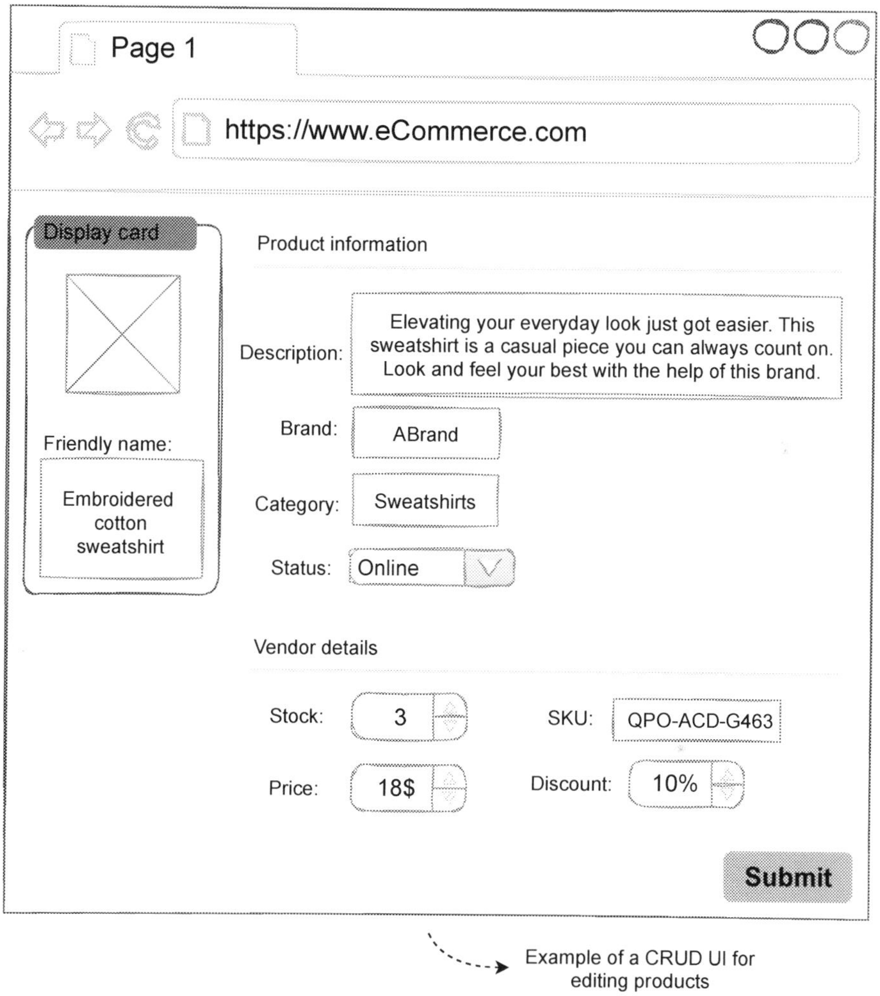

Example of a CRUD UI for
editing products

Figure 9-9. Example of a CRUD UI to submit a product edition

The product information is submitted in a single interaction; it's limited to data entry rather than a business process. This kind of approach is simple, straightforward, and easy to understand and benefits simple use cases where the application doesn't need to model a complex domain. The process is limited to transferring and manipulating a DTO (data transfer object); the service fetches the data, maps to a DTO, and passes it to the UI; the UI changes it and sends it back to the service to be saved.

As you might recall, when we discussed DDD, commands and events should reflect the user's intent; the very business domain value is imbued in their design. In CRUD style UI, the user's intent is often lost or has very limited meaning; the interaction is resumed in manipulating the current state.

Following this approach with more complex domains and more intricate business processes often leads to the application failing to capture the real domain workflow. You probably experienced this firsthand a time or another when the people operating the software had to edit information on a series of applications or UIs. The workflow of the operations is written down on a piece of paper or in someone's mind (like go to UI X and edit something, go to UI Y and change something else). Is that an intricacy of a given system/business, or just the failure of the system to model what the user needs to do? Certainly, this kind of design is valuable in simpler systems; more complex domains and processes might benefit from different approaches. The example in Figure 9-10 also highlights an additional challenge when mapping to a microservice architecture; there are different sets of information belonging to different domains.

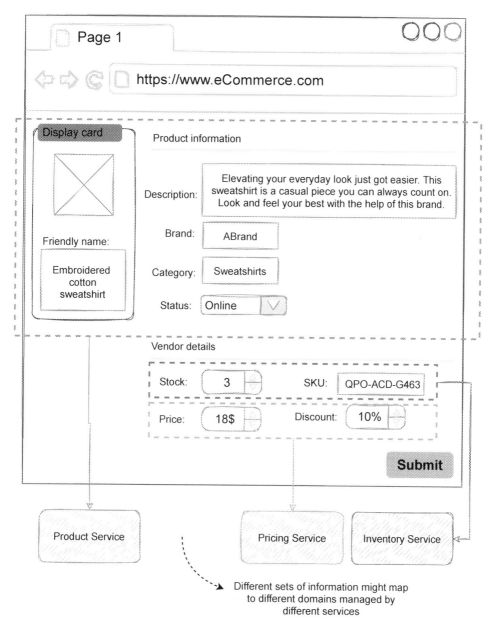

Figure 9-10. *CRUD UI coupling together different domains*

Having a UI aggregating different domains together isn't necessarily bad, and it often is a requirement by the business. But changing information in different domains usually implies different actions and intentions. It also begs the question of how to guarantee the consistency of a single update. For example, by pressing the Submit button, the inventory service might save the stock information successfully, while the product service might fail to submit the product information due to an error. What should we show when one service fails but the others succeed? Displaying an error message saying "Submission failed for part of the information" might be an approach but certainly is a dubious user experience.

Task-based UIs are typically built to help the user advance in a journey and guide him to accomplish a process. Each change also maps more cleanly to the user's intent, making it easier to map to commands for each domain. For example, we could model the UI to translate each user's action by segregating the different tasks, as illustrated in Figure 9-11.

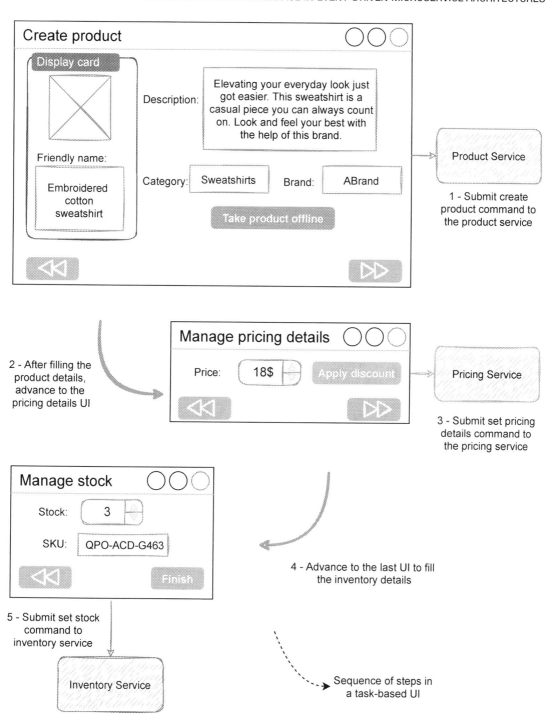

Figure 9-11. *Example of task-based UI for product creation*

Each context has a different screen and maps to a respective service and domain. For example, the screen to manage the product's price is dedicated to that task, reflecting the user's intent more clearly. This design also helps to translate the user actions to commands. A change product price command semantic is more meaningful and has more domain value than an edit product command.

Task-based UIs usually map more cleanly and have higher synergy with distributed architectures due to building commands for each segregated task. Each task has a separate command, which most likely will translate to an event with similar meaning, paving the way for more meaningful and domain-rich event streams. Event streams that capture the user's intent tend to be more valuable and more relevant for future requirements.

Typically, simple domains with straightforward processes don't benefit much from this kind of approach. If the user's operations are CRUD in nature, then a CRUD approach is obviously more beneficial. Event-driven architectures typically model complex domains; however, don't fall into the trap of applying this kind of design everywhere. In complex architectures, there are several domains; some are intricate enough to benefit from this approach, while others might hardly benefit from it.

Arguably, the most useful benefit we can extract from task-based UIs, even when we end up not using them, is the focus on why and how the user is trying to achieve its goal. The usability and the nature of the business process are the cornerstones of the design.

9.6 Event-Driven APIs

The asynchronous nature of event-driven APIs often transforms an otherwise synchronous operation into an asynchronous one. For example, the order fulfillment process in a single-process application like a monolith could be a synchronous process for the order submissions that have all the conditions to be fulfilled. However, in an event-driven architecture, the order fulfillment is likely the choreography of several event-driven services. Asynchronous operations might be more common throughout the architecture. To ensure a friendly web experience, we might shift from synchronous CRUD UIs, where feedback was immediate, to UIs that show the progress of the request as it advances in the workflow, displaying a status or alerts to the user.

With the advent of reactive UIs, event-driven frontend implementations are becoming increasingly popular. They have high synergy with the asynchronous approach; as the state advances, asynchronous updates can be delivered to the user seamlessly. Although older protocols like XMPP (Extensible Messaging and Presence Protocol) are still popular and traditionally used to provide this functionality, more recent and lightweight alternatives are available. WebSockets[2] have become quite popular recently as a solution for two-way communication and bi-directional traffic. Server-Sent Events[3] is also a valuable alternative approach, although focused on pushing new data to the client in one-way communication. WebHooks[4] are also an interesting approach to implement one-way notifications to clients using custom callbacks. All three approaches are valid choices for asynchronous real-time communication, much like event-driven microservice architectures.

It's peculiar how both backend and frontend embrace event-driven mindsets (although with very distinct use cases, tools, and at different scales), but the communication between them often uses synchronous HTTP API calls. In fact, for a long time, there was a scarce number of options to provide seamless backend asynchronous interfaces for UI applications to use. Microservice message brokers like Kafka or RabbitMQ might not be suitable to deliver asynchronous events to UI applications due to challenges with firewalls, lack of granular role or resource-based access control, and lack of clear standards and straightforward ways to access asynchronous events.

In fact, traditional synchronous APIs like REST are a common functionality in most platforms in no small measure due to clear, well-established standards. Standards like OpenAPI[5] simplified the development and integration of different systems without the need for complex coordination. AsyncAPI[6] is increasingly filling that gap in asynchronous APIs. It is an open source project based on OpenAPI that seeks to provide a specification for asynchronous implementations with a message-driven foundation. It supports several messaging protocols and provides tools to define the event schema and semantics to connect, subscribe, publish, and interact with the API. It also supports a wide range of tooling, similar to OpenAPI, like code generation, API discovery, and event management. It can be a valuable approach for documenting and designing your asynchronous APIs.

---

[2] Protocol definition in "The WebSocket Protocol," December 2011, `https://datatracker.ietf.org/doc/html/rfc6455`

[3] More information in "Server-send events," `https://developer.mozilla.org/en-US/docs/Web/API/Server-sent_events`

[4] Wikipedia page in "WebHook," `https://en.wikipedia.org/wiki/Webhook`

[5] Specification in "OpenAPI Specification," February 15, 2021, `https://spec.openapis.org/oas/v3.1.0`

[6] Specification in "AsyncAPI Specification," `www.asyncapi.com/docs/specifications/v2.0.0`

9.6.1 Event-Driven Combined with WebSockets

Let's work through an example of how an asynchronous functionality could interact with the UI using WebSockets. Let's say we have a UI to create products and the business only considers the product created once it is available on the product catalog to be managed. The product catalog is updated asynchronously, so it would be useful for the user to know when the product is available on the catalog. Figure 9-12 illustrates this example.

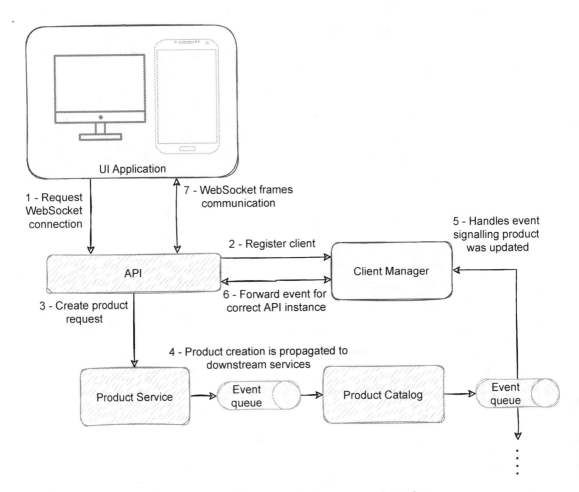

Figure 9-12. *Asynchronous product creation using WebSockets*

The user creates the product through the UI application, which triggers a request to the API component and the product service. The product service creates the product and publishes an event signaling that change, which the product catalog service uses to register that product in the catalog. The product catalog, which likely handles different streams to enrich a denormalized model of the products (similar to what we discussed in Figure 9-8), also publishes an event signaling the product creation.

The UI application first registers itself on the API and requests a WebSocket connection. The client manager is responsible for keeping track of the registered clients and handling the event signaling the product creation in the catalog. Each time a product is created, the client manager handles the event and informs the UI of successful product creation.

Why do we need the client manager component? Can't we just handle the events from the API? The challenge of delivering events to the frontend applications is delivering the correct events to the right clients. All components can (and likely will) be horizontally scaled, meaning there will be several instances of each component. If there are several product catalog services, UI applications, and API instances, how can we guarantee the events will be delivered to the correct client that created the product?

A possible solution could be for each of the API instances to handle all events and filter those that correspond to the clients connected to that instance. It can be an option for low-scale use cases; however, it quickly becomes impracticable for large event streams. The client manager can help manage all existing clients and deliver each event to the corresponding API instance, which has a WebSocket connection to the client.

9.6.2 Event-Driven Combined with Server-Sent Events

In use cases, we don't need a bi-directional communication channel; Server-Sent Events can be a valid alternative. Server-Sent Events is a subscribe-only protocol that provides a way to subscribe to an event stream and is a lightweight approach to deliver asynchronous data to the frontend applications.

The approach to the use case we discussed in the previous section with Server-Sent Events remains largely unaltered. Instead of using a two-way connection to the backend, the UI application opens a persistent connection to the API with the EventSource[7] object. The client manager component forwards the event stream to the API. Figure 9-13 illustrates the same use case we discussed before.

---

[7] More information in https://developer.mozilla.org/en-US/docs/Web/API/EventSource

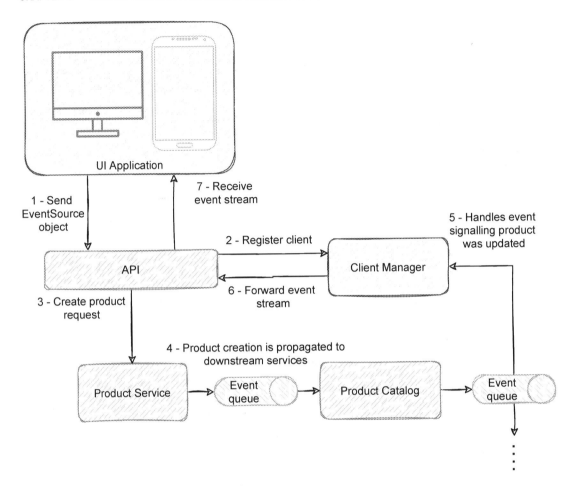

Figure 9-13. *Asynchronous product creation using Server-Sent Events*

Instead of having a bi-directional connection, the delivery of the event stream is one-way. Server-Sent Events also supports straightforward error handling, generating error events that can be more sustainable dealt with in the frontend application. One main difference from WebSockets is they use HTTP requests to maintain a persistent connection (also getting multiplexing over HTTP/2) instead of a dedicated protocol.

WebSockets tend to be more heavyweight in mobile use cases; since they establish a two-way connection, they require a full-duplex antenna, which in most use cases impacts the bandwidth and power consumption. Server-Sent Events implements unidirectional traffic through HTTP which, compared with WebSockets, tends to reduce the total data usage and battery power.[8]

9.6.3 Event-Driven Combined with WebHooks

Another alternative to implementing one-way asynchronous communication to the frontend applications is through WebHooks. WebHooks work in a reverse flow that we are used to; the subscriber registers a callback that the server will call to deliver the event stream (they are often dubbed as reverse APIs). Similar to Server-Sent Events, the communication occurs through HTTP and doesn't apply any specialized protocol.

The main difference from the other alternatives is the callback mechanism. Let's work through the same example we discussed in the previous section using WebHooks. The product creation flows through the product and product catalog service, and we deliver the corresponding event to the frontend application, as illustrated in Figure 9-14.

---

[8] Full article in Martin Chaov, "Using SSE Instead Of WebSockets For Unidirectional Data Flow Over HTTP/2," February 12, 2018, www.smashingmagazine.com/2018/02/sse-websockets-data-flow-http2/

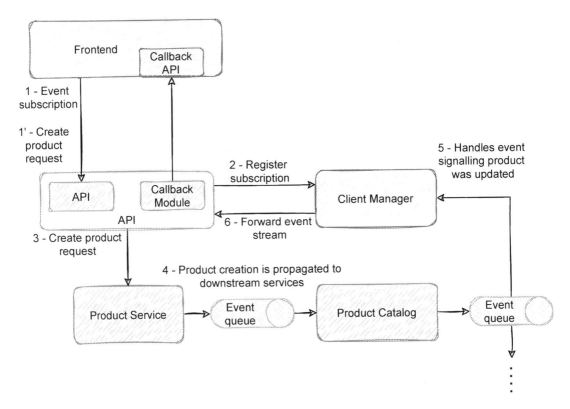

Figure 9-14. *Asynchronous product creation using WebHooks*

The frontend application subscribes to the event stream with an HTTP request to the API and registers a callback URL, which the backend will use to deliver the event stream. The product creation flows through the services, and the product catalog service will eventually generate an event signaling the change. The client manager will handle that event and deliver it to the callback module responsible for delivering the stream to the frontend application. To do so, the module will typically make a POST request to the callback API providing the new events.

The limitation of WebHooks resides in relying on an HTTP callback endpoint to deliver the events. Hosting a publicly exposed HTTP endpoint in user-facing applications like mobile apps or a browser is often impractical or even infeasible due to implementation and security concerns. Typically, WebHooks are applied to frontends or BFFs which are servers and can sustainably implement this feature. However, they are an interesting option when we need one-way communication for push notifications or event delivery.

9.7 Summary

- An aggregating layer can help optimize the bandwidth and response time when we need to aggregate data from different services. It's typically best applied to simple applications and contained use cases. We should avoid the pitfall of adding too much responsibility to the aggregating layer; if code has a place to gravitate to, it typically will.

- BFFs can abstract the downstream platform functionalities and provide higher segregation of responsibilities, thus avoiding adding too much responsibility to a single aggregating layer. They also enable a close optimization of the UI needs without the worry of coupling platform features to specific UI use cases.

- We can decompose a UI application into smaller components to best adapt to the underlying microservice platform. Decomposition can be done at the application, page, and section level; we can adapt each pattern to the most adequate use case.

- API composition is a useful and straightforward solution for obtaining the data to display in a small number of requests. However, in use cases that require comprehensive filtering and ordering requirements, building a dedicated model might be a reasonable approach to guarantee acceptable performance.

- Task-based UIs usually have higher synergy with distributed architectures due to building commands for each segregated task. They also are typically built to help the user advance in a journey and guide him to accomplish a process. Each change also maps more cleanly to the user's intent, making it easier to map to commands for each domain.

- Event-driven APIs can be a valuable alternative to traditional synchronous APIs in event-driven architectures. We can use them to asynchronously inform the user of changes in the ecosystems in a sustainable manner.

- To implement event-driven APIs, we can use WebSockets, Server-Sent Events, and WebHooks. WebSockets provide a way to implement two-way communication between the UI and the backend. Server-Sent Events and WebHooks are good options for one-way event delivery and push notifications.

CHAPTER 10

Overcoming the Challenges in Quality Assurance

This chapter covers:

- Understanding the different kinds of tests and their scope in the overall architecture

- The challenges of guaranteeing the quality of the end-to-end flow in event-driven services

- Using contract testing and consumer-driven contracts as core concepts in the quality assurance process

- Strategies to safely validate functionality in the production environment

As systems evolved from overly complex single units to constellations of highly distributed smaller components, in many ways and in many businesses, quality assurance seems to be left behind. It's peculiar how we evolved our architecture designs, development processes, and deployment strategies to accommodate the paradigm shift of highly scalable distributed architectures, but the practices of quality assurance remain roughly the same.

© Hugo Filipe Oliveira Rocha 2022
H. F. Oliveira Rocha, *Practical Event-Driven Microservices Architecture*,
https://doi.org/10.1007/978-1-4842-7468-2_10

We came a long way from the manual validations and lengthy regression testing of traditional applications and embraced, as we should, the joys of automated testing. However, to guarantee the correctness of the end-to-end flow as the end user sees it, we often rely on the same approaches we always did, by deploying all functionality in a quality environment and running manual or automated validations against the whole system. There is a mismatch between this approach and the very core principles of distributed microservice architectures and of independent deployment procedures and autonomous release cycles.

Despite the other kind of difficulties and limitations, monoliths provide the means to easily perform end-to-end validations. By having a single deployable unit, it's often possible (although not always easy) to deploy the application and its dependencies to test the end-to-end flow. When dealing with an architecture composed of dozens or even hundreds of independent components, it easily gets extremely complex to perform pre-production validations against the whole end-to-end flow. The practices of DevOps and continuous delivery promote a fast feature delivery flow in order to provide fast feedback. The autonomous release cycle of each independent service in microservice architectures is a way to achieve it. However, how are we able to accomplish independent deployments of each component while validating the integrity of the end-to-end flow?

The typical test categories ranging from unit to integration tests still apply to event-driven architectures. They provide higher decoupling characteristics which we can combine to achieve the more sustainable approaches we discuss in this chapter. Depending on the use case and the conditions of your company, you might still need to invest in complex end-to-end tests; however, as we will discuss at the end of the chapter, we will challenge you to adopt more sustainable and scalable approaches by combining a pre-production quality assurance process with safe production validations.

10.1 Microservice Testing Approaches and How They Relate to Event-Driven

There's a lot of confusion in the definition of the several types of tests. Integration, component, and end-to-end tests are often used interchangeably and change their meaning depending on the context. In this section, we will explain the different categories of tests, their scope, and how they apply to event-driven services.

There are several categories of tests in software engineering; you most likely came across several of them while developing new functionality. In the past, manual testing was a substantial step of the quality assurance process, although thankfully most businesses have been focusing on a more automation mindset. Most types of tests still apply to event-driven services, the same as they would in a traditional application or a monolith.

Event-driven architectures often imply a considerable number of components and frequent releases. As we will discuss in the next section, a strong automation mindset is pivotal for the success of these systems. Manual testing is still useful, but rather than having people doing a suite of repetitive tasks on every release, test automation frees them to do more meaningful work by interacting with the application in unexpected or creative ways (through, for example, exploratory testing).

10.1.1 Unit Tests

Unit tests validate functionality on a section of code inside a service. Typically, in the context of a function or class, there isn't any hard rule on how small they should be. Unit tests should be present throughout the several layers of the service's architecture. You might recall when we discussed the event-driven service's architecture in Chapter 3 and worked through the N-tier and clean architecture. Each service typically has several layers with dedicated responsibilities. Each of these layers will have unit tests to validate the layer's functionality on the smallest possible scope. Figure 10-1 illustrates how unit tests fit in the overall event-driven architecture.

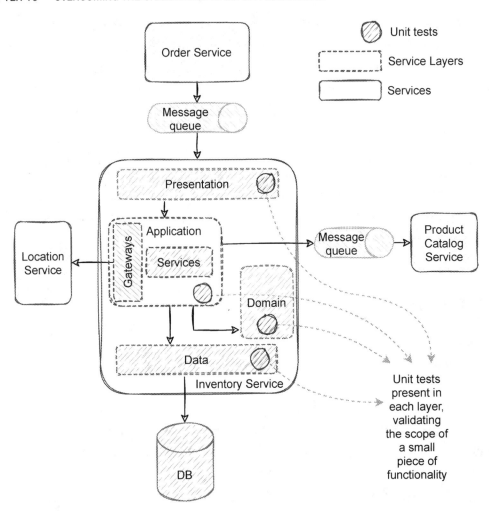

Figure 10-1. *Unit tests on an event-driven service*

Figure 10-1 illustrates the inventory service with several layers. It consumes events from the order service and publishes events to the product catalog service. It also does a synchronous request to the location service. Unit tests sit on each of the service layers validating solely the layer's functionality. If the piece of code the test is validating has a dependency on an external resource, like the database or external service or even another layer, the test mocks that request and focuses solely on the functionality implemented by that piece of code.

Although unit tests are fast and usually performant, it doesn't mean they are free. A pitfall I often see companies with strong unit testing culture fall into is creating unit tests for every line of code, whether it makes sense or not. Remember unit tests are code and have a maintenance cost; we need to maintain them. Code with hardly any logic likely doesn't need a test. People often measure quality by test code coverage; although it can be an indicator (among many) alone, it doesn't mean much, and struggling to have 100% code coverage won't benefit you much. Instead, it might hinder your velocity due to the maintenance overhead. Be pragmatic, measure the cost, and understand if the test makes sense.

Having said that, unit tests are the fastest feedback loop we have access to, they usually are extremely fast to run, and we can expect applications to have large quantities of them. They are extremely useful to validate small scoped functionality. They also are good as an indicator of the code organization; if a unit test is considerably large or has extensive responsibility, it's often an indicator the code might need to be refactored and divided.

10.1.2 Component Tests

Unit tests are great to validate localized and small scoped functionality inside a service layer but provide no guarantees on how the several layers interact with each other to compose the overall service features. Component tests fill that gap; they validate the full code flow inside a service, going through every layer, but only in that service's scope, removing external dependencies.

Component tests don't exert external dependencies like the database, external services, or message brokers; they focus only on the functionality inside the boundaries of the service. You can see it as testing anything the service does as a single process, without running anything else. Figure 10-2 illustrates the component tests scope.

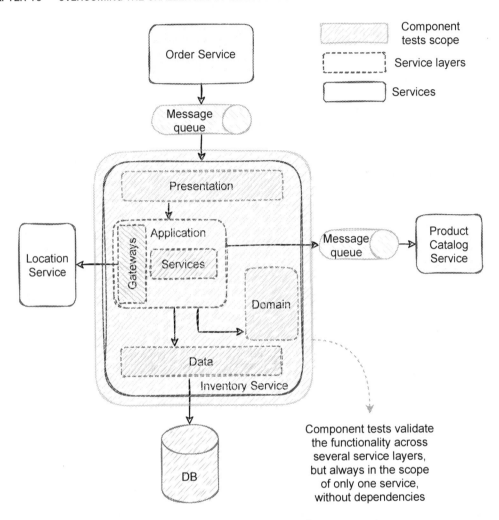

Figure 10-2. *Component tests scope in an event-driven service*

In this case, suppose the inventory service reacts to order created events to process stock, saves state in the database, and publishes a stock changed event. A component test for this flow could be the full flow of the order event processing without using the database, the message broker, or the location service.

A way to easily abstract the external dependencies is using dependency injection. While running the tests, the service can inject mock implementations and fake the normal or abnormal responses of external dependencies validating the correctness of the service.

Component tests are useful to validate the soundness of the sequence of steps or overall workflow of the service in a way unit tests aren't supposed to due to their limited scope. Well implemented, they can also be extremely fast due to the lack of direct dependencies; everything can be run in memory.

However, since they abstract the dependencies to the external resources, they don't prevent bugs in their direct implementation. For example, if the inventory service is using a SQL database, we could write a component test to validate the order created event processing logic, but if we had an issue in the SQL query, the test wouldn't likely be able to detect it since the repository would be mocked.

10.1.3 Extended Component Tests

A way to mitigate the risk of issues in the implementation of the external dependencies (like the example of the SQL query we just discussed) is to use an extended version of the component tests. Instead of completely removing the external dependencies, we can use the in-memory version of those dependencies. For example, if the service has a database, we can use an in-memory implementation of the database. It can behave the same way a database would, and it would allow validating the soundness of the query. Figure 10-3 illustrates the same use case but with in-memory components of the external dependencies.

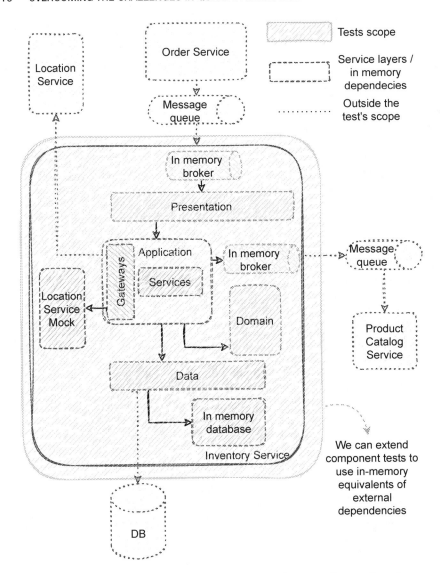

Figure 10-3. *Extended component tests with in-memory dependencies*

As you can see in the example, the external dependencies were replaced by their in-memory equivalent. The exception is the location service; it likely won't have an in-memory equivalent available since it is a service built in-house, but we can replace it with a mock or a stub. Extended component tests can paint a comprehensive scenario of the service and provide exceptionally valuable validations while not suffering from the drawbacks of managing external dependencies. They are able to validate the interactions with external dependencies while still being able to run extremely fast. The lack of external dependencies also facilitates the setup, running the tests locally, and simplifies the release process; since the release pipeline won't need to manage the dependencies, only the service and the tests.

If they sound too good to be true, it's perhaps they often are. In theory, it's a great setup, but implementing them in practice is often hard due to the inexistence of the in-memory replacements of the external dependencies. There are some providers of in-memory database equivalents, for example, Microsoft's in-memory entity framework provider,[1] that can provide similar features of a real database without using external components. However, these providers often fall short of the actual, real-life implementations. Often implementations don't fully match the full features of a real database. Transactions, the ACID guarantees, aren't real when run in memory; everything works instantaneously and without the restraints of a real database.[2] H2 database engine[3] is also an interesting alternative to emulate databases in memory; however, it suffers from similar limitations and doesn't provide compatibility to all functionality. What people often end up doing is having an integration test against a real database validating the same thing, which raises the question of why to have the extended component test in the first place.

If you are using Java, Kafka has an embedded Kafka implementation which is a very interesting in-memory equivalent. Since both Kafka and ZooKeeper (for older Kafka versions) are Java applications, it is possible to run them from Java code. However, it doesn't reflect all implications of a real Kafka cluster.[4] ElasticSearch also had an embedded alternative that could be used for testing; however, it was discontinued due to the difficulties of maintaining compatibility with new features (in this case security-related[5]).

A very promising alternative is using Testcontainers.[6] They can provide an easy way for tests to use and run containerized instances of most databases. RabbitMQ, Kafka, and most message brokers provide containers that are compatible with this approach.

---

[1] More information in "EF Core In-Memory Database Provider," October 27, 2016, https://docs.microsoft.com/en-us/ef/core/providers/in-memory/?tabs=dotnet-core-cli

[2] Full article by Jimmy Bogard, "Avoid In-Memory Databases for Tests," March 18, 2020, https://jimmybogard.com/avoid-in-memory-databases-for-tests/

[3] Home page at www.h2database.com/html/main.html

[4] Full article by Ivan Ponomarev and John Roesler, "Testing Kafka Streams – A Deep Dive," August 18, 2020, www.confluent.io/blog/testing-kafka-streams/

[5] More details by Clinton Gormley, "Elasticsearch, the server," August 30, 2016, www.elastic.co/pt/blog/elasticsearch-the-server

[6] Home page at www.testcontainers.org/

Although they aren't actually component tests but are perhaps halfway between integration and component tests (half-breed integration tests as we will discuss in Subsection 10.1.5), they can provide a reliable way to set up real dependencies with real-life scenarios. Unlike the H2 database engine, they provide full database compatibility,[7] since the actual database runs in a container.

For most use cases we've seen, teams tend to struggle to find reliable alternatives for external dependencies. But it really depends on the dependency; some of them might have valuable in-memory alternatives which we can use. They can complement integration tests well by limiting the number of integration tests and move most validations to faster and more reliable component tests. But most often than not, the alternatives are limited and can be used on somewhat niche or simple use cases.

10.1.4 Integration Tests

The meaning of integration tests has a lot of ambiguity, different references mention different scopes, and there's usually some confusion between component, integration, and end-to-end tests. We will define them with arguably the most consensual definition; tests designed to validate the communication and relationship with external dependencies. The tests validate the actual interaction with external components like databases, message brokers, other services, distributed caches, etc. We can approach them in two ways, on a smaller scope by validating only the interaction with each external dependency and nothing else or on a broader scope by validating the full business flow including the external components.

In the context of event-driven services, they usually include the interaction with the message broker but not with the service publishing messages. However, they usually include services with a synchronous dependency like an HTTP request. Event-driven services are decoupled by the event broker so it is a sound decision to relinquish other services in the message flow to the broader end-to-end tests. The consequence of direct synchronous requests between two services is higher coupling; thus, the requesting service can be directly affected by an issue with the target service. Hence, integration tests often include synchronous dependencies in their scope. Figure 10-4 illustrates the scope of integration tests.

---

[7] Further details at `www.testcontainers.org/modules/databases/`

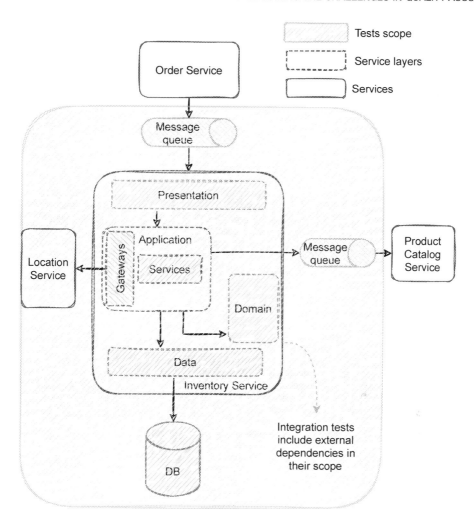

Figure 10-4. *Scope of integration tests*

These tests are often slower and more brittle than the ones we discussed until now. We need to guarantee there are the right conditions for the execution of the tests, the database needs to have the relevant data, caches need to be cleared, the existing messages in the broker must not affect the result of the tests, and so on. Guaranteeing these kinds of conditions on a daily basis can be complex to manage and often originate false positives. Containers can help with this; if we run containers and then remove them on a per test or per test session basis, it can help with these issues.

The direct dependency on the location service can be even harder to tackle. We need to guarantee we have a valid live version of the location service with relevant data for our test cases. If the location service has several dependencies, it can be even harder to manage since we have to guarantee each dependency is in a valid condition for the service to respond. Guaranteeing all of these conditions is no small feat and raises several questions on how to release the inventory and the location service. Should we run these tests in every release of both services? We will further discuss these concerns in Section 10.3.

10.1.5 Half-Breed Integration Tests

There's a distinction between the service's mainstream dependencies, like databases or message brokers, and synchronous dependencies to other services, for example, the dependency between the inventory and location service. Mainstream dependencies are typically more stable and predictable. We aren't continuously changing our databases or message broker's version; it remains stable for a considerable amount of time, and when we change them, it often is a carefully scheduled operation.

However, other services on the architecture are being developed by fellow teams in the organization which might deploy their services frequently. Each has its own peculiarities in schema, data, configurations, and dependencies. Setting up a test to validate the interaction between two or several services can be exceptionally challenging due to the need to get everything right plus the need to maintain the quality environment synced with the newly released versions.

A variation of integration tests that ease that process is to delegate the responsibility to integrate other services in the ecosystem to the realm of end-to-end tests. Half-breed integration tests mock or stub external service dependencies but maintain mainstream dependencies like databases or message brokers. They can validate the service's functionalities on a broader scope and be more reliable since these dependencies are often more predictable and easier to set up with containers. Figure 10-5 illustrates this scenario.

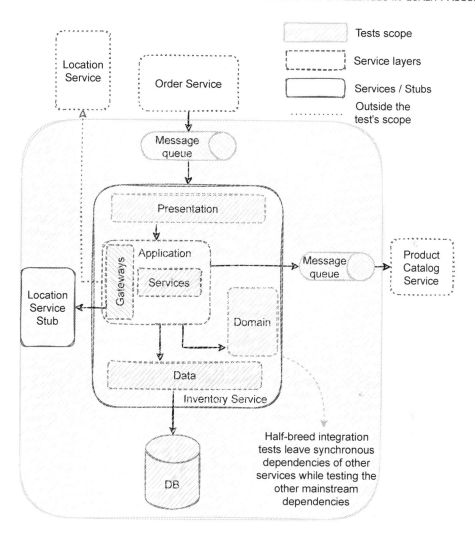

Figure 10-5. *Scope of half-breed integration tests*

These tests still need to maintain valid external components and guarantee the coherency of the data and message queues. However, it's only in the service's direct ownership, which greatly simplifies the test's development for the team governing the service. They don't need to worry about other services outside their ownership.

The tests still validate the interaction with the location service, but by mocking the request. In this case, using mocks is a good approach to simplify the overall setup while guaranteeing the correctness of some interactions between the two services. We no longer need to worry about deploying and maintaining a correct configuration and relevant data on the location service; we simply mock the calls we need to validate the flow of the inventory service. However, mocks suffer heavily from confirmation bias.

The teams will develop the mock's expectations according to what they believe the service will return, which can be troublesome when those assumptions are, or become, wrong. Either way, it's a great way to complement unit and component tests in a broader scope and guarantee the correctness of the overall flow of the service.

An interesting way I observed teams implementing them is having the tests bootstrap all the required preconditions for the tests and validating the end result. Figure 10-6 illustrates this approach with the inventory service handling of order created events.

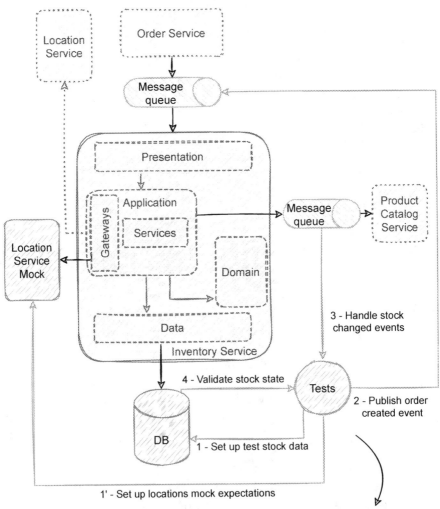

Figure 10-6. *Example of half-breed integration tests with the order created event flow in the inventory service*

Before running the actual tests, we bootstrap the inventory database by setting up data. For example, if the test case is when a new order is created, we decrease the stock quantity by one; we might need to set up the existing stock quantity before actually running the test. We also set up the expectations in the location service mock.

To trigger the start of the test, we publish an order created event to the inventory message queue. The service will handle the event and produce a set of expected results. For example, the service might decrease the stock and publish a stock changed event. We can then wait for the stock changed event by consuming the inventory service event queue. Once we receive the event, which signals the processing finished, we can validate the event's data and the state in the database. The main difficulty is to know when to stop waiting for the event; some test cases might not even publish anything, and we might want to validate that no event was published. For example, if the stock didn't change, the service won't send a stock changed event. Typically, we use a timeout but can increase the time the tests run significantly. An alternative can be sending a testing purpose event at the end of processing the order event. When the service finishes the processing, it publishes an event signaling the finish of the operation, whether it sent a stock changed event or not. Changing the code to be testable is a common practice in unit tests; however, in this case, it adds some complexity and adds code that is only used by the tests.

An interesting alternative is to monitor the order created event queue and wait for the inventory service consumer to acknowledge the successful processing of the event (e.g., in Kafka, wait for the consumer group to run out of lag). This way, we can be sure the service ended the processing without introducing additional developments in the service.

Guaranteeing the tests are autonomous has high synergy with applying a container approach to dependencies. We can run the database and message broker containers, set up the initial schema and data, run the tests, and in the end clean everything by disposing of the containers. This way, we guarantee no garbage data remains in a quality environment or data from older test runs don't end up affecting the current tests.

Mocking or stubbing the synchronous requests, like the dependency to the location service, provides the decoupling of the service with the rest of the ecosystem and enables autonomous releases. We no longer need to worry about configuring services out of the scope of the service we are releasing, and overall the tests enjoy higher stability and consistency. However, mocks are heavily biased, especially when defined only by the consuming team, and releases are susceptible to defects in the interface interaction between both services. No guarantee is made if the location service makes a change in its contract or behavior. A new release of the location service can be deployed live with its tests passing and break every other consumer.

To overcome this limitation, we can complement these tests with contract tests, consumer-driven contracts, and production tests. We will further these subjects in the remainder of the chapter. Another alternative is to use end-to-end tests, but they suffer from even more constraining issues. Overall half-breed integration tests are a great complement to component and unit tests, especially when we can't use extended component tests. They can provide broader scope validations of the behavior of the service along with the correct usage of its external dependencies.

10.1.6 End-to-End Tests

End-to-end tests validate the system as a whole, typically its correctness according to broad business rules. They often go well beyond the scope of a single service; they validate the business flow across multiple services and provide high-level, technology-agnostic, and business-facing validations. They are the type of tests that give the most confidence in the system since they cover a large ground. However, they have a mismatch with the distributed event-driven mindset, often have an overwhelming cost, and maintaining them is often extremely challenging.

Except for integration tests, all test categories we discussed until now are in the service's scope; if we include any of those tests in the service release pipeline, the service would only depend on itself. On the other hand, end-to-end tests include the collaboration with several services; if we are to release any service, we need to run the end-to-end tests. Figure 10-7 illustrates the end-to-end tests scope in the example we discussed until now.

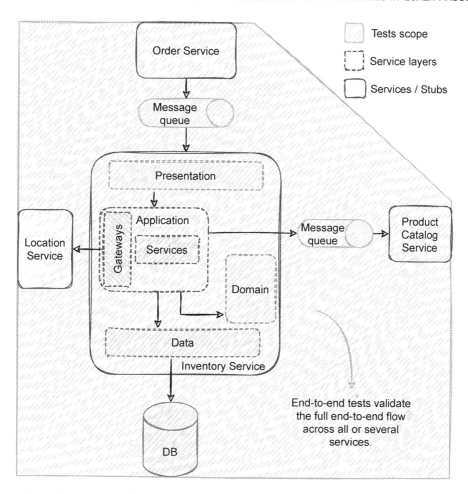

Figure 10-7. *End-to-end tests scope*

Not only the tests include the inventory service, its database, and message broker but also the location, order, and product catalog service. It would likely also include other upstream and downstream services, for example, the UI where the user submitted the order and the shipping and pricing services.

Releases

Since end-to-end tests target the entire microservice ecosystem, we must run the tests every time we release any service within the test's scope. These kinds of tests are slow by nature; they typically involve several services with several dependencies, ranging from databases, message brokers, distributed caches, etc. When the tests run into an issue, for example, if we are doing a release of the location service and the tests are failing, every other release of the order, inventory, and product catalog service would have to wait for the fix.

Remember when we discussed in Chapters 3 and 4 how services must be independent and autonomous, how event-driven architectures potentiate this characteristic and facilitate a truly continuous delivery mindset? This can easily escalate to a step back in that mindset; a service is no longer autonomously released; it depends on the successful implementation of several other services. It also leads to complex lockstep releases and quickly escalates to releasing everything in a single moment, which is what we need to avoid by adopting an event-driven architecture.

Data and Environments

Another substantially cumbersome challenge of end-to-end tests is state management. Services without state are easier to handle in an end-to-end context since no data bootstrap is needed. However, many services have data and need to have data initialized in order to run test cases. This is a common challenge; we discussed it before when we discussed integration tests, but in that case, the service only had to manage its data. In end-to-end tests, each service has to have relevant data, and worse, all data need to be consistent with each other.

In an integration test, the tests may initialize test data and run the tests against that data set. With end-to-end tests, the services not only need to initialize their state but need to make sure it is coherent with every other service. For example, it's not enough to set up test stock data in the inventory service, we also need to guarantee the external identifiers like the products we assign stock to must be the same as the ones in the order and product catalog service. The tests aren't in charge of only one service but require an orchestration across all services in the test scope just to set up the conditions for the test to run. This necessity often requires intrinsic coupling between the overall flow and business logic and the tests. This makes the tests exceptionally brittle and susceptible to changing requirements. Often tests become more complex than the functionality under test.

The complexity of distributed architectures often makes teams build an integrated quality environment where the end-to-end tests run. Maintaining this environment is often complex and time-consuming. We need to guarantee the services are updated every time a release is deployed live. It can be done automatically, but often the intricacies of each service, their configurations, lack of discipline managing the data stores and message brokers end up breaking the quality environment frequently. It quickly leads to having individuals or full teams dedicated to maintaining the environment stable.

Another downside of the data bootstrap in quality environments is leftover data from previous test runs. Message brokers and data stores tend to be a dumping ground for test data that often is responsible for causing the tests to fail with false positives. It also further deviates the quality environment from production. A good approach to this challenge is to build a system on demand, deploying containerized versions of the services and dependencies to an environment, and clean everything up in the end. However, the tests may take longer to run.

Governance

Since end-to-end tests span several services, it makes sense to run the tests in the release of every service in the scope of the test. But that will likely mean several teams might be involved in the development and ownership of those tests. Deciding who has the direct ownership of the tests can be troublesome; we can assign it to a team that is highly involved in the overall flow; for example, assign the order fulfillment test to the team that owns the order service. However, it can get tricky to manage when those tests fail because the stock wasn't reflected on the product catalog service. That team has limited context of that service; requesting assistance from the respective team might be the way to go but harder to effectively do if they don't have skin in the game.

Another alternative people sometimes take is to have a dedicated team to develop those tests. This can be even more difficult to manage; that team has limited context about the effective implementation of the services and makes the teams that own the services even more detached from the whole process. This team often becomes a gatekeeper for releases making teams losing even more autonomy.

A better approach can be to have the tests with shared ownership; each team is responsible to contribute and develop the tests. If the tests fail, the team who is releasing the feature is the driver to find the issue; if it involves other services, the corresponding teams must help understand the issue; communication is key. A possible downside of this approach is the lack of drive to resolve flaky tests; people trying to make the tests pass for their release even if they have to retry the tests a few times ("a dog with two owners dies of hunger"). However, it is a preferable approach to deal with the test's governance.

Approaches to Mitigate the End-to-End Tests Challenges

These are a few examples of the challenges of end-to-end tests. The context of end-to-end tests often varies from company to company; however, here is some advice to address these concerns:

- Do you really need end-to-end tests? Distributed architectures require the correct approaches and techniques to quality assurance rather than trying to apply old ones to a new context. We will detail alternatives to them in this chapter and make an informed decision whether they are worth the cost. Of course each company has its own context and risk tradeoffs, so will yours, but ask yourself how many end-to-end tests you need and if (or how) you can replace them. Often it's not about losing quality but making quality sustainable.

- Perhaps you don't need to run end-to-end tests on every release but rather on the end of larger projects or technical revamps. An approach I saw used to some success in larger projects, is to have each service deliver its features live, but disabled. Before enabling the functionality, the teams ran an end-to-end test to guarantee there are no issues in the high-level flow; if any is found, the team would develop a component or unit test to guarantee it doesn't happen again. Typically, large projects or major restructurings benefit from end-to-end tests; using them on an ad hoc basis and guaranteeing continuous quality through other means might be a useful approach.

- Perhaps you don't need to validate the whole end-to-end flow. Often a segment of the whole flow is more critical than the remaining flow; validating that segment has more value than exercising the complete flow. Measure stability over test coverage and make informed decisions.

- Using a containerized environment that bootstraps, runs the test suite, and cleans everything up can be a good approach to difficult state management issues later on. It can also be a stepping stone for running the tests locally in the developers' computers instead of using a shared quality environment. Running the tests locally can also be a good approach to avoid lockstep releases where an issue in one service blocks the releases of the other services. However, even when adopting infrastructure-as-code practices, this approach gets trickier with complex flows. Not only bootstrapping the whole constellation of services can be extremely confusing and time-consuming, but also maintaining it requires substantial effort. With high numbers of services, it might be hard to have a machine with resources capable of running every service and its dependencies. Focusing on a critical part of the end-to-end flow can be a reasonable option.

- Guarantee autonomous management of data and event schemas, event streams, and data stores. You must strive for guaranteeing the setup of the environment is automatic. Every change in the schema by the teams must have an associated script or process; the process to deal with event's breaking changes must be accounted for in the quality environments in an automatic way, avoiding manual corrections in the quality environments.

- If you do need end-to-end tests, guarantee you only have a very limited amount. Most validations can be done by combining the other types of tests (unit, component, and integration) and highly contain the responsibility of end-to-end tests. Use them only for critical high-level flows and focus on clear business processes.

End-to-end tests can be applied successfully to small architectures with a very limited number of components which likely only one team manages. If this is your case, it might make sense to have them; however, they tend to get worse as we add more components and the architecture evolves. It gets even worse when we lose autonomy to release functionality, which typically is severely aggravated when multiple teams are involved in the same tests.

10.2 Applying Contract Tests and Consumer-Driven Contracts to Event-Driven

Contract tests are often associated with schema validations, like breaking, forward, or backward changes, as we discussed in Chapter 8. But they go further than that; they validate the correctness of a producing service against the expectation of a consumer. Automatic schema validation is pivotal in event-driven services and can be provided by schema registries (like Avro in Kafka[8]). Contract tests go beyond agnostic schema validation rules; they validate the inputs and outputs of producing services against the needs of consumers. This section will discuss their scope in event-driven architectures and how we can combine them with consumer-driven contracts.

Contract tests typically sit in the boundary of a service with an external interface. Their focus is the compliance of the producing service with what consumers expect. Figure 10-8 illustrates the scope of contract tests in the same example we discussed until now.

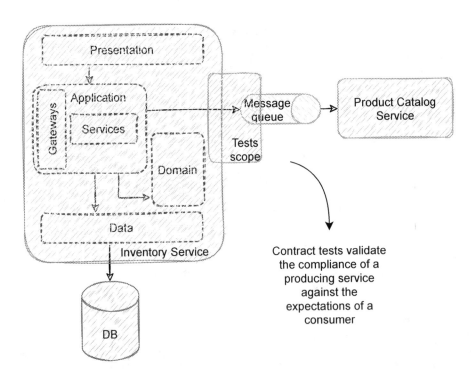

Figure 10-8. *Contract tests scope*

---

[8] More details in "Schema Validation on Confluent Server," https://docs.confluent.io/
platform/current/schema-registry/schema-validation.html

In this case, the product catalog service consumes stock events produced by the inventory service. An interesting contract test we could add to the inventory service is guaranteeing every information needed by the product catalog service is being published. We can use mock or in-memory replacements of the message broker to achieve better performance and stability. However, many use cases benefit from having a dependency to a message broker due to serialization and compatibility concerns. The tests can guarantee the consumer is able to read the message by consuming the events in the same way, using the same schema, serialization protocol, headers, etc. For example, sometimes different consumers have different serialization protocols for different event streams, and it's easy to mess up the configuration. This way, we can have a broader guarantee that the consumer will be able to read the message.

It can also guarantee some business logic the consumer is relying upon. Some events might have data in some fields in certain situations. For example, if we have multiple steps in the creation of a product, the first step might fill only the mandatory data, and the remainder of the information will be enriched later in the process; for example, we can create the product and add stock later. However, stock requires the size to exist in the product; for example, we add stock to an XS size. In this case, the product service might expect that all stock to be associated with a product size. A possible validation could be when the stock is greater than zero, the size is also published. These kinds of validations go further than direct schema validations; they guarantee an expected behavior in the producer, which if broken will cause issues in the downstream components.

Until now, we discussed how the team managing the inventory service could unilaterally add contract tests to the service. A valuable iteration of contract tests is to align them with consumers, typically referred to as consumer-driven contracts. In Chapter 8, we discussed the importance of consumer collaboration in the schema definition. This approach takes that collaboration one step further; the team managing the producing services has the mission to understand and guarantee the expectations of the consumer services in direct cooperation with the consumer teams. Consumers can even implement the tests in the producing service to guarantee their expectations. Figure 10-9 illustrates this scenario.

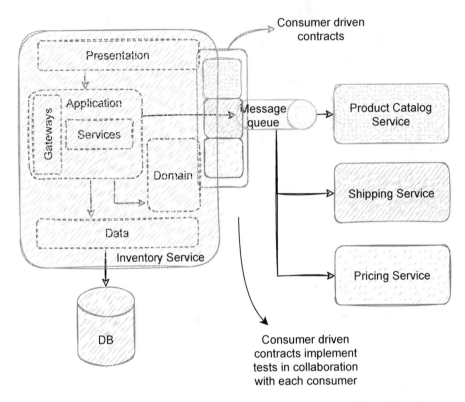

Figure 10-9. *Inventory service consumer-driven contracts with multiple consumers*

If we run the contract tests for each release of the inventory service, we have greater confidence that the functionality we are releasing won't break existing consumers. They also encourage communication between both teams. Communication is pivotal in guaranteeing quality and understanding the needs of consumers; coding them down in the form of tests is a great way to guarantee their expectations are being met. Ownership of a correct message flow in every release is distributed to the different teams involved, which usually helps to guarantee everyone is on the same page.

Business processes are often choreographed with a series of events in event-driven architectures. Applying contract tests and consumer-driven contracts to every component in the flow can be a way to guarantee more scalable validations of the end-to-end flow.

10.3 Test Categorization and Purpose

The types of tests we discussed until now have different purposes and scope. Categorizing the different kinds of tests can help make sense on how and when to apply them. Brian Marick defined four quadrants for test categorization[9] that helped to clear a lot of misunderstandings when discussing the various categories. We can think of it by having tests focused on verifying what is expected against finding unforeseen corner cases or unexpected use cases. In the original Marick's categorization, those test categories can also be more oriented to business or technology, as illustrated in Figure 10-10.

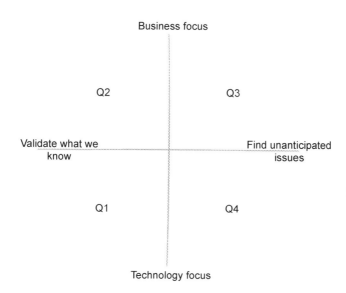

Figure 10-10. *Test categories divided by their focus and purpose*

Using this categorization, we can find some examples for each quadrant:

- Q1: Fully automated tests oriented to verifying what we developed works as we expect it to work. Can be unit, component, or integration tests.

---

[9] See article "Agile testing directions: tests and examples," August 22, 2003, www.exampler.com/old-blog/2003/08/22/#agile-testing-project-2

- Q2: Automated (or manual) tests to verify if we developed the correct functionality as defined by the business. Typically, functional and acceptance tests, including business validations of the application.

- Q3: Manual exploratory tests dedicated to finding issues with the application. These tests are creative in nature and are oriented to people interacting with the application in unexpected ways.

- Q4: Tests to verify the non-functional requirements and technical limits of the application. Can be performance and load tests, security validations, and other quality attributes like availability, correctness, or reliability. It usually relies on automation or specialized tools.

Although this categorization makes a lot of sense, some areas can be subjective. For example, if an acceptance test finds an issue with the application, we could, if possible and if small scoped enough, develop an automated unit test to guarantee the issue doesn't happen again. Unit tests can be used to guarantee the soundness of business rules as long as they are small scoped enough (typically in the context of a specific part of the code like a function), although that unit test would now be technology-focused rather than business-focused.

Quality assurance practices have come a long way from the extensive manual testing plans. It's actually pretty obvious the advantages of not having a single person or a team of individuals performing a repetitive set of actions every time there's a release (there's even the tale of a test engineer who automated his job for six years without the company noticing[10]). Test automation isn't just smart, it becomes a necessary condition to successfully scale a distributed architecture. If you think about it, extensive manual regression tests might be an option in a single deployable component like a monolith, but when you have to operate dozens or even hundreds of autonomous components with several daily releases, it quickly becomes unviable to scale the number of manual testers to cope with the growing number of releases.

However, it doesn't mean there's no place for manual testing. Repetitive tasks should and need to be automated, but there's a rightful place for curious and creative ways to break the application. Automating repetitive tasks frees quality engineers to do much more meaningful and creative work of interacting with the application in unforeseen and unexpected ways through, for example, exploratory tests. Manual testing can also be

---

[10] News in www.payscale.com/career-news/2016/05/programmer-fired-after-6-years-realizes-he-doesnt-know-how-to-code

relevant for use cases where we simply can't automate due to the effort or cost involved; I mostly saw this happening with extensively large legacy applications. In event-driven architectures due to the component's high decoupling and the large number of independent components, a strong test automation culture is advisable.

All the categories discussed in this and the previous sections are in the context of pre-production testing. As we will discuss at the end of the chapter, production testing approaches that we will discuss in this chapter can be categorized into the different quadrants of Figure 10-10. Production testing is an increasingly adopted practice that helps overcome the challenges of quality assurance in complex distributed systems and can be extremely valuable as a complement to traditional pre-production approaches.

10.4 End-to-End Quality Without End-to-End Tests

For years, end-to-end testing was the quintessential bastion of quality and a beacon of trust in the tempestuous releases of new functionality. In truth, they can be a valuable quality assurance strategy in monolithic applications. However, as we discussed in Section 10.1, they have serious downsides when applied to fully distributed microservice architecture. Event-driven architectures nurture several fully decoupled, independent, and scalable components, and as we will see in this section, end-to-end tests have strong dissonance with the event-driven approach. The approach to quality assurance requires different strategies and a shift in the traditional mindset.

Despite the adoption of microservice architectures, many companies continue to have an approach to quality the same way they always did, by deploying all functionality in an environment and running the test suite against the whole system. I always found it peculiar how we faced the limits of monolithic databases with ACID properties by moving to highly distributed architectures, featuring high numbers of components asynchronously communicating with each other, often with different database technologies with weaker consistency guarantees, and still managed to maintain the consistency needs for the business to run. But our approach to quality is still deploying and running tests against every single functionality in a single place. We were able to develop patterns to deal with something as complex as consistency and state management across distributed components, but why are we unable to have a similar approach to quality assurance? Why do we need to apply the old quality assurance approaches to a fundamentally new context?

In the same way, we don't lock every single microservice database to achieve atomicity; we shouldn't deploy every single component and block each service's release to guarantee quality. The distributed nature of event-driven architectures requires an approach to quality and quality assurance strategies that preserve boundaries and independent releases. One of the most valuable characteristics of event-driven architectures is the decoupled nature of its components. This enables the architecture to be truly evolutionary; features can be implemented separately from each other; services are autonomous and independently released. It allows for teams to truly own their services and do their work without the shackles of dependencies, approvals, or gatekeeping processes. End-to-end testing is a deliberate and confident step in the opposite direction. We face all the challenges we discussed throughout this book to achieve this clear segregation, single responsibility focus, well-defined domains, autonomy, and decoupling and, many times, to throw it away in the quality assurance process.

Adopting a truly decoupled and distributed architecture requires the correct approaches to quality assurance, instead of forcing traditional techniques to a radically different environment. One way to do this is to combine some of the strategies we discussed in Section 10.1. We can approach end-to-end quality as the sum of the quality of each component, as illustrated in Figure 10-11.

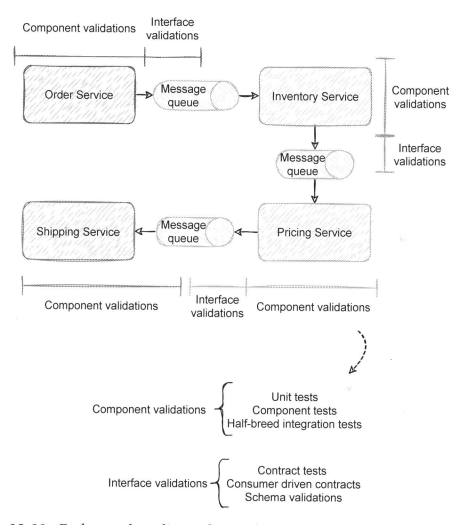

Figure 10-11. *End-to-end quality as the combination of quality assurance practices in each component*

Each component needs to guarantee its quality independently, through unit, component, and half-breed integration tests. Integration tests across several services were intentionally left out since they suffer from many of the same downsides as end-to-end tests, but at a smaller scale. Each service must guarantee its correctness through its own tests, including its part in the end-to-end flow. It is pivotal that each team has a higher-level vision of the larger flow in order to understand and implement the validations of their components (this builds on the concepts we discussed in Chapter 4). The compatibility with other services is guaranteed through schema validations, contract tests, and consumer-driven contracts. Not only do they guarantee there are no unexpected changes in the event's schema but also guarantee the expectations and behavior of downstream services are maintained. This is the situation where the sum of the parts is greater than the whole.

Typically, failures in the end-to-end flow map to one or a set of components, which can validate that condition in the scope of only the corresponding components. However, this approach requires close communication and alignment with each team, which consumer-driven contracts intend to tackle, at least partially.

I wouldn't say this approach is failproof, it isn't; however, neither are end-to-end tests. Maintaining a copy of the live environment is extremely expensive and time-consuming, and the result is a poor reproduction of the live environment at best. Production tends to be highly dynamic with differing usages, throughputs, and conditions that vary through time. An environment that only runs the tests doesn't really stand near to the live conditions. These environments often use a small number of machines with resources far smaller than production (to contain costs) but fail considerably in replicating the performance and concurrent conditions of live environments. They also typically stand in the same network host or in network conditions that minimize or eliminate several network failures like network partitions. They often only have a subset of the production data (if any) which can't really reproduce all the possibilities of data existing in production, for example, event streams covering every current or past use case. Configurations, network topologies, and connectivity conditions are often replicated but without any guarantee they remain the same as the live environment. After all, how many times did we run end-to-end tests only to find there were still issues after releasing the functionality?

End-to-end quality as the sum of its parts doesn't guarantee there won't be issues either. Would you be able to write a test for every single condition a service can fail? Probably not. Test suites excel in validating the known failures of the system. End-to-end tests are just one approach, perhaps valuable in monolithic applications, but extremely inadequate in distributed systems.

So, am I saying the only way is to live with the problem? Not at all. Pre-production quality assurance techniques can be complemented with testing in production approaches to mitigate many of these issues, which we will discuss in the next section.

10.5 Testing in Production

I know what you're thinking, "I don't always test my code, but when I do, I do it in production." Well, I'm pretty sure you probably have your own tales of testing in production the same way as I have, but that's not quite it. Testing in production has become increasingly relevant in the context of microservice distributed architectures as a way to complement pre-production tests or even as the only feasible way to provide comprehensive end-to-end quality assurance guarantees. This section will discuss those approaches and how we can use them in event-driven architectures.

As we discussed in the previous section, pre-production tests can have limited coverage of the possible failure modes of a complex distributed system. It can become even more challenging when usage patterns change over time. Trying to cover every possible failure mode often requires such a complex testing logic and infrastructure that can even match the system under test. Besides being limited, leaving the burden of end-to-end quality assurance to exclusively pre-production strategies will invariably and substantially delay the release and feedback cycles. With the right tools and practices, we can use the production environment to increase our confidence in our quality and release process in a sustainable and comprehensive way, instead of trying to use a poor imitation of the live environment.

The most challenging aspect of implementing this practice is often getting people on board with the approaches. People used to the traditional testing practices and oblivious to the challenges of distributed architectures often frown at the very suggestion of testing in production. Sometimes we put unmeasured faith in automated testing, perhaps the same way as we did in dedicated quality teams that did manual regression testing in an era before automated tests, without honestly facing the viability of alternatives. The live environment is often looked at as a pristine forbidden artifact that shouldn't be touched (sometimes with good reason), but we should also consider that the correct approaches can greatly benefit quality assurance processes without endangering the live conditions (Cindy Sridharan has a great series of articles that further these topics that I recommend[11]). To be fair, health checks to services deployed in the live environment are a way to test in production. Often features are behind feature toggles, or we release functionality to only a segment of users; all of this can be seen as testing in production. Business validations occurring behind testing or sandbox users aren't unheard of. Testing in production might

---

[11] Full articles by Cindy Sridharan, "Testing Microservices, the sane way," December 31, 2017, https://copyconstruct.medium.com/testing-microservices-the-sane-way-9bb31d158c16

seem radical, but often they already are part of our processes, embracing them as what they really are; a powerful tool to fully achieve end-to-end quality can provide a more sustainable and transparent approach to quality assurance.

10.5.1 Shadowing

A common challenge of pre-production testing is the diversity, quantity, and accuracy of the data. Shadowing (also known as mirroring) is a strategy to expose new releases to production data without impacting the user. It can be extremely useful to guarantee new releases are able to interact successfully with real, real-time requests.

We often use mock data or generate data for our tests. There is a range of tools to generate random data based on given contracts (e.g., AutoFixture), which simplifies the data generation process. Despite its usefulness, generated data is random or manually set up, which always struggles to represent a comprehensive sample of the real production data. Random data can easily generate scenarios that don't make sense and even cause instability in the test suite. For example, if we are generating a stock changed event, the tool can easily generate random values for product identifiers with unexpected size. Although it might be useful to test those scenarios, a test like that might fail in one run and pass in the next. It is better to test deliberate scenarios than generating brittle tests through random data generation, thus the need to carefully set up the random data. Random data also tends to deviate considerably from real production traffic, and even when they are accurate, they hardly mirror the variety of scenarios we find in production.

Mocked or stubbed data suffer from similar challenges. They are also particularly susceptible to bias; we often set up mocked data with what we are expecting to receive. What we receive and what actually exists in production can be very distinct. In production, there are also edge cases with data that we don't expect, and thus we don't create test cases for those use cases. This is often a source of issues with teams with a high test automation culture. Unfortunately, when this happens, we can only detect it in production, despite the high coverage we think our tests have. As an alternative approach, we can also copy data from production. But typically we copy only a sample of data, which differs greatly in quantity and might not have samples for every use case.

With shadowing, we can help prevent these issues by replaying current production traffic to new releases. Let's work through a use case; imagine we are deploying a new version of the inventory service and its consuming order created events. Figure 10-12 illustrates this scenario.

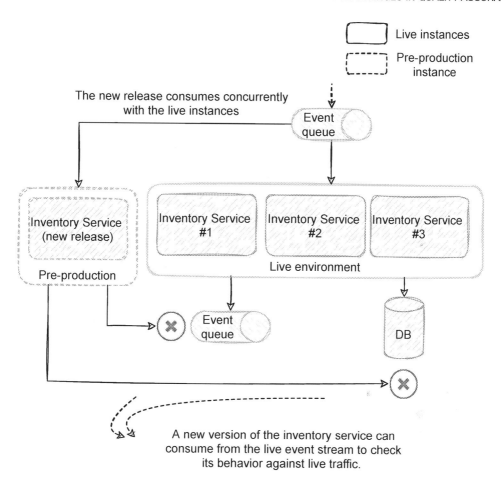

Figure 10-12. *Shadowing in an event-driven service*

In this example, we have the inventory service with three instances in the live environment and a new version of the service we want to deploy. Before actually installing live and replacing the existing instances with the new version, the new release consumes concurrently the same events the live instances are consuming. For example, if we are using Kafka, we can simply have a separate configuration for the pre-production environment and use a different consumer group configuration for the new release. Since the new version will have a consumer group and the three instances will share a different one, the new version will consume the same events the three instances are consuming.

It is important to notice the new release is deployed in the live environment the same as a live instance and has access to all its resources, but with different configurations. The main goal is guaranteeing the service is able to correctly process live traffic with the new features. So the service will process the live event stream, and we can automatically detect changes in error rate and have automatic validations of the service behavior. We also need to guarantee the pre-production instance doesn't effectively change the live state. The new instance will consume the messages, apply its business logic, but shouldn't save state in the database or publish events to the event stream. We can implement that by having different configurations that inject fake message broker and database implementations.

An interesting metric to monitor could be the throughput of the service. But since we are using fake implementations of the external dependencies, it wouldn't be accurate. We also wouldn't be able to validate the implementation against a real database or message broker. We can further elaborate on this pattern by having a separate data structure or event queue with the pre-production data. Figure 10-13 illustrates this scenario.

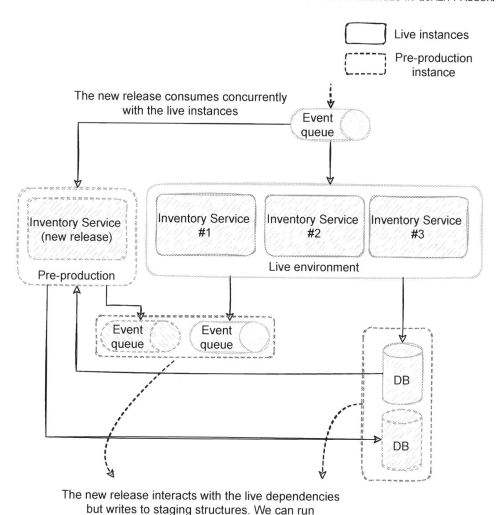

Figure 10-13. *Shadowing in an event-driven service with live dependencies interaction*

In this example, the new release reads from the live event stream and the live database but writes to different structures than the live instances. For example, the new release can publish to a staging queue inside the same broker and write to a staging table inside the same database. This guarantees the new release is able to write successfully to the external dependencies. We can also monitor relevant deviations in the new release's throughput since it should be roughly the same as the live instances (lag will be different and likely to increase in pre-production since only one instance is processing against three). We can also run automatic validations to compare both event streams and detect deviations. If we are generating unexpected events or events with incorrect data, when compared to the real live event stream, it would be an indication to invalidate the release and automatically fail the deploy. We can do the same with the database's state.

Shadowing can also be applied to synchronous requests, albeit with the support of an external tool like a proxy. The proxy can duplicate requests to a pre-production instance similar to what we discussed with the inventory service. Figure 10-14 illustrates this scenario.

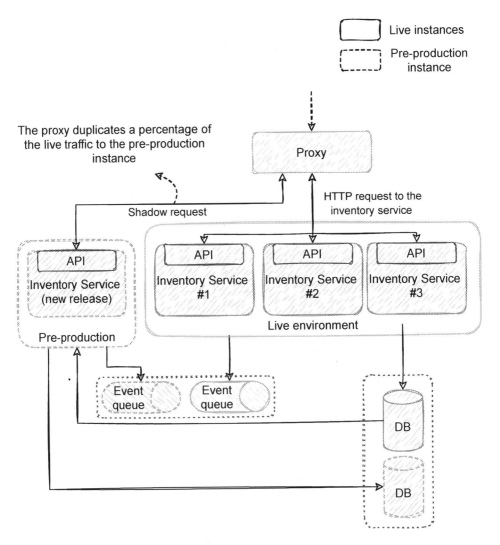

Figure 10-14. *Shadowing in with synchronous requests*

In this example, the inventory service exposes an API to both writes and reads. With the help of the proxy, we can duplicate a segment of the live traffic to the pre-production instance. Some tools support this functionality out of the box; for example, HAProxy supports this kind of functionality seamlessly.[12] Reads don't have any impact; we can simply redirect a portion of the reads to the new version and validate its results against the live instances. If we want to validate writes, we can take an approach similar to what we discussed with purely event-driven services by writing to a staging structure and validating both.

Shadowing is exceptionally useful by allowing us to test new functionalities against real-time, live traffic without impacting the user. The downside is we have a new instance consuming from live resources; although they usually can (and should) handle the load of an additional instance, we need to guarantee the dependencies (like the broker and database) are prepared for it. Either way, it is an especially valuable and simple technique to guarantee new releases won't run into issues when exposed to live traffic, without the limitations of sampling data from production to quality environments.

10.5.2 Canaries

A popular approach to production validation is canaries. Canary involves exposing only a segment of end users to new functionality, instead of making it available to everyone instantly. Unlike shadowing, this approach only minimizes risk; end users are still exposed to the new functionality, but on a smaller scale. This section will detail the several approaches we can take in implementing canaries.

One possible approach is to deploy one instance with the new version and add it to the pool of production instances. Since traffic is distributed across all instances, the new version will receive a part of the live traffic where the already existing instances will receive the remaining, as illustrated in Figure 10-15.

---

[12] More details by Nick Ramirez, "HAProxy Traffic Mirroring for Real-world Testing," July 23, 2019, www.haproxy.com/blog/haproxy-traffic-mirroring-for-real-world-testing/

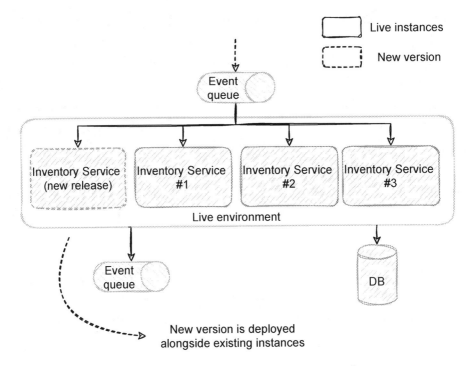

Figure 10-15. *Canarying by sharing the live instances pool*

Typically, traffic is approximately equal across all instances. In this example, since there were three instances in live and we added the new one to the instance pool, the new instance will receive only one fourth of the live traffic. In case there's an issue, only one fourth of the traffic will be impacted and we can roll back the release.

Alternative approaches can forward only a selected segment of traffic to the new version. We can first direct only internal traffic to the new instance; for example, the internal teams can first interact with the new version before rolling it out for the entire public. This approach is easier with synchronous requests and a proxy that can selectively deliver requests to specific instances using a location or header. With event-driven services, it can be harder since services would have to selectively process or ignore events that weren't directed to them or implement a custom routing algorithm. A further iteration of this approach is to divide traffic by relevant business information, like country or user segment. This approach is even more relevant with a lower number of instances (in this case, 25% of the traffic would be processed with an error).

The main issue with canaries is when there are issues, end users will be faced with an error. In event-driven services, it also means an invalid build was temporarily running against live data. Roll backing no longer completely solves the issue since downstream event streams or the database might be corrupted. An approach to mitigate this is what we discussed in Chapter 7 by rewinding the queue to the state before the deployment. A further challenge is to deal with database or event schema changes which require a more careful approach. A possible solution is to avoid breaking changes and do forward and backward schema changes instead of deploying the breaking change in a single deployment, as we discussed in Chapter 8. However, it adds complexity in favor of security and stability.

10.5.3 Feature Flagging

A common way to implement testing in production is through feature flagging, where new features are deployed but disabled by a feature flag. We can test the functionality's correctness and compliance with non-business requirements like throughput and response time and activate it when we are confident the feature works as expected. Deactivating the feature is also straightforward since it only involves switching a configuration.

Feature flagging varies in scope; it can be all or nothing where we either activate or deactivate the functionality. Or it can be more intricate processes where we roll out new functionality to increasing amounts of end users for a given time period, similarly to canaries. There are also several types of toggles; they can range from toggling business functionality and non-functional requirements to security and experimentation features.

The concept is straightforward; we have a set of configurations that activate functionality depending on whether they are active or not. They can be more elaborate configurations when we only want to activate a segment of live traffic, for example, a configuration with all the countries we want to activate the feature to at that time. When processing an event, we decide which path to follow based on the event's data or headers; if it is an event from a configured country, we activate the new features.

A common pitfall is the complexity some toggles have and how they sometimes become entwined with the core business logic. Following especially closely the single responsibility principles and dependency inversion can help decouple the toggle logic with the reminder service's functionality. It is also important to have a strict rule to clean old flags when they are no longer needed. The build-up of several feature toggles through time can make the service needlessly complex. The added complexity will also reflect in the test suite since it should test both paths while the toggle exists. Thus, a strong discipline to refactor and clean old toggles is important. Although feature flagging is often a simple and straightforward strategy, some toggles extend through long periods of time, making extensive use of this approach more complex than it needs to be. However, with the right code refactoring concerns, it is a simple and incremental approach to expose functionality to live data.

10.5.4 Production Automated Testing

A further development of production testing practices is to run automated tests directly against production instances. This approach is arguably the most radical and requires strong alarmistic, monitoring, metrics gathering and control over the release process. With the right approach, combined with the traditional pre-production strategies, it can provide the most comprehensive coverage of the test cases that we can't or are too costly to set up in pre-production environments.

To be fair, this approach is perhaps one of the most mature stages a company can implement. A common evolution path is typically to start with traditional end-to-end testing and automated component tests and then implementing strong logs collection, metrics, and tracing. Then move to more straightforward approaches like feature flagging and canaries. Shadowing could arguably be the next logical step, while production automated testing is the very last.

The approach involves having a test suite that runs directly on new releases on production instances. This way, we can have test cases that test the full integration with the service dependencies. If the tests pass, we are sure there are no unforeseen cases that weren't picked up in the pre-production tests. Let's work through the use case of the inventory service we discussed until now. The service receives events, processes them, and publishes stock changed events to downstream services, in this case, the shipping service, as illustrated in Figure 10-16.

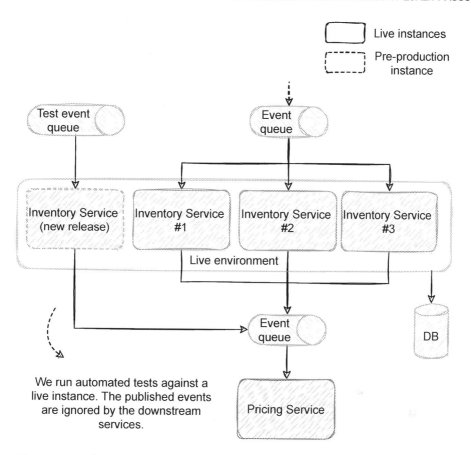

Figure 10-16. Production automated testing example

The new release is deployed alongside the remaining inventory service live instances. The test suite publishes events to the test event queue which are processed by the new version. If the service publishes events, it will publish to the real event stream and, in this case, should include a header indicating they are test events. The shipping service will use that header to ignore those events. The interaction with the database gets trickier, reads are fine, but when handling writes, there's the concern of polluting the database with testing data. We can have a staging structure like we discussed in the shadowing strategy or ignore test data by signaling those records. An alternative could be having specific users or segments of data dedicated to testing, for example, sandbox clients that we know are only for testing. Many companies already do some kind of business validations directly in live recurring to these kinds of clients; running automated tests against them instead of manual validations might not sound so far-reaching.

With this approach, we can validate that the interfaces with other services are working according to the expectations of the inventory service. All validations also occur in concurrency with the whole ecosystem instead of having only the tests running. We can also realistically validate non-functional requirements like response time or throughput. As we discussed, besides all the things that can go wrong with traditional quality assurance approaches, distributed systems have a myriad of failure modes that are infeasible to reproduce in quality environments. These types of approaches can be a valuable addition to assure new functionality works as expected.

10.6 Summary

- There are several quality assurance strategies we can implement in event-driven services. They can range in scope and quantity; combining them can be a valuable approach to guarantee comprehensive test coverage.

- Unit and component tests only depend on the service, are usually fast and stable, but have limited scope. Extended component tests can be a valuable way to validate the interaction with external dependencies but can be hard to find the right in-memory replacements.

- Half-breed integration tests can be a good compromise between including standard dependencies and other services. Standard dependencies like message brokers or databases are typically easier to set up and are more stable than other services in the architecture.

- Integration and end-to-end tests are extremely challenging to implement consistently. They also quickly restrict the release process and the team's autonomy. There are approaches we can take to minimize these challenges, but they will always be costly to maintain. A more sustainable approach is to combine pre-production with testing in production approaches.

- Contract testing and consumer-driven contracts are a great way to validate the interfaces with other services and encourage collaboration and communication with both the producing and consumer teams.

- An alternative approach to full end-to-end tests in event-driven services is to combine pre-production approaches like unit, component, and half-breed integration tests with interface validations like schema validations, contract tests, and consumer-driven contracts.

- Shadowing can be an excellent approach to validate new functionality with live traffic without impacting the end user.

- Canaries and feature flagging can be valuable to gradually expose new functionality to increasing quantities of users. They can minimize the risk with new releases and limit the footprint of possible issues.

- One of the most mature approaches to quality assurance in event-driven architectures is automated testing in production. It can help in guaranteeing the coverage of failure modes pre-production approaches aren't able or are too costly to detect.

Index

A

AddStock command, 37
Anemic domain model, 128
Anemic satellite services, 154
Apache NiFi, 59
API composition
    aggregating data, 372
    denormalized view, data, 375–377
    ElasticSearch, 374
    event-driven architectures, 375
    filtering, 374
    information, 374
    limitations, 377
    ownership, 377
    pitfall, 377
    pricing domain logic, 377
    product listing page, 372, 373
    requests, 374
    user's order details, 377
Asynchronism, 173
Atomicity, consistency, isolation, and
    durability (ACID), 187
Atomicity, consistency, isolation, and
    durability (ACID) 2.0
    at-least-once semantics, 303
    business process, 305
    CALM, 303
    consuming messages, 302
    distributed systems, 304
    duplicated events, 305
    event handling, 305

    event processing, 303, 304
    event schema, 305
    event versioning, 305
    exactly-once semantics, 303
    order, 305
    product service, 302, 303, 305
    properties, 304
    retrying, 302
    StockOut *vs.* StockChanged event,
        304, 305
Automated testing, 394
Availability, 196
Avoiding message leak
    acknowledgement, 307
    at-least-once/at-most-once
        semantics, 307
    auto acknowledge interaction, 306
    issues, 307
    Kafka, 307
    message broker, 306
    poison events, 308
    pricing service, 307
    RabbitMQ, 307

B

Backends for frontends (BFFs)
    benefits, 365
    design, 365
    functionalities, 362
    limitations, 365

© Hugo Filipe Oliveira Rocha 2022
H. F. Oliveira Rocha, *Practical Event-Driven Microservices Architecture*,
https://doi.org/10.1007/978-1-4842-7468-2